"With the revival of natural theology in the ⸻ an outbreak of fresh, rigorous arguments for ⸻ existence. In turn, this has raised afresh new issues about the relationship between Christian philosophy and theology with science. Interestingly, little attention has been given to questions about the origin of consciousness, especially self-awareness. But that is no longer the case. In *On the Origin of Consciousness*, Dr. Ventureyra has produced a stunning book, based on wide and careful research, that brings the resources of a philosophically informed theology to bear on showing that such a theology explains the origin of consciousness better than do the natural sciences. Along the way, Ventureyra treats us to a rich study in metaphysics, systematic and natural theology, philosophy of mind, and philosophy of science. I am enthusiastic about this book and highly recommend it."

—**JP Moreland**, Talbot School of Theology, Biola University

"Sometimes you read a book where you disagree with just about everything the author claims—starting with the dedication! And yet . . . You learn and you rethink. I feel exactly that way about Scott Ventureyra's *On the Origin of Consciousness*. I intend that as high praise."

—**Michael Ruse**, Florida State University

"Consciousness can become less mysterious when we see our universe as created by God. Scott Ventureyra helps to prove it by this very wide-ranging and interesting book."

—**John Leslie**, University of Guelph

"Dr. Ventureyra's book, *On the Origin of Consciousness*, is surely the most complete and most thoroughly researched treatment of the subject from a theological standpoint. Readers may not agree with all of the author's conclusions, but they will be deeply impressed with the comprehensiveness of his discussions of this very difficult philosophical-theological question. There is no doubt that a study of *On the Origin of Consciousness* will stimulate further intellectual labour on a subject of critical importance."

—**John Warwick Montgomery**, University of Bedfordshire

"A refreshingly robust defence of the contributions of theology and scripture to understanding consciousness that also deftly handles scientific and philosophical aspects. The clear position developed and the trajectories for future research that are traced will be important for the future theology and science debate."

—**David Grumett**, University of Edinburgh

"Ventureyra's *On the Origin of Consciousness* is not only a very good read; it provides a fertile primer for grasping the metaphysical significance of consciousness. But it is the careful examination of the origins of consciousness through the prism of contemporary scientific, philosophical and theological contexts that gives this enquiry resonance. Ventureyra offers readers in philosophical theology, epistemology of theology, philosophy of mind, and philosophy of science a model study of how to think about the origins of consciousness—conscientiously."

—**Robert M. Berchman**, Director General and Academic Fellow,
 Foro di Studi Avanzati, Gaetano Massa, Roma

"*On the Origin of Consciousness* presents a Christian theological understanding of consciousness. In developing his argument, Scott Ventureyra provides a comprehensive overview of different models for the interaction between faith and science, and he describes the role philosophy plays in guiding the integration. What makes the book unique is his insightful interactions with the work of such intelligent design researchers as Bill Dembski and myself. He identifies the concept of information as not only central in the discussion of the origin and development of life but also in understanding consciousness' origin and operation. Ventureyra's approach is both compelling and practical. I highly recommend this book for anyone interested in how theology can help guide scientific research on consciousness and in the topic in general."

—**Stephen C. Meyer**, best-selling author of *Darwin's Doubt*

"Scott Ventureyra's compelling book applies my interactive method for relating theology and science (CMI) to the problem of consciousness. In doing so, Ventureyra creatively describes contributions theology might make to the scientific understanding of the origin and emergence of consciousness in nature. I am very pleased to recommend this book to both technical and general readers in theology and science."

—**Robert John Russell**, Graduate Theological Union, Berkeley, California

"Scott Ventureyra's *On the Origin of Consciousness* is a rich, albeit somewhat eclectic, work. Although there are many points at which I disagree—Scott takes the emergentism of Teilhard de Chardin and Philip Clayton much more seriously than I think is warranted—I found the book a rewarding read."

—**Robert Larmer**, University of New Brunswick

"Scott Ventureyra's *On the Origin of Consciousness* is a brave and illuminating book that could easily serve as an advanced primer on the topic. The book starts from the obvious but no less striking premise that unlike physics, biology, and even psychology, consciousness is not a surprising phenomenon to theology. In fact, theologians expect consciousness, understood as the existential basis for humanity's relationship to God. This suggests that theologians should be central to the emerging interdisciplinary study of consciousness. Ventureyra makes good on this proposal by showing the mutual bearing that theological and scientific arguments have on each other. While himself a traditional Christian, he is mindful not to overstate the probative character of theological arguments. Here Ventureyra updates the appeal to philosophy as an honest broker between the claims of science and theology that had been instrumental in legitimizing of the Scientific Revolution in the seventeenth and eighteenth centuries. An especially welcome feature of this book is the extended, sympathetic, yet also critical treatment of the work of Pierre Teilhard de Chardin."

—**Steve Fuller**, University of Warwick, Author of *Dissent over Descent*

"As remarkable as science's progress has been, it has been completely stumped trying to explain its own foundation—the existence of conscious, rational agents like ourselves. In *On the Origin of Consciousness* Scott Ventureyra explores how theology and philosophy may be able to rescue science from its doldrums."

—**Michael J. Behe**, author of *Darwin's Black Box*

"Dr. Ventureyra's *On the Origin of Consciousness* provides an excellent analysis of the interactions between theology and science. It gives a clear explanation of the different creation-evolution models. It also outlines some of the promising modern theories of consciousness. The most intriguing aspect of Ventureyra's book is his proposal of God's action through the connection between information and consciousness, something which can open new lines of research in the theology and science dialogue."

—**Miguel A. Rodriguez**, former Biochemistry Teaching Labs Coordinator at the University of Ottawa, Canada

"In *On the Origin of Consciousness*, Ventureyra offers a critique of naturalistic explanations for the emergence of mind. Yet he also offers a positive account for how theology can contribute to the quest for a satisfactory account. This book is well-researched, insightful, and an exemplary model for how to integrate scientific, philosophical, and theological questions."

—**Sean McDowell**, author of *The Fate of the Apostles*

"The twofold strength of this exceptionally well-argued volume resides in its rational commitment to Christian Theism while allowing a rich variety of sub-positions to serve as potential paths for reaching the ultimate goal of explaining human consciousness. Though all trails cannot be ultimately or equally successful, Ventureyra argues persuasively for a carefully-delineated cadre of options from which to achieve the final goal. The result poses a profound and growing amalgam of insurmountable problems for Naturalism."

—**Gary R. Habermas**, Liberty University

"Wanting to specify God's role in the origin of consciousness, Dr. Ventureyra painstakingly presents a critical overview of theories in neuroscience, philosophy, and especially different entangled theologies. A useful categorization of the theories, although overlapping, is a major contribution; but the field remains ever a jungle. Nonetheless, this lay of the land might serve as a welcome provocative prelude to other takes on the matter."

—**Daniel A. Helminiak**, University of West Georgia, author of
Brain, Consciousness, and God: A Lonerganian Integration

"Scott Ventureyra has tackled one of the most challenging issues in the field of science and theology: how to account theologically and scientifically for the origins of consciousness. In a wide-ranging and thoroughly-researched book, he develops a distinctive and sometimes provocative account, which will offer both stimulation and challenge to anyone with an interest in these questions."

—**Neil Messer**, University of Winchester

On the Origin of Consciousness

On the Origin of Consciousness

*An Exploration through the Lens of the Christian
Conception of God and Creation*

Scott D. G. Ventureyra

WIPF & STOCK · Eugene, Oregon

ON THE ORIGIN OF CONSCIOUSNESS
An Exploration through the Lens of the Christian Conception
of God and Creation

Wipf & Stock
An Imprint of Wipf and Stock Publishers
199 W. 8th Ave., Suite 3
Eugene, OR 97401

www.wipfandstock.com

PAPERBACK ISBN: 978-1-5326-5517-3
HARDCOVER ISBN: 978-1-5326-5518-0
EBOOK ISBN: 978-1-5326-5519-7

Permission from Fortress Press to use figure 4 (appendix 1 of this book) of Robert
John Russell's *Cosmology: From Alpha to Omega.*

Manufactured in the U.S.A.

This book is dedicated to the God of all mercy and love;
the co-Creators of all existence: God the Father, God the Son,
and God the Holy Spirit.

Contents

Acknowledgements

THIS BOOK IS A result of my thesis work on the science and theology interaction, and in natural theology and philosophical theology. In some senses it is a continuation of my master's thesis, which focused on Robert John Russell's "Creative Mutual Interaction"(CMI). It applies the CMI to the origin of consciousness and goes further in its argumentation to explain its plausibility in the universe we find ourselves in. It certainly embodies my insatiable fascination on the question of origins. Although I do not presume this work provides a definitive answer to the question of the origin of consciousness, I hope that it can act as an impetus to stimulate deeper thought on the matter within an interdisciplinary framework. I argue for a holistic approach to science, philosophy and theology while also respecting each discipline's limitations.

First, I would like to thank my parents, Enrique and Maria-Elba, for their unwavering support, encouragement, love and faith in me. They have always emphasized the value of education, so I hope this book is a testament to that. The long hours of thought and writing are my way of expressing my gratitude towards their consistent support and love. Their graciousness has made the completion of this book possible.

Second, my daughter, Julianna, for her innocence and the light she shines onto an increasingly dark world. I thank her patience for the many hours I couldn't spend playing games with her. I also thank Julianna's mother, Tanya, who looked after our precious daughter when I was busy with my research and writing.

Third, my thesis supervisor, Professor Maxime Allard, for agreeing to take this project on several years ago. Despite some profound disagreements, I am indebted to his vision, support, wisdom, patience, and openness. Throughout my years at the Dominican University College (DUC) in Ottawa, he had helped me in many different capacities. A large reason that this book was eventually possible was because of his support.

Fourth, I thank Fr. David Bellusci for his friendship and for his introduction to other scholars in the Canadian Jacques Maritain Association. Walter and Barbara Schultz, and William Sweet, for their insights and help in different capacities throughout the earlier stages of this project. Fr. Hervé Tremblay for his support over the many years I was at DUC. Professor James Pambrun at Saint Paul University in Ottawa, for his introduction of Robert John Russell's Creative Mutual Interaction to me back in 2008.

Fifth, I thank all others, including my sister Valerie (for sporadically entertaining our parents over the last couple of years), my godmother, Ethel Blum, for her consistent love, my late godfather, Leslie Ivan (and his wife Maureen), for his love and for letting me be part of his remarkable transition, in heart and mind, toward faith in God. Fr. Joseph Escribano for his spiritual guidance in difficult times throughout my doctoral work. Dr. Michael Froeschl for his attentive medical care. I am also thankful to Nick Lukach, a true disciple of Jesus, for helping rekindle a faith that I thought may have been forever lost. This encounter has unquestionably precipitated this path into exploring Christian theology and its relationship to science. Angela for patiently listening to me verbally flush out my ideas before the defense. I also thank many other friends, professors, and acquaintances who over the years have offered countless stimulating conversations. I am also indebted to the great scholars of today and of the past, for providing boundless inspiration through their valuable insights.

Abbreviations

AC	Argument from Consciousness
AIR	Attended Intermediate-Level Representation Theory
CENTAC	Cumulative Evolutionary Natural Theological Argument from Consciousness
CTL	Category Theory Logic
CTNS	Center for Theology and the Natural Sciences
CMI	Creative Mutual Interaction
DAP	Divine Action Project
DCC	Divine Collapse Causation
DE	Directed Evolution
ECA	Embodied Conscious Agent
FINLON	First Instantiation of a New Law of Nature
FINLONC	First Instantiation of New Law of the New Creation
fMRI	functional Magnetic Resonance Imaging
IBE	Inference to the Best Explanation
IDT	Intelligent Design Theory
IIT	Integrated Information Theory
KCA	The Kalam Cosmological Argument
LLII	Leibniz's Law of the Indiscernibility of Identicals
MSRT	Mirror Self Recognition Test
ND	Neo-Darwinism
NDE	Near Death Experience
NDT	Neo-Darwinian Theory
NE	Naturalistic Evolution

NIODA	Non-Interventionist Objective Divine Action
NOMA	Non-Overlapping Magisterium
NT	New Testament
NTE	Non-Teleological Evolution
OCD	Obsessive Compulsive Disorder
OEC	Old Earth Creationism
Orch-OR	Orchestrated Objective Reduction
PE	Planned Evolution
PSII	Psychophysical-Semantic Integrated Information
QEEG	Quantitative Electroencephalography
QFT	Quantum Field Theory
QM	Quantum Mechanics
RSMEs	Religious/Spiritual/Mystical Experiences
SRP	Scientific Research Program
TE	Theistic Evolution
TRP	Theological Research Program
UCD	Universal Common Descent
YEC	Young Earth Creationism

Introduction

Introductory Remarks

THE ORIGIN OF CONSCIOUSNESS intimates some of the most profound questions a human person can ask. It is deeply interconnected to many perennial questions, although refined through the constant development of our understanding of ourselves and the cosmos. The questions revolving around consciousness are intimately linked to other recalcitrant questions, such as: Does God exist? What is God's nature? Why does anything exist at all? What is the structure of reality? Why are the constants, initial conditions, and laws of physics the way they are? What is mind? Where did mind come from? Is our perception accurate with how reality actually is? Is the cosmos intelligible? What is human nature? Do we have free will? Are we morally responsible for our actions? And a multiplicity of other related questions. To be sure, these questions have been approached in many distinct ways throughout the ages. There is no definitive consensus amongst theologians, philosophers, and scientists. Despite there being disagreements, as there typically are with theological, philosophical, and scientific issues, this does not mean that progress in learning more about ourselves and reality is not possible, at least in the sense that we can inch our way closer to truth.

As twenty-first-century humans, we find ourselves in an era of utter awe and discovery with the rapid advancement of the natural sciences and the exponential development of technology, all of which serve as indispensable aids to scientific, philosophical, and theological inquiry. Through this ever-evolving correspondence between our understanding of the natural sciences and technological development, it is astonishing, for instance, to observe the features of "low life" (microorganisms) endowed with specified complexity,[1]

---

1. Specified complexity refers to the arrangement of the structure of something. It is a designation for the organization of a particular thing, commonly used to describe functionally integrated systems such as organisms and their components but can also refer to a computer program, literature, recipes, a telephone book, etc. For instance, a

something that has been only possible because of our advancement in technology. Most remarkable is the fact that we can unravel a world far more intricate than any computer or device we have been able to design. This is especially true with the informational content embedded on the spine of the double helical DNA molecule. Indeed, our technology has allowed us to discover an exquisite world of "nano-technology" that is far more sophisticated than our own, yet vastly more primitive (e.g., even primordial singled-celled organisms such as eukaryotes or prokaryotes bacteria), exhibiting much lower orders of specified complexity and obvious cognitive capacities than humans possess. Such advancements provoke us to reflect deeply on our philosophical and theological outlooks. The success of the modern sciences has raised a series of intriguing questions revolving around a string of variant phenomena: the universe itself, the physical laws that govern the universe, the information necessary for the existence of the first cell and consciousness, particularly as related to the human mind. The intelligibility of the cosmos and our advancement in the natural sciences, with corresponding technological advancement, presupposes an inherent rational order and structure to reality.[2] It is not a requirement of existence that our minds correspond with how reality actually is and that we are able to gain understanding of it with our various theological, philosophical and scientific "instruments." Yet this is the intriguing state we find ourselves in.

It is worth noting that consciousness as a human phenomenon is a term and an idea that has undergone a variety of changes over the years. This is particularly true with advancements in the neurosciences. Some maintain that the findings of neurosciences have had a deep impact on how we are to understand mental states as they are related to the neurophysiology of the brain. Others suggest that such findings, although very interesting to a variety of disciplines including psychology, psychiatry, neuroscience,

---

strew of letters arranged in a random manner may be complex, but it does not necessarily specify anything; however, a series of letters organized in a particular fashion as we observe with the English alphabet to formulate certain words, phrases or sentences, can be considered as specified complexity since it conveys a certain pattern or message based on both its complexity and specificity in the arrangement of the letters and words. The same is true in life, whether within a cell or in the arrangement of trillions of cells like those that make up the human brain. See Orgel, *The Origins of Life*, 189; Davies, *The Fifth Miracle*, 112; Dembski, *No Free Lunch*, 19.

2. In chapter 8, we will briefly discuss a philosophical and theological argument (Lonergan) and a scientific argument (Gonzalez/Richards) related to intelligibility and the correspondence between the two. For works supporting the inherent rationality, structure and comprehensibility that permits the very endeavor of science, see Klaaren, *Religious Origins of Modern Science*; Jaki, *The Origin of Science and the Science of its Origin*; Hooykaas, *Religion and the Rise of Modern Science*; Whitehead, *Science and the Modern World*; Lindberg and Numbers, *God & Nature*.

biology, etc., are nonetheless irrelevant to philosophical and theological understandings of consciousness.[3] This is applicable to those who believe in substance dualism.[4] There are also disputations over how to interpret what the ancients believed about consciousness.[5] There is, so to speak, an evolving understanding according to which prior to the period of Teilhard (a thinker whose notion of evolution and consciousness we will explore in chapter 4 of this book) there may have been a different understanding of consciousness than the one we find in our present day. J. P. Moreland's version of substance dualism will be explored. In the final section of this book, we will also explore the thoughts on consciousness of Bernard Lonergan and Daniel Helminiak, and Philip Clayton.

Two Prongs and Why

This book endeavors to develop a theological understanding of the origin of consciousness through the Christian conception of God and creation. This is something that had not been explored until now with any great depth, aside from the work of Pierre Teilhard de Chardin. This book is primarily a work of theology set in the science-theology interaction and, as such, will have strong ties to several branches of both philosophy and science.[6] As a work in theology, it ultimately affirms St. Anselm of Canterbury's (1033–1109) motto: *fides quaerens intellectum*. One is not suspending reason in such an exercise; rather one is engaging in loving God with all of one's mind (Matt 22:37) and actively seeking an ever-deepening understanding of God through this commitment.[7] This book affirms that God is the Creator of all, both things visible and invisible (Col 1:16). Any meaningful work of Christian theology presupposes the truth of Christian theism, but it is a work that engages deeply with the rational endeavor of natural theology,

3. This is true in J. P. Moreland's exposition of substance dualism which will be explored in chapter 8.

4. Moreland, *The Soul*, 74–116.

5. See Caston, "Aristotle," 751–815. Victor Caston has pointed out that, for well over thirty years, philosophers have debated, for instance, on whether Aristotle had a notion of consciousness. Nonetheless, he agrees that both sides are correct to one degree or another and that Aristotle had a concept of perception.

6. It is tied to various branches of philosophy, including philosophy of science, philosophy of mind, and philosophy of religion. It is also closely tied to various branches of science, including evolutionary biology, neuroscience, cosmology, physics, and chemical evolution.

7. See Anselm, *Monologion* chapter 68. Here Anselm argues that a dead faith is one that merely accepts what one "ought" to believe without further investigation. See Thomas Williams, "Saint Anselm."

which has traditionally relied on different philosophical tools and concepts. Natural theology is a rational means to infer the existence of God and the purposiveness in nature through empirical observation of the created world and human intellect.[8] Moreover, the current enterprise of natural theology not only relies on philosophical reasoning, but also modern science (as will be seen with the Cumulative Evolutionary Natural Theological Argument from Consciousness [CENTAC]). However, any engagement with naturalism will have to be rather brief and cannot be expected to be exhaustive. An in-depth refutation of naturalism is beyond the scope and project of this book. A work responding to such critics would have to be a separate project in and of itself. Given this, it should be stated that this book is of an exploratory nature and as such, is meant to initiate a dialogue on the examination of the origin of consciousness from the perspective of Christian theological interactions with science—a dialogue which has so far not taken place. It does not intend to have a final say on the matter, its purpose being to inspire future research into one of the most difficult areas of human intellectual endeavors. For example, in this book, some of the arguments presented in chapter 5 have a long history and have found many defenders and detractors; however, by no means can this book address all of the arguments, counter arguments, rebuttals, and defeaters. These arguments have been subject to vigorous debates in both philosophy and theology journals. What can be said is that they are taken seriously by detractors and have sufficient support to justify sound arguments in defense of theism in general and Christian theism in particular (when taken as part of a cumulative case).

There are two broad prongs I wish to explore with respect to this book. The first has to do with a methodological question, namely, what fruitful contribution can Christian theology provide the sciences?[9] Put more specifically, in which ways can the Christian conception of God and creation shed light on potential research avenues into the discernment of the origin of consciousness? It is my contention that through our developed understanding(s) of science, philosophy, and theology, we can answer this question in a more precise fashion than was possible in the past. The question of consciousness, as I will demonstrate throughout this book, requires the cooperation of a variety of disciplines within theology, philosophy, and science. It cannot be examined adequately in isolation, i.e., as a purely scientific question since it overlaps with both theology and philosophy. Neither do I purport to argue that Christian theology alone can account

8. See Brent, "Natural Theology," lines 1–5.

9. Here I use the term sciences in a broad sense to cover natural sciences, neuroscience, the humanities, etc. In the first chapter, we will explore a modified version of Robert John Russell's program suggested by William Stoeger.

for consciousness since philosophical and scientific engagement are also required. It would be a gross misunderstanding to suggest otherwise. It must also be understood that the science of consciousness is a developing enterprise which is still in its speculative stages since consciousness is not observable through conventional scientific-empirical means.

This book affirms that Christian theology is not in conflict[10] with, but can support, scientific hypotheses and conclusions. Indeed, scientific theories dealing with the subject of origins will inevitably have theological implications and points of intersection. The very interactions of these three disciplines form a synergy, including interdependence with one another. Synergy is not a vague term used to mask any problem, but the reality in which we must deal with the inseparability of the three disciplines. However, it must be acknowledged that each of the three disciplines still have their own set of epistemological options, structures, and limits. What must be kept in mind is that this synergy among the three is not taken for granted by all scholars, although those involved in the science-theology dialogue, as we shall see in chapter 2, are closely tied despite a series of objections (such as the verificationist principle and the criterion of falsification). Philosophy's important role in the science-theology dialogue illustrates this in chapter 2. Alan Padgett asks the following question: What role does philosophy play in theological reflection?[11] His answer demonstrates how theology cannot be separated from philosophy:

> For one thing, philosophical training can bring clarity and logic to the reflective, systematic, and constructive tasks of Christian theology. Philosophy may also provide key ideas necessary to explicate revelation. More than this, philosophers may pose problems of internal coherence within the patterns of life and thought that are Christian tradition, religion, and theology. This is a valuable service, and one which theologians have not ignored over the long history of engagement with philosophical partners. Philosophy can also pose other questions to the Christian religion, giving shape in sharp and poignant ways to the problems of our place and time.[12]

---

10. If there is such a thing as a conflict between science and theology, it is mainly at a superficial level, for example, the claim of evolutionary psychology that religion is nothing more than an aid for survival. According to philosopher Alvin Plantinga's evolutionary argument against naturalism, the real conflict lies between naturalism and science. See Plantinga, *Where the Conflict Really Lies*; Ventureyra, "Scratching the Surface," Review of *Where the Conflict Really Lies*.

11. Padgett, *Science and the Study of God*, 93.

12. Ibid., 93.

What I mean by synergy, in the context of the origin of consciousness, is that the interaction and combination of theology, philosophy, and science is greater than the sum of the individual disciplines bearing on the question at hand. It is not to say that any of these disciplines is invading in the territory of the other. For instance, science will not dictate questions about the nature of the Holy Trinity, nor will theology impose a method of multiplying microbial organisms, etc. Science, for example, has absolutely nothing to say directly about God's nature (as understood in classical theism). This would be the domain of philosophical theology. But that is not to say that certain findings of the natural world, gathered through scientific observation, cannot say anything about God's action which may reveal something about His nature. Moreover, science takes for granted the existence of space, time, and matter— science is inoperable without these in place. This implies that engagement over metaphysical nothingness is the domain of philosophy and engagement upon spiritual beings is the domain of Catholic theology.

A bidirectional approach helps examine the complex interaction between science and theology, which itself is a philosophical question, one having to do with how theology can influence science on the origin of consciousness. The response to this first question reveals the first prong of this book, which examines the approach of physicist and theologian Robert Russell, whose novel approach to the science-theology discourse, Creative Mutual Interaction (CMI), allows for a bidirectional interaction between the two disciplines. CMI involves eight pathways; five from science to theology and three from theology to science. All pathways have been examined throughout the book but there will be a stronger focus on the latter three. I must emphasize again that theology's interaction is not meant to denigrate or subsume the sciences. The sciences do have many interesting things to say on consciousness, which will be explored in detail in our application of Russell's CMI to the origin of consciousness, but the point, as renowned philosopher of mind David Chalmers says, is this:

> The problem of consciousness lies uneasily at the border of science and philosophy. I would say that it is properly a scientific subject matter: it is a natural phenomenon like motion, life, and cognition and calls out for an explanation in the way that these do. But it is not open to investigation by the usual scientific methods. Everyday scientific methodology has trouble getting a grip on it, not least because of the difficulties observing the phenomenon. Outside of the first-person case, data are hard to come by. This is not to say that no external data can be relevant, but we first have to arrive at a coherent philosophical understanding before we can justify the data's relevance. In this book

> I reach conclusions that some people may think of as "anti-scientific": I argue that reductive explanation of consciousness is impossible, and I even argue for a form of dualism. But this is just part of the scientific process. Certain sorts of explanation turn out to not work, so we need to embrace other sorts of explanation instead. Everything I say here is compatible with the results of contemporary science; our picture of the natural world is broadened, not overturned.[13]

I completely endorse Chalmers's insights here, but I do part ways when he later reveals his naturalistic inclinations. This is where the second prong of the book, which is intertwined with the first, provides justification for the origin of consciousness. Therefore, I maintain that Christian theology has something to contribute to this interaction in a number of ways. The second prong is also one that I contend will help in discerning the origin of consciousness, but this is to be detailed in chapter 1 with respect to Russell's "CMI." The precise ways in which Christian theology make a contribution to the sciences in terms of explaining the origin of consciousness will be detailed in chapter 7.

Second is the question of content: Does Christian theism, in light of the Christian conception of God and creation, provide a plausible explanation for the origin of consciousness? In other words, do particular arguments in natural theology, philosophical theology, and systematic theology provide a plausible explanation for the origin of consciousness? Philosophical theology is the application of philosophical tools to analyze theological concepts. In this book, it is used to understand the nature of God in the doctrine of divine simplicity. Unlike both philosophical theology and natural theology, systematic theology attempts to formulate a coherent picture of both special and general revelation.[14] Moreover, it is worth noting that systematic theology takes into account both philosophy and science, but unlike natural theology and philosophical theology (general revelation), draws also on biblical texts (special revelation).

It is my contention that the Christian conception of God and creation can help provide a satisfying response to this question. However, in order

---

13. Chalmers, *The Conscious Mind*, xiv. To be sure, albeit controversial, there are several developing scientific theories of consciousness that attempt to account for its nature and origins. These will be examined later in greater detail and include the following: Integrated Information Theory, see Tononi and Koch, "Consciousness: here, there and everywhere?" 1–18. There are others such as Stuart Hameroff and Roger Penrose's Orchestrated Objective Reduction (Orch-OR Theory): see Hameroff and Penrose, "Reply to criticism of the 'Orch OR qubit'—'Orchestrated objective reduction' is scientifically justified," 94–100.

14. Geisler, *Systematic Theology*, 14.

to require a truly compelling response, it would require much more rigor since the development of each of these arguments has entailed book-length treatments and/or dissertations by scholars who have defended them. The arguments also have a long history of back-and-forth rebuttals in peer-reviewed journals and anthologies. Thus, it is not my intention to retrace the history of each of the arguments in natural theology, philosophical theology, and systematic theology, nor am I arbitrating between the many debates surrounding them individually. My intention is to simply propose plausible paths for the science and theology dialogue and an overall explanation for the origin of consciousness. Nevertheless, individually, these arguments are strong and defensible in the face of the strongest detractors. However, cumulatively these arguments, in my estimation, are even more powerful and persuasive. The reason I state this is because they paint a picture of a universe where the likelihood of the origin of consciousness is quite high given the plausibility of the premises of each argument. My goal is solely to provide a sketch of these arguments in order to give the background information pertaining to this particular universe whereby Christian theism provides a plausible explanation for the origination of consciousness. For this purpose, I utilize CENTAC. The steps in this line of argumentation include: the Kalam Cosmological Argument (KCA), the fine-tuning of the laws of physics and biology, the origin information necessary to build the first organism, and evolutionary convergence where biological complexity meets consciousness in its human form. Further argumentation in philosophical theology to affirm God's nature includes the notion of God's simplicity, which is in part derived from the implications of CENTAC. The systematic theological arguments, which further indicate the nature of consciousness as manifested in humanity, work in addition to CENTAC, further delineating the type of God responsible for the origin of consciousness, specifically the Christian God. These arguments include: the image-likeness of God, the origin of moral consciousness and the Trinitarian Mode of Creation.

It is worth pointing out that CENTAC on its own would be akin to what Blaise Pascal had famously named "the Philosopher's God," but the closer and more intimately involved this God becomes with His creation (e.g., the fine-tuning of the laws of biology, the origin of information for the first replicating system and the origin of self-consciousness) the closer to theism, and then eventually to Christian theism one gets with the systematic theological arguments. It would be wholly inadequate to suggest that an argument such as the Kalam Cosmological Argument or any of the others in CENTAC could possibly affirm the Christian conception of God since in isolation these arguments are not meant to do so. Thus, the second prong of the book is in combination and conjunction with the arguments of CENTAC, divine simplicity, and the ones I offer in systematic theology, according to which we get a fuller picture of the Christian God. We could, of course, go on arguing for other justifications of Christian theology such as Jesus's divine self-understanding and the historical evidences of Jesus's resurrection, but this would take us beyond the scope of the origin of consciousness. It is also worth mentioning that each of the arguments of CENTAC, taken on their own, only demonstrate a very generic type of God, even a deistic understanding of God. But when the arguments are cumulatively understood, in conjunction with the systematic theological ones—a specific Christian understanding of God is revealed. In developing these arguments, I intend to present a reasonable explanation for why the Christian conception of God and creation helps affirm the origin of consciousness. This will be explored in chapters 5 and 6.

One may now ask the following questions: What is the value of the second prong to the book? And how is it connected to the first prong? At least intuitively, the nature of our own consciousness seems indicative of an ultramundane consciousness, but its justification is dependent on additional argumentation. This is partly because of the objection that humans have never experienced nor directly encountered a disembodied consciousness. Humans of course encounter other minds all the time; they engage in acts of self-consciousness when they think and reflect about their own existence and thoughts. They also experience God in a personal way throughout their lives. However, to have a direct encounter with God as a disembodied consciousness is something that is not typically pursued on the level of involving rational argumentation.[15]

It is worth indicating that due to the very nature of consciousness, it appears to be a subject-dependent type of "thing." Furthermore, it seems not only plausible but reasonable to think that the connection between consciousness and matter is contingent and not necessary. Therefore, careful consideration between complexity and consciousness is necessary. This being said, further argumentation is needed to draw the connection between finite/contingent consciousness and necessary consciousness, i.e., God (eternal consciousness among many other attributes). Thus, the second prong provides a backdrop and justification for finite consciousness pointing toward the eternal existence of God. From the implications of CENTAC, some insights toward several attributes of God are revealed, such as being

15. Unless one is engaging in argumentation for God's existence, but such arguments do not directly link God's disembodied nature with His existence; rather they are derived from the implications of arguments like the Kalam Cosmological Argument or other cosmological arguments. For a unique work that attempts to provide epistemic warrant for belief in God and other minds, see Plantinga, *God and Other Minds*.

uncaused, immaterial, spaceless, timeless, changeless, and inconceivably intelligent and powerful. Some of these attributes will be argued in chapter 5. This prong, alongside the systematic theological arguments, in my estimation, points persuasively not only to the existence of the Christian God as understood by classical Christian theism, but also to an explanation as to why consciousness ever originated in this universe. In other words, it is the sort of thing you would expect to originate given such an understanding of the universe and the data of human consciousness.

In response to the second question, it is worth noting that the second prong is embedded within the pathways and guidelines of the first prong of the book. For the purposes of the book, I see the two prongs mutually informing one another. This is precisely where philosophy plays a vital role in not only mediating between both science and theology, but also deeply interconnecting the two great disciplines. In my estimation, it is naïve to think that science, theology, and philosophy can be neatly segregated from one another (we will return and elaborate more on this in chapter 1). Through Russell's CMI and my use of it, a synergy appears between science, philosophy, and theology; strongly bonding the three disciplines together. The second prong is intimately linked to the arguments in natural theology, philosophical theology, and systematic theology. These arguments help form a basis for providing the background information for the possibility of the origination of consciousness, i.e., it sets up a universe allowing not only for the possibility of the origin of consciousness, but for its high likelihood since we start with mind or consciousness, not matter or metaphysical nothingness alone. As this is a work primarily in theology, a major presupposition, although a highly plausible one (as demonstrated through CENTAC), of this book is that the emergence of consciousness is impossible without mind in the first place. If all that exists is matter somehow self-assembling itself through the laws of physics and chemistry into more numerous and large segments of complex matter, then the question of how consciousness emerges in the absence of a source consciousness is troubling. Naturalistic emergence merely asserts that complex forms of matter give rise to something fundamentally different, but a detailed, cogent, and plausible explanation is never truly provided. It is truly an example of getting something from nothing. The only "viable" alternative to a world where consciousness results from God would be panpsychism, whereby consciousness is a fundamental property of matter. However, this position is fraught with difficulties, including the combination problem.[16] Nevertheless, it is still very well

16. This seems like the final subterfuge for naturalists to attempt to circumvent God in their reliance on an archaic explanation of consciousness (dating back to Thales and East Ancient Buddhism). The combination problem is a significant problem for

possible that God could cause matter to be conscious, as demonstrated in Teilhard de Chardin's law of complexity-consciousness. However, as already stated, the connection between consciousness and matter is contingent: it is not at all obvious that it is a necessary connection. Moreover, consciousness always belongs to a subject: it is owned, not ownerless. The burden of proof would be on the one making the assertion.

In the minds of scientific materialists or naturalists, coupling theology and its potential contribution to the outlined questions may seem unnecessary and irrelevant to the study of this already complex question.[17] However, naturalists such as philosopher William Lyons acknowledge how out of place immaterial substances are in the naturalist universe. He succinctly states the following:

> [physicalism] seem[s] to be in tune with scientific materialism of the twentieth century because it [is] a harmonic of the general theme that all there is in the universe is matter and energy and motion and that humans are a product of the evolution of species just as much as buffaloes and beavers are. Evolution is a seamless garment with no holes wherein souls might be inserted from above.[18]

---

panpsychism: it has to do with how consciousness accumulates in its miniscule forms, as found in sub-atomic particles, so as to combine and form into consciousness in its more elaborate forms and to experience qualia and self-consciousness. For a first articulation of the problem, see James, *The Principles of Psychology, Vol. 1*. For an appraisal of the problem, see Chalmers, "The Combination Problem for Panpsychism,"; Goff, "Why Panpsychism Doesn't Help Us Explain Consciousness," 289–311. For general problems, see Searle, "Consciousness and the Philosophers," 43–44. For an informative paper which explains that some panpsychists such as Chalmers should not hold on to panpsychism and for a second position of organizational invariantism simultaneously, see: Sebastián, "What Panpsychists Should Reject: On the Incompatibility of Panpsychism and Organizational Invariantism," 1833–46. Sebastián explains the tension involved in holding seemingly mutually exclusive propositions in his abstract:

> Some philosophers, like David Chalmers, have either shown their sympathy for, or explicitly endorsed, the following two principles: Panpsychism— roughly the thesis that the mind is ubiquitous throughout the universe—and Organizational Invariantism—the principle that holds that two systems with the same fine-grained functional organization will have qualitatively identical experiences. The purpose of this paper is to show the tension between the arguments that back up both principles. This tension should lead, or so I will argue, defenders of one of the principles to give up on the other.

17. In the introduction, I will further outline the problems with the conflict model and the independence model (with those of faith and outside) in order to justify the CMI program. This will involve a detailed discussion of critical realism, Lakatosian research programs and epistemic holism in chapter 2.

18. As quoted in J. P. Moreland, *Consciousness and the Existence of God*, 2. For

Nonetheless, by its very nature, the science-theology dialogue moves far and beyond such narrow views. Although this book is intended to be exploratory in nature, it is my contention that the assumptions brought forth by metaphysical materialism and naturalism[19] are not warranted and have led us down blind alleys in unraveling the difficult questions of being. As I will explain further below, part of the endeavor of the science-theology dialogue and of the use of critical realism as a methodological tool is to argue against various forms of reductionism, such as epistemic, ontological, causal, and eliminative.[20] This was a major attraction of Ian Barbour's work to thinkers like Robert J. Russell.[21] Therefore, I do think there are a number of good reasons as to why this question is worth exploring. As we shall see, Lyons sentiment is not at all uncommon to philosophical naturalists: there is an acknowledgment of the difficult and indeed mystifying element to the very presence of consciousness in a material universe.

Philosopher Thomas Nagel realizes that the reductive materialistic picture cannot account for the origin of information necessary to build the first replicating system or for the phenomenon of consciousness. He thus poses the pointed question: "If physics and chemistry cannot fully account for life and consciousness, how will their immense body of truth be combined with other elements in an expanded conception of the natural order that can accommodate those things?"[22]

On the other hand, there are some non-materialists, and even some Christian theists who disagree with the methodology I propose, i.e., with the notion that theology can influence science. This is a term that Russell uses for the bidirectional interaction of science to theology and theology to science. It is important to note what Russell means by "influence"[23]:

> At the outset, however, I want to stress that by "influence" I am *not* assuming that theologians speak with some special kind

---

original quote see Lyons, *Modern Philosophy of Mind*, iv.

19. That is beyond the dictates of methodological naturalism. Scientists who are not philosophically informed tend to conflate methodological naturalism with metaphysical naturalism—the view that all that exists is nature. The two are very distinct; methodological naturalism is proper to modern scientific investigation.

20. For an interesting paper which challenges reductionist assumptions underlying much of neuroscience which are identified more with ideology than science, see Tortorello, "What is Real about Reductive Neuroscience?," 1–20.

21. See Russell, *Cosmology*, 4–5.

22. Nagel, *Mind & Cosmos*, 8.

23. It is a term that Russell uses in a synonymous fashion to the term interaction. He does not go too deeply in defining what he means by "influence" but uses the guidelines as a means to demonstrate what he means by that word.

of dogmatic authority. Quite the contrary; the overall context should be an open intellectual exchange between scholars based on mutual respect and fallibility of hypotheses proposed by either side . . . The asymmetry between theology and science should now be quite apparent: Theological theories do not act as data for science, placing constraints on which theories can be constructed in the way the scientific theories do for theology. This, again, reflects the prior assumption that the sciences are structured in an epistemic hierarchy of constraints and irreducibility. It also safeguards science from any normative claims by theology. Together these eight paths [of the CMI] portray science and theology in a much more interactive mode. I suggest calling this *"the method of creative mutual interaction."*[24]

As shown by Russell, the role between theology and science is not equivalent, as will be discussed in chapters 2 (especially 2.7) and 7. Following Russell, what I mean by influencing is providing a conceptual framework for science to operate from. The other ways that theology influences the sciences are through providing philosophical assumptions underlying the sciences. I also mean that theology, through particular doctrines, can provide a criterion to select from rival scientific theories. This will be explored more deeply when we engage in our application of the science-theology interaction to the origin of consciousness.[25]

To the question why one should explore the question of the origin of consciousness in terms of theology's fruitful contribution to the natural sciences, one could respond with a simple "why not?" But a much more satisfying response is to demonstrate that there is a strong bidirectional influence between science and theology. Despite the many scientific and technological developments over the past few centuries, theology has something to contribute to this conversation concerning the origin of consciousness. Isolating the disciplines of science, philosophy, and theology does not bring us any closer to resolving the deep questions of being. We indeed live in one world where there are deep connections and interactions between the physical, intellectual, and spiritual. These are all essential elements to the human person and indeed the world around us. To neglect one over the other is to neglect the nature of nature. The question with respect to the origin of consciousness has fascinated the minds of thinking human persons since the beginning of recorded history. Inevitably when one ponders any sort of question that is worth one's while, a subsequent question emerges:

24. Russell, "Eschatology and Scientific Cosmology: From Conflict to Interaction," 105.

25. See chapter 7.

Why should one want to explore the question at all? The following list provides reasons as to why one would want to approach this question from this angle. Before I provide these reasons, it should be noted that not all of them will be explored in great depth throughout this book. However, they can act as springboards for future research:

1. The verification principle and its close associate, the falsification principle, had stifled many philosophical and theological questions revolving around revelation and God. With their collapse, many of the questions in theology, philosophy of religion, and philosophy of mind have opened up again, where a dialogue and dialectic can develop.[26]

2. The science and theology interaction with respect to the origin of conscience is intimately connected to who we are as human persons and how we reflect upon ourselves.

   a. This interaction relates to the concept of our created capacities in reference to God, namely being created in God's image-likeness.

   b. It will be worthwhile to explore this connection between consciousness and the *imago dei* doctrine.[27]

3. Considering the great advancement in the sciences and information revolution, the time is ripe for this kind of exploration: such advancements are a significant aid to understanding ourselves and the cosmos.[28]

4. In turn, it seems as though both philosophy and theology have benefited from these advancements. Nonetheless it is worth bringing to attention that philosophy and theology presuppositions/assumptions are embedded within scientific notions and theories, which can also act as guides and be used both implicitly and explicitly.[29]

5. The burgeoning interaction between theology and science in recent years has set the stage for addressing deep questions about consciousness.

---

26. See Moreland and Craig, *Philosophical Foundations for a Christian Worldview*, 154–56; Craig, "Theism Defended," 901–90. This discussion on the verification principle and the falsification principle will continue in chapter 2.

27. This will be explored below in a couple of systematic theology arguments regarding self-consciousness and its closely related concept of moral consciousness.

28. This will be seen below through research guidelines in chapter 7 regarding different theories of consciousness.

29. This will be explored below with Russell's Creative Mutual Interaction and different understandings of divine action.

a. Although what the natural sciences and the neurosciences say to theology in terms of constraints is very important, I contend that what theology has to say to them is equally important.

b. An important aspect of this book will be to demonstrate that theology has something positive to say about the origin of consciousness and personhood. I wish to explore what sort of research avenues theology can inspire to the natural and neuro-sciences.

c. Advancements in nonmaterialistic science with discernment of the mind-body problem.[30]

6. The question of God and creation in understanding the origins and emergence of consciousness opens the gateway within contemporary culture to tackling suppressed ethical dilemmas. This can be done through providing justification for our ability to talk more forthrightly about those who hold strictly natural and materialist perspectives on the meaning of personhood, human dignity, freedom of choice, euthanasia, brain death, vegetative states, abortion, and other moral issues related to the human person with respect to the origins and nature of consciousness.

---

30. These ideas will be further explored in our research guidelines under the section "Dualist Notions with Scientific Implications (A Spiritual Neuroscience?)." The following texts attempt to present a scientific case for substance dualism: Jeffrey M. Schwartz's work has actually been guided by the presupposition that the mind is separate from the brain. He has been able to help thousands of patients combat obsessive compulsive disorder without prescribing medication, relying instead on mental capacities that have an effect on the neurophysiological makeup of the brain. Mario Beauregard received his PhD in neuroscience and is currently affiliated with the Department of Psychology, University of Arizona, which is renowned for its Center for Consciousness. See Schwartz, *Brain Lock: Free Yourself from Obsessive Compulsive Behavior*; Schwartz and Begley, *The Mind & The Brain*; Schwartz, Stapp, and Beauregard, "The Volitional Influence of the Mind on the Brain, with Special Reference to Emotional Self-Regulation," chapter 7; Schwartz, Stapp, and Beauregard, "Quantum Theory in Neuroscience and Psychology: A Neurophysical Model of Mind-Brain Interaction," 1309–27; Schwartz, et al., "Mindful Awareness and Self-Directed Neuroplasticity: Integrating Psychospiritual and Biological Approaches to Mental Health with a Focus on Obsessive Compulsive Disorder," chapter 13; Beauregard and O'Leary, *The Spiritual Brain*; Schwartz, *You Are Not Your Brain*; Beauregard, *Brain Wars*.

The Science & Theology Dialogue

Historical Considerations

While recent centuries may well document a divide that has developed between theology and science, prior to the age of Enlightenment the relationship between science and theology seemed more collaborative. Many of the leading scientists of the day assumed that the universe was intelligible, rational, and could be discerned by the human mind. For example, both the theological assumptions of *creation ex nihilo* and the contingency of the world played a dominant role within the rise of modern science.[31]

In this section, we will examine the thought of John Philoponus, the first thinker of antiquity to bring rigor to the doctrine of *creation ex nihilo*. He also demonstrated that theological doctrines could be deeply connected to philosophy and science (or more accurately natural philosophy). From there a brief word on the development of science and its relation to theological and philosophical thought from the early modern era will be offered. Then brief reflections will be provided by nineteenth- and early-twentieth-century thinkers such as Charles Darwin (1809–1882), Alfred Wallace (1823–1913), and Gilbert Keith Chesterton (1874–1936). Pierre Teilhard de Chardin (1881–1955) will be briefly considered in this section, although his thought on God, consciousness, evolution, and creation will be examined in chapter 4. Brief references to contemporary scientists and philosophers such as Thomas Nagel, who have reflected deeply on the nature of reality, creation, science, the human person, and consciousness, will also be made.

John Philoponus

A strong historical example is found in the preserved writings of John Philoponus. Philoponus's belief that God created the universe out of nothing played a significant role in questioning the reigning philosophy of his time.[32] Many Christians and Jews were embarrassed by the doctrine of *creation ex nihilo* and were divided over whether God created from pre-existing matter through reorganizing it or created matter itself from nothing.[33] The reason for this embarrassment was precisely because of the natural philosophical consensus that pointed toward an eternal past. As philosopher and

31. Russell, "Eschatology and Physical Cosmology," 285.

32. The prevailing philosophic (pre-scientific) view from the time of the pre-Socratic materialists up until as recently as the early twentieth century modern science was that the universe was infinite in the past.

33. Sorabji, "Infinity and Creation," 208.

renowned Philoponus commentator, Richard Sorabji notes: "Up to AD 529, Christians were on the defensive. They argued that a beginning of the universe was not impossible. In 529, Philoponus swung round into the attack. He argued that a beginning of the universe was actually mandatory, and mandatory of the pagans' own principles."[34] Instrumental to Philoponus's approach was a separation between Creator and creation. This belief allowed him to argue not only that the past was finite, but also that the sun is made of fire, which he acknowledged as a terrestrial substance, as opposed to a celestial substance.[35] Thus, Philoponus established that heavenly bodies are not divine and are subject to decomposition, thereby collapsing a central Aristotelian doctrine before a Christian doctrine.[36]

Philoponus's Christian worldview permitted him to also create a coherent system of thought where he could provide argumentation and evidence to support his belief system—one that was fruitful to scientific discovery. Some examples include not only his criticism of Aristotle's doctrine of the eternity of the world but also his criticism of Aristotle's theory of light[37] and the Aristotelian view of dynamics. Historians of science have noted that Philoponus's rigor was beneficial to the future direction of cosmology.[38] Moreover, he was able to do so, without sole recourse to sacred texts, but through arguments grounded in experience.[39] Philoponus's integrative approach to what he observed in reality with his Christian faith allowed him to develop a prototypic natural theology that has developed throughout the centuries up until the present thanks to the work of Islamic, Jewish, and Christian theologians and philosophers.

As history has shown, philosophy and theology have played a large role in the rise of modern scientific theories. Philoponus was an early example of such an influence. According to Sorabji, interestingly, Galileo makes mention of Philoponus more recurrently than Plato in his early works. To get a real sense and appreciation for Philoponus's thought, one must realize the impact of Philoponus's ideas on medieval and early modern philosophy and science. Sorabji, who has spent a significant amount of time studying Philoponus's works, notes that Bonaventure was falsely credited for Philoponus's ingenious arguments against an eternal past.[40] Seven hundred years

---

34. Sorabji, "Infinity and Creation," 210.

35. Lindberg and Numbers, *God & Nature*, 38–39.

36. Ibid., 38–39.

37. Christensen, "Aristotle and Philoponus on Light."

38. Lindberg and Numbers, *God & Nature*, 39.

39. Ibid., 39.

40. Sorabji, "Infinity and Creation," 210.

later, Bonaventure was merely recirculating the same arguments, which had been preserved by Muslim theologians. Furthermore, it is interesting to note, recent scholarly works trace the scientific revolutionary notion of the introduction of impetus theory (the force with which a body moves) into dynamics back to Philoponus. This notion became known to Europe through Muslim philosophers.[41] Philoponus's critiques of the eternality of the universe are found in three major phases.[42] Thus, Philoponus's understanding of reality, which was heavily influenced and guided by his Christian faith, brought about several fruits that are relevant to this very day. His theological and philosophical reasoning is confirmed by modern empirical science, which affirms that that the universe is not eternal in the past. This affirmation is made through two lines of reasoning: the expansion of the universe (as argued by the standard big bang model) and the second law of thermodynamics. Both of these can be remarkably traced in Philoponus's thought. Even though the evidence provided by the empirical sciences is typically provisional and can indeed change in the future, we have good reasons to believe in the beginning of the universe, as established by modern scientific data. Philoponus in the sixth century exemplifies a strong consonance[43] between science and theology in the Early Middle Ages.

41. For further details, see: Richard Sorabji, "John Philoponus," and "Infinity and Creation."

42. First, *Against Proclus's "On the Eternity of the World 1–5"* (De aeternitate mundi contra Proclum) (529). See Philoponus, *Against Proculus's "On the Eternity of the World 1–5,"* vii. According to Sorabji, this text is "one of the most interesting of all post-Aristotelian Greek philosophical texts, written at a crucial moment in the defeat of paganism by Christianity"; Second, *Against Aristotle on the Eternity of the World* (De aeternitate mundi contra Aristotelem) (530–34). See Wildberg, "John Philoponus," In this second phase, Philoponus examines Aristotle's work *On the Heavens*. According to Herbert A. Davidson, it is unclear how accurately Simplicius actually quotes Philoponus since his vitriol may indicate the possibility of deliberate misrepresentation, which is evidenced by several incongruencies. There is also reason to believe that there are sources of Philoponus's work on *Against Aristotle* independent from Simplicius's commentaries, e.g., certain Arab thinkers such as Farabi. This work has been lost but is mainly known through citations in Simplicius's commentaries on Aristotle's *De Caelo* and *Physics*. See Davidson, "John Philoponus as a Source of Medieval Islamic and Jewish Proofs of Creation," 357–59. Third, a treatise titled *On the Creation of the World* (De opificio mundi) that survived in fragments and that provides a series of arguments for *creation ex nihilo*. See again: Wildberg, "John Philoponus."

43. A termed frequently used by philosopher Ernan McMullin to signify the confluence and consistency between theological notions and scientific affirmations. See Hess and Allen, *Catholicism and Science*, 134–37; Barzaghi and Corcó, "Ernan McMullin's Thought on Science and Theology: An Appreciation," 512–23.

The Early Modern Era[44]

The assumptions regarding the intelligibility and rationality of reality came to shape much of the empiricism in science, as well as the use of mathematics to describe natural processes.[45] Indeed, theological insights and understanding inspired developments in modern scientific thought. This is especially true of great scientific minds such as Isaac Newton, Johannes Kepler, Rene Descartes, Galileo Galilei and Nicolas Copernicus, who posited that the structure of physical reality was knowable.[46] These explicitly theological ideas, according to which there is intelligibility and comprehensibility in reality because of God's role as Creator,[47] inspired scientists to adopt a type of reverse engineering mode of thinking (where humans could possibly even modify and perfect creation) in order to understand how things were created (this was precisely the mode of thinking possessed by Isaac Newton).[48] This would in turn help to perceive how the universe functioned. The point here is that, from the early modern period until the early twentieth century, scientists were explicitly aided by theological thoughts and notions to discern the existence and operation of nature. The inescapable thought here is that modern science was born out of a Christian worldview: these theological notions set a framework for scientific research and discovery. Throughout history theological thought and science have gone hand in hand more often than not. They seem to be more partners than foes, despite the popular depiction of their relation. However, on a number of occasions, science does the work of science and has nothing to say regarding theology, and vice versa. This is especially true when the sciences deal with arguably metaphysically neutral questions such as the number of elements in the periodic table or the physical and chemical properties of water that permit it to change into three different states. Yet when one is dealing with questions such as cosmological or biological origins, Einstein's theories of special or general relativity and their implications on our views of time, the relationship is not so clear.

44. This term is used for simplification. For an understanding of the real complexities that lie behind the Copernican Revolution and the important relationship between history and scientific movements, see Blumenberg, *The Genesis of the Copernican World.*

45. Russell, "Eschatology and Physical Cosmology," 285.

46. Grant, "Science and Theology in the Middle Ages," 59.

47. As has been aforementioned, this will be examined in a section on Lonergan and his argument for God based on the intelligibility of reality.

48. Fuller, *Dissent over Descent,* 51.

Over 150 years ago, the majority of scientists believed that God's creation seemed to have a stronger affinity with a certain scriptural interpretation.[49] In 1605, Francis Bacon famously proposed his doctrine of "two books," one pertaining to natural revelation (physical reality), and the other to supernatural revelation (biblical texts). He sought to achieve the outmost progress of understanding for both types of revelations.[50]

However, many contemporary scientists believe that such appropriations are neither apparent nor as obvious as they used to be; some scientists, influenced by postmodernism, even say that they are non-existent.[51] It is also important to note that, although philosophical or theological assumptions are often not explicitly fleshed out, they play a significant role in the development of scientific theories, even if the scientist(s) may not be completely aware of such frameworks or presuppositions.[52]

Sentiments from the Nineteenth Century to the Present

In 1863, the geologist Charles Lyell (1797–1875), who mentored Darwin in the methodology employed for abductive reasoning throughout the *Origin of Species*, and Thomas Henry Huxley (1825–1895), who is known as Darwin's "bull-dog," wrote their respective works on the origin of humanity from an evolutionary perspective. Lyell allowed for mainly physical explanations for all of human features[53] except with respect to the human intellect (consciousness) and moral sensibilities which, in his view, were directly attributable to God's creative action. Huxley, on the other hand, sought to explain *all* features of humanity by physical processes. Charles Darwin did not weigh in on the questions until 1871 with the publication of *The Descent of Man*. Jon H. Roberts, a religion and science historian, makes the following observation:

49. Moore, "Geologists and Interpreters of Genesis in the Nineteenth Century," 323. The hermeneutics involved in Genesis has a very complex history which is partially explored throughout this article. The nineteenth-century professionals, including geologists such as Lyell and others, alongside German Old Testament scholars, presupposed that nature should interpret Genesis, that is to say that we should use the findings of science and work back to understand the text rather than the other way around.

50. Moore, "Geologists and Interpreters of Genesis," 322.

51. Postmodernism incoherently holds to the view that there is no such thing as objective/universal truth, but of course such a statement is self-refuting since any negation of an objective truth is an inevitable affirmation of it. If this were actually the case, the whole endeavor of science, theology and philosophy would collapse. Indeed, so would any form of communication.

52. Russell, "Eschatology and Physical Cosmology," 285–86.

53. Roberts, "Religious reactions to Darwin, 84.

In attempting to demonstrate that even human intellectual, spiritual and moral attributes could be understood within an evolutionary context, Darwin employed two interwoven strategies. First, he sought to persuade his readers that the mental differences between the human species and the higher animals were differences of degree rather than kind by showing that those higher animals possessed, in incipient form, numerous mental endowments—powers and aptitudes such as the capacity for improvement, the ability to use tools, and even religious impulses—that had frequently been thought of as uniquely human. Second, through a process of imaginative historical reconstruction, Darwin sought to show that even humanity's possession of moral sense, which he regarded as 'the best and highest distinction between man and the lower animals,' could be explained 'exclusively from the side of natural history.'[54]

Thus, any discontinuity between the human mind and that of lower primates is avoided by naturalistic evolutionists from Darwin forward. Darwin exemplifies this view when he states in *The Descent of Man* that:

> The difference in mind between man and the higher animals, great as it is, certainly is one of degree and not of kind. We have seen that the senses and intuitions, the various emotions and faculties, such as love, memory, attention, curiosity, imitation, reason, etc., of which man boasts, may be found in an incipient or even sometimes in a well-developed condition, in the lower animals.[55]

Interestingly, and in an opposing direction, Wallace, who was best known for his co-discovery of natural selection (alongside Darwin in 1859), thought that natural selection could explain most organic physical phenomena but not the the origin of life nor the origins of human consciousness:

> Let us fearlessly admit that the mind of man (itself the living proof of a supreme mind) is able to trace, and to a considerable extend has traced, the laws by means of which the organic no less than the inorganic world has been developed. But let us not shut our eyes to the evidence that an Overruling Intelligence has watched over the action of those laws, so directing variations and so determining their accumulation, as finally to produce an

---

54. Roberts, "Religious reactions to Darwin," 85.
55. Darwin, *The Descent of Man and Selection in Relation to Sex*, 126.

organization sufficiently perfect to admit of, and even to aid in, the indefinite advancement of our mental and moral nature.[56]

Chesterton in his classic *Everlasting Man* written ninety years ago, had the following insight:

> The matter here is one of history and not of philosophy so that it need only be noted that no philosopher denies that a mystery still attaches to the two great transitions: the origin of the universe itself and the origin of the principle of life itself. Most philosophers have the enlightenment to add that a third mystery attaches to the origin of man himself. In other words, a third bridge was built across a third abyss of the unthinkable when there came into the world what we call reason and what we call will. Man is not merely an evolution but rather a revolution. That he has a backbone or other parts upon a similar pattern to birds and fishes, is an obvious fact, whatever be the meaning of the fact. But if we attempt to regard him, as it were, as a quadruped standing on his hind legs, we shall find what follows far more fantastic and subversive than if he were standing on his head.[57]

Despite the significant increase in our knowledge of cosmology, physics, chemistry, bio-chemistry, and the neurosciences, these three singular "events": the origin of the universe, that of life, and that of mind (consciousness) remain even more daunting to unravel, particularly from a strict naturalistic perspective, than they did in 1925 when Chesterton reflected upon them. For instance, the evidence in cosmology has been pointing more intensely and persuasively to a definite beginning, with the layering of confirmatory scientific evidence, which includes George Lemaître's hypothesis that an expanding universe must be traced back to a "primeval atom." In this section, I will not delve into specific details regarding the scientific advancements with respect to the origin of the universe and life, even though in subsequent sections I will explain the relevancy of such events for this book.[58] The other key point to extract from Chesterton's insight is his recognition of the exceptionality of the human person: he states that "Man is not merely an evolution but rather a revolution." Chesterton intuits that although humanity has evolved the same physical components as the lower primates, there is something radically novel that is unique to humans. Moreover, while the animal kingdom displays extreme levels of complexity,

---

56. Wallace, "Sir Charles Lyell on Geological Climates and the Origin of Species," 394.

57. Chesterton, *The Everlasting Man*, 158.

58. See chapter 5 on Natural Theology/Philosophical Theology Arguments.

the complexity of human features, despite the high degree of complexity of the brain, is not what makes the human person exceptional. Rather it is, *in part*, the existence of a high level of consciousness, the ability to ponder great thoughts of existence and the like.

Teilhard, seeing that consciousness was present in rudimentary forms of matter and that it had reached its current and local pinnacle in human consciousness, expounded panpsychism. He offers an interesting outlook as a paleontologist and a theologian. All of these different views regarding human consciousness share the radicalness of its presence in humanity.

There seems to be an inherent fascination with questions of origin embedded in deeply inquisitive minds. This inner fascination with respect to the exterior and the interior world is ultimately driven by a quest to find or get closer to truth. The search is propelled by this hunger, thirst, and desire that can only be satiated, quenched, and fulfilled through the source of ultimate truth (a necessary being responsible for *all there is*).

Among Christian thinkers, the position is not clear-cut on consciousness. However, a fundamental point of agreement between various outlooks on the origin of humans is that humans that originally bore the full image-likeness of God would have had to be morally self-reflective agents in order to have the ability to sin. There is nothing in evolutionary thought, whether through the Modern or Extended Synthesis, which precludes this. Although Darwin himself and subsequent evolutionists have held that the difference between humanity and animals was one of degree, not of kind, such debates regarding continuity versus discontinuity between humans and their precursors seem inconclusive at present. Some speculate that either consciousness itself is an emergent property of the brain or that God intervened at a certain moment to create this immaterial aspect of humanity. The former option is monistic and held by Christian thinkers such as the philosopher Peter van Inwagen.[59] The latter, substance dualism, is supported by biophysicist and geneticist Francis Collins. Both are live options for the Christian believer. Despite the anatomical continuity between humans and their precursors, it seems as though there is a fundamental disjunction in terms of level of consciousness. Thus, one can see the importance of seeking an explanation for this apparent disjunction.

---

59. See van Inwagen, *The Nature of Rational Beings: Dualism and Physicalism*, chapter 10.

The Current State of Affairs

This book is about understanding the origins and emergence of consciousness through the creative mutual interaction between science and theology
based on the conceptions of the Christian God and creation.

The current state of the interaction involves a wide range of points of
intersection that raises questions concerning the very viability and coherence of such a dialogue. Such points of intersection should include big bang
cosmology, the fine-tuning of the laws of physics, quantum physics, origin
of life studies, evolutionary biology, consciousness, the origin of objective
morality, free will, the intelligibility of the cosmos, artificial intelligence, and
the mind-body problem in the neurosciences. Without a doubt, the field
of science and theology is of such breadth and diversity that approaches to
such an interaction become equally diverse.

In order to promote some comprehensive understanding of the
diverse approaches, a number of theologians have attempted to develop
representative typologies of the approaches that define the dialogue. For
example, Ian Barbour (1923–2013), a pioneer of the science and theology
dialogue and a recipient of the 1999 Templeton Prize for his contribution
to the advancement of religion and science, has developed a well-known
fourfold typology for science and theology. It consists of the following
main typologies: conflict (scientific materialism and biblical literalism),
independence (contrasting methods and differing languages), dialogue
(presuppositions and limit questions, methodological parallels and nature-
centered spirituality), and integration (natural theology, theology of nature
and systematic synthesis).[60] As is quite evident, Barbour's typologies contain a wide range of possibilities with respect to the relationship between
science and theology. In addition, there are typologies proposed by Ted Peters, Willem Drees, and John Haught.[61] However, some critics have maintained that such typologies cannot encompass the full set of complexities
and specific features of the dialogue between theology and science due to

---

60. See Barbour, *Religion and Science*, 77–106; Barbour *Religion in an Age of Science*,
3–31. For an application of several of Barbour's typologies to Christian spirituality and
biological evolution, see Ventureyra, "Science & Christian Spirituality: The Relationship between Christian Spirituality and Biological Evolution," 1–20.

61. Barbour, *When Science Meets Religion: Enemies, Strangers, or Partners?*, 4. John
Haught's typology has a slight variation to Barbour's; see Haught, *Science and Religion*.
Ted Peters' typology consists of eight categories; under Conflict he has three sub-
categories; see Peters, *Science and Theology: The New Consonance*. William Drees has
the most, with nine categories; this is good for precision but can add confusion as the
classification of each may not rest well under a particular category. See Drees, *Religion,
Science and Naturalism*.

the fact that the very number of complexities and distinct features do not lend themselves to neatly designed categories.[62]

The common field of natural science and theology is a burgeoning discourse with the potential for valuable new discoveries and insights. Despite popular caricatures that the two great fields are at odds with one another, they have had much to say to one another in mutual cooperation throughout history. Such cooperation continues to this very day. Ever since the 1960s, a number of peer-reviewed journals devoted to the dialogue have sprung into existence. They include: *CTNS: Theology and Science Journal, The European Journal of Science and Theology, Zygon: Journal of Science and Religion*, and the latest addition: *Philosophy, Theology and the Sciences*. Indeed, the field is growing and gaining interest from scholars of a variety of disciplines.

Until the modern era, particularly until the development of evolutionary theory (Darwinism/Neo-Darwinism), many of the explanations of consciousness tended to be philosophical and/or theological in their core. In recent years, the study of consciousness has involved research in a variety of scientific disciplines, including biology, chemistry, biochemistry, genetics, physics, neuroscience, psychology, and a host of others. Moreover, modern philosophy, particularly philosophy of mind, has inspired a large number of works probing into the nature of consciousness, how it can be understood, and how it came to be. Even though theological explanations prior to the modern scientific era have provided speculations into the nature of consciousness, it seems as though reformulated notions in theology might offer a mutually creative interaction with the sciences which probe into this phenomenon.[63]

---

62. Barbour, *When Science Meets Religion*, 4.

63. In the section on "Different Christian Understandings of Consciousness," we will explore the work of J. P. Moreland, Bernard Lonergan and Daniel Helminiak, and Philip Clayton, who have all sought to reformulate or rethink their theologies in light of modern neuroscience. It is worth noting that an important co-edited volume on neuroscience and "the person" communicating different scientific, philosophical and theological positions was published under the title *Neuroscience and the Person: Scientific Perspectives on Divine Action*. Philosopher Nancey Murphy provides an interesting assessment of some of the historical-theological positions on the nature of personhood in the introduction of this volume. In addition, this work contains an important series of essays, but they are not directly relevant to this book since we are focusing on looking at the fruitful contribution of theology to the natural sciences, to the understanding of the emergence and origins of consciousness. This work delves into a series of constraints that the neurosciences impose on theology and provides points for dialogue between God and consciousness. This will be discussed below, in the application of Russell's Creative Mutual Interaction to the origin of consciousness in terms of constraints from neuroscientific findings on how conscious states are affected by brain states.

Much of the writing on the origin of consciousness focuses on the cor-relation between complexity and consciousness. This will be examined in the chapter on Teilhard, but it is common to many scientific theories of consciousness which focus on information.[64] Interestingly, geneticist John Craig Venter, along with two hundred co-authors, offers the following ca-veat regarding the connection between complexity and consciousness:

> In organisms with complex nervous systems, neither gene num-ber, neuron number, nor number of cell types correlate in any meaningful manner with even simplistic measures of structural or behavioral complexity . . . Between humans and chimpan-zees, the gene number, gene structural function, chromosomal and genomic organization, and cell types and neuroanatomies are almost indistinguishable, yet the development modifications that predisposed human lineages to cortical expansion and de-velopment of the larynx, giving rise to language, culminated in a massive singularity that by even the simplest of criteria made humans more complex in a behavioral sense . . . The real chal-lenge of human biology, beyond the task of finding out how genes orchestrate the construction and maintenance of the mi-raculous mechanism of our bodies, will lie ahead as we seek to explain how our minds have to organize thoughts sufficiently well to investigate our own existence.[65]

It is quite intriguing to witness leading biologists such as Venter and his team, who are highlighting the mystery of the irreducibility of con-sciousness. Hence, science alone is insufficient to offer a satisfying or even "true" explanation of consciousness.

In his 2012 book titled *Mind & Cosmos: Why the Materialist Neo-Dar-winian Conception of Nature is Almost Certainly False*, Thomas Nagel had pointed out that a reductive materialist interpretation of evolution is leading us down blind alleys in discerning the emergence of mind and information.[66] Although metaphysical naturalism should be contrasted with methodologi-cal naturalism,[67] it seeks to explain certain phenomena within the universe

---

64. Examples of scientific theories of consciousness which take complexity and in-formation seriously include: Integrated Information Theory (IIT) and Psychophysical Semantic Information Integration (PSII).

65. Venter et al, "The Sequence of the Human Genome," 1304–51. As cited in Rolston, *Science and Origins*, 93.

66. See Nagel, *Mind & Cosmos*, 41.

67. For an explanation of methodological naturalism and its differentiation from metaphysical naturalism, see: de Vries, "Naturalism in the Natural Sciences: A Chris-tian Perspective," 388–96.

that it is not capable of despite the great achievements in multiple domains of scientific inquiry. To be certain, Nagel is optimistic about the possibility of finding an overarching naturalistic explanation for consciousness, he is just not sure *how* such an explanation will realistically be found.

Regardless of one's worldview, the origin of consciousness is an event that is challenging to understand in the history of the universe. It raises questions such as why such a phenomenon ever came about and why it came about when it did. It also raises the question as to *how* such a phenomenon came about. Without it, the practice of science or theology would be impossible. These questions deserve careful attention since they deal with the essence of what it is to be human. Theology can shed light in potential research avenues, particularly in regards to the emergence of consciousness, since consciousness is consonant with a Christian theistic worldview where everything emanates from a transcendent principle understood as an eternal "mind."

Part of this book seeks to overcome the resistance of the natural sciences, to the input of theology, in the provision of research guidelines concerning the origin of information and consciousness (the two, in my estimation, are inextricably linked). As we shall see, several scientific theories of consciousness are intimately associated with notions and theories of information. This is also very much connected to God's action in the world. In order to present an overall coherent picture of how God acts in the world, one must use an approach that is consistent with both what we observe in nature and with our interior life, the latter including conscious activity. We will explore several arguments in systematic theology in favor of our connection with God, but also the potentiality of God's interaction within the universe through quantum mechanics and informational structures.

Some Preliminaries

Throughout the course of history, particular thinkers, depending on their traditions and presuppositions, have had different understandings of terms which are distinct but related to consciousness, including mind, soul, spirit, and psyche.[68]

68. The terms soul, mind, spirit, psyche and consciousness are deeply interconnected to one another. Despite this deep interconnection, their definitions have been blurred, thus, overlapping with one another. At times, certain thinkers throughout history have used the terms interchangeably and have conflated their meanings with one another (which seems to be the case of some contemporary discussions). We will leave, for the most part, the terms of soul, mind, spirit and psyche aside and focus on consciousness.

Defining Consciousness—How It Will Be Used in This Book

A helpful framing of consciousness is provided by philosopher Eric Lormand, who understands consciousness as involving "intentionality, introspection (and the knowledge it specifically generates) and the phenomenal experience."[69] These three aspects are of particular relevance to this book since they are all intimately related to the nature and origin of embodied consciousness.

Introspection involves the interiority of one's own conscious thoughts and self-reflective capacities, e.g., awareness of self. Over 1,600 years ago, Augustine alluded to such an understanding of consciousness in reference to the precept "Know yourself," in the sense of self-awareness.[70] This is the *main meaning* of consciousness that we will retain throughout this book. It corresponds to what I understand self-consciousness to embody. The awareness of self or self-consciousness (those are the expressions we will use throughout this book)[71] signify precisely the same things. Self-consciousness entails a recognition of individuation, i.e., that one is an individual being separated from other beings and the surrounding physical environment.[72] Moreover, it is the recognition and understanding of one's own existence and the ability to reflect about one's own existence and thoughts, a consciousness of consciousness. It is a first step toward moral consciousness,[73] fathoming one's own finitude, the aptitude for higher intellection, such as is involved in the understanding of one's self, others, nature, and God. However, intentionality[74] and phenomenal experience are also important as they are not so neatly disentangled from introspection, nor from one another.[75]

69. Lormand, "Consciousness," 167

70. Augustine, *De Trinitate X*, ix, 12; for a continued discussion on Augustine's understanding of self-awareness, see also X, x, 13–16.

71. Just to be clear, my use of self-consciousness is akin to self-awareness and is distinguished from self-consciousness as associated with guilt and embarrassment; see Rochat, *Others in Mind*. Psychologist Philippe Rochat has done much work on the origins of self-consciousness with guilt, but also in terms of self-awareness, which we will examine later in the book (chapters 5 and 7).

72. See Jabr, "Self-Awareness with a Simple Brain."

73. See Locke, *An Essay Concerning Human Understanding*, Chapter XVII. In this chapter titled, "Of Identity and diversity," Locke links self-identification with moral responsibility. With self-consciousness comes moral responsibility, particularly because of the ability to realize the weaknesses of others and how to inflict emotional and physical pains on others. It is the realization of not only others' vulnerability but of our own as well. We will briefly examine the role of moral consciousness in chapter 6.

74. Siewert, "Consciousness and Intentionality."

75. See Kind, "Qualia." Lines 18–28. Amy Kind explains the connection between phenomenal and intentional aspects of mental states:

As humans we experience all three understandings of consciousness to different degrees, depending on our cognitive, introspective, intentional, and phenomenal capacities.[76] Intentionality refers to particular mental states, including thoughts, beliefs, desires, and hopes, which are aimed at some object or state of affairs. Phenomenal experience involves what is known as qualia (singular quale), which are understood as phenomenal properties of experience, such as a specific sort of intrinsically characterized mental state, e.g., seeing the color green, having a sweet taste, smelling roses, hearing Mozart's "Great G minor symphony," and feeling a sharp pain. It is what Chalmers has likened to a theater of experience but with touch, taste, and smell. Since we have recognized that the introspective, intentional, and phenomenal capacities of consciousness are bound together, it is interesting to note that neuroscientist Antonio Damasio does not think that phenomenal consciousness is possible without a higher order of consciousness such as this book is concerned with: self-consciousness. Damasio, in fact, argues that phenomenal consciousness is dependent on self-consciousness.[77] This has startling implications, but this is his controversial claim, nonetheless.[78]

Some mental states—for example, perceptual experiences—clearly have both phenomenal and intentional aspects. My visual experience of a peach on the kitchen counter represents the peach and also has an experiential feel. Less clear is whether all phenomenal states also have intentional aspects and whether all intentional states also have phenomenal aspects. Is there really something that it is like to have the belief—even the occurrent belief—that there is a peach on the counter? What could be the representational content of the experience of an orgasm? Along these lines, the nature of the relationship between phenomenal consciousness and intentionality has recently generated considerable philosophical discussion. Some philosophers think that phenomenal consciousness can be reduced to intentional content, while others think that the reductive relationship goes in the other direction. Still other philosophers deny both claims.

The same is true with respect to the connection between introspection and either intentionality or phenomenal experience.

76. One can think of Helen Keller who was deaf and blind as lacking aspects of phenomenal experience or of people with intellectual disabilities (people with Down's syndrome), and others with perhaps other types of deficiencies when it comes to moral capacities such as those with autism or psychopathic/sociopathic traits and personalities.

77. See Damasio, *Self Comes to Mind*, 181, and 182–88.

78. Block, "What Was I Thinking," Review of *Self Comes to Mind*, has the following criticism:

Is this discussion of any practical importance? Yes. Phenomenal consciousness is what makes pain bad in itself and pleasure good. Damasio's refusal to regard phenomenal consciousness (without the involvement of the inflated self [self-consciousness] as real consciousness could be used to justify the brutalization of cows and chickens on the grounds that they are not self-conscious

Yet, it is important to understand that Damasio recognizes that in order to have self-consciousness, it must have evolved from precursors such as phenomenal consciousness.[79]

Discussions revolving around phenomenal experiences necessarily involve the distinction between subjective versus objective states. The only way one can examine subjective states is through entering into the experiential point of view held by the subject.[80] This raises the problem of whether phenomenal states can be reduced to physical states. According to Nagel, such a thing is possible if subjective states can be reduced to objective states (i.e., non-subjective).[81] As mentioned earlier, responses to this problem include eliminative materialism, which denies the existence of mental phenomena, as well as John Searle's approach, which involves "microphysical properties of the brain."[82] Nagel invokes some undiscovered nonphysical entities he has named "proto-mental properties."[83] Others like Frank Jackson and James van Cleve have emphasized the irreducibility of consciousness as emergent.[84] This latter approach is favored by Christian panentheist philosopher Philip Clayton, as we shall see.[85] Other philosophers and scientists opt for a sort of dualism. The question of consciousness is no doubt an open one, as Brian McLaughlin alludes to in his 1995 dictionary article,[86] but not much has changed twenty years or so forward. Human persons undergo unconscious states such as those experienced through anesthesia or in a coma, which means that we may be alive but not conscious. Even if one is fully conscious, one is not aware of the many physical changes our bodies endure, e.g., cell division, blood circulation, growth of nails/hair, etc.

---

and therefore not conscious. Damasio, in response to those who have raised such criticisms in the past, declares that in fact he thinks it "highly likely" that animals do have consciousness. But this doesn't square with the demanding theory he advances in his book, on the basis of which he denies consciousness in dreams and in "vegetative state" patients who can answer questions. He owes us an explanation of why he thinks chickens are conscious even though dreamers and the question-answering patients are not.

79. See Damasio, *The Self Comes to Mind*, 178–88; Damasio, *The Feeling of What Happens*. In his 1999 book, *The Feeling of What Happens*, Damasio lays out his hierarchical case for consciousness, where each level as acquired by evolutionary development is dependent on the antecedent.

80. See McLaughlin, "Philosophy of Mind: Consciousness," 605.

81. Ibid., 605.

82. Ibid.

83. Ibid.

84. Ibid.

85. See the final section of chapter 8.

86. McClaughlin, "Philosophy of Mind: Consciousness," 605.

This book affirms the unity and the real non-illusory existence of consciousness. As such, it runs contrary to those who defend the eliminative materialist position, such as Steven Pinker, Daniel Dennett, and Paul and Patricia Churchland, who are more or less on the fringe today, with respect to the science of consciousness studies.[87] Chalmer's assessment of the ability of eliminative materialism and materialism in general, to explain consciousness is especially illuminating:

> I should note that the conclusions of this work [*The Conscious Mind*] are conclusions, in the strongest sense. Temperamentally, I am strongly inclined toward materialist reductive explanation, and I have no strong spiritual or religious inclinations. For a number of years, I hoped for a materialist theory; when I gave up on this hope, it was quite reluctantly. It eventually seemed plain to me that these conclusions were forced on anyone who wants to take consciousness seriously. Materialism is a beautiful and compelling view of the world, but to account for consciousness, we have to go beyond the resources it provides. By now, I have grown almost happy with these conclusions. They do not seem to have any fearsome consequences, and they allow a way of thinking and theorizing about consciousness that seems more satisfactory in almost every way. And the expansion in the scientific worldview has had a positive effect, at least for me: it has made the universe a more interesting place.[88]

I would add that the fully articulated version of the arguments in chapters 5 and 6 present significant challenges to both the materialist and naturalist frameworks.[89] They elucidate the origin of the universe and its resistant features, including the precisely calibrated laws, constants, and initial conditions, which allow for the origin and evolution of life, specified biological complexity, and consciousness. In chapter 8 of this book, I examine three distinct Christian views concerning consciousness, including

87. For a defense of eliminative reductionism, see: Churchland, "Eliminative Materialism and the Propositional Attitudes," 67–90. Churchland, *Matter and Consciousness*; Dennett, *The Intentional Stance;* Dennett, *Consciousness Explained*; Dennett, *From Bacteria to Bach and Back*, chapter 14; Churchland, *Neurophilosophy*; Pinker, *How the Mind Works*. For several powerful critiques of eliminative materialism, see: Baker, *Saving Belief*; Boghossian, "The Status of Content," 157–84; Boghossian, "The Status of Content Revisited," 264–78; Reppert, "Eliminative Materialism, Cognitive Suicide, and Begging the Question," 378–92; Stich, *Deconstructing the Mind*.

88. Chalmers, *The Conscious Mind*, xiv.

89. There are several strong critiques of naturalism with respect to ontology, epistemology, value theory and natural theology. See Craig and Moreland, *Naturalism*; Wagner and Warner, *Naturalism*.

Moreland's substance dualism, the Lonergan-Helminiak model (which I have dubbed the Tripartite Transcendent Model), and Clayton's emergent monism. These Christian views are supportive of this book. They present three distinct Christian interpretations of the origin of consciousness. They also demonstrate that one is not restricted to one particular understanding of consciousness. Openness to different models exemplifies this (as is the case with chapter 8). It is an approach of prudence, realizing that scientific findings are never ultimately conclusive, but provisional, and always subject to change.

Ultimately, consciousness can be understood as a feature of the mind,[90] simultaneously and seemingly paradoxically, as the most obvious and mysterious. It is directly accessible through a first-person perspective, but to fully encapsulate what it is and having access to what it is that others are experiencing through consciousness is one of the most baffling mysteries. Chalmers has dubbed this the "hard problem" of consciousness, namely, "the question of how physical processes in the brain give rise to subjective experience." [91] The subjective experience is what we have called the phenomenal experience, which entails qualia. Moreover, the essential difficulty is this inaccessibility to the interiority of the thought of others, while attempting to create a science to understand such inner workings. While there may be a science of the neural correlates of consciousness, which entails the minimal set of neuronal interactions and mechanisms sufficient to discern a particular conscious precept,[92] there is no science allowing us to know the content of a particular thought based on the physical neuro-chemical inner workings of the brain. In other words, we are faced with a fundamental irreducibility: subjective mental experiences cannot be reduced to neurobiological experiences. What I mean by the origin of consciousness[93] is the commencement of self-consciousness or

90. Dennett, "Consciousness," 161.

91. Chalmers, "The Puzzle of Conscious Experience," 62–68. The hard problem is contrasted with the "easy problems" of integrating information, mental states, memory, since what is required for such explanations is the provision of a particular mechanism to carry forth the said function.

92. See Koch, *The Quest for Consciousness*; Chalmers, "What is a neural correlate of consciousness?" 17–39.

93. See Jaynes, *The Origin of Consciousness in the Break Down of the Bicameral Mind*. In this famous book, the psychologist Julian Jaynes observes that one way of resolving the issue of the origin of consciousness is to claim there is no such thing at all. It is an alarming solution, yet a clever one. Those who have sought to abolish embodied personhood have attempted to do the same with God, who would entail a disembodied mind possessing self-reflection. This book seeks to refute such reductive positions by arguing that consciousness is very real, but that its existence is plausibly explained through the Christian conception of God and creation. Jaynes asks:

If consciousness emerged in evolution, when? And as the first flush of a

self-awareness that human(s) experienced in the history of biological/
anthropological evolution on our planet. This is what we call the initial
realization of the "I," as distinguished from other beings. In essence, the
beginning of the existence of such a phenomenon, closely associated with
this understanding of self-consciousness, is the rise of moral awareness
and its close ties to self-consciousness. These will form part of the systematic theology arguments in chapter 6. It is worth noting that there are
varying degrees of self-consciousness: child to child, child to adult, adult
to adult, based on different cognitive capacities and experiences. Nonetheless, what is fundamental is the introspective aspect, which distinguishes
human beings from other beings.

It is difficult to speak of the place where consciousness originated since
it is a nonphysical thing. This is true for both monists and dualists. Those
who are physicalists must look for a causal connection between consciousness and the brain. This would be tremendously difficult in pinpointing
where such a thing first transpired, but not completely without hope given
the burgeoning of information science. One could ask what it was that dif-
fered, in terms of physiological changes in a human brain, that experienced
that initial state of self-awareness. To speak of self-consciousness as something originating gradually presents a difficulty, since it is something that
did not exist at one point and then did exist at a later point. There is a great

---

theoretical breakthrough waned, it was seen that nothing about the problem
had really changed. It is these specifics that need to be answered. Certainly,
one way of solving the problem of consciousness and its place in nature is to
deny that consciousness exists at all . . . It is an interesting exercise to sit down
and try to be conscious of what it means to say that consciousness does not
exist. History has not recorded whether or not this feat was attempted by the
early behaviorists . . . What a startling doctrine! But the really surprising thing
is that, starting off almost as a flying whim, it grew into a movement that occupied central stage in psychology from about 1920 to 1960 (13).

Interestingly it still has had much tract with eminent philosophers such as Daniel
Dennett, Paul Churchland, Patricia Churchland, Alex Rosenberg, and psychologists
like Steven Pinker and Susan Blackmore in contemporary discussions. Jaynes' view on
the origin of consciousness is just as startling and controversial. In a nutshell, he claims
that at one point the bicameral human mind appeared, that is that the brain being par-
titioned into two sections, one for speaking and the other for listening to commands,
began to have a break down around the second century BC. Before this breakdown,
humans did not exhibit consciousness, in terms of intellection and self-awareness.
This seems to contradict much of standard anthropological evolution and, as we shall
see, Teilhard's notion of consciousness and self-reflection, which would have occurred
much prior to the period that Jaynes mentions. I would take awareness of one's finitude
as a major development of self-consciousness, which exists much prior to Jaynes' claim
about the origin of the breakdown of the bicameral mind; this seems evident through
textual and archeological evidence. Jaynes further argues that language is a necessary
condition for consciousness, but not a sufficient one since language predated consciousness. However, it could not have come about without the existence of language.

chasm between beings who possess self-reflection and those who do not. It is not like the study of the origin of a particular organ, which may or may not leave a physical trace through paleontological evidence. Similar problems mar origin of life studies, in determining the origin of information necessary to build the first replicating system. Even though we have a pretty good idea of the origin of life based on indirect evidence, pertaining to the atmospheric and planetary conditions necessary for self-replicating organisms to survive and flourish.[94] However, ascertaining how life actually first appeared still eludes us. Many experiments are being done to break this gap in knowledge. Similarly, we have indirect evidence of the existence of human self-consciousness through archeological finds, e.g., human art and inscriptions and tools for hunting.

It seems that the inner physiological workings of the brain would not reveal such a thing as consciousness, even if we could somehow miraculously have access to such a thing. If one were to put a human/human precursor under laboratory observation, perhaps certain portion(s) of the brain would light up, but this would not reveal the content of the areas concerned. Hence the hard problem of consciousness would remain, even though one might observe that there was a change in the behavior of the subject.

Complexity and Consciousness

It is important to note that within our universe there is a strong positive correlation between complexity[95] and levels of consciousness, although such a correlation does not fully explain the degree of consciousness in each organism, nor indicate the quantitative proportionality between complexity and consciousness. The conceptual connection between the two is difficult to ascertain. Nonetheless, when we observe the complexity of lowlife microorganisms, we see the effect of information bearing systems, but not the degree of interwoven complexity that we observe in higher organisms and their functions, such as, for example, ants and their degree of inner organization and cooperation. Much in the same way there is a profound complexity, except more so in the comparison of humans to lower mammals, even the great apes. Computer scientist Melanie Mitchell has worked on understanding complex systems and understands complexity in a qualitative sense to mean "a system in which large networks of components with no central control and simple rules of operation give rise to complex collective behavior, sophisticated information processing, and adaptation

94. See Farabee, "Paleobiology: The Precambrian: Life's Genesis and Spread."

95. Complexity can be seen as generally used to characterize something with many parts, where those parts interact with each other in multiple ways. However, there is no consensus on a specific quantitative definition.

via learning or evolution."[96] This seems to correspond quite accurately with the definition of the organismal complexity I was referring to above. Yet, to define complexity in a quantitative way seems much more difficult. Mitchell asks: "Just how complex is a particular complex system? That is, how do we measure complexity? Is there any way to say precisely how much more complex one system is than another?"[97] These are intriguing questions without definitive answers, as of yet, Mitchell admits.

Mitchell ponders the intimate involvement of information to biology and how it acquires meaning or purpose in teleological terms. She asks, in relation to conscious beings:

> [W]ho or what actually perceives the meaning of situations as to take appropriate actions? This is essentially the question of what constitutes consciousness or self-awareness in living systems. To me this is among the most profound mysteries in complex systems and in science in general. Although this mystery has been the subject of many books of science and philosophy, it has not yet been completely explained to anyone's satisfaction.[98]

I agree with Mitchell that no satisfactory materialistic or naturalistic account has been brought forth as of yet. Moreover, Mitchell admits that there is no single science of complexity or complexity theory in place as of yet. She admits that the struggle has to do with defining terms. She also provides a historical context of relevant terms that have been notoriously difficult to ascertain, which include: information, computation, order, and life. [99] Thus, there is an intimate connection between information processing capacities, complexity, and consciousness. This will be explored further in the works of Teilhard and other thinkers. I contend that there is a deep correlation and connection between the two.

Emergence

Emergence functions as a possible candidate for providing an explanation for the origin of consciousness, through a scenario envisioning emergent evolution. The emergence of a particular phenomenon forms a particular picture of its origins. Origin is a broader tent for understanding the coming into being at a particular time of a particular phenomenon, in our case, consciousness. Chalmers notes that the concept of emergence has

---

96. Mitchell, *Complexity*, 13.

97. Ibid., 13.

98. Ibid., 184.

99. Ibid., 3–111.

generated much confusion.[100] He distinguishes between strong and weak emergence to help clarify discussions.

Emergence refers to the appearance of a property at a certain instance, which, prior to that instance, did not exist since particular conditions for its existence did not exist. An example of an emergent property would be wetness in the universe, which is derived from water molecules sticking to a particular surface that are weakly attracted to each other. The constituent parts of the water compound, oxygen and hydrogen, do not possess the property of wetness. Only when they are combined can wetness emerge. Another example is a ferromagnet being heated gradually until it suddenly loses its ability to magnetize at a particular temperature known as the Curie point.[101]

The difficulty is that there is not just one standard definition of emergence. As Bedeau and Humphreys observe, definitions of emergence include "irreducibility, unpredictability, conception novelty, ontological novelty, and supervenience. Some definitions combine a number of these ideas. There are various kinds that may overlap."[102] The important thing to recognize about emergence, if the concept is to be coherent, is that it is both dependent on fundamental/basic phenomena and at the same time independent from it. The subject of emergence is vast, complex, and not entirely understood at this point. A modern synthesis of it will require more thought. Searle explains how the concept relates to consciousness:

> Consciousness is a causally emergent property of systems. It is an emergent feature of certain systems of neurons in the same way that solidity and liquidity are emergent features of systems of molecules. The existence of consciousness can be explained by the causal interactions between elements of the brain at the micro level, but consciousness itself cannot be deduced or calculated from the sheer physical structure of the neurons without some additional account of causal relations between them.[103]

Emergence and its relationship to the origin of consciousness will be briefly examined in Clayton's understanding of consciousness.[104]

---

100. Chalmers, "Strong and Weak Emergence," 244.

101. Bedeau and Humphreys, "Introduction," 1.

102. Ibid., 3.

103. Searle, "Reductionism and the Irreducibility of Consciousness," 69.

104. See section 8.4.

Which Christian Conception of God?

Before we conclude our section on preliminaries, a brief word on the Christian conception of God will be necessary. The Christian conception of God that I am working with has been referred to by philosophers and theologians in the Anglo-American tradition of philosophy and theology as the classical Christian conception of God.[105] Aside from the classical Christian God being a tri-personal God as revealed through the salvific designations of God the Father, God the Son, and God the Holy Spirit, the classical Christian conception of God shares in the attributes of what is known as classical theism. The God of classical Christianity is considered to be a maximally great being who also has the attributes of omniscience, omnipotence, omnipresence, and omnibenevolence. Some classical Christian theists go on further to support God's aseity, simplicity, immutability, impassibility, and timelessness. The purpose of maintaining this classical conception of God is to refute naturalism, pantheism, polytheism, process theism, and open theism. This is the position maintained by the greatest Christian philosophers and theologians of the church, including Augustine, Anselm of Canterbury, and Thomas Aquinas.[106] The classical Christian conception of God framed as such and with the arguments in natural theology, philosophical theology and systematic theology will be expounded in chapters 5 and 6 and will lend support to this view of God.

It is worth noting that while these attributes are accurate descriptors in understanding the nature of God for complex composite beings such as ourselves, they actually do not fully encompass the nature of God. God's nature, as will be argued, is one of simplicity: there are no real distinctions within God, i.e., God represents unity without distinction in the doctrine of divine simplicity.[107] God's simplicity has been rejected by thinkers such as Alvin Plantinga and William Lane Craig, in part because they take these distinctions as being very real.[108]

---

105. See Pojman and Rea, *Philosophy of Religion*, 2. It is worth noting that this is also known as the God of classical theism minus an explicit Trinitarian view. One should also note that not everyone agrees that this should be dubbed "classical theism" or the "classical Christian conception of God," the view being that this is a seventeenth- and eighteenth-century apologetic strategy. However, contrary to this view is Brian Leftow's position which states: "[Classical theism] entered Christianity as early as Irenaeus and Clement of Alexandria and became Christian orthodoxy as the Roman Empire wound down. Though more and more challenged after 1300, it remains orthodox." See Leftow "God, concepts of," 3165.

106. Ibid., 3160–69. Especially pages 3165–67.

107. This will be examined in great depth in chapter 5. See also James Dolezal's quote from his YouTube interview in the conclusion.

108. Dolezal's defense of this is a good refutation of such views.

Christian Theology as an Explanation
for the Origin of Consciousness

These distinctions are important in understanding the origin of consciousness through the Christian conception of God. Important to the discussion will be the interaction of brain states with conscious events. This raises another distinction aside from substance dualism and property dualism, which suggests that while the human person is essentially a physical or material substance in a monistic material world, there are physical and mental properties as well. Mental properties arise from the brain but are not reducible to it. Embodied consciousness as it is manifested in the universe through human persons had a point of origination such that it did not exist prior to this incipient event. This brings about questions about the cause or causes, and necessary conditions for consciousness.

Russell's CMI from paths 6 to 8 focuses on theology influencing science and seems to provide some modest ways in which Christian theology can influence science, which we will explain in more detail in chapters 1 and 7. This brings up the question of what it is about consciousness that can be explained by Christian theism, i.e., by the Christian conception of God and creation. In chapter 7, I explore a number of explanations of how theology can interact and even guide scientific research. Chapters 5 and 6 provide the argumentation that sets up a universe with the likelihood of the origination of consciousness. The arguments in natural theology need not only be seen as arguments for God's existence, but also as ways of explaining why something in the universe is the way it is. God functions as a cause and/ or explanation for such phenomena. The concept of divine simplicity, for example, provides an undergirding for all of reality, including the physical universe. The Christian conception of God acts as the first cause of finite physical reality (whether the universe or multiverse), as the fine-tuner of the laws, constants, and initial conditions of both physics and of biology, which are necessary for the existence of matter, the evolution of life, and embodied conscious agents, which eventually develop self-consciousness. Once certain conditions are explained by a plausible cause for finite material existence, the parameters that are necessary for material existence and life then become more likely to emerge, through convergent evolution, the origin of self-consciousness. The origin of self-consciousness represents what Russell calls a First Instantiation of a New Law of Nature (FINLON). From the incipient moment of self-consciousness this capacity became available to human persons, even though sometimes it has been inaccessible to certain beings in vegetative states or those who experience severe cognitive dysfunction.[109]

109. This would be related to the problem of natural evil but an exploration of this is beyond the scope of this book.

Nonetheless, I suggest that such an instance in the universe prior to the incipient moment could not exist. This FINLON for self-consciousness will be argued for in chapter 5 in the section on convergent evolution, where biological complexity and consciousness ultimately intersect. It will function as a refined version of Teilhard's law of complexity-consciousness. This raises questions about creation and evolution, which will be explored in chapter 3. It also gives rise to questions about divine intervention/action (this will be examined when we explore the concept of Non-Interventionist Objective Divine Action (NIODA) in chapter 7.4), which will be key to making the CMI work with respect to the origin of consciousness. Divine action will be explored with respect to quantum mechanics (QM-NIODA),[110] Plantinga's notion of divine collapse causation (DCC),[111] and informational processes. Informational structures are necessary not only for the origin of consciousness in general and for self-consciousness specifically, but also for the origin of life, which has a close connection to consciousness. Scientific theories of consciousness, which will be explored in chapter 7, demonstrate some affinity with concepts of information. Moreover, the arguments from systematic theology which use Scripture, philosophy, and science through William Dembski's Trinitarian Mode of Creation provide a conceptual basis for how the Trinity interacts within creation to bring about the possibility of self-consciousness. All these provide explanations as to why Christian theism can help us to understand the origin of self-consciousness. Yet, these explanations are not meant to suggest that we cannot unravel the natural world and understand its variant phenomena, including consciousness. Regardless of the metaphysical or religious framework we use, we all have the

110. The preferred interpretation of QM for Russell and others involved in NIODA is the Copenhagen interpretation (also known as the orthodox interpretation). It was developed by Niels Bohr and Werner Heisenberg in the late 1920s. This interpretation suggests that physical systems only have definite properties after they are measured. Once a measurement is taken it affects the system. This in turn causes the set of probabilities to be relegated to only one of the possible values subsequent to the moment of measurement. This event is known as a wave function collapse. See Section 7.4.2; Herbert, *Quantum Reality: Beyond the New Physics*.

111. It is important to note that Plantinga does not offer DCC as an alternative to QM but rather a different interpretation of QM, i.e., Ghirardi–Rimini–Weber theory (GRW); a theory which seeks to avoid the measurement problem. The measurement problem revolves around questions pertaining to how or even whether a wave function collapse occurs. The difficulty lies within the inability to observe this process directly. See Ghirardi et al., "A Model for a Unified Quantum Description of Macroscopic and Microscopic Systems." It is worth noting that the Copenhagen interpretation of QM speculates that a collapse occurs whenever a subatomic particle is measured. Another difficulty lies in discerning what is meant by "measurement." This is a heavily debated question. GRW is a response to the vagueness or imprecision regarding the term "measurement," in this context. See sections 7.4.1 and 7.4.2; Albert, *Quantum Mechanics and Experience*, 80–111.

same evidence in front of us. A universe, life, and consciousness all exist. Determining how they came to be is the task before all of us. I propose that we use different theories of consciousness, models of evolution, and Christian understandings of consciousness in order to attempt to understand their origins as well. It is definitely not one or the other; it is the conjunction and cooperation of all three disciplines that brings us closer to understanding the origin of consciousness. This line of reasoning is consistent with J. P. Moreland's incisive assessment concerning the concept of God as Creator:

> Theological concerns are important to science at several levels. One of the main ways theology interfaces with science is by providing rational conceptual problems for scientific theories. This often is achieved via philosophy; for example, the theological concept of God as Creator is studied as a philosophical concept (an agent who acts in various ways that can be specified and from which conceptual and empirical implications for science can be drawn.) In general, the integration of science and theology is a philosophical question.[112]

Thus, as Moreland acknowledges, there is a deep synergy between philosophy, science, and theology, and it is unreasonable to separate the three. More will be said on this in chapter 2.

Overview

The structure of the book is important to the development of its twofold argumentation. First it explores the fruitfulness of theology influencing the sciences with respect to the origin of consciousness. Secondly it elucidates why the Christian conception of God and creation gives a plausible, though not definitive, explanation for the origin of consciousness. Therefore, it will be important to first establish Robert J. Russell's "Creative Mutual Interaction" (CMI) before moving onto other components of the book. From there we will examine the importance of philosophy in the science and theology interaction. Understanding God's role as Creator with respect to creation and evolution will be vital to understanding the origin of consciousness, since it demonstrates the method which God employed to bring about consciousness. From there we will analyze Teilhard's thought as a test case regarding evolution and complexity to consciousness in understanding the origin of consciousness. Having examined the test case it will be important to present the arguments from philosophical

---

112. Moreland, *Christianity and the Nature of Science*, 57.

theology, natural theology, and systematic theology that explain why the Christian conception of God and creation make it possible to understand the origin of consciousness. After laying a case for CENTAC and the systematic theological arguments, we will apply our findings to the CMI model for the origin of consciousness. Finally, a look at some prominent Christian views on consciousness, which can be applied to understanding the origin of consciousness, will be reviewed.

Although this book is primarily a work of theology, it interacts with many other relevant disciplines. Since this book is at the interface of the science-theology dialogue, several scientific concepts in cosmology, biology, chemistry, and neuroscience will be explored. It also involves reflection on some of the sub-disciplines of these fields. This work engages with philosophical theology, philosophy of religion, philosophy of science, and philosophy of mind. Indeed, due to the very nature of the subject, there will be an inevitable engagement with many different concepts and academic disciplines. The method of theology used in this book consists of a series of arguments from natural theology, philosophical theology, and systematic theology showing that the Christian conception of God and creation provides both a plausible explanation and a guarantor for the origin of consciousness.

In chapter 1, I will provide important details regarding Robert John Russell's CMI. I will proceed by providing information about Robert John Russell and the Center for Theology and Natural Sciences (CTNS), which he founded. I intend to situate the significance of Russell's work in the science-theology dialogue. From there I will reveal an insight that inspired this research project and eventually led to the usage of Russell's methodology. I will then discuss the significance of Russell's CMI and its applicability outside of his own work, revolving around cosmology, resurrection, and eschatology. It is my contention that the CMI model will apply adequately to the topic at hand. I will also explore some of the constructive criticisms and appraisals that have been offered by friendly critics.

In the second chapter, I will discuss the role of philosophy in the science-theology interaction. In so doing, I will explore some popular misconceptions about the significance of philosophy to science, logical inference as it applies to science, the inescapability of presuppositions within scientific theories, and how presuppositions influence the formulation of scientific theories. To this end, I will use Russell's favorite example, Fred Hoyle's Steady State Model. I will then successively examine the philosophical bridge of critical realism, which has been a significant tool for the interaction between science and theology for a number of thinkers, Russell's move from critical realism to CMI, and, finally, the issue of whether science and theology are commensurable disciplines. One of the main objects of this chapter is to demonstrate that the use of philosophy is fundamental to the science-theology dialogue, particularly when it comes to the question of the origin of consciousness.

The third chapter will look at the differing conceptions revolving around creation and evolution. I will first systematize the notion of creation as it applies to Christian theology. From there I will examine different meanings of evolution as these tend to get conflated in scientific, philosophical, and theological discussions. I will then explore different understandings of theistic evolutionary models. I will propose to use one model or a combination of models for purposes of this book.

In chapter 4, I will examine the thought of Teilhard de Chardin. This chapter is not meant to be a full application of Russell's thought, but an examination of the early attempts at thinking deeply on evolutionary science and its relationship to theological doctrines and thought. Nonetheless, some of the insights gathered in this examination can be applied in the form of research guidelines. Indeed, Teilhard was a pioneer in merging evolution with theology. Although much of the science he used is outdated, his general framework is of interest, particularly his notion of complexification/consciousness. This chapter will pay close attention to Teilhard's concepts of evolution, complexity, and consciousness. Much of his work deserves to be examined critically, although criticisms in recent years have been few and far between, many theologians and scientists having come to sympathetically read Teilhard to suit their needs. An honest appraisal encompassing both serious criticisms and the fruits of his work would be left for a separate endeavor.

Chapter 5 will examine various natural theology and philosophical theology arguments supporting the notion that the origin of consciousness (self-consciousness) is plausibly explained by the Christian conception of God and creation. It will present a cumulative evolutionary natural theology type of argumentation involving modern scientific findings and their philosophical and theological implications. In relation to this, the Kalam Cosmological Argument, and the Teleological Argument, in three different forms: the fine-tuning of the universe, the origin of life, and convergent evolution for the origin of self-consciousness, will be examined. We will also look at Russell's concept of FINLON as it applies to the origin of consciousness through exploring convergent evolution.

Chapter 6 will take a look at various arguments from systematic theology as they relate to the origin of consciousness, including the image-likeness that humans share with God, and our moral consciousness, the latter being understood as a development of our self-consciousness and a Trinitarian Mode of Creation.

In chapter 7, we will apply Russell's CMI model to the origin of consciousness. We will first examine the influence of scientific research programs on theological research programs according to five paths. Second, the influence of theological research programs on scientific research programs will be examined, according to three paths. From there, a series of speculative and exploratory research guidelines will be proposed in terms of bidirectional research from science to theology and vice versa. A brief exploration of Teilhard's concept of "ultra-physics" will be taken into account. The following prominent theories of consciousness will be explored: Integrated Information Theory (IIT), Psychophysical Semantic Information Integration (PSII), Orchestrated Objective Reduction (Orch-OR), and dualist notions with scientific implications. Russell's important research program on divine action—Non-Interventionist Objective Divine Action (NIODA) will be examined with some considerable depth so as to flesh out its implication on the origin of consciousness. Dembski's development of information will be explored in light of quantum mechanics and NIODA. From there a look at Russell's concept of FINLON will be explored in light of the origin of consciousness.

Chapter 8 will look at three distinct understandings of consciousness: Moreland's notion of substance dualism, Helminiak's development of Lonergan's concept of consciousness (which I dub the Lonergan-Helmniak Tri-partite Model) and, finally, Clayton's emergent monism. All of these understandings, I argue, are compatible with the central claim of this book, i.e., that the origin of consciousness is plausibly explained by the Christian conception of God and creation. The conclusion will offer a series of reflections, including a thread that ties all the parts of this book together and explains why the Christian God provides a plausible explanation for the origin of consciousness.

Chapter 1

Robert John Russell's
"Creative Mutual Interaction"

THIS CHAPTER WILL EXPLAIN who Robert John Russell is, his CMI program, and the reasons that have led me to apply the CMI method to the origin of consciousness. It also provides some relevant appraisals and criticisms of the CMI.

1.1 Robert John Russell

It would be worthwhile to provide some background information on Robert John Russell since I will be utilizing his general framework regarding the interaction between science and theology. A word on Russell's education is relevant since it has played a significant role in the development of his CMI.

Robert Russell earned an undergraduate degree in physics from Stanford, and an MS and PhD in physics from University of California.[1] He also received a minor in religion while completing his undergraduate degree in physics. Moreover, he has completed a M.Div. and an MA in theology from the Pacific School of Religion.[2] This extensive academic training has given him an excellent background to assess the importance and significance of the disciplines of science and theology. His background in physics has given him an in-depth understanding of modern physics, evidenced by his writings, as well as hands-on experience in the applications of physics. This is something that a theologian would lack unless he had done a great amount of research and reading on his own, as is the case with thinkers like Wolfhart Pannenberg and William Lane Craig. Russell's training in the natural sciences provides him with invaluable insights that can be relevant to both the fields of science and theology. Although Russell does not possess a doctorate

1. Russell, *Cosmology*, 1.
2. Ibid., 2.

in theology, he has demonstrated his competence in the fields of theology, and science and theology, as attested by his long publication list.[3] As a result of his unique academic training, Russell is well equipped to tackle the issue of theology's contribution to the natural sciences.

1.2 The Center for Theology & the Natural Sciences

Russell is the founder and director of the CTNS at the Graduate Theological Union, Berkeley, California. This center has been fruitful for the disciplines of science and theology. It has helped Russell to develop much of his thinking and to write extensively in the field of science and theology. The CTNS has cultivated an environment whereby both scientists and theologians are able to critically question one another while pursuing a fruitful dialogue. The CTNS has made a major contribution to the dialogue. What was unthinkable thirty years ago seems to be possible now, namely lively exchanges between theologians and scientists that permit a greater understanding of each field and their interaction with one another.

1.3 An Insight Revealed by Steve Fuller's Thought Coupled with Nagel's Vision

In reading works in the science and theology/religion field, I began to think about some of the issues that were not directly addressed in what I had read. Years ago, I happened to be listening to a debate between Steve Fuller and Jack Cohen, a reproductive biologist at the University of Warwick. Upon listening to this debate, a key insight emerged that was necessary and significant for this entire research endeavor. It not only influenced my master's research but also inspired subsequent thought. This insight, coupled with Nagel's critique of reductive materialism's ability to explain consciousness, has inspired this work. The main insight, revealed through Fuller's thought, was the notion that theology can contribute something fruitful to the natural sciences.[4]

---

3. Ibid., 328–36.

4. Steve Fuller is a professor of sociology at University of Warwick in England. Fuller earned his doctorate in the history and philosophy of science and served as an expert witness in the 2005 trial in the *Tammy Kitzmiller, et al. v. Dover Area School District* case, which had to do with the teaching of biological evolution and intelligent design. He has published two books revolving around the Intelligent Design (ID) controversy in recent years: *Science vs. Religion* and *Dissent over Descent*. Fuller, who is religiously agnostic, contends that the concept of Intelligent Design, irrespective

Moving forward, in light of recent thought, such as Nagel's criticism of reductive materialistic explanations and its trivialization of the dilemma at hand concerning the origin of consciousness, I pose the following questions: Is there a fruitful opportunity for theology to speak to the sciences? Can theology offer potential research programs? If a full blown naturalistic explanation does not seem plausible or forthcoming, can theology offer a fertile ground for scientific research for those willing to approach the issues with a new set of questions and outlook(s)? This is precisely the direction

---

of whether there exists a designer (whether it be a supernatural entity or a natural entity), can lead to greater insights about certain features of the universe, as opposed to purely undirected natural processes. Some of the features include biological structures such as the bacteria flagellum and the information processing component (genetic code) of the double helical DNA molecule. The main point that Fuller attempts to iterate is that ID can lead to a better understanding of how certain biological features (like the bacteria flagellum) function and came to be built (regardless of whether it was through design or natural processes). His views seem consonant with those of scientists like Isaac Newton, who wanted to envision reverse type engineering scenarios, in order to enter into the mind of God, in order to discern the structure and function of the universe. It is important to note that the concept of ID is extremely controversial in scientific, philosophical, and theological circles. One of the reasons why it is controversial is that it challenges a major component of the modern scientific method—methodological naturalism. Many defenders of ID adhere to an interventionist type of creation which runs contrary to Robert Russell's methodology. Robert Russell's research program embodies a non-interventionist objective divine action (NIODA), which attempts to explain how God may act (since God is both transcendent and immanent) in the universe without direct intervention or violation of the laws of nature. Aside from the above-mentioned controversy, I used this notion which was initiated by Fuller, but transformed it into something more applicable to my research regarding the field of science and theology. This is what inspired the question: "what fruitful contribution can theology make to the natural sciences?" So, if theological thought had an implicit influence on the history of modern sciences by aiding many of the great scientists to unravel the natural world, that is to say God's creation, where can this place or relation be located today? This was the main concern that occupied my thought in my master's thesis. See Ventureyra, *Theology's Fruitful Contribution to the Natural Sciences: Robert Russell's 'Creative Mutual Interaction' in Operation with Eschatology, Resurrection and Cosmology.* For predominantly scientific and some philosophical criticisms of ID, see Perakh, *Unintelligent Design.* For scientific, philosophical, and theological criticisms and defenses, see: Pennock, *Intelligent Design Creationism and Its Critics*; Dembski and Ruse, *Debating Design.* For a full-blown defense of Intelligent Design, see Dembski, *The Design Revolution.* For a thorough explanation of NIODA, see: Russell, "Cosmology, Evolution, and Resurrection Hope," 28–29, 78. More will be said on NIODA in a later section. For helpful discussions on occasionalism and divine action, see: Sangiacomo, "Divine Action and God's Immutability: A Historical Case Study on How to Resist Occasionalism," 115–35; Schmaltz, "Occasionalism and Mechanism: Fontenelle's Objections to Malebranche," 293–313; Freddoso, "God's General Concurrence with Secondary Causes: Pitfalls and Prospects." 131–56.

which brings more substance to my original question regarding theology's fruitfulness to the natural sciences.

1.4 Warrant for Using Russell's Creative Mutual Interaction (CMI)

Taking into consideration the various attempts highlighted in the above-mentioned typologies, regarding the science-theology interaction and their acknowledged complexities, the aim of this book is to explore one approach: one developed by physicist and theologian Robert John Russell. Because of its own methodological developments and its strategy of developing some precise guidelines for the interaction, Russell's work deserves, in my judgment, particular attention. In this work, I will explore the contribution that theology makes to the scientific understanding of the origins and emergence of consciousness. Although I will briefly explore how the sciences influence theology, that will not be the focus of this work. Nonetheless, I will provide a brief outline of such a component of the science-theology interaction (as will be discussed by the eight pathways [five from science to theology and three from theology to science]). I wish to develop my warrant for selecting Russell's approach for this book by prefacing it with a brief comment.

It is worth pointing out that an initial interest in Russell's work resulted in a master's thesis which documented his methodology as applied to the concepts of eschatology, resurrection, and cosmology.[5] Since my master's thesis, I have gained many other insights as I sifted through much of the literature in science and theology, the natural sciences, the neurosciences, philosophy of mind, and philosophy of religion. This will be illustrated by the arguments about the fruitfulness of theology's contribution to the origin of consciousness.

I would like to briefly outline some of the various merits of Russell's methodological approach to science and theology, as illustrated by his notion of CMI and his willingness to confront some of the toughest questions in the field of science and theology. A look at what some of his colleagues have observed will also be of interest.[6]

5. See Ventureyra, *Theology's Fruitful Contribution to the Natural Sciences*, 6–8, for the original explanation of Fuller's insight.

6. It is significant to note that Robert Russell's accomplishments and work within the discipline of science and theology have not gone unnoticed. This has been exemplified with the publication of Peters and Hallanger, *God's Action in Nature's World: Essays in Honour of Robert John Russell*. It includes contributions from scientists, philosophers, and theologians such as John Polkinghorne, Paul Davies, William Stoeger, Ian Barbour,

Several years ago, Russell applied his CMI methodology to the theological thought of the eminent theologian, Wolfhart Pannenberg (1928–2014). Russell utilized some of Pannenberg's insights, in interaction with both philosophy and modern physics. One of these valuable theological insights is revealed by Pannenberg in the following quote:

> Is there conceivable any positive relation between the concept of eternity and the spatio-temporal structure of the physical universe? . . . This is one of the most arduous but also one of the most important questions in the dialogue between theology and the natural science . . . Without an answer to the question regarding time and eternity, the relationship of God to this world remains inconceivable.[7]

In this work titled *Time in Eternity: Pannenberg, Physics and Eschatology in Creative Mutual Interaction*, Russell explores concepts of time, eternity, physics, and eschatology, as well as their mutual interactions.[8] Many of the refinements in Russell's thought exemplified throughout this work will be examined throughout this book.

According to Ted Peters, Russell's CMI is his most important contribution to the field. In support of this, Ted Peters states that:

> [I]t seems to me, the single most valuable contribution of Robert John Russell to the blossoming field of Science & Religion is his conceptual contribution. Taking advantage of his training in both physics and theology, Russell has brought to the dialogue some of the most insightful and revolutionary proposals for breakthrough into a new domain of shared understanding. Beyond warfare, beyond two languages, beyond dialogue, beyond the pursuit of consonance, Russell has advanced us to the stage of creative mutual interaction between natural sciences and Christian theology.[9]

This quote is highly significant since it points to Russell's extension of the discipline of science and theology, beyond the standard engagement, through the establishing of a conceptual framework based on reciprocal

---

Arthur Peacocke, Nancey Murphy, Philip Clayton, and others.

7. Quote by Wolfhart Pannenberg in "Theological Questions to Scientists" as cited in Russell, *Time in Eternity: Pannenberg, Physics and Eschatology in Creative Mutual Interaction*, 1.

8. See Russell, *Time in Eternity*.

9. Peters, "Robert John Russell's Contribution to the Theology & Science Dialogue," 17.

influence. This is something that occupies a significant portion of Russell's research program on CMI.

The method of Russell's CMI is significant for a number of reasons. It is best represented diagrammatically (see appendix 1 below). The CMI provides a detailed interaction of a total of eight pathways. Five of these involve science speaking to theology, i.e., theology "appropriating the discoveries" of science. These pathways can be designated by SRP à TRP. The three other pathways, which are the larger focus of this book, are from theology to science and are designated by TRP à SRP. Theology here can take initiatives to potentially influence science or scientific theories as a whole or to inspire particular research programs.[10] As Russell stresses:

> In short, each side can find new insights and challenges from the other while retaining their independent identities as authentic fields of discourse and discovery. Moreover, by reflecting on all eight paths *taken together,* we can discern something about the interaction of theology and science as a whole which we have *not* appreciated to date by taking each path separately. Finally, the overall perspective might also tell us something about the direction for "theology and science" in the future, shedding new inspiration for novel research programs that combine new work in theology as well as new work in science in a dynamic and ongoing interaction.[11]

Russell's approach is indeed novel, as will be appreciated by the appraisal and constructive criticisms offered by his colleagues. More will be discussed on the importance of philosophy as a mediator between the two great disciplines in our next chapter. It is also important to note that the novel element of this book comes from its application to the origin of consciousness and the speculative approach that I take in suggesting potential research guidelines in helping to move the discernment of the origin of consciousness forward. This will also be done by providing a series of arguments in natural theology, philosophical theology, and systematic theology that are intimately linked to the origin of consciousness and the CMI model.

---

10. This will be examined in greater detail when the origin of consciousness is applied to the CMI in chapter 7.

11. Russell, *Cosmology,* 22.

1.5 Is Russell's CMI Applicable to Disciplines Outside of Physics?

The question of the origin of consciousness has yet to be approached from the perspective of theology offering insights to the sciences. It is worth mentioning that various philosophical treatises have been laid out on the subject of consciousness, but none precisely framed as I propose in this book: What fruitful contribution can theology make to explain the origin of consciousness? It is the Christian conception of God and creation which will aid in this. Moreover, through this book, I seek to demonstrate through a series of philosophical and theological arguments that the Christian conception of God and creation provides a plausible explanation for the origin of consciousness.

One may wonder if Russell's in-depth academic training in physics raises doubts about the applicability of his methodologies to the relation between theology and a science other than physics. Is there something inherent within Russell's methodology that constrains it necessarily to the physical sciences? I do not see any reason to believe so. Russell's methodology seems malleable and flexible enough to adapt to other academic disciplines. Astronomer and cosmologist William Stoeger, SJ, (1943–2014) shared this outlook.[12] This leads us to ask why one should examine Russell's work in an attempt to answer the question of theology's fruitful contribution to the natural sciences. I see Russell's methodology as being sufficiently versatile to not only extend to other natural sciences, such as chemistry and biology, but also to the neurosciences and even to the humanities. This is a case in point made by Stoeger, who was a major participant in the science-theology dialogue and is quite familiar with Russell's program. Stoeger actually proposed a generic reformulation of Russell's eight pathways of CMI that are applicable to all natural and human sciences:

Scientific Research Programs influencing Theological Research Programs (SRP à TRP)

> Path 1: Theories in the sciences can act directly as data that place constraints on theology.

---

12. Stoeger, "Relating the Natural Sciences to Theology," 31. The reason I do not list the eight paths of Russell's CMI prior to Stoeger's reformulation is because Russell's original paths are quite specific to physics and cosmology, whereas in this book we are concerned with the origin of consciousness.

Path 2: Theories in the sciences can act directly as data either to be 'explained' by theology or as the basis for a theological constructive argument.

Path 3: Theories in the sciences, after philosophical analysis, can act indirectly as data for theology.

Path 4: Theories in the sciences can also act indirectly as data for theology when they are incorporated into a fully articulated philosophy of nature (for example, the process philosophy of Whitehead).

Path 5: Theories in the sciences can function heuristically in theology by providing conceptual inspiration, experiential inspiration, practical/moral inspiration, or aesthetic inspiration.

Theological Research Programs influencing Scientific Research Programs (TRP à SRP)

Path 6: Theology can provide some of the philosophical assumptions underlying the sciences.

Path 7: Theological theories can act as sources of inspiration or motivation for new scientific theories.

Path 8: Theological theories can lead to 'selection rules' within the criteria for choosing scientific theories.[13]

A detailed explanation of how Russell's eight pathways (through Stoeger's reformulation) can relate to an understanding of the origin of consciousness, through the Christian conception of God and creation, will be provided later in chapter 7.

1.6 CMI: Some Criticisms and Appraisals

In *God's Action in Nature's World,* a number of Russell's colleagues working on the interactions between science and theology present their assessment of Russell's CMI, outlining the general difficulty raised by the notion of theology influencing science. These essays provide constructive criticisms of

13. See Appendix 1. These eight pathways are Russell's pathways adapted to theories of physics (cosmology and eschatological scenarios of the future of the universe), with theological constructs related to the resurrection. I've included headings dividing the first five pathways from the last three. This is how they appear in Stoeger's proposal, which works well in a generic sense for our purposes. Stoeger, "Relating the Natural Sciences to Theology," 31–32.

Russell's program in order to help stimulate further thought. All agree the CMI attempts to provide a framework allowing for a unique bidirectional influence from science to theology and vice versa.

This critical engagement among theologians, philosophers, and scientists is of tremendous significance for the ability of theology to make contributions to the natural sciences since it provides a fertile ground for the open exchange of ideas. This becomes possible only through an open-mindedness of scientists to the understanding implicit within the disciplines of theology and philosophy.

Philosopher Philip Clayton makes the following observation about Russell's edited volume *Neuroscience and the Person*:

> Finally, as far as I can tell, none of the contributions to Russell's CTNS/VO volume, *The Neuroscience of the Person* [sic], required neuroscience to be done differently. The individual contributions either summarize existing neuroscience or offer philosophical or theological *interpretations or applications of* neuroscientific results. But such work represents only a *one-way influence* [emphasis added], not creative mutual interaction.[14]

Clayton's observation is consistent with what I had mentioned above regarding this volume co-edited by Russell on neuroscience. This provides a warrant for navigating in unchartered waters, regarding the influence theology can have on the sciences (neurosciences), since there has not been a creative mutual interaction with respect to the question of consciousness, and particularly its origin.

Imre Lakatos (1922–1974) suggested that science goes beyond the verification or falsification of isolated hypotheses. Science in its entirety is a research program that comprises a number of assumptions and hypotheses. Scientific research programs are much more complex than typically recognized. Lakatos explains this complexity:

> I claim that the typical descriptive unit of great scientific achievements is not an isolated hypothesis but rather a research programme. Science is not simply trial and error, a series of conjectures and refutations. 'All swans are white' may be falsified by the discovery of one black swan. But such trivial trial and error does not rank as science. Newtonian science, for instance, is not simply a set of four conjectures—the three laws of mechanics and the law of gravitation. These four laws constitute only the 'hard core' of the Newtonian programme. But this hard

---

14. Clayton, "'Creative Mutual Interaction' as Manifesto, Research Program and Regulative Ideal," 58.

core is tenaciously protected from refutation by a vast 'protective' belt of auxiliary hypotheses. And, even more importantly, the research programme also has a 'heuristic', that is, a powerful problem-solving machinery, which, with the help of sophisticated mathematical techniques, digests anomalies and even turns them into positive evidence. For instance, if a planet does not move exactly as it should, the Newtonian scientists check his conjectures concerning atmospheric refraction, concerning propagation of light in magnetic storms, and hundreds of other conjectures which are all part of the programme. He may even invent a hitherto unknown planet and calculate its position, mass and velocity in order to explain the anomaly.[15]

At its core, a scientific research program (SRP) is a method of problem solving based on the collection and interpretations of data. It also is used to provide warrant and sometimes to modify certain hypotheses.[16] According to Clayton, this is true when the research program is applied to a particular "test-case."[17] Clayton believes this to be a very difficult challenge. He states the following:

> CMI remains an intriguing research program and religion-science scholars may wish to attempt to establish the full bi-directional interaction that it describes. But, apart from the exceptions listed above, [for instance, in the construction of cosmological theories,[18] i.e., Hoyle's atheism in the formulation of the Steady State Model] one cannot yet detect that the research program has been successful when applied to the actual cases. Indeed, in some ways it faces an uphill battle: the practice of contemporary natural science is now more resistant to outside influences—especially religious influences—than at almost any other time in the history of science. *Interpretations* of science, *applications* of science and the *ethics* of scientific research are deeply influenced by non-scientific factors, and rightly so. But the core methods and basic results of 'pure science' appear at present to be as insulated from the impact of religious ideas as they could possibly be.[19]

15. Lakatos, *The Methodology of Scientific Research Programmes*, 4. We will return to this issue of falsification and demarcation in section 2.7.

16. Ibid., 4.

17. Clayton, "'Creative Mutual Interaction' as Manifesto," 58.

18. Ibid., 57.

19. Ibid., 58.

It is precisely this outlook that Clayton elucidates, which requires responding to. What's more is that Clayton believes that the CMI, understood as a research program from a Lakatosian perspective, does not represent a "progressive problemshift." A problemshift occurs in the examination of the progress or degeneration of a research program.[20] This book endeavors to penetrate this resistance of the natural sciences, since they have experienced difficulties in explaining certain phenomenon, including the origin of information and consciousness. This is where theology can make a significant contribution.[21]

J. Wentzel van Huyssteen also recognizes the difficulty and importance of the contribution of theology to the sciences. He states:

> The most challenging aspect of an interdisciplinary dialogue between theology and the natural sciences, however, may be for theology to lift up the specific limitations of this conversation. This implies a quite specific appeal from theology to the sciences: an appeal for a sensitivity to that which is particular to the broader, non-empirical, or philosophical dimensions of theological discourse. This respect for disciplinary integrity means that Christian theology has an obligation to explore conceptual problems that may not be empirically accessible, but that can indeed creatively interact with the data from science because they may complement and enrich the worldviews in which science is embedded.[22]

Van Huyssteen is touching upon precisely what I think is needed to provide a fruitful engagement where science has its limitations on its explanatory power and scope without the influence of philosophy and theology. This problematic arises specifically in the question of the origin of consciousness, as will be explored throughout this book. For instance, notions revolving around consciousness only have empirical verifiability in terms of brain function but not on consciousness itself because of its, at least apparent, irreducibility to the brain. Theology can challenge the philosophical assumptions that are inherent to the sciences.[23]

---

20. Lakatos, *The Methodology of Scientific Research Programmes*, 33–35.

21. This is a restatement of what was said in the introduction; now as it applies to Clayton's quote. Interestingly, Clayton will help affirm this point when we analyze his views on consciousness. See the last section of chapter 8 on Clayton's view of consciousness.

22. van Huyssteen, "'Creative Mutual Interaction' as an Epistemic Tool for Interdisciplinary Dialogue," 68.

23. Ibid., 69.

Van Huyssteen further suggests in order to avoid vague blanket terms such as "theology and science," one should focus "on specific theologians, [who are] doing very specific kinds of theologies, attempting to enter into interdisciplinary dialogue with very specific scientists, working with specified sciences on clearly and identified problems."[24] This book seeks to assess the work, thought, and methodology of certain theologians, particularly Teilhard de Chardin for his insights on the origin of consciousness while looking toward Russell's methodology in the fruitfulness of theology influencing science. Moreover, the work of particular scientists and philosophers on consciousness, cosmology, physics, origin of life studies, and evolutionary biology will be examined.

Clayton raises a further critical issue about the CMI, which is worthy of mention: namely that it may not be able to meet its ambitious goal of being fully integrative; of wholly exhibiting a bidirectional influence from science to theology, particularly from theology to science.[25] Instead, he thinks the CMI may function best through a regulative ideal. Clayton uses Kant's notion of the "highest ideal" as an illustration of a regulative ideal.[26] Clayton further argues that only one being, if such a being existed, could function as a highest ideal, one that, as he explains, would be similar to Descartes's utilization of God as a guarantor for human reason.[27] Likewise, the regulative ideal, for Kant, the use of God, as being the "idea of the highest good" functions as ground that allows for the coherency of human reason and intelligibility. This notion of intelligibility will be explored when we examine Bernard Lonergan's argument for God's existence based on intelligibility.[28] It will also be examined in light of some modern scientific findings regarding astrophysics and astrobiology suggesting a correlation between Earth being a habitable planet and one by which scientific observation can be made. This correlation of intelligibility between theological, philosophical, and scientific findings plays a key role in the origin of consciousness as understood by the Christian conception of God and creation. Clayton argues that Russell's CMI could function as a regulative ideal for the science-theology dialogue similar to Kant's notion that the idea of God is a regulative ideal for reason.[29]

Clayton views the CMI as functioning at the highest level of "dialogue" between science and theology, especially because of the bidirectional

24. Ibid., 70.
25. Clayton, "'Creative Mutual Interaction' as Manifesto," 58–59.
26. Ibid., 59.
27. Ibid.
28. See chapter 8.
29. Clayton, "'Creative Mutual Interaction' as Manifesto," 60.

influence even if it fails as a research program, and does not meet the criterion for a "progressive problemshift." Clayton's skepticism arises from Russell's application of his research program to the notions of resurrection and eschatology. It will be important to see how Clayton would view the endeavor of this book on the origins of information and consciousness in its application to the CMI. For instance, he expresses doubt about *creation ex vetera* being a possibility lending itself to scientific inquiry given the empirical evidence revealed from modern cosmology. Similarly, he sees major problems with the concept of resurrection:

> physicists, biologists and empirical historians do not, and in my view should not, do their actual scientific work differently as a result of the resurrection claim (though they may well live differently because of it). Where such religion-to-science applications have been attempted in these fields, they have not resulted in acknowledged 'progressive problemshifts' within the relevant fields themselves.[30]

Clayton certainly raises a tremendous obstacle for the CMI with respect to theology influencing science in the application of resurrection and eschatology. The question may be asked: Is this because of the methodology employed in the natural sciences, which tends to create obstacles to certain theological considerations? Clayton, who echoes, Lakatos's problemshift, is opposed to Popper's criterion of falsification, which would completely remove a particular scientific theory off the table.[31] But rather, Lakatos's method explores two kinds of problem shifts: "progressive" and "degenerative" ones. A research program such as CMI can be considered progressive if it creates "novel facts"[32] as opposed to anomalies (that have no positive impact). "Novel facts" arise when a particular theory is more empirically fruitful than its competitors, and anomalies will arise more frequently that are not directly explicable by the theory in question, when it is empirically weak.[33] This will be of aid in discerning between potential theories which can help explain the origin of consciousness. These will be explored when we apply Russell's CMI to the origin of consciousness while considering various prominent scientific theories of consciousness. It will be useful to explore the concept of NIODA, which could in a sense act as a way of blocking some of theology's influence on the sciences. Some clarifications

---

30. Ibid., 60–61.

31. Ibid., 57. See Lakatos, "Falsification and the Methodology of Scientific Research Programmes," 34–36.

32. Clayton, "'Creative Mutual Interaction' as Manifesto," 57.

33. Ibid., 57.

and modifications will be proposed based on criticisms by Alvin Plantinga, quantum mechanics, and Dembski's work on information and its relationship to God's action. In that case, these barriers are imposed by methodological constraints applicable to the sciences or rather philosophical interpretations of science. The controversial question of the warrant of methodological naturalism arises—is it always viable? If not, would this open the fruitfulness of the CMI in a bidirectional influence? It seems this could offer an interesting avenue of research and further exploration to the interconnection between science and theology: "The fact that we will not finally remove the epistemic gaps between the scientific study of the natural world and theological reflection on its ultimate origins is no reason not to explore their interconnections as fully as possible."[34] This is the advice we shall follow. This book will endeavor to attempt to move the CMI beyond a regulative ideal to a fully viable bidirectional interaction between theology and the sciences. This is something that we will discover; Clayton is not as resistant as he seemed at the time he labeled the CMI merely a regulative ideal. Information, consciousness, and God's action, and their deep interacting connection, will be of vital importance.

Despite the various criticisms, I am led to believe that the virtues and methodology of Russell's CMI surpasses the typologies proposed by Ian Barbour, Ted Peters, John Haught, and Willem Drees, in terms of addressing the specific features, complexities, and details of the field of science and theology. This is primarily because it provides an avenue for theology to contribute something to the sciences which seems to be lacking in much of the other proposed methodologies. Even though, as will be shown, I do not subscribe to every aspect of Russell's methodology, it is nonetheless the best methodology for demonstrating the potentially fruitful contribution of theology to the sciences.

1.7 Conclusion

In this chapter, we examined who Russell is, the significance of the CTNS, and his contribution to the science and theology interaction. We examined his CMI and provided warrant for its usage over other programs. We then examined its applicability to scientific questions outside of physics, since this is the domain in which Russell has centered research on his CMI. Finally, we examined a series of constructive criticisms from his colleagues, comprised of philosophers, theologians, and scientists. In this last section, we paid particular attention to Clayton's concern regarding

34. Ibid., 61.

whether the CMI functions as a Lakatosian problemshift. This is an issue that I believe is better resolved through my transformation of Russell's CMI with respect to the origin of consciousness. This will be detailed in both our next chapter concerning the role of philosophy, and the development of the CMI in chapter 7.

Chapter 2

The Role of Philosophy in the Science-Theology Interaction

2.1 Introduction

IN THIS CHAPTER, WE will examine the various functions that philosophy plays within the interaction between science and theology. Logic is at the heart of both science and theology. So are a number of presuppositions. Philosophy helps form epistemological bridges between seemingly dissimilar disciplines, such as the natural sciences and theology. It is vital for the endeavor of science on its own and cannot function without the use of presuppositions. It also plays a critical role in demonstrating consonance between theological doctrines and scientific finding. Rationality and comprehensibility are at the root of the science and theology interaction, which is facilitated by philosophy. The very existence of consciousness and the fact that we can even be introspective allows us to engage in philosophical thought. God acts as a guarantor for not only the existence but correspondence between thought and reality—this will be explored with critical realism. Having examined Russell's CMI and various criticisms and appraisals of his program, it will be worthwhile to examine the role of philosophy in the science-theology interaction. Both theology and science are infused with philosophical assumptions such as the intelligibility and comprehensibility of reality, which allows for the discernment of meaning and truth. This is especially true as it relates to the nature of information and the different understandings of consciousness, which will be explored in a subsequent chapter. The ability to be introspective, being self-conscious of one's self and the world around us, allows for us as rational beings to engage in both the endeavors of science and theology. It is this introspection, this look within, that allows us to look without and ask profound philosophical questions of meaning and truth, which are embedded within the great disciplines of science and theology.

The interrelationship between philosophy, theology, and science is indeed a complex one. Reflecting upon these interconnections reveals that the three disciplines cannot be neatly segregated from one another since they overlap and are quite intertwined. Philosophy, science, and theology are all inextricably linked to one another. As I will show, science cannot proceed without the use of philosophy, nor can theological thinking. Although, I agree with Russell's emphasis on the importance of philosophy acting as a mediator between theology and science,[1] my view is that philosophy is more than a mediator and is always in operation throughout both scientific and theological thought. My section examining the commensurability of science and theology illustrates the importance of philosophy to this program. As was mentioned earlier, the integration of science and theology is largely a philosophical issue. Moreover, I also believe that part of this has to do with Russell's avoidance of natural theology (my use of CENTAC strays from Russell in that respect), which is the bedrock of this book. Russell opts out for a theology of nature and thus his approach in viewing the influence of theology to science will be more minimalist, although his theology of nature is of a maximalist persuasion.[2] The distinction in our method will be exam-

1. See Russell et al., *Physics, Philosophy and Theology: A Common Quest for Understanding*.

2. In contrast to natural theology which functions as a rational endeavor to adduce God's existence and purpose in nature through understanding the natural world (sans the aid of biblical revelation), a theology of nature begins through the Christian tradition via religious experience, and historical and biblical revelation. Moreover, a theology of nature suggests that certain Christian doctrines may require revision in light of modern scientific findings. Both approaches have their fruits and purposes. Although Russell acknowledges the force of some natural theological arguments (i.e., the fine-tuning), he has two misgivings. The first is related to the provisional nature of science (and even controversial standing of some of these arguments in the scientific community)—things are subject to change. The second is that they don't reveal anything about the Christian God. See Russell, *Cosmology*, 48. On the first point I agree, but this is why I think an inference to the best explanation can aid in seeing which alternatives fit best with the evidence. This requires philosophical appraisal. The second is also true but the purpose of these arguments especially when formulated separately are not meant to "bring" you to the Christian God (see page 8 where I deal with this objection). They can bring you to a broad theistic type of belief. They are also not meant to dispense with biblical revelation and tradition. This is also why I use the systematic theological arguments which bring us closer to the Christian God than the natural theological arguments. Nevertheless, the natural theological arguments cumulatively provide a compelling case for a personal God once you get into biological fine-tuning, the origin of life, and convergent evolution and the origin of consciousness. It is worth mentioning that I use the term minimalist in terms of the impact theology may have on science. A theology of nature demonstrates the influence is predominantly from science to theology. Whereas the natural theological arguments, demonstrate a philosophically informed theology which can at least adduce that concepts of the Christian God and creation to function as a better explanation than mere natural causes for life and consciousness. In turn, these can influence and guide research into the origin of

ined further in section 2.7. I also use philosophical theology and systematic theological arguments, which rely heavily on philosophical reflection.

Alvin Plantinga has remarked that "philosophical reflection is not much different from just thinking hard."[3] This simple affirmation can be taken to be akin to thinking rigorously about things, be it science, theology, or any other discipline. Therefore, good philosophy involves proper thinking in all fields of inquiry.

2.2 Philosophical Shortcomings of Scientific Materialism

The same is true of the discourse between science and theology. Ardent reductive materialists, in their naivety, have sought to denigrate and eradicate philosophy from scientific understanding. This incoherent thought remains prevalent and has had a damaging effect upon Western culture. When prominent popularizers of science such as Richard Dawkins,[4] Lawrence Krauss,[5] and Stephen Hawking[6] make bold declarations regarding philosophy, theology, and religion in general, they stifle the general understanding of the relationship between philosophy, science, and theology. They repre-

---

consciousness. Nevertheless, Russell acknowledges the importance of theology influencing science in a number of ways including grounding the assumptions inherent to science which transcend scientific endeavors; how theology can help select between rival scientific theories; and how it can inspire/motivate future science. Although, Russell's theology of nature is of a maximalist persuasion as Peters suggests, it and its application to the CMI seem insufficient to affirm that the origin of consciousness is plausibly grounded by the Christian conception of God and creation. His use of the CMI and a theology of nature, in my estimation, does not function as a genuine problemshift in the science-theology dialogue. For an explanation of a maximalist theology of nature, see Peters, "Natural Theology versus Theology of Nature," 2.

3. Plantinga, *God, Freedom and Evil*, 1.

4. See Ventureyra, "Dawkins' Unholy Trinity: Incoherency, Hypocrisy and Bigotry."

5. See Kraus, *A Universe from Nothing: Why There Is Something Rather than Nothing*. Krauss has created a lot of confusion regarding the concept of nothing. He equates nothingness with a quantum vacuum as opposed to the general meaning philosophers and theologians mean by nothingness, i.e., "not anything." Clear philosophical thinking would have prevented this, but his denigration of philosophy has brought much well-deserved ridicule his way. David Albert appropriately states: "But all there is to say about this, as far as I can see, is that Krauss is dead wrong, and his religious and philosophical critics are absolutely right. Who cares what we would or would not have made a peep about a hundred years ago? We were wrong a hundred years ago. We know more now. And if what we formerly took for nothing turns out, on closer examination, to have the makings of protons and neutrons and tables and chairs and planets and solar systems and galaxies and universes in it, then it wasn't nothing, and it couldn't have been nothing, in the first place." See Albert, "On the Origin of Everything"; Siniscalchi, "A Response to Professor Krauss on Nothing," 678–90.

6. Lennox, *God and Stephen Hawking: Whose Design Is It Anyway?*

sent only one position out of the panoply of positions in the science and theology dialogue, namely, conflict—i.e., that there is a supposed conflict between science and Christian belief. This position is widely held in popular culture. This point is especially important in examining the different understandings of consciousness as defended by Christian philosophers such as Moreland, Lonergan, and Clayton. This will be further argued through these understandings of consciousness and their relationship to information and God's action. Such argumentation will allow us to build a cumulative argument for why the Christian conception of God and creation functions as a plausible explanation for the origin of consciousness. This standpoint can be contrasted with the prevalence of scientific materialism. Russell's program of CMI actually demonstrates the cooperative and mutually beneficial interdependence of science and theology, which acts a response to scientific materialism. Similar to the commentary, contra the "new atheism" by Murphy on Russell's CMI,[7] is echoed in this book, i.e., arguing that consciousness is plausibly explained through the Christian conception of God and creation can indirectly act as a remedy to the prevalence of reductive materialist thought revolving around consciousness.

Nonetheless, philosophy is indispensable to scientific endeavors. Three components are fundamental to science: presuppositions, evidence, and logic.[8] All methods of knowledge must use presuppositions and logic, including theological reflection. So, philosophy is very intimately involved in both science and theology.

Although science has been notoriously difficult to define, the endeavor of science involves collecting data through empirical evidence; evidence that is observed by the five senses. It is important to note that there are different kinds of sciences, including empirical, experimental, observational, theoretical, and historical science.[9] The reason for making these distinctions between different types of sciences is to show that philosophy has different levels of involvement within scientific theories. Further in the book, through a mediating philosophy, we will argue there is a deep consonance and influence between philosophical-theological arguments and science with respect to God's consciousness and finite consciousness.

---

7. Murphy, "Robert John Russell Versus the New Atheists," 193–212.

8. This is observed by a scientist who is well versed in philosophy. See Gauch, *Scientific Method in Practice*, xv.

9. See Rau, *Mapping the Origins Debate: Six Models of the Beginning of Everything* 23–24.

2.3 Logical Inferencing in Science

An important contribution of philosophy to science is the use of logical inferencing, since empirical observation alone is insufficient.[10] The two broad
kinds of logical inferencing include deductive and inductive. Deductive
reasoning involves going from general to specific, whereas inductive moves
in the opposite direction from specific particulars to broader, more general-
ized deductions.[11]

A third way of utilizing logical inferencing—which is used by scientists
engaged in interpreting the past—is known as abductive reasoning, namely
the use of presently acting causes to make reasonable inferences about the
past. Both Darwin and Lyell made use of such methods. Lyell mentored Darwin and used this method of argumentation in his *Principles of Geology*,[12] by
which he argued if you want to explain events of the past, you should utilize
presently acting causes instead of devising exotic explanations. Darwin employed such reasoning in his *On the Origin of Species*.

Such a methodology is particularly useful in making inferences to the
best explanation to rule out competing hypotheses.[13] Inference to the best
explanation[14] has its uses in attempting to demonstrate the cause of singular
occurrences in the past, such as the origin of consciousness, which is the
very endeavor of this book. It is also a valid method to investigate the origin
of the universe, the origin of life, the Cambrian explosion, and the resurrection of Jesus.[15] Abductive reasoning, as opposed to deductive reasoning, does not guarantee the conclusion with certainty. Similarly, abductive
reasoning, as opposed to inductive reasoning, does not give us a conclusion
with a particular likelihood since inductive arguments are not considered as
valid or invalid but rather as strong or weak in their probability. In spite of
this, abductive reasoning is extremely useful for ascertaining events of the
past. The use of deductive, inductive, and abductive reasoning is essential to
the debates concerning origins. Logical inferencing will play an important
role for the central argument in this book concerning the Christian conception of God and creation for the origin of consciousness.

10. Lederman, "Syntax of Nature of Science Within Inquiry and Science Instruction," 304.

11. Gauch, *Scientific Method in Practice*, 157–59.

12. See Lyell, *Principles of Geology*.

13. Lipton, *Inference to the Best Explanation*, 1.

14. Inference to the best explanation has the same meaning as abductive reasoning.
See Douven, "Abduction."

15. Ventureyra, "Warranted Scepticism? Putting the Center for Inquiry's Rationale
to the Test," 1–26.

2.4 The Inescapability of Presuppositions

Hugh Gauch states that: "[a] presupposition is a belief that is necessary in order for any of the hypotheses to be meaningful and true but that is non-differential regarding the credibility of the individual hypotheses. The hypotheses originate from the question being asked that is the ultimate starting point of an inquiry, and then presuppositions emerge from comparing the hypotheses to see what they all have in common."[16]

Throughout the early 1900s logical positivists suggested that science is solely based on evidence and logic without any room for assumptions and presuppositions. However, philosophers of science have demonstrated the falsity of such claims.[17]

There are a series of presuppositions that are implicit to science and any human endeavor for understanding reality. For example, beliefs such as the existence of the physical world outside of our minds and that our perception, at least roughly, corresponds with how reality actually really is. We may ask why the coherent study of theology, philosophy, and science is possible. For instance, the duality of contingency and intelligibility allows scientists to perform science. Thomas Torrance argues that the: "[c]orrelation with rationality in God goes far to account for the mysterious and baffling nature of the intelligibility inherent in the universe, and explains the profound sense of religious awe it calls forth from us and which, as Albert Einstein (1879–1955) insisted, is the mainspring of science."[18] This is in line with the Christian doctrine of *creation ex nihilo*, Russell notes:

> Historians and philosophers of science have shown in detail how
> the doctrine of creation *ex nihilo* played an important role in
> the rise of modern science by combining the Greek assumption
> of the rationality of the world with the theological assumption

16. Gauch, *Scientific Method in Belief*, 81.

17. See Craig, "God is Not Dead Yet," 22–27; Craig, "Theism Defended," 901–3. Related to this notion of presuppositions and refutation of logical positivism with respect to it, is the reaction in the second half of the twentieth century to positivism/verificationism when it comes to the question of God. This is particularly relevant since some of the arguments I will use will be related to natural theology and its relation to science and theology. Section 2.7 will continue this discussion. Arguments concerning God's existence have had a revival since the 1960s with thinkers such as Alvin Plantinga, William Alston, Stuart Hackett, Richard Swinburne, Dallas Willard, William Lane Craig, and J.P. Moreland. This in part was due to the collapse of verificationism, which suggested that for a sentence to have meaning it should be empirically verifiable, i.e., by the senses; therefore knowledge of God was impossible and rendered meaningless. The interesting thing about this verification principle is that it was revealed to be incoherent itself, by its own very criteria since it could not be verified by the senses. So, in part, because of this there has been a burgeoning of arguments for God's existence in the Anglo-American philosophical realm.

18. Torrance, "God and the Contingent World," 347.

that the world is contingent. Together these helped give birth to the empirical method and the use of mathematics to represent natural processes.[19]

So, it is the very belief in the Christian doctrine of creation that acts as a guarantor for the rationality of the universe that scientists can unravel.[20] The universe is dependent on God and wholly other from God, a belief that allowed for the rise of modern science. This coupled with God's action as will be explored in our chapter on NIODA serves to demonstrate consonance between the concept of the Christian God and creation and the origin of consciousness. This realization corresponds with transition from critical realism to CMI as will be explored below.

2.5 Presuppositions in Influencing/ Formulating Scientific Theories

When it comes to science dealing with origins, which is more intimately connected with the historical sciences (through use of abductive reasoning) than the experimental science—theological and philosophical commitments can influence scientific theories. Thus, reasonable objectivity from scientists when it comes to issues of origins may be possible, but perhaps unsound. However, this is not a strike against the development of a particular theory; weighing the evidence is always significant since one can accept, discard, or augment the particular scientific theory, based on the preponderance of the available evidence. Russell's CMI embraces such instances. He has praised the a-theological commitment of Fred Hoyle in the development of his Steady State Model. Hoyle's philosophical naturalism caused him to reject the standard big bang model in favor of his own Steady State Model, which rejected t=0. As Russell reflects:

> I mused the story of Fred Hoyle who had constructed steady state cosmology, in which the universe is eternally old with no t=0, and who had done so in part to undermine big bang cosmology which was being invoked by Christians to support the existence of God. Hoyle became my hero, for he had been willing to take his theology (that is, atheism) seriously and build a cosmology that to him represented the implications of atheism in the context of science: an eternal universe with no beginning. In my mind he had bridged the whole worlds of theology and

19. Russell, "Eschatology and Scientific Cosmology: From Conflict to Interaction," 105.

20. Barbour, *Religion and Science*, 90. For an extensive treatment of this in his chapter 1 of the same text, see "The Medieval World-Drama."

science—in the way thought impossible by my seminary men-
tors! Why I wondered, silently, couldn't others do so too, especially those cosmologists who were theists?[21]

This cuts to the heart of CMI's fruitful contribution to the natural sciences,
hence pathways 6 to 8 of theology influencing science. It is the very endeav-
or of this book. This is precisely why I chose Russell's CMI to understand the
question of the origin of consciousness through the Christian conception of
God and creation.

It is worth noting that both theological and a-theological constructs
involve philosophical beliefs about reality. A theological belief may be justified without philosophical rigor or reflection, but its justification necessitates the work of philosophy. The doctrine of *creation ex nihilo* may be
a Christian belief but to argue for its veracity, one would need to utilize
scientific evidence and philosophical argumentation to establish its truth.

2.6 Philosophical "Bridges": From
Critical Realism to CMI

The utilization of critical realism has been instrumental to the development
of the science-theology dialogue. It has permitted diverse fields to interact
with one another. But what precisely is critical realism? Critical realism is
an epistemological tool used to bring into dialogue seemingly disparate
fields of inquiry such as the natural sciences and theology. It is worth noting
that although Russell acknowledges critical realism's significant historical
and methodological contribution, he only takes serious interest in it with
respect to its use of analogy.[22] Critical realism has played a crucial role in
the development of the CMI model, whether acknowledged implicitly or
explicitly, and provides a way of understanding the complex interactions
between science, philosophy, and theology.[23] This book will continue to
develop these ideas, as one shall see. Central to critical realism are two of the
presuppositions we mentioned above: first, that there is an objective world
outside of our minds and our perceptions of it, and second, that we can
ascertain reliable data of this particular world. However, critical realism also
affirms, as Ross McKenzie and Benjamin Meyers observe,

---

21. Russell, *Cosmology*, 20.

22. Russell, *Cosmology*, 5; see also 6, 21, 57, 60, 72, 122, 129, 226, 258, 303, 306.

23. It is to be preferred to other methods of interactions such as absolute idealism,
naïve idealism/naïve realism, critical idealism, instrumentalism, and determinism, see
Hiebert, "Epistemological Foundations of Science and Theology," 5–10.

that knowledge is constructed by fallible humans in particular social contexts, and that our knowledge of the world is at best approximate. This view is critical because it allows knowledge to change when confronted with more evidence about the nature of reality itself. It is critical also because it claims that theoretical concepts are only approximate and provisional representations of reality, rather than exact representations that correspond intrinsically to reality.[24]

Critical realism holds to an objective understanding of the world while recognizing that the development of the sciences, social sciences, philosophical, and theological constructs are ultimately provisional and always subject to revision.

Russell posed the following questions, which illustrate the need for a mode of interactive philosophy such as critical realism:

> The question of methodology lies at the heart of the interdisciplinary field of theology and science: How are we to relate fields as apparently different as the natural sciences, the philosophy of science, the philosophy of religion, [philosophy of mind] and systematic and philosophical theology? And how are we to accomplish all this while keeping in mind the kinds of knowledge claimed, languages used, methods of theory construction, and types of data involved seem to dissimilar?[25]

Russell denotes that science itself raises a number of questions revolving around theology which involve deep philosophical reflection. In a "Faith and Reason" TV program on PBS, Russell was posed the following question, which relates to the importance of philosophy in the science-theology interaction: "How do you see a model for getting scientists and theologians together more?" He responded by stating:

> I think part of the problem of getting scientists and theologians together is the need for the mediation of philosophy. That is, science really raises philosophical questions of a fundamental nature, why is the Universe contingent, and understandable by mathematics, and discoverable through external methods. And theology depends upon the notion of experience, and text, and tradition, and why those count as data for a theory, or why they're epistemic.

---

24. McKenzie and Meyers, "Dialectical Critical Realism in Science and Theology: Quantum Physics and Karl Barth," 49.

25. Russell, *Cosmology,* 4.

Well, these are philosophical questions on both sides. And
so we need the three groups, the philosophers, the theologians,
and the scientists to get together, but also to get together realizing that it's not a turf war, we're not trying to replace one with
the other one, or put solutions from one to the other one. We're
trying to learn from each other. My motto is, if a theologian engages with a scientist and then decides that her own theological
research is more fruitful from the interaction, we've succeeded.
And if a scientist engages with a theologian and finds that interesting philosophical questions raised by her science are given a
deeper perspective, or perhaps moral issues are given a deeper
understanding, and she feels more confident about her science,
and more interested in it personally, then we've succeeded.[26]

In this response, one can see the seeds and appeal of a critical realist approach which eventually led to the development of his CMI. What is
revealed through this quote is the importance of cooperation between philosophers, theologians, and scientists in order for his CMI to be fruitful and
bidirectional. It is the correspondence between these three great disciplines.
Indeed, science and theology as we have recognized are permeated with
philosophical assumptions. It is these philosophical assumptions that can
bring the two disciplines closer together. I will endeavor to demonstrate
through God's action (while avoiding occasionalism and crude interven-
tionism) that this lies in the different understandings of consciousness; ones
that can be informed by scientific theories of consciousness through informational structures in the universe by God's action.

We can now ask ourselves precisely where it is that Russell finds the
fruit of critical realism as it applies to the science and theology interaction.

In recent years, scientist-theologians such as Ian Barbour, John Polkinghorne, and Arthur Peacocke (1924–2006) have used critical realism as a
common methodological tool for science and theology.[27] Russell, in expli-
cating his journey from critical realism to his CMI, utilizes the thoughts of
both Barbour and Peacocke.

26. An interview with Robert John Russell on a TV program titled "Faith and Reason," broadcast on September 11, 1998. The excerpt was taken from a transcript found
at: http://www.pbs.org/faithandreason/transcript/bobr-frame.html.

27. See Barbour, *Myths, Models and Paradigms*; Peacocke, *Intimations of Reality*;
Polkinghorne, *Belief in God in an Age of Science*, chapter 5; Allen, *Ernan McMullin and
Critical Realism in the Science-Theology Dialogue*, chapter 1. Allen's work examines the
relationship of natural theology to the science and theology dialogue through an exploration of critical realism in the particular context of understanding the dispositions
of the three above mentioned theologians. Allen is in agreement with McMullin's criticism of these scholars' epistemological work as being more descriptive than anything.

Barbour's approach of critical realism functioned as a bridge for relating science and theology. Russell praises Barbour's critical realism on two fronts: 1) that it is primarily rooted in secular disciplines such as philosophy of science and philosophy of religion—leaving it open to a variety of "theological purposes" for not only Christian scholars but scholars of other religions. 2) Its compatibility with non-reductionist metaphysical perspectives including "non-reductionistic metaphysical perspectives, including physicalism (cf. Murphy), emergent materialism (cf. Peacocke, Clayton), dual-aspect monism (cf., Polkinghorne), panexperientialism (cf. Ian G. Barbour) and [Russell's own choice of emergent monism]."[28]

It was Barbour's insight that: "the basic structure of religion is similar to that of science in some respects, though it differs at several crucial points" that came to play an inspirational role within Russell's own methodological thoughts.[29] This key insight and the careful attention that Barbour paid to the similarities and differences between science and religion, which he transposed into diagrams, provided Russell with profound insights into the development of his own methodological ideas leading up to his methodology of CMI (Creative Mutual Interaction).

Stoeger intimates that this realization and utilization of "methodological analogies" between science and theology has been an important component of Russell's CMI. In other words, Russell, through following the thought of Ian Barbour with respect to tracing crucial similarities between the sciences and theology, has facilitated the possibility of a critical evaluation of the contents of both fields.[30] It seems quite evident that Barbour's notions regarding the similarities between science and theology allowed for a development of Russell's CMI. The CMI, because of Barbour's insight, was able to take the shape it did, namely a structure involving interaction between science and theology, while being mediated through philosophy.

Russell was most impressed with Barbour's use of analogy between scientific and theological reasoning. Russell sees this as the bridge between science and theology. He quotes Barbour: "the basic structure of religion is similar to that of science in some respects, though it differs at several crucial points."[31] I will explore these similarities and dissimilarities

28. Russell, *Cosmology*, 5. It should be noted that although Russell in this quote lists Clayton's position as emergent materialism, it would be more accurate to list Clayton as an emergent monist as he describes himself. This is Clayton's position on the origin of consciousness.

29. Russell, *Cosmology*, 6.

30. Stoeger, "Relating the Natural Sciences to Theology," 31.

31. Russell, *Cosmology*, 5. I will delve into the similarities and differences between science and theology when providing a fuller discussion of Russell's CMI.

in discussing the structure of Russell's CMI, as they are important to the trajectory of CMI.

Related to discovering the similarities and dissimilarities between science and theology is a method explored by theologian James Pambrun, who recognizes both the continuity and discontinuity between, for instance, human language and affirmations about God and God's love: "On the one hand, it affirms a real discontinuity between human language and the truth of God's love. On the other hand, it affirms a real continuity in so far as it affirms a real capacity for human understanding to say something of the truth of God as Creator."[32] In an attempt to bridge the distinctness of these seemingly opposing affirmations, Pambrun bears on the importance of thinking analogically,[33] which, as we have witnessed, Russell finds important in scientific and theological judgment. This "bridge" akin though distinct[34] from Barbour's critical realism is labeled as "acts of understanding" for Pambrun, "by showing how both science and theology testify to the generosity and integrity of understanding. [This] article points to an existential lieu where both partners can recognize, in the authentic quest of the other, a reference common to their own efforts."[35] This lieu, or act of understanding, functions ultimately as a linkage between science and theology, i.e., philosophical reflection. Russell, in a similar vein, has declared that philosophy is a mediator between the two disciplines of science and theology.

Pambrun stresses that God cannot be known in the same way we come to know physical and contingent existence, hence the distinction between scientific and theological understanding. Such an understanding for the theologian begins with the revelation of God as Creator, through which one can come to know part of the Divine Mystery through God's effects.[36] Pambrun offers an astute insight into analogical thinking whereby both the theologian and the scientist can meet on common ground through distinct enterprises:

> Analogy appeals to our intelligence in act within a light which
> reveals the world as world, that is, as creation capable of a free
> and genuine encounter with God. In this way, it possesses a
> double reference. One is to the integrity open and unrestricted

32. Pambrun, "Science, Theology and Acts of Understanding," 71.

33. Ibid., 73–78.

34. Pambrun recognizes that although the methodologies between science and theology are sufficiently distinct, their similarities lie in what he and Lonergan refer to as "acts of understanding."

35. Pambrun, "Science, Theology and Acts of Understanding," 79.

36. Ibid., 77.

desire of reason to understand. The other is God's own desire for an encounter. But analogy refers to the first in light of the second. It alludes to the experience of reason as a light in such a way that it discovers within itself a further light by virtue of which it enlightens. Can this testimony, anthropological and existential in nature, not be an area where the scientist and the theologian encounter one another? I have proposed that such a field consists of a reflection, philosophically mediated and informed, on acts of understanding.[37]

This opens the door on the question of the origin of consciousness with respect to God and His Creation in light of the science and theology dialogue. This concept of analogy that Pambrun brings to the fore will seemingly serve as an useful aid in reflecting upon these difficult concepts; concepts that would be impossible without God who serves as the ultimate guarantor and "regulative ideal" for thought, reflection, and consciousness itself.

We have witnessed, although implicitly, that Pambrun does not provide an endorsement of critical realism, at least as it has been implemented by major thinkers in the science-theology dialogue. He sees the fruits of philosophy as a mediator between science and theology, yet at an explicit level, critical realism has been criticized by several thinkers.[38] The critical realist approach to the science and theology dialogue has been scrutinized scholars such as William Stoeger, philosopher Ernan McMullin (1924–2011) and theologian Paul Allen. McMullin has expressed major reservations in the applicability of critical realism to theology, as it is applied to the natural sciences.[39] Both McMullin and Allen have criticized these scholars' epistemological work (i.e., the works of Barbour, Peacocke and Polkinghorne). The suggestion is that they are fundamentally descriptive and do not prescribe an explanatory account of human rationality, while they opt for an approach that is "both oriented to a scientific understanding of the world while positively open to the question of God."[40] Stoeger has stressed that "if critical realism is valid for the natural sciences but not for

37. Pambrun, "Science, Theology and Acts of Understanding," 78.

38. Alister McGrath has offered his own criticisms, which will not be delved into here due to space and relevance. See McKenzie and Meyers, "Dialectical Critical Realism in Science and Theology: Quantum Physics and Karl Barth," 50–51; McGrath, *A Scientific Theology*.

39. McMullin, "Realism in Theology and Science: A Response to Peacocke," 39–47.

40. Allen, "A Philosophical Framework within the Science-Theology Dialogue: A Critical Reflection on the Work of Ernan McMullin," 74. As quoted in Stoeger, "Relating the Natural Sciences to Theology," 35.

theology, then it is very difficult to see how we can support reflective direct interactions between the natural sciences and theology."[41] Stoeger probes further to illustrate the problematic of critical realism as applied to the science-theology dialogue, since the objects of natural science and theology radically differ: "God and God's relationships with what is not God—is not really articulable or definable, as we have already stressed."[42] Now this may be the case with apophatic language, but the mere recognition of the problem does not facilitate the purpose of this book, which is to explore the Christian conception of God and creation in understanding the origin of consciousness. Although the irreducibility of both God and consciousness to the material world leaves us with such a problematic, appropriate philosophical and theological discourse on God can help us discern the origin of consciousness, in spite of linguistic difficulties. Stoeger recognizes through McMullin and Allen's insights that "human rationality insists on going beyond those methodological limits [those of the natural sciences], prospecting for alternative evidential grounds and procedures of validation in its transcendental forays, and finally the discovery of such alternative grounds and procedures."[43] Thus, human rationality is not constrained by the methodology of the sciences, leaving openness to theological methods as well, and creating a bridge between the differing methods.

Stoeger continues building toward the discernment that science, for instance, cosmology, raises questions which it cannot answer itself because of its limitations. This is precisely where philosophical and theological reflection will bear its fruit, as he states:

> Focusing on cosmology, after it has reached certain conclusions about the dynamics, structure, history, and destiny of the universe, it raises further questions which it cannot answer, but which certainly seem legitimate. These include questions about the ultimate origin and destiny of the universe, about its meaning and purpose, about the role of consciousness and mind, about the source of values.[44]

This is where theology alongside philosophical reflection can make its contribution to the question of the origins and emergence of consciousness. It seems as though cosmology, evolutionary biology, and the neurosciences, as they unravel the natural world and the processes and phenomena contained within it, raise questions beyond their scope to answer. Hence, as this book

41. Stoeger, "Relating the Natural Sciences to Theology," 34.
42. Ibid.
43. Ibid., 35.
44. Ibid.

will labor to demonstrate, the Christian conception of God and creation can help in this puzzling mystery.

2.7 On the Commensurability of Science and Theology in Russell's CMI

At this point, we may deal with one last philosophical issue: whether there is a presupposition present, namely that science and theology are epistemologically on par, or whether science and theology are commensurable in Russell's CMI? The answer involves a larger explanation, but I contend that they are not epistemologically equivalent. A first point to make is that, as has been discussed, there is a synergy between philosophy, science, and theology that cannot be ignored. As Moreland observes: "It is foolish to say, with popular opinion, that science by definition rules out theological or philosophical concepts."[45] Both philosophy and theology are embedded within scientific theories. They also provide inspiration for scientific theories. Although Russell argues that theology can "influence" science in a number of ways (as set out in his paths 6 to 8) he does not explicitly state whether they are commensurate.

Although the CMI promotes the bidirectional interaction between science and theology, it stands against the claim that they are epistemologically equivalent. Nowhere within paths 6 to 8, for instance, does this imply an epistemological equivalence. The mode of influence is not questioning the findings of science but rather the direction of research. However, in other instances the influence of theology on science is not all so clear. For instance, Russell acknowledges that NIODA is explicitly a theological program not a scientific one, as he states:

> NIODA is part of a theology of nature, not a natural theology ("physical-theology"). This is a project in constructive theology, with special attention to a theology of nature . . . This hypothesis should be taken not as a form of natural theology, nor as one of a physico-theology, and most certainly not as an argument from design. Instead it is part of a general constructive Trinitarian theology pursued in the tradition of *fides quarens intellectum*, whose warrant and justification lies elsewhere and which incorporates the results of science and the concerns for nature into its broader framework mediated by philosophy. Although I believe God's special action is intelligible in the context of, and coherent with, our scientific view of the world because of indeterministic

45. Moreland, *Christianity and the Nature of Science*, 56–57.

character of the natural processes as suggested by plausible philosophical interpretation of quantum physics, such special action cannot be discovered by the natural sciences as such nor can it be based on them. Where faith will posit it, science will see only random events described, as far as they can be by science, by theories of physics, chemistry, biology, ecology, and so on. The positive grounds for an alleged divine action are theological, not scientific. This hypothesis is not drawn from science even though it aims to be consistent with science.

Science would not be expected to include anything explicitly about God's action in nature as part of its scientific explanation of the world. Theology, however, in *its* explanation of the world, can and should include both. This is as it should be for the mutual integrity of, and distinction between, the two fields of inquiry, and for the order of containment entailed by emergence views of epistemology which requires theology include and be constrained by while, transcending science in its mode of explanation. [46]

There are a number of crucial points to unpack from this dense quote. The first point is that although I am utilizing Russell's CMI, I am not following in his steps of adhering to merely a theology of nature. I am venturing into creating my own natural theological argument, albeit an evolutionary natural theology, following Teilhard's footsteps, but with significant differences as will be demonstrated with CENTAC. I believe CENTAC, along with the arguments from philosophical theology (divine simplicity) and systematic theology, will help bring a genuine explanation from Christian theology to science in understanding the origin of consciousness by providing both first cause and final cause arguments that can potentially help guide future research (which will be explored in chapter 7). An understanding provided by Allen will help in illustrating the significance of natural theology with respect to the science-theology dialogue and critical realism (in light of the works of Barbour, Peacocke, and John Polkinghorne).[47] In particular, this will be seen in the discernment of God as Creator, which is an essential pillar to this book for understanding the origin of consciousness:

One approach in which the issue of critical realism has been framed is natural theology. Natural theology is a form of reflection that takes its structure of questioning from the discipline

46. This is provided in a first point in response to a number of facts which he regards as misconceptions. See Russell, *Cosmology,* 125–26.

47. Allen, *Ernan McMullin and Critical Realism in the Science and Theology Dialogue,* 13–47.

of philosophy and its point of departure from the world as given, to speak about God as creator . . . The experience of God as creator is pivotal for the entire Christian theological tradition. It is the chief locus of concern in both natural theology and the science–theology dialogue.[48]

It is my hope that I am able to advance the science-theology dialogue further through the use of my understanding of natural theology, as it applies to the origin of consciousness, beyond the tensions that Allen elucidates in the works of Barbour, Peacocke, and Polkinghorne.[49] Moreover, in my estimation, this will help bring forth genuine progress to the CMI method as a "progressive problemshift" that was a criticism of Clayton in chapter 1.6.

Secondly, I, much like Russell, as stated in my introduction, follow the motto of *fides quaerens intellectum*.[50] The interesting point to be made here is that Anselm was following this motto in his formulation of his famous natural theological argument; the ontological argument.

Third, what does Russell mean by random events? This we will explore in the context of Neo-Darwinism in chapter 3. This does not present a rational obstacle to faith, which requires a quasi-fideistic interpretation, as it seems is being offered here.

Fourth, it is true that science should not contain anything explicitly about God and causation. Nonetheless, faith does present a point of contact and tension, which will be explored in chapter 7. From NIODA we do get the sense that there is still a *real* issue of demarcation between science and theology and vice versa for Russell concerning the CMI method. That is to say, they are mutually interacting with serious constraints. I contend that a theology of nature and the language that Russell uses, codifies such an understanding. To see how, we can list a number of the other remaining facts associated with NIODA:

48. Ibid., 13.

49. Allen indicates there seems to be a confusion of terminology and frameworks within Polkinghorne's work, regarding revealed theology, systematic theology, natural theology, and philosophical theology:
Polkinghorne strongly implies that the arguments offered within the natural theology tradition are insufficient by themselves. For Barbour and Peacocke, the natural/revealed theology distinction, does not base their theological notions, as it does for Polkinghorne. Complicating the issue is the fact that Polkinghorne later labels revealed theology as systematic and natural theology as philosophical theology.
See Allen, *Ernan McMullin*, 34; Polkinghorne, *Scientists as Theologians*, 12.

50. This motto closely resembles St. Augustine's "*crede ut intelligas*"—I believe so I may understand. See Ramirez, "The Priority of Reason over Faith in Augustine," 123–31; Ventureyra, "Augustine as an Apologist: Is Confessions Apologetic in Nature?" 1–34, especially the section: "Augustine's View of Faith and Reason."

1. *NIODA is part of a theology of nature, not natural theology.*

2. *NIODA is not meant to "explain" how God acts or "prove" that God acts.*

3. *NIODA is not a gaps argument in either the epistemic or ontological sense of the gaps.*

4. *NIODA is not undermined by the fact that scientific theories can be given multiple and mutually contradicting interpretations.*

5. *God's action is not reduced to the status of natural cause.*

6. *God's action is hidden from science.*

7. *NIODA is a distinct category from that of miracle.*[51]

To be sure, I am appreciative of what Russell is attempting to do here. He does not want to tread on scientific territory through imposing theological doctrine or assumptions upon science. I agree with this, but then the question arises as to whether anything really significant or intelligible can be affirmed aside from simple declaration? How does Russell square off his concept of FINLON and in particular First Instantiation of the New Law of Nature of the new creation (FINLONC), for example, with respect to his claims regarding the resurrection of Jesus? He makes the distinction when he states:

> Together, these two insights represent what I call the "first instantiation contingency." As previously noted, I refer to it by the acronym FINLON, or "the first instance of a new law of nature." FINLON refers in specific to the resurrection of Jesus as the first instance of a radically new phenomenon in the world. But within the context of the coming New Creation the resurrection of Jesus will be the first instance of a regular new phenomenon, the general resurrection from the dead and life everlasting. It might better be termed "the first instance of a new law of the New Creation" (FINLONC).[52]

In proverbial terms, is Russell trying to "have his cake and eat it too"? On one level, Russell explains, there is a genuine influence of theology to science, but on another, is he still neatly segregating the two disciplines with philosophy, potentially policing between the two? But yet here, Russell is laying the bold claim that FINLONC is actually transpiring in our universe after the resurrection of Christ.[53] If this is the case, then it is true that theology is

---

51. Russell, *Cosmology,* 126–29.

52. Russell, *Time in Eternity,* 181.

53. Ibid., 179–85.

intersecting in a profound way with natural science and should be discernible from the *actual* created order. This becomes a matter of interpretation through the lens of faith, but to be sure there is a genuine claim about cause and effect being made by Russell that does affect not only natural science but nature. If true, Celia Deane-Drummond, who is both a biologist and Catholic theologian, has sympathized with Russell's program, but expressed serious doubt of its efficacy as a biologist.[54] Ultimately, I'm not sure of the precise resolution, but there is a definite tension between Russell's NIODA and the theological claims being made. Whether they are necessarily coherent or incoherent is a matter of closer scrutiny.

Throughout this chapter I have argued that philosophy is fundamental, to not only science but to the science-theology dialogue. There are three essential elements to Russell's CMI that are exemplary in demonstrating that science and theology are not epistemically equivalent, nor commensurate with one another, including critical realism and Lakatosian "problemshifts".

A number of issues must be disentangled. First, having already examined the concept of critical realism, which functions as a philosophical bridge between science and theology, we can outline several important points to keep in mind:

1. Critical realism holds to an objective understanding of the world but the data and development of every field including science and theology are not conclusive but provisional.

2. Scientists and theologians are not in a turf war, no one is trying to subsume each other's disciplines.

3. Critical realism is primarily rooted in the secular disciplines of philosophy of science and philosophy of religion. This leaves it open to various theological purposes.

4. Critical realism is compatible with non-reductionist metaphysical perspectives.

5. We must be mindful of both the differences and similarities between science and theology.[55]

It is notoriously difficult to define the methods of either theology or science. For the sake of simplification, in a very broad sense, theology involves a

54. This was expressed in the Q&A period of her keynote address March 26–28, 2015, at the conference *Re-Imagining the Intersection of Evolution and the Fall* hosted by Garrett-Evangelical Theological Seminary and sponsored by *The Colossian Forum on Faith, Science and Culture, BioLogos and the Stead Center for Ethics and Values* in Evanston, Illinois.

55. These are points that have been made throughout section 2.6.

particular method which uses Scripture, reason, tradition, and experience (all of which are not neatly segregated and overlap with one another).[56] The scientific method differs, since it involves observation, measurement, and experiment, and the formulation, testing, and modification of hypotheses.[57] We cannot get involved in all the distinctions between science and theology here, but each method is clearly distinct. However, given these distinctions in method, does this mean that they never intersect? That they do not have any similarity? That they have nothing to say to one another? The similarities are typically cognitive, not epistemological.[58] Both disciplines engage in some sort of experience, understanding, judgment, and thinking or acting in a specified way.[59] Allen further elucidates this cognitional similarity between science and theology:

> These kinds of cognitional operations are part of being human, but when we pay attention to the patterns of their use in an intellectual inquiry, such as theology, we can take special delight in knowing what kind of thing we know. For instance, an interpretation of Gen 1:1 is simply that: an understanding. An understanding does not in and of itself preclude a variety of judgements or decisions that potentially flow from that particular understanding. So, this is Lonergan's point about method: it is always cognitionally based. And, when we know what we are doing (literally), our theology becomes more disciplined, less prone to bias or ideology and better communicated. Lonergan's eight taks [sic] are what he terms 'functional specialties' by the way.[60]

Barbour, in his book *Myths, Models and Paradigms*, had suggested that the method of theory construction through imagination, metaphor,

56. For a rigorous analysis of the method involved in theology, see Bernard Lonergan, *Method in Theology*. See also, Teevan, *Lonergan, Hermeneutics and Theological Method*. For a recent exposé, which provides a historical overview of the development of a theological method and its close interaction with philosophy and science, see Allen, *Theological Method: A Guide for the Perplexed*.

57. Gauch, *Scientific Method in Practice*.

58. For a series of important works that look at the similarities between science and theology which may overlap in method but more so cognitively, see Macintosh, *Theology As an Empirical Science*; Montgomery, *The Suicide of Christian Theology*; Pannenberg, *Theology and the Philosophy of Science*; Schlesinger, *Religion and Scientific Method*; Schoen, *Religious Explanations: A Model from the Sciences*; Sherry, *Spirit, Saints and Immortality*.

59. Lonergan, *Method in Theology*, 3–26; Allen, *Theological Method*, 209–10, 223–28; Smedes, "Does Theology Have a Method? An Interview with Paul Allen,"; Lonergan, *Insight*, 765–68.

60. Smedes, "Does Theology Have a Method? An Interview with Paul Allen."

and model; the ways data are interpreted by theory and the existence of metaphysical and aesthetic elements in theological paradigms are rather analogous to their role in science.[61] Suggesting that science and theology merely occupy separate domains of inquiry involves what is known as the demarcation problem, namely that of neatly separating theology and science. But this seems highly unrealistic. Philosophers such as Alvin Plantinga, Basil Mitchell, J.P. Moreland, and theologians such as J. Wentzel van Huyssteen and Arthur Peacocke have questioned the strict separation of theology and science.[62] Why should they differ qualitatively in every respect? For instance, when it comes to questions of origins, such as the origin and nature of the cosmos, life, and humanity (including consciousness), both science and theology seem to make propositional claims about such things. It could be that science or theology could be right or wrong about such things. The monotheistic religions of Judaism, Christianity, and Islam make claims about space and time that may agree or disagree with particular scientific claims. Moreover, it is undeniable that many scientific theories have metaphysical and theological implications, for example, big bang cosmology, the cosmological explanations for the fine-tuning of physical constants, and evolutionary biology. The finitude of the past implied from the standard big bang model, at the very least, is consonant with a belief in *creation ex nihilo*. Although the method of empirical description of such an event would be a scientific explanation, it does not preclude a profound point of intersection between metaphysics and theology—this will be examined with the KCA in chapter 5.

There are thinkers who maintain that modern science and theology must either be compartmentalized or in conflict. A famous example of conflict would be Alfred Jules Ayer's verification principle, whereby theological and metaphysical claims were tantamount to nonsense since they could not be verified.[63] Interestingly, Ayer's verification principle made the claim that a sentence is only meaningful if the proposition being expressed within it could be verified empirically. Unfortunately, such a criterion was realized to be incoherent since by its own criterion, it could not be verified. Moreover, another claim collapsed, namely that theology and metaphysics make reference to unobservable entities, whereas verificationism referred to only

61. See Barbour, *Myths, Models and Paradigm*, chapters 4, 5, 7, 8 and 9.

62. All of these authors believe that Christian theism provides a rational explanation for the world as a whole. See Mitchell, *The Justification of Religious Belief*; Moreland, *Christianity and the Nature of Science*; Plantinga, "When Faith and Reason Clash: Evolution and the Bible," 8–32; 5; van Huyssteen, *Essays in Postfoundationalist Theology*, 231; Peacocke, *Theology for a Scientific Age*, 134.

63. See Ayer, *Language, Truth & Logic*.

observable entities; however, this was inconsistent with many of the scientific theories which regularly make reference to unverifiable and unobservable entities such as forces, fields, atoms, quarks, and universal laws.[64] The verification principle then mutated into the falsification principle, first presented by Antony Flew at the Oxford University symposium of 1948 with his paper "Theology and Falsification."[65] It too suffered the same fate.[66] In an intriguing turn of events, many years later, both Ayer and Flew realizing their errors and recanted their previously held philosophical views.[67]

Philosopher of science Karl Popper (1902–1994) suggested that falsifiability would make a much better criterion for demarcating science from religion and pseudoscience (non-science). So, now in opposition to being verified, scientific theories can be falsified through the grounds of prediction and observation, whereas metaphysics and theology were unfalsifiable by such criteria.[68] But again, this proved to be extremely difficult. Falsification has been shown to be much too simplistic in its criterion. Rom Harre observes, "There is a widespread myth that scientists do experiments to test hypotheses."[69] So to what extent is falsification relevant? Moreland indicates that "falsification is certainly relevant to science. Whether it constitutes a necessary or sufficient condition for science, however is quite another matter."[70]

It is difficult to see exactly how Popper's criterion of falsification is helpful overall to the construction and development of scientific theories or to the science-theology interaction. Popper's student Imre Lakatos (whose notion of scientific research programs and "problemshifts" have already been briefly examined), shrewdly observed a way forward,[71] which is an important component to the CMI (even though it would require further

---

64. Meyer, "The Demarcation of Science and Religion," 18–26.

65. Flew, Hare, and Mitchell, "Theology and Falsification," 96.

66. Moreland and Craig, *Philosophical Foundations for a Christian Worldview*, 155.

67. Antony Flew, having spent his whole academic career as an atheist, explicitly accepted the existence of a deistic God. He based his acceptance on design arguments including Intelligent Design ones, with a specific openness and fondness for the Christian conception of God. See Flew and Varghese, *There is a God*. Ayer acknowledged that *Language, Truth and Logic* was a work full of mistakes, see Ayer, "The Existence of the Soul," 49.

68. See Popper, *Realism and the Aim of Science*, chapter 2.

69. Harre, *Great Scientific Experiments*, 108 as quoted in Moreland, *Christianity and the Nature of Science*, 33.

70. Moreland, *Christianity and the Nature of Science*, 33.

71. Lakatos, *The Methodology of Scientific Research Programmes*, introduction and chapter 1.

development). Lakatos's scientific research program provides a refutation of Popper's falsification criterion:

> Popper's demarcation criterion can indeed be easily 'falsified' by using the meta-criterion proposed in the last section; that is, by showing that in its light the best scientific achievements were unscientific and that the best scientists, in their greatest moments, broke the rules of Popper's game of science.[72]

Falsification is incredibly difficult to attain since both scientific theories and indeed pseudoscientific theories are extremely malleable and adaptable. Interestingly, by Popper's criterion of falsification, a scientific theory of biological evolution such as Neo-Darwinism is considered to be non-scientific.[73] But who is prepared to make such claims today? A much better way forward is suggesting that a theory like Neo-Darwinism or other theories of origins can conform to an "inference to the best explanation" (IBE or abductive reasoning), which was already examined in this chapter. This method of IBE is useful not only to science, but also to historical, philosophical, theological, and religious utterances.[74] These new developments in the philosophy of science demonstrate that there are ways forward beyond the problem of demarcation, as employed in the science-theology dialogue, which suffers from the inherent presupposition of a Popperian interpretation of science. The CMI purposefully avoids a series of potential pitfalls, as Russell notes with respect to the "bridge" of critical realism:

> It is worth noting at the outset that there are two key attractions to Barbour's work: 1) its use of nontheological arguments for the construction of the "bridge"; and 2) its compatibility with a variety of metaphysical systems. 1) Being based primarily on the secular disciplines of philosophy of science and philosophy of religion, critical realism can be used for a variety of theological purposes not only by Christian scholars seeking dialogue with science but to a large extent by scholars in any religious tradition or by those involved in inter-religious dialogue who likewise wish to engage in conversations about the natural sciences. One need not be committed to process theology, as Barbour is (and I am not), let alone be a Christian (as we both are) to employ

---

72. Ibid., 146

73. Popper, "Darwinism as a Metaphysical Research Program," 144–55.

74. For IBE's application (with some modifications) to theological utterances, see van Holten, "Theism and Inference to the Best Explanation," 262–81; Meyer, "The Demarcation of Science and Religion," 18–26; Peter Lipton, *Inference to the Best Explanation*.

Barbour's "bridge" in relating nonreductionistic metaphysical perspectives, including physicalism (cf. Murphy), emergent materialism (cf. Peacocke, Clayton), dual aspect monism (cf. Polkinghorne), panexperientialism (cf. Ian G. Barbour), and my own choice, emergent monism). This is because its primary purpose was not to deploy a specific metaphysics to frame the science/theology dialogue. Instead it was to clear the ground for dialogue by arguing against the strident critiques on at least four fronts: a) against those challenging religion as such by arguing for epistemic, ontological, causal, and eliminative reductionism; b) against those attempting to insulate religion from science by arguing for ontological dualism (including vitalism, and Cartesian and Platonic forms of substance dualism)[75] or for "two language" compartmentalizations of science and religion (as in Protestant neo-orthodoxy and existentialist theology [this would also include the methods of Jacques Maritain and Karl Barth]); c) against the supporting one of several philosophical interpretations of science (including naïve realism, instrumentalism and positivism) while supporting an alternative view of religion; and d) against those claiming that scientific reasoning is radically different than theological reasoning. In their place, Barbour argued for a) anti-reductionism in all its forms, b) an overlap between scientific and theological language through the common use of metaphors and models, c) a critical realist view of both science and religion, and d) an analogy between scientific and theological reasoning. [76]

Aside from Jacques Maritain who had a view of different "degrees" and kinds of knowledge that also compartmentalize science from religion,[77] and Karl Barth with his skepticism of the cognitive meaningfulness of religious language espousing fideism[78] (as mentioned in point c) in Russell's quote above), there has been the Wittgensteinian view that theological utterances are part of a distinct "language game."[79] Wittgenstein believed that there

75. In chapter 8, I argue for the compatibility of Moreland's version of substance dualism with the CMI despite some difficulties that I outline. I also suggest that William Hasker's emergent dualism may be a better idea of dualism, although Moreland's dualism is different from Cartesian and Platonic dualism.

76. Russell, *Cosmology*, 4–5, see also 25–26n 7–10. Russell sees analogy as the most important component and contribution to the science-theology dialogue. Earlier in the chapter, I discussed Pambrun's use of analogy in science and theology.

77. See Maritain, *The Degrees of Knowledge.*

78. See Taliaferro, "Philosophy of Religion," section on "God's Existence."

79. See Wittgenstein, *Lectures and Conversation.*

is no cognitive meaning to statements about God. Thus, "language games" relegates religion to be about attitude while science/metaphysics are about facts. This does not hold to scrutiny, because utterances such as "God exists," "Jesus is fully divine and fully human," or "God created the universe" are claims about reality—classical theism has deep metaphysical commitments, and this type of relegation of religion to attitude seems only applicable to liberal forms of Judaism/Christianity and something like Zen Buddhism.[80] There is much that can be said about Wittgenstein's "language games" and his fideistic outlook but that would take us beyond the scope of this book. I believe enough has been said to demonstrate that it does not pose a serious threat to the science and theology interaction.

Finally, it is worth mentioning the position of a thinker that we will be examining in chapter 8 for his understanding of consciousness: psychologist and theologian Daniel Helminiak, in his work *The Human Core of Spirituality*, although not addressing directly the question of the origins, labors to provide an answer to the question: "What is a human being and what is spirituality?"[81] Helminiak disagrees with the proposition that theology can contribute something fruitful to the natural sciences. He indicates that:

> the fact is that science, and no longer religion, sets the standard of acceptable explanation . . . the valid fruits of science are well established, and the scientific mentality is widely diffused. What does not stand up to rigorous criticism and square with 'the best available opinion of the day' is not given real credence and cannot long stand . . . If religious and scientific issues are to form one coherent explanation, that explanation must be systematically formulated. That is, it must meet the criteria of scientific thinking.[82]

He presents a position contrary to the work involved in this book, denying the potentially fruitful interaction between theology influencing the natural or human sciences, opting it seems for Barbour's[83] conflict typology; not a bidirectional influence as we seek to demonstrate in this book. Furthermore, at another instance, it seems Helminiak is supporting Barbour's independent typology; although Helminiak acknowledges God as Creator, he believes that using the concept of God in dialogue with science is a pointless exercise:

80. Forrest, "The Epistemology of Religion."

81. Helminiak, *The Human Core of Spirituality*, 14.

82. Ibid., 12.

83. See introduction for a brief discussion of Ian Barbour's famous typologies regarding science and theology.

For that reason and with good logic, it is taken for granted here that human spirit is not divine [this is in response to Eastern traditions and beliefs such as Hinduism]. So spirituality will be discussed apart from discussion of God. This is not to oust God from all consideration. It is merely to place the question of God in its appropriate place. If God is understood as Creator, what can discussion of God add to an understanding of human spirituality? Granted that God created us human beings and granted that God gave us the human nature we have and granted that part of being human is to have human spirit, what more can appeal to the Creator-God of the Universe add to this discussion? To understand human spirituality, one would have to look to this created human reality and examine it in itself. Noting that God created it helps not one bit in understanding its nature. The nature, was indeed, given by God but to understand the nature one must look to it, not to God, in order to understand the universe, though the sky and the universe are created by God, we must attend to human spirit itself and not to God, in order to understand spirituality. Once this state of affairs is clear, treatment of human spirituality must proceed apart from discussion of God.[84]

Interestingly, in his recent work on consciousness, Helminiak seems to have revised his position slightly when he suggests that:

The understanding of God as Creator has its validity. Of course, there is no suggestion that we actually understand what *Creator* means or how creation happens. Nonetheless, the term does indicate a reasonable answer to a legitimate question about the empirical existence of things and, thus, focuses and constrains our further thinking about God. From an overall perspective, this answer accords with the thrust of dynamic human consciousness because the answer is reasonable. *Creator* implies necessary being that would account for the universe of contingent being . . . the theory of God as Creator is conceptually and methodologically robust.[85]

Now Helminiak admits the fruitfulness of the question of God as Creator although we cannot really know precisely how God creates. However, the exploratory nature of this book seeks to examine this in a tentative way: how and by what possible means God could originate self-consciousness. Thus, contrary to Helminiak's position(s), the very pursuit of this book will

84. Helminiak, *The Human Core of Spirituality*, 15.
85. Helminiak, *Brain, Consciousness and God*, 353.

examine the Christian conception of God as Creator in understanding the origin of consciousness.

Though, much more can obviously be said on the various approaches, indeed many books could be devoted to just this theme. It attempts to segregate theology and science, whether from a secular or religious perspective, but I believe sufficient reasons to reject the demarcation problem as a genuine issue to the science-theology interaction have been presented.[86]

Lakatos's method of scientific research programs is our next topic of discussion. Lakatos's scientific research programs are vital to demonstrating that Russell's CMI does not presuppose that science and theology are epistemically equivalent or commensurate with one another. Although we have made a few observations earlier regarding Lakatos's research programs, it is important to mention that this method is a much better way forward from Popper's criterion of falsifiability. It allows for the complex interactions within both scientific and theological theories whereby many of the hypotheses and theories are quite malleable. Theories are considered to be progressive problemshifts if they not only confirm data but also come up with "novel facts," making them empirically progressive.[87] Theories which do not fit such criteria and allow "proliferation of rival theories" demonstrate a degenerative problemshift.[88] Progressive problemshifts will demonstrate longevity and fruitfulness. The fact that theories have an inherent capacity for explanatory flexibility does not mean they should be deemed non-scientific. Lakatos illustrates this flexibility when he states: "Neither the logician's proof of inconsistency nor the experimental scientist's verdict of anomaly can defeat a research program in one blow. One can be 'wise' only after the event."[89] Thus, unlike Popperian falsification, Lakatos offers a much more realistic interpretation, which is applicable to the science and theology interaction.[90] Russell claims a strong reliance on this method. Although he structures the CMI model in terms of both scientific research programs (SRP) and theological research programs (TRP), this method is not further developed.[91] This could be leveled as a criticism against Russell's CMI, but

---

86. An interesting approach is to examine the fruits of a particular idea/theory through asking whether it is good philosophy, science or religion on its own without focusing on the demarcation problem. See Haarsma, "Is Intelligent Design 'Scientific'?" 55–62.

87. Lakatos, *The Methodology of Scientific Research Programmes*, 32–35.

88. Ibid., 111–3.

89. Ibid., 149.

90. See Murphy, *Theology in the Age of Scientific Reasoning*, chapters 4 and 6.

91. After a brief mention on the significance of Lakatos' methodology in the introduction, he is only mentioned in notes or in passing. See Russell, *Cosmology*, 2, 9, 16,

this could also be an avenue for future development and strengthening of the CMI method. Adding to the discussion in section 1.6, my particular interests lie in Lakatos's notion of a problemshift.

Another essential component of the CMI is the notion of epistemic holism.[92] Epistemic holism allows for the autonomy of both science and theology, but with the provision that they interact in a meaningful way. Disciplines are dependent on those found at the lower levels, but are not reducible. This allows for theology to make novel claims without imposing itself on the sciences.

2.8 Conclusion

Throughout this chapter, we have witnessed the vital role that philosophy plays in the science and theology interaction. Philosophy plays an indispensable capacity in the formulation of both scientific and theological theories. Philosophical reflection also plays a critical role in maintaining the authenticity and integrity of not only the reflective aspects of each discipline, but also of their interactions. This is an essential component to the endeavor of this book. It will be of significant aid to assessing the relevancy of philosophical and scientific theories of consciousness, their role in discerning the origin of consciousness, and how they interact with the Christian conception of God and creation. Philosophy also plays an integrative role in the development of CENTAC in its relevancy to the origin of consciousness as well. Although science and theology differ epistemologically, I believe there is sufficient evidence to show that the two disciplines cannot be neatly segregated and have points of contact, particularly when it comes to the subject of origins. There are also aspects that need future development, i.e., Lakatosian research programs, which will only strengthen CMI. We now turn to the creation and evolution debate and its relationship to understanding God as Creator through the different alternative models.

22, 26, 30, 31, 79, 88, 247.

92. Epistemic holism is a notion that is important to both emergence and supervenience. It is also important to Russell's CMI. Epistemic holism can be illustrated through envisioning the discipline of physics as being on a lower level of the epistemic holistic hierarchy, thus placing constraints on disciplines which are on higher levels such as biology, psychology and theology. The idea is that, for instance, biology depends on physics: if adequate biological theories are to be formulated, they ought not contradict well-established physics such as quantum mechanics or relativity theory. Yet, the upper levels are emergent, meaning that they are dependent on the lower levels, but not reducible to them. This allows for theology to make novel claims about the world that may not come about through biology, physics or psychology for instance. See Russell, *Cosmology*, 7.

Chapter 3

Creation & Evolution

3.1 Introduction

HAVING LAID OUT RUSSELL's CMI and the role of philosophy in the science and theology interaction, we now turn to a fundamental component to this book: the Christian conception of creation. Central to the question pertaining to the origin of consciousness are the notions of creation and evolution. In attempting to understand and explore the very endeavor of this book, a particular understanding of both evolution and creation is necessary. It must be an understanding that is consistent with how we understand the concepts of consciousness, origins, and emergence. There very well may be several possibilities between notions of creation and evolution, but I will attempt to adduce the best explanation given our current scientific knowledge. Therefore, it will be of use to explain each of the major models (of how God acts in the world—they all incorporate different amounts of evolutionary development, as per the definitions). From there we can evaluate how they line up with explaining the origins of consciousness.

In this chapter I will bring precision to both terms while providing a variety of different understandings of each. For our purposes, the following question will be important to bear in mind: how can theology bring clarity without blindly choosing side(s) between the panoply of positions regarding evolution and creation—which of the differing options is most consistent with reality and Christian faith? As we shall see, many of the most compelling positions intersect between various conceptions of both evolution and creation.

In order to provide a meaningful response to the question at hand, one must adequately delineate all the relevant terms and their contextual meanings. It seems as though much conflict and tension has arisen with respect to the notions of evolution and creation precisely because the two terms have neither been clearly defined nor identified. Both of these terms must be carefully delineated since much of the theological literature tends to use these terms quite loosely, particularly that of evolution.[1] The purpose of this chapter will be to provide proper contextual definition of these terms. Moreover, it will be to examine which of the number of options available to Christianity is most consistent with reality and Christian faith. It is important to note that Christian theologians engaging in discussions revolving around creation and evolution must do this is in a clear and responsible fashion in order to alleviate obtrusions and confusion for the faithful. It is worth noting that the concepts of creation and evolution extend to a number of fields in the natural sciences such as physics, chemistry, and biology, while also influencing many other disciplines in the human sciences such as neuroscience, psychology, and anthropology. The broadly used term "evolution" extends into all fields of inquiry including economics, business, sociology, and a plethora of others. Once clear definitions of creation and evolution are provided, it will be useful to list some major categories by which creation relates to evolution. From there we can make some careful assessments on which of the differing options are most consistent with Christian theology. Before proceeding, it is worth noting that all of the options available to us, whether strictly creationist options or theistic evolutionary ones, involve an in-house debate between Christians. These are not meant to convince naturalists or outsiders of the Christian faith, particularly non-theists, but to demonstrate that Christian theism is compatible with a number of creation and/or evolutionary models. The Christian in this context, given the multiplicity of models, can freely follow the evidence wherever it leads without being constrained by one position such as naturalistic evolution. It is also worth pointing out that this creation and evolution debate is significant to the origin of consciousness in examining the possible methods by which God acts in the natural world to bring consciousness into existence. As

---

1. Looking through many texts that deal with evolution, there is often a paucity in explaining what the term means and the multiple definitions that do exist. See, for instance, Barbour, *Religion and Science*, 50–72. In this seminal work on science and religion, Barbour does not provide us with a distinction between the different definitions of evolution; instead, he provides us with different alternative theories of evolution—where different thinkers may agree on universal common descent (see below) but disagree on the mechanisms, God's actions, and what they are able to produce. He denotes the differences between Alfred Wallace, Charles Darwin, Jean-Baptiste Lamarck, and Asa Gray. He also considers a variety of mechanisms as well. See Haught, *Responses to 101 Questions about God and Evolution*. Here again we do not see a precision on the term of evolution. We see the same is true in Russell's work *Cosmology*. It seems that in the theological literature and in the science-theology dialogue, in general, it is just taken for granted, however, as we shall see these definitions help bring clarity to the debate. We can witness where the agreements and disagreements lie with those on polar opposite spectrums of the creation-evolution debate and everything in between.

mentioned earlier, it is also closely tied to Teilhard's "evolutionary natural theology," CENTAC, and the systematic theological arguments.

3.2 Systematizing the Notion of Creation

Creation in its most basic form is a reference to the "the act of making or producing something that did not exist before: the act of creating something."[2] However, the term "creation," as it is understood in theology, has several distinct meanings which differ from how one discusses the word creation in everyday English language. The accounts found both in Gen 1:1–2:3 (in the "priestly" tradition), which utilizes a seven-day schema to explain how God brings everything into being through his word, and in Gen 2:4–25 (through the "Yahwist" source) demonstrates more than anything a mythological framework. Theologian Peter C. Phan observes that these accounts in Genesis illustrate God's role as Creator by showing that:

> God is the Lord not only of Israel but also of other peoples and of the whole universe; that the world is essentially good; that it is utterly dependent upon God and hence created out of nothing and not out of pre-existing matter; that human beings, created in God's image and likeness, exercise dominion over the world but also bear responsibility toward it; and finally, that human beings must praise and trust in God because of God's creative act.[3]

An essential role that these creation narratives also serve to demonstrate is the distinctiveness of Yahweh over the gods of other creation myths, such as the Babylonian myths.[4]

A vital point to be made about the term "creation" is that it implies a distinction between creature and the Creator, signifying a profound division between Creator and creature. It could be simply put that what is not God is the work of God. God is an eternal and necessary being, whereas the universe is nonetheless considered to be contingent and, in modern cosmology, finite. Traditionally, Christian theism affirms that there is an "abyss" between God and the world. Yet, an essential component of biblical theology has always been that Yahweh created and sustained the world.[5] It

---

2. Online Merriam-Webster Dictionary.

3. Phan, "Creation," 210.

4. Phan, "Creation," 210; Bouteneff, *Beginnings*; Brueggemann, *Interpretation of Genesis*; Dalley, *Myths from Mesopotamia*.

5. Frey, "Creation: Systematic Theology and Ethics," 720.

is also worth mentioning that within systematic theology, there is nothing unequivocal that the church says regarding creation.[6] In other words, there are many different positions within the church regarding how to interpret God's creation, as will be seen in the number of options available to us. The endeavor of this chapter is to try to find the most accurate position regarding creation and evolution with respect to reality and Christian theology. One further clarification should be made that if Christian theology is true, it is on par with reality. Although this assumption may be implicit, I feel as though it should be explicit for the purpose of this study.

Creation is used as a term to replace the term "nature," but in a manner which exemplifies an aspect of faith such as belief in a first cause, for instance.[7] It is also used to signify a teleological view replacing a purely mechanistic or naturalistic view of the existence of the world and everything contained within it. In chapter 5, we will explore in greater depth some of the arguments that support God as Creator and, in turn, can be used to show the potential influence of theology on science, especially concerning the origin of consciousness.

Church doctrine covers four fields concerning creation: (1) God as the Creator, (2) *creation ex nihilo*, (3) the world and human beings as creation, and finally (4) God's relationship with creation (providence; theodicy).[8] This book will cover the first of these three fields. We have already examined the first point briefly and it will be a continuous point of interest throughout this book. The implications of the second point will be examined more thoroughly in chapter 5.2. The overall initiative of this book encapsulates the third point of creation.

When we examine specific methods by which God can act to bring about such things as life and consciousness below, we will be able to ascertain which type of approach to creation-evolution is most appropriate to tackle the origin of consciousness.

3.3 The Different Meanings of Evolution

An informative article written by historian of science Michael Keas and philosopher of science Stephen Meyer entitled "The Meanings of Evolution" delineates six meanings of the word "evolution," as are used in textbooks for the broad fields of physics, chemistry, and biology. This article provides the most helpful delineations and distinctions regarding the term. It is sloppy

6. Ibid., 722.

7. Ibid.

8. Ibid.

scholarship to conflate one meaning with another as is so often done in discussions revolving around evolution. The purpose of including these definitions here is to create transparency and help bring clarity to explorations regarding the origins of consciousness.

In addition to the six definitions it offers, I have included two other important definitions provided by Catholic philosopher and theologian Jay Wesley Richards in his introduction to *God and Evolution* (which are meanings 7 and 8)[9]

1. Change over time; history of nature; any sequence of events in nature.

2. Changes in the frequencies of alleles in the gene pool of a population.

3. Limited common descent: the idea that particular groups of organisms have descended from a common ancestor.

4. The mechanisms responsible for the change required to produce limited descent with modification, chiefly natural selection acting on random variations or mutations.

5. Universal common descent: the idea that all organisms have descended from a single common ancestor. This definition is often times referred to as "the fact of evolution."[10]

6. "Blind watchmaker" thesis: the idea that all organisms have descended from common ancestors solely through an unguided, unintelligent, purposeless, material processes such as natural selection, acting on random variations or mutations; that the mechanisms of natural selection, random variation or mutation, and perhaps other similarly naturalistic mechanisms, are completely sufficient to account for the appearance of design in living organisms.[11]

9. Definition #7 is a very common usage of the term evolution that should be distinguished from the more technical usages in the realm of evolutionary biology and/ or cosmology (definition #1). Definition #8 is important since it designates an inherent teleology as we will explore below with St. Augustine.

10. It is worth pointing out that prominent biologists like Craig Venter leave open the possibility for multiple origins of life. Prominent philosopher and biologist Massimo Pigliucci is also open to this idea and suggests it does not threaten the status of evolution in terms of common descent and material mechanisms. Although, multiple origins of life would—in my mind—further undercut overarching materialist scenarios for evolution in a cosmic sense.

11. Meyer and Keas, "The Meanings of Evolution," 136–37. In these definitions, the authors do not take into account differing mechanisms nor different "theories" of evolution as noted in footnote 1. Yet, the definitions are all adaptable to various different models/theories of evolution. Definition #6 would depend on the metaphysical and religious outlook at play. There are two other definitions: See Richards, *God and Evolution: Protestants, Catholics and Jews Explore Darwin's Challenge to Faith*, 30.

7. A metaphor describing the rise, development, success, and collapse of sports careers, business enterprises, nations, and so forth, through a process of competition.

8. Progress or development through time of something that existed initially in a nascent form, such as a child emerging from an embryo or an oak tree from an acorn. This idea was common in pre-Darwinian views of biological evolution, which led to Darwin avoiding the word "evolution" in his *Origin of Species* [in the first six editions of *Origin*]. Contemporary Darwinists, following Darwin, generally reject this understanding of biological evolution, which suggests a purposeful or teleological process. Nevertheless, language that implies progress frequently appears even in the writings of those who reject it.

It will be useful to make a few qualifying statements regarding these definitions of evolution in terms of their relevance to this book. Definitions 2, 3, 4, 5, 6, and 8 focus on the realm of biology. Although certainly applicable to biological development, the first definition extends beyond such explanations. It can be applied to many avenues including origin of life studies (abiogenesis) and cosmic evolution as studied by cosmologists. The standard big bang model exemplifies this definition where the universe experiences an expansion from $t=0$, which continues to the present moment. The universe has evolved from a hot and dense state to eventually a cooling down that led to the formation of galaxies, stars, and planets. It also in relatively recent years encompassed the question of the evolution of humans, including all human traits such as consciousness, free will, reason, and a soul (if one accepts the existence of these phenomena). These are controversial phenomena to explain, and naturalists have assumed that physical seamless evolutionary explanations will suffice to explain all of them, but they have been reluctant to provide any such explanations. Nagel's recent book, as was mentioned in chapter 1, is a case in point, along with the positions of various thinkers outlined in the introduction.[12] Nonetheless, this definition in its most basic sense refers to one state or event in nature changing into another.

Definitions 2 and 3 exemplify standard observational data regarding changes that organisms go through. The fourth definition is agreed upon to a large extent, although at times perhaps the mechanisms of change may be questioned even for limited descent by a minority of scientists, but it is generally accepted. The fifth definition of evolution referring to universal

12. See Nagel, *Mind & Cosmos*; Beilby, *Naturalism Defeated?* Plantinga outlines his argument from reason, against naturalistic evolution, with critiques and appraisals from other philosophers. It also includes a rejoinder to his critics by Plantinga.

common ancestry is differentiated from the mechanisms of change (i.e., natural selection and random mutation). It is compatible with various mechanisms of change, though a Darwinian one is usually associated with Universal Common Descent (UCD), namely the view that all organisms are ultimately modified descendants, from one organism in the past. As we shall see, this is the main point of commonality that characterizes theistic evolution. This is the key component to theistic evolution, despite all the other differences among the diverse models of theistic evolution (as will be shown later in this chapter).

It is worth noting that Gen 1:1–2:3 and Gen 2:4–25 allow for a number of differing interpretations with respect to understanding human origins. Some of these interpretations include the following perspectives: young earth creationism, old earth creationism, naturalistic evolution, and theistic evolution (encompassing non-teleological evolution, planned evolution, and directed evolution). It is important to note that each of these positions possesses their own set of challenges, whether scientific, philosophical, and/or theological. This book will not take a literalist interpretation of Genesis. I will not delve directly into these debates, but will outline the distinctions, in order to set a clear path for argumentation regarding how the Christian conception of God and creation will aid in understanding the origin of consciousness.

The most controversial of all eight definitions of evolution is the sixth one, the blind watchmaker thesis. This combines UCD with naturalistic mechanisms (namely natural selection and random mutation with the possibility of other naturalistic mechanisms; endosymbiosis, self-organization, etc.), without the possibility of any direction or purposiveness from an intelligent agent. This definition makes the grandest claims out of all the other definitions of evolution. A few points are worth making regarding this definition. This definition is an explicit reference to Richard Dawkins's metaphor for Neo-Darwinian (and Darwinian)[13] evolution, whereby all organisms were derived from a single common ancestor through an unguided, purposeless form, via natural selection acting on random mutations. It is essentially an allusion to William Paley's watch analogy and teleological design. However, in this definition of evolution, natural processes act as a designer substitute for God or any other intelligent cause. This is why biologists such as Richard Dawkins, Ernst Mayr, and George Gaylord Simpson draw philosophical and theological conclusions from this view/definition of evolution. George Gaylord Simpson states it simply in his book *The Meaning of Evolution*: "Man is the result of a purposeless and natural process that

---

13. See Dawkins, *The Blind Watchmaker*.

did not have him in mind. He was not planned."[14] Statements of this sort should be apparent to the shrewd observer as metaphysical or a-theological claims, more than any corroborated and observed scientific observation.

Definition #7 seems self-explanatory and is commonly used by a large number of individuals. Definition #8 was actually used by St. Augustine in *The City of God*. It is predominantly theistic or at the very least teleological (assuming someone who may be a Deist and believe in God's purposive action through cosmic, chemical, and biological evolution, etc.).

3.4 Creationism

First, there is Scientific Creationism,[15] which seeks to impose a particular interpretation upon Genesis 1 and 2 through collecting empirical evidence in the natural world to corroborate this particular interpretation. Scientific Creationism is typically associated with young earth creationism (YEC), which entails the belief that God created the world in six, twenty-four-hour days—usually within the past 10,000 years.

Adherents to old earth creationism (OEC)[16] hold to mainstream scientific consensus with respect to the age of the universe and the earth. However, they believe that God created particular things, which include galaxies, planets, ecosystems, the first replicating cell, a variety of life, humans, human souls, and so on, but through a direct way such as a "primary" or "efficient" cause.[17] There is disagreement amongst OECs as to when and where God creates particular things, but there is agreement that nature on its own could not produce these particular things without God's direct intervention.[18]

Are these fit models to explain the origins and emergence of consciousness? To be sure, these models *could* explain how consciousness originated—through an intervening act of God at a given moment in the

14. Simpson, *The Meaning of Evolution*, 345. These sorts of statements are not unique and can be encountered throughout biology textbooks. For example, in Douglas Futuyma's widely used college textbook, *Evolutionary Biology*, it says: "By coupling undirected, purposeless variation to the blind, uncaring process of natural selection, Darwin made theological or spiritual explanations of the life processes superfluous." See Futuyma, *Evolutionary*, 5.

15. For various works supportive of Scientific Creationism (Young Earth Creationism), see Whitcomb and Morris, *The Genesis Flood*; Morris, *Scientific Creationism*; Duane T. Gish, *Evolution the Fossils Say No!*; Sarfati, *Refuting Evolution*.

16. See Ross, *More Than a Theory*; Ross, *Navigating Genesis*.

17. Richards, *God and Evolution*, 11.

18. Ibid.

universe's history. But they raise further questions, such as whether it is something that God does systematically over and over again at the birth of a new human. This raises the issue of traducianism or creationism for the creation of consciousness and the soul.[19] I do not think either of these models is adequate for the explanations we seek. The intention of this book is to be in line with modern scientific discovery and evidence, but only to question certain findings of science if there is sufficient reason, whether scientifically and/or philosophically, to consider them suspect but not necessarily a priori.

Both these positions seem to be internally coherent if one accepts certain premises and assumptions.[20] I find the first view of YEC problematic for a number of reasons. It tends to contradict the majority of the findings of modern science, whether it is in biology, geology, physics, or cosmology. Moreover, the reason it does so is because of an assumption that Gen 1:1–2:3 and Gen 2:4–25 should be read in a particular narrow and literal sense. It should be pointed out that perhaps there are legitimate reasons to reject aspects of modern scientific theories, but it seems that it should be done through scientific means, without the influence of particular assumptions garnished by how a biblical text is read and understood. YECs may dispute they have evidential grounds for their claims against modern scientific theories, but as of yet, their case is quite weak. However, one of the strengths of this particular view, if it turned out to be true, is that it ties many of the concepts of sin and biblical timelines neatly, without having to explain why such great amounts of time were taken for species to go extinct and humans to finally emerge. In other words, some tough theological problems of how death and suffering enter the world through human sin would be simplified.

OEC is more in line with modern scientific findings. The major problem with this view, in my opinion, is that God is portrayed in a sense as a tinkerer, appearing sporadically in time throughout the development of His Creation. It favors an interventionist mode of creating species over the cumulative evidence there is for UCD, including the most recent and

19. Moreland, *The Soul*, 183. Traducianism is the view that both our body and soul is passed onto us from our parents, so we need to have the parents that we do to possess the soul and consciousness we have. On the other hand creationism is the view that our parents are responsible for our bodies but our souls are directly created by God.

20. For an interesting exposition on several different views regarding creation and evolution, YEC, OEC, and theistic evolution, see Moreland and Reynolds, *Three Views on Creation and Evolution*.

compelling: homological biochemistry and genetic code; selectively neutral similarities and phylogenetic trees.[21]

3.5 Intelligent Design

The term Intelligent Design (ID)[22] has been mentioned several times already. ID is the minimalist claim that the universe and certain features within the universe, whether biological or not (solar systems, laws of physics, constants of nature, etc.), are best explained by a designing intelligence.[23] It will be worthwhile to outline several basic ideas that emanate from ID. Much confusion surrounds the concept of ID, as it is often mischaracterized through media outlets and by many academics who offer bland platitudes as criticisms since they have not taken the time to read the works and understand the arguments of prominent ID advocates.[24] There are a lot of emotional responses toward ID found in the media and among academics, but it seems that often it is based on misunderstandings.[25] In order to adequately criti-

21. See the following recent articles that support the theory of universal common descent. Theobald, "A Formal Test of the Theory of Universal Common Ancestry," 219–22; Steel and Penny, "Origins of Life: Common Ancestry Put to the Test," 168–69; Than, "All Species Evolved From Single Cell, Study Finds."; Yonezawa and Masami "Was the universal common ancestry proved?" E9.

22. The following titles are a list of books that lay out the case for ID. For an interesting historical survey of ID, see Woodward, *Doubts about Darwin: A History of Intelligent Design*. For the original works which ignited debates about design, critiquing Neo-Darwinism and materialistic origin of life scenarios, see Denton, *Evolution: a Theory in Crisis*; Thaxton, Bradley, and Olsen, *The Mystery of Life's Origins*. For more recent ID works inspired by the aforementioned texts, see Behe, *Darwin's Blackbox*; Dembski, *The Design Inference*; Denton, *Nature's Destiny*; Dembski, *The Design Revolution*; Behe, *The Edge of Evolution*; Meyer, *Signature in the Cell*. For a text providing several positions for ID, see Dembski and Ruse, *Debating Design*; Stewart, *Intelligent Design*. For texts critical of ID, see Pennock, *Intelligent Design Creatonism and its Critics*; Perakh, *Unintelligent Design*; Petto and Godfrey, eds., *Scientists Confront Creationism*.

23. Dembski, *The Design Revolution*, 33–37.

24. These document inaccuracies among critiques of ID are from the American Association for the Advancement of Science (AAAS) and National Academy of Sciences (NAS). In particular, the article by John West found that when the AAAS released a press release condemning ID, he contacted those behind the statement and found that AAAS "board members voted to brand intelligent design as unscientific without actually reading for themselves the academic books and articles by scientists proposing the theory." See West, "Intelligent Design Could Offer Fresh Ideas on Evolution"; Luskin, "The Facts about Intelligent Design: A Response to the National Academy of Sciences' Science, Evolution, and Creationism."

25. There are many examples of these, but I will list only a few. I'll provide a series of emotional quotes with the corresponding sources: "The current Intelligent Design movement poses a threat to all of science and perhaps to secular democracy itself. . . .

cize a particular notion, one should understand it as accurately as possible, since otherwise one runs the risk of attacking a caricature instead of the actual idea.[26]

Intelligent Design is a controversial view revolving around the origins of various phenomena within the universe and the universe itself. It makes the minimalistic claim that the universe itself, certain features of the universe, and living systems are best explained by an intelligent cause as opposed to a purely undirected process. It is distinct from creationism and natural theology although some of its proponents may adhere to such notions. Moreover, although ID exponents may criticize many tenets of evolutionary theory, they also claim to have a positive basis for their reasoning, which is dependent upon standard modes of scientific reasoning. ID extends into various domains including cosmology, physics, chemistry, biology, and neuroscience, and also into the humanities, so it is not restricted to biology (a popular misconception).

ID remains contentious in philosophical, theological, and scientific discussions since it seeks to challenge the efficacy of methodological naturalism as a reliable methodology for the natural sciences.[27] It is important not to conflate methodological naturalism with that of metaphysical naturalism. ID may very well challenge both after further philosophical reflection, but to be taken seriously as a research program it should not purposely make metaphysical claims about the nature of this so-called intelligent cause. Proponents argue that it may have theistic implications, but

---

Replacing sound science and engineering with pseudo-science, polemics, blind faith, and wishful thinking won't save you when the curtain of 'Dark Ages II' begins to fall!" See Berman, "Intelligent Design: The New Creationism Threatens All of Science and Society"; "[I]ntelligent-design theory and its companions are nasty, cramping, soul-destroying reversions to the more unfortunate aspects of 19th century America. Although I am not a Christian, I look on these ideas as putrid scabs on the body of a great religion." See Ruse, "Faith & Reason," 54–58, 134–36; "It is absolutely safe to say that if you meet somebody who claims not to believe in evolution, that person is ignorant, stupid or insane." See Dawkins, "Put Your Money on Evolution," sec. 7, 34; "If, for example, a student were [sic] to use examples such as the bacterial flagellum to advance an ID view then they should expect to be marked down," see Luskin, "Want a Good Grade in Alison Campbell's College Biology Course? Don't Endorse Intelligent Design," at *Evolution News & Science-Today;* and finally, Lynn Margulis states: "Honest critics of the evolutionary way of thinking who have emphasized problems with biologists' dogma and their undefinable terms are often dismissed as if they were Christian fundamentalist zealots or racial bigots." See Margulis and Sagan, *Acquiring Genomes,* 29.

26. Russell himself has criticized ID; see Russell, "A Critical Response to Cardinal Schönborn's Concern over Evolution," 193–98.

27. For a comprehensive critique and a series of proposed alternatives to methodological naturalism for the sciences see Bartlett and Holloway, *Naturalism and Its Alternatives in Scientific Methodologies.*

the "research program" is distinct. Critics maintain that ID has no place in scientific discussions for typically four reasons: 1) it is not science or that it possesses no scientific evidence, 2) it has no peer review publications, 3) that it is unfalsifiable, and 4) that it has been falsified. These issues revolve around what is known in the philosophy of science as the demarcation problem—between what can be classified as science and non-science. As one can see, critics sometimes offer contradictory criteria. If it is falsifiable it would adhere to the criterion of falsification as offered by the epistemology of philosopher of science Popper. But if it is not science, then it would be unfalsifiable. The same goes for the claims of it being unscientific. If it is unscientific is it falsifiable?[28]

Defenders of ID will point to the growing body of research being done at the Biologic Institute in Seattle, a non-profit research organization that was started in 2005. The scientists work from the framework and hypothesis that life appears to be designed because it is actually designed. The scientists working at this organization believe that this approach will be more heuristically fruitful than the reigning paradigm of Neo-Darwinism. Critics will point to the scarcity of peer-reviewed publications for ID.[29]

Intelligent Design, if incorporated in a wider Christian theistic understanding, could function as an explanation for the origins and emergence of consciousness.[30] That is, if the designer is identified as the Christian God. A theological criticism of ID is that it makes a case for an unknowable deity

28. See section 2.7 for our discussion on the demarcation problem. This is an issue closely associated to ID.

29. There is also the Evolutionary Informatics Lab originally fronted by mathematician William Dembski (he has since left the movement) and engineer Robert Marks III. The debates geared around ID and evolution rage on not only in scientific and philosophical circles but also among theological ones. These issues are much more nuanced than are popularly treated. See Fowler and Kuebler, *The Evolution Controversy*. It is a good way to begin to look at a detailed discussion of the differing positions. There is a vast literature both sympathetic and critical of ID. It is worth mentioning that some non-religious thinkers such as David Berlinski, Thomas Nagel, and Bradley Monton, although opponents of theistic explanations in general, are supportive of ID as a research program. They also value the profound scientific and philosophical questions ID proponents have raised concerning current scientific theories, such as the Modern Synthesis of evolution (Neo-Darwinism). In contrast, a number of theistic scientists such as Kenneth Miller, Francis Collins, and Karl Giberson have been highly critical of ID. Francis Collins, who was the director of the Human Genome Project, although he is critical of ID in biology, seems to accept ID within cosmology and astrophysics. This is made clear in his book: *The Language of God*.

30. For instance, Moreland outlines and contrasts various ID (from a Christian theist slant) and Evolutionary Psychology research programs. See Moreland, "Intelligent Design and Evolutionary Psychology as Research Programs: A Comparison to Their Most Plausible Specifications," 112–38.

and that it cannot be distinguished from deism. Proponents of ID respond that the nature of the designer remains elusive while the deduction of design is arguable. The question then is whether God created consciousness through secondary causes or intervened as articulated in YEC or OEC? Since ID is compatible with a variety of interventionist creation positions and even theistic evolution (as we will explore below) the question is left open. The only definition of evolution that runs contrary to ID is #6. If operational through secondary causes in a theistic evolutionary model, then ID could be of interest concerning the proposition set forward by this book. This remains to be seen.

It is worth noting that ID has different degrees of overlapping with the five theistic models outlined (including the three theistic evolutionary ones below). I disagree with Rau that ID's association is only restricted to YEC, OEC, and directed evolution.[31] I contend that ID, when extended to the origin of the universe and as an explanation for the fine-tuning of the physical laws, constants and initial conditions, would encompass planned evolution (PE) and Non-Teleological Evolution (NTE) as well.[32] Interestingly this is a stance that the philosopher of physics and atheist Bradley Monton agrees with in his book *Seeking God in Science: An Atheist Defends Intelligent Design*, in terms of the origin of the universe and the fine-tuning.[33] I will explain this further in the appropriate sections.[34] So, as a theist, ID is almost inescapable even though it has many negative connotations and has been deemed a dirty term by many. This not only includes non-theists who are opposed to anything with a modicum of religious undertones, but also to theists (those in the PE and NTE camps and even YEC and OEC who criticize the ID program for leaving the designer unnamed).

Intelligent Design is one explanation of how consciousness could have originated and emerged in our universe, i.e., through the designing act of intelligence, which many proponents of ID who are YECs, OECs, or TEs would agree to. However, it is obviously not a necessary position to hold. This could also be through designing a process as with the fine-tuning or through direct intervention. This will be discussed in more detail later.

31. Rau, *Mapping the Origins Debate*, 54.

32. Robert Russell, in a critical article on ID, confines his criticisms of ID to biology and not to physics, as he states: "Other possible meanings of 'Intelligent Design,' which refer, for example, to the 'fine tuning' of the fundamental laws of physics that ultimately make the evolution of life possible and which involve the so-called 'Anthropic Principle,' are not the subject of this essay." See Russell, "Intelligent Design is Not Science and Does Not Qualify to be Taught in Public School Science Classes," 132.

33. Monton, *Seeking God in Science*, 75.

34. See chapter 5, sections 5.2 and 5.3.

3.6 Theistic Evolution

In my estimation, one of the three following TE models is most conducive to a broad picture of God's creative action concerning the universe with life itself, the variety of organisms, and human consciousness. UCD is the best explanation for the diversity of life on Earth. It is empirically superior and theologically superior to both YEC and OEC. Theologically, theistic evolutionary models in general avoid turning God into a tinkerer as OEC does. Empirically it offers greater explanatory scope and power than both YEC and OEC, particularly more so than YEC. UCD offers great explanatory scope since it is based on the corroborative nature of modern scientific fields, such as geology, paleontology, and genetics. It also adheres to cosmic evolution (OEC does as well) following the corroborative sciences of cosmology and astrobiology. It is indeed the best explanation of several lines of evidence, including the fossil record (e.g., transition from fish to amphibians), geographical distribution, comparative physiology, and biochemistry (e.g., DNA sequencing, endogenous retroviruses), and comparative anatomy (e.g., homologous structures).

Gerald Rau has performed a great in-depth study regarding creation and evolution with his text *Mapping the Origins Debate: Six Models of the Beginning of Everything*.[35] He has done a tremendous service to those involved in such dialogues/debates. He has cut through much of the rhetoric and emotions that characterize most of the debates about origins. It is the most instructive work, outlining competing theories concerning origins, since Thomas B. Fowler and Daniel Kuebler's *The Evolution Controversy: A Survey of Competing Theories*. However, it encompasses a greater scope of subjects, since it is not strictly confined to discussions regarding biological origins. Fowler and Kuebler's work distinguished four of the differing schools of thought: The Neo-Darwinian, the creationist, the Intelligent Design, and the Meta-Darwinian.[36] The Meta-Darwinian school includes the same mechanisms of natural selection and random mutation but questions the degree that such mechanisms are responsible for generating phenotypic and genotypic novelties. This view of evolution involves other mechanisms such as punctuational change, stasis, hierarchical selection,[37] exaptation, punctuated equilibrium,

---

35. See Gerald Rau, *Mapping the Origins Debate*, 38.

36. See Fowler and Kuebler, *The Evolution Controversy*, 7, 277–326.

37. Punctuational change, stasis, and hierarchical selection are mechanisms of punctuated equilibrium (equilibria) theory, which was a viable extension to Ernst Mayr's idea of allopatric speciation that was proposed by Stephen J. Gould and Niles Eldredge: "Punctuated equilibrium is an interpretation of the fossil record, where it is posited that evolution goes through rapid pockets of change and large periods of

neutral theory, developmental mutations: evo-devo, morphogenic fields, self-organization/complexity theory, and endosymbiosis. Meta-Darwinism is also synonymous with what is known as the Extended Synthesis.[38]

In *Mapping the Origins Debate*, Rau outlines six extremely helpful models: naturalistic evolution (NE), OEC and YEC which we have already examined. Under the broad tent of theistic evolution (TE), Rau proposes three sub-categories: non-teleological evolution (NTE), planned evolution (PE), and directed evolution (DE).[39] For the purpose of this study, I will use Rau's three typologies concerning theistic evolutionary models.

3.6.1 Non-Teleological Evolution

Non-teleological evolution affirms that there has been no supernatural intervention since the creation of the universe.[40] Some proponents of such a position include the theologian John Haught, the late nuclear physicist, theologian, and pioneer of the science and religion typologies, Ian Barbour, and the late biochemist and theologian, Arthur Peacocke.[41] NTE is quite similar to NE but does not deny the existence of God and certain theistic realities. Rau would equate such views with a variety of forms of deism, even though many classified in such camps of thought would vehemently deny such associations. As Rau indicates:

> Thus it is basically a deistic perspective, although many proponents would not willingly accept that moniker. Many authors who support NTE espouse a liberal Christian theology, such as

---

stasis to explain the paucity in the record connecting different taxonomies, through a gradual incremental visible change," See Gould and Eldredge, "Punctuated equilibria: the tempo and mode of evolution reconsidered," 115–51.

38. Pigliucci and Müller, *Evolution: The Extended Synthesis*. For a more basic introduction to these issues, see Suzan Mazur, *The Altenberg 16*.

39. Rau, *Mapping the Origins Debate*, 37–38. It is worth pointing out that some thinkers will argue for more models than proposed by Rau. It is also conceivable that there could be intertwinements between one model and another, but these seem to cover the basic distinctions between the broader categories of theistic evolution. It is also worth noting that while several thinkers/scientists may agree with one another on the broad categories, it does not mean they are in accordance with every aspect, but that they share major agreements with respect to the characteristics of each model.

40. Rau, *Mapping the Origins Debate*, 43. Rau does not explore the views on particular theological issues such as grace, the incarnation, and resurrection, etc. in the thinkers that he classifies under NTE.

41. See Peacocke, *All That Is*. Peacocke, in the first part of this book, explains how God is involved through naturalistic processes, distinguishing it from metaphysical naturalism.

process theology. Scientists who come from a pantheistic world-view, whether Buddhist, Hindu, or New Age, in which super-natural and natural are one and the same, would also logically favor a position similar to NTE.[42]

Non-teleological evolution is very similar to a completely naturalistic vision of the universe with the exception that NTE holds that God exists and is the ultimate cause and reason for the existence of the universe. NTE proponents also claim that God is in the sustaining of the universe and in the process of evolutionary development, although how one explains God's action in a concrete way is rather difficult to envision. The precise distinc-tions from naturalistic mechanisms acting on their own and God's involve-ment are extremely vague at best. This view is said to not follow a plan or direction, so that the origins and emergence of consciousness may remain as elusive as under a fully naturalistic vision of reality. Haught, for instance, sees the universe as being set up by an "aesthetic cosmological principle." He sees beauty as emerging from nature's autonomous essence. He illustrates this point by using Alfred North Whitehead's metaphysics, namely that the purpose of the universe is to evolve into maximal beauty "and along with beauty, the possibility of subjective enjoyment."[43] It is interesting to notice that Haught does not acknowledge that God is the formal, efficient, or final cause of any phenomenon within the universe. It seems as though this is largely in order to avoid a potential god-of-the-gaps explanation. While this concern is certainly understandable, if God acts as an explanation for something, one need not invoke the god-of-the-gaps, since it could be that positive knowledge of something could provide us warrant for coming to such a conclusion, as opposed to resorting to ignorance. Nonetheless, this argument for the universe's goal to evolve into maximal beauty still leaves one vulnerable to attacks revolving around how one can possibly know such a thing. The argument could just as easily be made that ugliness, imbalance, pain, suffering, cold, desolation, meaninglessness, and void fill and pervade the universe. The point is that any system that makes a positive claim about reality can be countered, so Haught opens the door to objections, just as much as the creationist, ID proponent, or other TE positions. Russell for instance does not follow Barbour, Peacocke, or Haught in their utilization of process theology, although he admits there are useful insights that can

42. Rau, *Mapping the Origins Debate*, 43.

43. Haught, *Response to 101 Questions about God and Evolution*, 140. The context of this view is in response to the question: "According to process theology, what is the purpose of the evolving universe?" Haught claims that he does not agree with all of process theology's claims but sees merit in its views about nature's autonomy and evo-lutionary processes.

be gleaned from such a methodology.[44] According to the four fields that church doctrine covers, mentioned in section 3.2, the notion of creation, NTE seems rather ambiguous to points 3 and 4. However, Peacocke has made statements that seem to align better with traditional views of God as Creator. For instance, Peacocke, in discussing God's immanence in the evolutionary process has said that: "God is the Immanent Creator *creating in and through the processes of natural order* . . . and that all the processes revealed by the sciences, especially evolutionary biology, are in themselves God-acting-as-Creator."[45]

In an article arguing that Nagel could benefit from the theological insights of Teilhard and Lonergan, Haught has suggested: "Yet a materialist view of nature still can't show—without seeming like alchemy—how the lustrous gold of human intelligence emerged from the dross of primordial cosmic mindlessness simply by adding the elixir of deep time. Something else must be going on."[46] He goes on to explicate Lonergan's insight "that if our worldview is out of joint with what goes on in our minds—in every act of attending, understanding, knowing, and deciding—then we need to look for another worldview. He would agree with Nagel, that materialism doesn't work, not least because, it logically subverts the trust required for our minds to work at all."[47] Everything that Haught points out is very reasonable and logical, but is it plausible under his own very specific worldview? These deductions are very reasonable to make under a broad theistic worldview, but is it logically consistent, given his view of a non-teleological universe?

When taken to its logical conclusion, such a position, despite orthodox-sounding statements, does not provide any greater explanatory scope for the origins and emergence of consciousness. This is true since it holds that all of nature is autonomous, without any *real* telos aside from the autonomy being set up for the emergence of the beauty Haught speaks of. Haught also points to the intelligibility of the universe,[48] which is a very difficult thing to explain from a materialistic or naturalistic perspective. These do not provide much warrant for that, without ascribing to God as the source of all being. That is something that would be neither rationally discernible nor necessarily distinguishable from a completely naturalistic universe (as the atheist observes it). The emergence of beauty is left to

44. Russell, *Cosmology*, 5.

45. Peacocke, "Welcoming the 'Disguised Friend'—Darwinism and Divinity," 474.

46. Haught, "Darwin's Nagging Doubt: What Thomas Nagel Could Learn From Theology."

47. Haught, "Darwin's nagging doubt," 11.

48. Ibid.

chance and natural law without any forethought by God. Moreover, the ability to discern this beauty and the intelligibility of the cosmos through an emergent consciousness seems a difficult pill to swallow, in a universe that was not planned. If they say it was planned then it cannot operate solely by natural law, which is to say that the natural law was set up in such a way to allow for these phenomena to come about. So, God would foresee these things before they transpire. Language and precision of terms are left to ambiguity in the NTE model.

Ultimately, it seems as though the theologians who uphold the extreme autonomy of the universe on one hand reject the reductive materialistic scenarios and/or purely naturalistic explanations on the other. They do this through denying God as the ultimate Creator and sustainer in one breath while allowing for the emergence of maximal beauty, consciousness, and intelligibility in the next and seem to be committing what George Orwell called *doublethink*: "the power of holding two contradictory beliefs in one's mind simultaneously and accepting both of them."[49] One is left to wonder if in such a universe, consciousness would ever emerge. It seems to reveal the same problems as the NE model.

3.6.2 Planned Evolution

Planned Evolution holds that there is a specific intention and plan that was implanted into the universe at the moment of creation.[50] It is a form of teleological evolution and is a monotheistic position.[51] PE suggests that God certainly can intervene in creation but does not do so because the original creation was perfect.[52] Some major advocates of PE include Canadian dentist, theologian, evolutionary biologist, and first tenure track professor of science and religion, Denis Lamoureux, cell biologist Kenneth R. Miller,[53] medical doctor and biophysicist Francis Collins[54] (leader of the Human Genome Project and founder of BioLogos[55]), physicist Howard van Till,

49. Orwell, *Nineteen Eighty-Four*, 264.

50. Rau, *Mapping the Origins Debate*, 45.

51. Ibid. Unlike NTE, which is malleable enough to entertain Hindu, Buddhist, and polytheistic positions, PE is strictly monotheistic.

52. Rau, *Mapping the Origins Debate*, 45.

53. See Miller, *Finding Darwin's God*; Miller, *Only a Theory*. Miller considers himself both an orthodox Darwinist and an Orthodox Catholic.

54. See Collins, *The Language of God*.

55. BioLogos is a non-profit organization that seeks to reconcile evolutionary biology with the Christian faith. They also seek to demonstrate, in more general terms, that there is no inherent contradiction between science and biblical Christianity.

and geneticist, medical doctor, and first prominent dissenter of Darwinism, Michael Denton.[56]

Van Till has outlined his position for theistic evolution, which he has dubbed "The Fully Gifted Creation" or "Robust Formational Economy Principle."[57] He has suggested that God creates from the outset with "functional integrity." What he means by this is as follows:

> . . .wholeness of being that eliminated the need for gap-bridging interventions to compensate for formational capabilities that the Creator may have initially withheld from it" so it is "accurately described by the *Robust Formational Economy Principle*—an affirmation that the creation was fully equipped by God with all of the resources, potentialities, and formational capabilities that would be needed for the creaturely system to actualize every type of physical structure and every form of living organism that has appeared in the course of time.[58]

So, in van Till's view,[59] God sets up the universe by causing the big bang and fine-tuning the laws of physics to have the capacity for cosmic evolution, and eventually chemical and biological evolution as well, without the need for any intervention since God created the universe with the capacity to bring about his ever-unfolding planned creation. The issue to be confronted here is how to articulate a model for evolutionary creation, which makes sense of the singular events that seem intractable for a seamless evolving creation. How do we make sense of singular events like

---

56. Denton has claimed to be religiously agnostic, but it seems clear that he believes in some sort of God. He also has been associated with the ID movement but at times has seemed to distance himself from the ID movement. Despite this, The Discovery Institute (one of the main ID think tanks) has promoted and published some of his recent work. See Denton, *Evolution: Still a Theory in Crisis*; Denton, *Fire-Maker*; and his documentary *Privileged Species* was released by the Discovery Institute in March 2015. One could say that Denton's work is broadly sympathetic toward ID, at least when it comes to demonstrating teleology in nature and that there is fine-tuning of the laws of physics, chemistry, and biology.

57. See van Till, "The Fully Gifted Creation," 161–218.

58. van Till explains his views about Evolutionary Creation (Theistic Evolution). See "Functional Integrity (Fully Gifted Creation, Robust Formational Economy Principle)," entire page.

59. For a pointed criticism of van Till's theistic evolutionary views, see Richards "Making a Virtue of Necessity: van Till's Robust Formational Economy Principle," 129–45. Richards argues that van Till's position is theologically weak and ultimately unjustifiable since he seeks to be at all costs, in line with the philosophy of science principle, methodological naturalism, even if it compromises his scientific and theological understanding.

the origin of life, the Cambrian explosion, mammalian radiation, and the origin of consciousness?

On the other hand, Miller and Collins, for instance, have not developed an evolutionary theology to explain the compatibility of God and evolution. However, Denton has come up with a fascinating model himself, which has many points of intersection with Lamoureux's but does not make an explicit case for the Christian God, although he leaves the option open. Interestingly, Denton was deeply influenced by Lawrence Henderson in his book *The Fitness of the Environment* (1913).[60] This text "examines all the properties of the key building blocks of life—water, carbon dioxide, carbon compounds, and the basic biochemical processes like hydrolysis and oxidation."[61] In Denton's second book, *Nature's Destiny: How the Laws of Biology Reveal Purpose in the Universe*, he expanded on Henderson's work through the aid of modern scientific evidence. Henderson's *Fitness* showed that universal laws were finely calibrated to produce an environment extremely fit for life. Denton extended this concept to suggest that "life's constituent forms [that] are "lawful" rather than contingent assemblages of matter."[62] He suggests that the "possibility of evolution by natural law—the idea that physical law may be a major determinant of organic order . . . [and that] many simple organic forms were indeed determined by natural law—the round shape of the cell and the flat shape of the cell membrane are well known examples."[63] Moreover, he envisioned Stuart Kauffman's ideas of self-organizational processes as directing evolution "[through] prearranged paths, by mechanisms which would not have necessitated any sort of specific directed mutations in the DNA sequence space."[64] Denton believes his claims are quite consistent with some of Kauffman's[65]: "We will have to see that we are all natural expressions of a deep order. Ultimately, we will discover in our creation myth that we are expected after all."[66] The notion of natural law influencing the direction of the evolutionary process, coupled with Kauffman's speculations of self-organizational processes, provides an interesting alternative to the Neo-Darwinian model of evolution, a potential paradigm shift in how we view evolution. The merit in Denton's work is that he conceives of ways in

60. Denton, *Nature's Destiny*, xvi–xvii.

61. Denton, "An Anti-Darwinian Intellectual Journey: Biological Order as an Inherent Property of Matter," 167.

62. Ibid., 169.

63. Ibid., 170.

64. Ibid., 171.

65. Ibid., xvii.

66. Kauffman, *At Home in the Universe*, 112.

which the universe's laws have capacities to bring forth emergent systems, and how human consciousness was part of the plan. Denton presupposes an intelligible structure which unravels these laws of physics and biology, to bring forth greater complexity and radical new phenomena such as life and consciousness. This appears to be a more plausible method than an outdated Neo-Darwinian model. But is it sufficient in any way, to bring about all of the universe's novel features? As compelling as models like that of Denton and even van Till appear, it's difficult to say if these self-organizational capacities are sufficient for something like the origin of life and consciousness.[67] Lamoureux, who seems to agree with many of Denton's views, offers a less theologically porous version of PE, but it is seemingly consistent with the Christian conception of God and creation. Lamoureux's position regarding PE is the most rigorous and developed.

Lamoureux has labeled his model: evolutionary creation. Lamoureux states that this position is "purpose driven and not the result of blind chance." Stated more precisely, this position claims that "the Father, Son, and Holy Spirit created the universe and life through an ordained, sustained, and design-reflecting evolutionary process."[68] So, we can see a repudiation of the sixth definition of evolution. Although he does not reject the mechanisms of natural selection and random mutation, he does not interpret them necessarily as a "blind watchmaker" which renders the universe devoid of design. Lamoureux discusses Denton's model and seems to be in large agreement. He suggests that:

> It is important to recognize that though Denton presents sci-
> entifically credible data, its organization into a comprehensive
> theory of evolution, which features directionality and teleology,
> is in the first stages of development. Nevertheless, *Nature's Des-
> tiny* challenges the secular belief that evolution is driven only
> by blind chance and Denton's identification of law-like evolu-
> tionary mechanisms certainly points toward intelligent design.
> [Notice that the term is not capitalized in Lamoureux's usage of
> it, he does not endorse ID[69] as defended by ID proponents, but

67. It should be noted that when I mention the origin of life and the origin of consciousness together, I am not conflating the two but I am referring to the two separately although they both represent instances of FINLON and are interconnected through information somehow.

68. Lamoureux, *Evolutionary Creation*, xiii. Lamoureux uses evolution as an apologetic strategy among those skeptical about the compatibility of modern science, particularly biological evolution and Christianity. He sees this as one of the most contentious issues of our time and that clarification of this false opposition can indeed bring many individuals into the Christian community.

69. See Johnson and Lamoureux, *Darwinism Defeated?* Here Lamoureux provides

indeed believes that Intelligent Design is involved throughout the universe].[70]

Lamoureux goes on to state:

> The terms employed to describe scientific data are striking: co-incidences, fine-tuning, delicately balanced, precisely organized, just right, uniquely fit, and chain of coincidences. Significantly, many of the authors cited are not Christians. In other words, their appeal to anthropic data cannot be attributed merely to religious bias. This evidence stands on its own in providing a rational argument, and I contend a rather obvious conclusion.[71]

Thus, it is evident that Lamoureux believes the Trinitarian God is responsible for the plan of the universe, which involves the ubiquitous nature of evolution throughout the history of it. The question arises: is Lamoureux falling victim to *doublethink* as we have seen with Haught and those who adhere to an NTE model? It seems that he is not, since he labors to try to give an argument for why nature has a capacity to produce singular phenomena, such as the origin of life and consciousness. Lamoureux has alluded to the Christian God as the best explanation for the finely tuned laws of nature, which are part of the plan of the evolutionary process. This plan has led to life and human consciousness, which is capable of discerning and using science. Still, Lamoureux leaves us unsure through this explanation how exactly it all occurs. The most proximate answer to this is his suggestion of "front loaded evolution." So, how does this exactly work? Lamoureux suggests that God at the moment of the creation of the universe: "loaded into the Big Bang the plan and capability for the cosmos and living organisms, including humans, to evolve over 10–15 billion years."[72] How all of this is possible, we are not sure. Lamoureux makes reference to "spiritual realities" which he seems to equate to notions of consciousness, mind, and soul (immaterial aspects of the human person) when he iterates:

> Finally, spiritual mysteries are associated with both the embryological and evolutionary processes that created humans. Men and women are utterly unique and distinguished from the rest of creation because they are the only creatures who bear the

---

some compelling argumentation against Phillip Johnson's conception of ID. Phillip Johnson is considered as the father of the ID movement. He wrote the book *Darwin on Trial*, which challenged Darwinism.

70. Lamoureux, *Evolutionary Creation*, 89.

71. Ibid., 90.

72. Ibid., 2.

Image of God, and they are the only ones who have fallen into sin. Christians throughout the ages have debated where, when, and how these spiritual realities are manifested in the development of each individual. Yet history reveals that the church has not come to a consensus on these questions, leading to the conclusion that these issues are beyond human understanding. God's Image and the entrance of sin into the world during human evolution are also a mystery. Christian evolutionists accept without any reservation the reality of these spiritual characteristics but recognize that comprehending their origin completely is beyond our creaturely capacity to know.[73]

Lamoureux is certainly correct in pointing out that there is no consensus on these issues. Especially if we consider the position of prominent Christian philosophers/theologians who are physicalists, such as van Inwagen, Joel B. Green, and Nancey Murphy.[74] There are others such as NT scholar, N. T. Wright, who at times affirms generic dualism with affirming an intermediate disembodied state between death and the final resurrection, while disavowing dualism in one context then affirming it through particular NT passages in another.[75] They deny the existence of an immaterial soul and that the Scriptures affirm such a reality. Nonetheless, this book sympathizes with Lamoureux's perspective that aspects of the origin of these spiritual realities delve into the supra-rational realm. However, where I disagree is that we can at least make progress in understanding such phenomena. This is precisely where theology can make a contribution through research programs and guidelines.

---

73. Ibid.

74. In my estimation, Christian physicalists, such as the thinkers mentioned above, seem to wrongly equate generic dualism, (i.e., that the soul/mind/self is immaterial, distinct from the physical body) with Platonic dualism. Platonic dualism is different than generic dualism, since it upholds a view that the body does not have much intrinsic value and is viewed as evil, whereas the soul can have immortal existence without God's sustaining power. Furthermore, under Platonic dualism, a disembodied state of the soul is the ultimate state. Such is not the case for the position of the substance dualist, who upholds a Christian view of both the body and soul whereby humans are composites of the two interacting with one another. Christians who are substance dualists adhere to the view that the body and soul will be re-unified at the general resurrection, so that neither of these essential human components are given preference over the other. Both are vital. Having said that, there is a text that wrestles deeply in a novel way through a physicalist/materialist understanding of the human person. See Corcoran, *Rethinking Human Nature.*

75. See Moreland, *The Soul,* 67; Wright, *The Resurrection of the Son of God,* 131–34, 190–206, 366–67, 424–26; Wright, "Mind, Spirit, Soul and Body: All For One and Contexts."

Directly linked up and related to this discussion of "spiritual myster-ies" and the origin of consciousness is the topic of the origins of humanity. There are a variety of views on the origins of humanity, and consequently by association, consciousness as well, among supporters of PE. Fr. Neuner, SJ and Fr. Jacques Dupuis, SJ, weigh in on the issue with a contemporary outlook:

> In the context of other errors, Pius XII treats two questions regarding the origin of the human person. Firstly, the human being's origin through evolution from other living beings: while formerly evolution was rejected as irreconcilable with the bibli-cal account of creation (which was interpreted in too literal a sense), and as implying a materialistic conception of the human being, the question is now left open to scholarly investigation, provided that the creation of the soul by God is maintained. Secondly, monogenism or polygenism, i.e. the question whether the human race must be conceived as descending from a single couple or can be considered to originate from several couples: polygenism is rejected because 'it does not appear' [or 'it is not at all apparent'] to be reconcilable with the doctrine of original sin inherited by all from Adam. Recent theology, however, is seeking explanations of original sin under the supposition of polygenism, and so tries to remove the reason for its rejection.[76]

Lamoureux holds to a gradual polygenist view[77] where a group of in-dividuals possess consciousness and a soul or at the very least a stamp of the divine (being created in the image of God).

Recently, an interesting position, although admittedly highly specula-tive, has emerged by two Catholic thinkers, Mike Flynn[78] and philosopher Kenneth Kemp to demonstrate that there is no contradiction between a monogenist theological account of human origins and modern genetics

---

76. Dupuis and Neuner, *The Christian Faith*, 169.

77. Lamoureux, *Evolutionary Creation*, 290–91. Lamoureux makes the distinction between: (1) evolutionary monogenism, where God selects a single pair from a popula-tion of pre-evolved humans; (2) punctiliar polygenism, where God intervened in this view and stamped His image into all of the evolving pre-humans; (3) gradual polygen-ism, where "This approach asserts that the Image of God and human sinfulness were gradually and mysteriously manifested through many generations of evolving ances-tors. The origin of spiritual characteristics that define and distinguish humanity is not marked by a single punctiliar event in history . . . Their manifestation during human evolution is similar to that in embryological development. Consequently, there never was/were an Adam/s or Eve/s."

78. Flynn, "Adam and Eve and Ted and Alice," entire page.

and evolutionary biology.[79] What is important is a distinction between what it means to be human in a metaphysical sense as opposed to solely in a genetically and physiological sense. Briefly, they argue that God could have infused souls or higher consciousness into one of the thousands of couples, representing an "Adam and Eve." The descendants of this couple, infused with souls, mated with other couples that did not have souls and eventually the population of humans all had higher consciousness, because of this interbreeding and the ones without these souls eventually died off. So, consequently, no contradiction is apparent from claiming that every modern human is descended from a population of perhaps several thousand and also from a particular couple. This is because the notion of humans who have descended from this "original" couple does not necessitate the reception of all their genes from them.[80]

But does Lamoureux's "front loaded" explication as to how life and humans were created in the image of God have sufficient explanatory power? Meyer has critiqued this notion. Meyer has argued that Lamoureux's position does not work if "(a) all the information necessary to produce the first and subsequent forms of life was present in the initial conditions of the universe, or whether (b) the laws of nature added new information during the subsequent 'self-assembly' process. In any case, both proposals are scientifically problematic."[81] Meyer critiques the notion that the laws of nature have the capacity to generate information (that is specified and complex):

> Scientific laws describe (by definition) highly regular phenomena or structures, ones that possess what information theorists refer to as redundant order. On the other hand, the arrangements of matter in an information-rich text, including the genetic instructions of DNA, possess a high degree of complexity or aperiodicity, not redundant order . . . To say that the processes that natural laws describe can generate functionally specified informational sequences is, therefore, essentially a contradiction in terms. Laws are the wrong kind of entity to generate the phenomenon in question. The claim also betrays a categorical confusion. Physical laws do not generate complex sequences, whether functionally specified or otherwise; they describe highly regular, repetitive, and periodic patterns.[82]

79. Kemp, "Science, Theology, and Monogenesis," 217–36.

80. Ibid., 232.

81. Meyer, "The Difference it doesn't Make," 153–54.

82. Ibid., 154–55.

Meyer's pointed criticism makes it difficult to see how Lamoureux's "evolutionary creation" will be able to explain the origin of information and human consciousness. This is true in spite of its many fruits that acknowledge the necessity of the Christian God's initial creative action at the beginning of the universe and in finely tuning the laws and initial conditions of physics. There seems to be a missing ingredient to explain this "non-material" aspect of the material universe. Although a step forward from NTE, it seems to be lacking the necessary component(s) to increase its explanatory power and scope for explaining the origins and emergence of consciousness. One may ask, where is this new information coming from to bring about the origins and emergence of consciousness? As Meyer has demonstrated, it cannot come from the laws of physics or the initial conditions of the universe. PE seems to contain the necessary basic conditions, but not ones which are sufficient for our project. Unless there is a plausible way that one can demonstrate that the laws of physics and initial conditions of the universe contain sufficient information, to be disbursed throughout the evolution of the universe, to account for singular events such as the origin of life, the origins and emergence of consciousness, the origin of free will and moral values, a truly comprehensive solution does not seem to be forthcoming at this point in time.[83]

3.6.3 Directed Evolution

The final model of theistic evolution, DE, is also another form of teleological evolution, in some ways similar to PE. DE declares that God, even after bringing the universe into being, continues to act within it. Unlike PE, in DE, God intervenes throughout the history of the universe, although proponents are divided over whether such a thing is scientifically detectable or not. Supporters of this view include the prolific quantum chemist,

---

83. See Whitworth, "The Emergence of the Physical World from Information Processing," 221–49. Whitworth considers the fundamental role that information plays in processing and reality (whether physical or virtual). He states that: "Modern information science can suggest how core physical properties like space, time, light, matter and movement could derive from information processing. Such an approach could reconcile relativity and quantum theories, with the former being, how information processing creates space-time, and the latter how it creates energy and matter." This indicates that information is fundamental to the shaping of reality. Could front loading be operative in such an understanding of reality?

Henry Fritz Schaefer III,[84] physicist Loren Haarsma,[85] and the famous bio-chemist Michael Behe,[86] who coined the term "irreducible complexity"[87] as a criterion for ID. It should be mentioned that although a number of advocates of ID can be classified as proponents of DE, this by no means suggests that ID and DE are commensurate. ID is a wide tent but most proponents of ID do not adhere to DE.

Proponents of DE may vary on the issue of monogenism and poly-genism, most likely favoring monogenism, but either option is open. DE views the relationship of science and theology as interactive.[88] Rau explains the variants within this view of TE regarding God's action: "For those who think that God's intervention is scientifically detectable, it makes sense to ask whether a particular event has a natural or supernatural cause. Al-though natural causation is expected for most events, the large number of low probability events that have occurred at each level of origins is taken by this group as evidence for God's direction."[89]

A strong defender of DE is Behe. Behe, who argues that "junk" DNA is not in fact "junk," has responded to a prominent critic of ID (Kenneth Miller) who has argued that the presence of non-functional pseudogenes cannot be explained by ID but is better explained by a higgledy-piggledy process of gene duplication gone wrong.[90] Moreover, Miller, associates the activity of a "designer" with respect to "irreducible complexity" as a recent geological event (as YEC proponents might suggest) but points out that in-ferring design is not dependent on a recent creative or designing act. Behe's

84. See Schaefer, *Science and Christianity: Conflict or Coherence?* Schaefer has pub-lished over 1,500 scientific papers and was a nominee for the Nobel Prize in Chemistry several times.

85. See. Haarsma and Haarsma, *Origins.*

86. See Behe, *Darwin's Black Box*; Behe, *The Edge of Evolution.*

87. Behe, *Darwin's Black Box*, 39. Behe defines it as "A single system which is com-posed of several interacting parts that contribute to the basic function, and where the removal of any one of the parts causes the system to effectively cease functioning."

88. Rau, *Mapping the Origins Debate*, 47.

89. Ibid.

90. Miller, "Life's Grand Design," 29–30. Even though he does not directly weigh in on the Behe and Miller debate, Francis Collins has also addressed the issue of pseu-dogenes and "junk" DNA; Collins uses "junk" DNA as a strong argument against ID. While everyone in the scientific community agrees that most of the DNA is non-pro-tein coding, there is a debate going on about whether the non-protein coding regions of DNA (estimated to be at 95 percent of total DNA) have any function. For many years, "junk" DNA was used as evidence against ID by prominent evolutionists such as Dawkins and Jerry Coyne. Ironically, around the same time, Collins' own research team was publishing a number of these papers that argue for a high degree of functionality in these non-protein coding areas. See Wells, *The Myth of Junk DNA.*

response involves his own idea of front loading not through the laws of physics, but rather one that would come into play within the first cell:

> The irreducibly complex biochemical systems that I have discussed in this book did not have to be produced recently. It is entirely possible, based simply on an examination of the systems themselves, that they were designed billions of years ago and that they have been passed down to the present by the normal processes of cellular reproduction. Perhaps a speculative scenario will illustrate the point. Suppose that nearly four billion years ago the designer made the first cell, already containing all of the irreducibly complex biochemical systems discussed here and many others. (One can postulate that the designs for systems that were to be used later, such as blood clotting, were present but not "turned on." In present-day organisms plenty of genes are turned off for a while, sometimes for generations, to be turned on at a later time). Additionally, suppose the designer placed into the cell some other systems for which we cannot adduce enough evidence to conclude design. The cell containing the designed systems then was left on autopilot to reproduce, mutate, eat and be eaten, bump against rocks, and suffer all the vagaries of life on earth. During this process *pace* Ken Miller, pseudogenes might occasionally arise and a complex organ might become non-functional. These chance events do not mean that the initial biochemical systems were not designed. The cellular warts and wrinkles that Miller takes as evidence of evolution may simply be evidence of age.[91]

Is this front loading of the first cell plausible? The question hinges on another question: What happens to components of the DNA that are not manifested in the phenotype? Well, it cannot be selected, so these mutations accumulate over many generations until perhaps certain genes are rendered unusable.[92] If this is true, the designer has to intervene numerous times to stop the genes from becoming useless. Such an activity of the designer would most likely be impossible to validate through scientific testing. It also has theologically disastrous consequences, since it would render God powerless with very little foresight and lots of inefficiency. One conceivable way of circumventing these criticisms is by suggesting that the discovery of the functionality of "junk" DNA or pseudogenes can potentially backfire on Miller's criticism. Perhaps this layering upon layering of complexity that we are discovering in genetics and epigenetics in recent

91. Behe, *Darwin's Black Box*, 227–28.
92. See, Miller, "Review of Darwin's Black Box," 36–40.

years can be more supportive of front loading, than an explanation like exaptation or perhaps exaptation and front loading have more of a correspondence with one another than meets the eye?[93]

Behe's speculative scenario should be considered in the context of a response to Miller's criticism of ID and irreducibly complex molecular machines. Nonetheless, Behe has used this line of reasoning in public forums in an attempt to explain how "irreducibly complex" machines have come about through the evolutionary process. This is a question of how the designer did it. As of yet, ID has not explained how and when the designer designed a particular organelle or biological structure. ID proponents focus on the discernment of design rather than how it happened. They claim that once this is established, then the *how* can be discussed. The main point in raising this issue is that some of those who adhere to DE are ID exponents and one would want to know how this view of theistic evolution measures up to others. ID itself is theistic friendly, but refers to a generic designer, not to the Christian conception of God, but can be used in a broader framework to support such. Nonetheless, DE on its own must answer whether it is capable of explaining phenomena like the original of life and consciousness in a way that's more plausible than NTE or PE?

Philosopher Brendan Sweetman in his recent book *Evolution, Chance and God* provides an erudite case against naturalism while he offers an Augustinian-type outlook on evolution, where God endows the universe with certain potencies that lead to the development of humankind (as expressed in definition #8 of evolution). Sweetman explains that God created a deterministic universe where every species was planned for, focusing less on the universe's autonomy as prescribed in NTE: "The species that emerged therefore *had* to emerge and are not random."[94] So, pondering whether God created in a deistic way, or with special interventions along the way, he suggests that "the scientific evidence [won't] help us much here," at least for the present moment. He also counters views of chance expounded by thinkers such as Polkinghorne and Peacocke to further support his deterministic evolutionary position. One thing to note is that Sweetman doesn't really look seriously at the origin of life studies, nor does he look at issues of the emergence of consciousness.[95] When taken to their logical conclusions, sci-

93. Exaptation refers to a particular trait serving a particular function at one point in evolutionary history, then throughout the course of evolution comes to serve another. The following article compares the explanatory power of both exaptation and genetic front loading. Brayton, "Exaptation vs Front Loading," entire page.

94. Sweetman, *Evolution, Chance and God*, 169.

95. See for instance the rigorous case that Stephen Meyer builds for ID in terms of the origin of the information for the first self-replicating life, Meyer, *Signature in the Cell*.

ence and philosophy in this domain seem to resist physicalist explanations regardless of the proclamations made by proponents supportive of such conclusions. Since many of the supporters of DE are either exponents of ID or at least sympathetic to ID, it will be well worth quoting a very pointed observation made by Sweetman that completely resonates with me, as I struggle to find which of these competing models best describes reality:

> ID theorists occasionally suggest that God could design the plan of living things, including the irreducible complexities, into the blueprint of the universe from the beginning of creation, and then there would be no need of God's direct intervention in biological systems in acts of special creation. [This is something that is line with Lamoureux's view of ID (intelligent design as he refers to it) even though he dissociates himself from ID proponents.] However, this claim is contrary to the way ID theory is normally represented and would seem to make it indistinguishable from more traditional forms of the argument from design, especially if ID theorists then add that only *random* natural selection could not produce biological complexity, but that *directed* (i.e., non-random) natural selection *could* do so. If they nuance their view in this way, then their only original claim would appear to be that ID is part of science, not philosophy or theology. Their other claims would be indistinguishable from theistic evolution, a view they reject.[96]

I must confess there is something that is theologically unsatisfactory, unpalatable, and most of all, heterodox to describe God creating a universe, which requires repeated interventions, especially as described above, with regulating genes. It runs the risk of making God appear to be an incompetent fumbler who has not properly created his creation from the incipient moment. However, there is also the analogy of God acting like an artist or a composer of a great musical piece, which has not been fully realized. This

---

96. Sweetman, *Evolution, Chance and God*, 221n14. See my notes above in section 3.6 on ID. For the demarcation problem see, Meyer, *Signature in the Cell*, 400–401, 419, 430–31. In reference to Sweetman's quote and ID proponent's suggestion of a process instead of intervention as a possibility of ID, see Dembski *No Free Lunch*, 335; Behe, *Darwin's Black Box*, 229–33. Sweetman also discusses whether ID is science or not, but in his section on ID theory (found on page 191) echoes what IDers like Meyer have stated: regardless of whether ID is considered science or not, what matters is whether it is true or not: "the public controversy about ID has often been about whether or not it should be described as science (and so discussed in biology classes), this is ultimately a secondary matter because it is really only a debate about how ID is to be classified, whereas the real question must be about whether or not it is true."

plays into notions of time, God's action, and God's foreknowledge, which would take us beyond the scope of this chapter.

3.7 Conclusion

Inevitably, we ponder which of these creation-evolution models is the most appealing. This is a question that seems to appeal to our aesthetic and/or theological preferences. Either way, what is important is to see which of these models has the greatest explanatory power and scope. It seems that the singular events such as the origin of life and the origin and emergence of consciousness are not well explained by a seamless evolution but rather as something very distinct occurring at a specific point in time. One may wonder why I have mentioned seemingly singular events such as the origin of life alongside the origin and emergence of consciousness. The reason is that the origin of life is a necessary condition for consciousness to emerge in the universe; without life, no organisms of higher consciousness could develop. It creates a cumulative case against naturalistic outlooks, since it compounds the problem for naturalism and physicalist interpretations when taken together. This is what I see as a strong epistemic background against the naturalist case, which opens the gate for theology to influence scientific study (the origin of the universe, the fine-tuning argument, and the intelligibility of the universe, compound this issue for naturalism). This is why I have developed CENTAC in chapter 5.

This type of intervention does not necessarily need to be a crude injunction, but it could be more subtle such as God acting through quantum mechanics and chaos[97] or through a universe that is informationally porous. A point worth iterating is that the universe is only a closed system under a non-theistic view. Under Christian theism the universe is open to God's action, but this is a point we will return to in chapter 7. The DE model aligns best with the evidence of cosmic and biological evolution while not succumbing to certain methodological conventions and constraints utilized in modern science. This would demonstrate an inability to explain the phenomena at hand. Is it possible to find a happy medium between NTE, PE, and DE? One which is consistent with the evidence at hand and where God is not reduced to a hapless tinkerer?

Overall, we have brought precisions to the different understandings of the terms of "creation" and "evolution." We have seen that in most cases, evolution is complementary and non-contradictory to theological notions of creation. We have also assessed several creation and evolutionary models,

97. See Poe and Davis, *God and the Cosmos.*

all of which are adhered to by Christian thinkers. We have seen that most of the models fail either because they contradict scientific evidence or because they have theological and/or philosophical shortcomings. To be sure, none are exempt from sharp criticisms. Despite some shortcomings, DE seems to be the most robust and flexible model to explain the origins and emergence of consciousness. It is worth noting that Russell's CMI and the constraints set forth by NIODA[98] would come nearest to NTE and PE versions of theistic evolution. I would argue more closely to PE.

In dealing with theistic evolution through NIODA, Russell provides three *stringent* criteria:

> 1) God's acts are objective and specific without such actions things would have turned out differently. (Claims about divine action involve counterfactuals). 2) God's acts are hidden to science: science sees strictly random events. This entails that divine causality cannot be reduced to secondary or natural causality, the subject of scientific inquiry. 3) God's action is non-interventionist and both epistemic and ontological "gaps" arguments are rejected. (God acts in special events in nature without suspending God's general action which undergirds the regularities of nature. Moreover our claim that God acts is not based on what science does not understand but on what it does understand.)[99]

It raises a very important epistemological issue between what is not understood by science and the limitations of scientific knowledge, as these two things are very distinct. Russell very well acknowledges the limitations of science. The question is how to discern between the two. Either the current methodology of science (i.e., methodological naturalism) would need revision in order to incorporate resistant phenomenon, or if it is not possible to incorporate it into science (whether its methodology is revised or not), it may be a question left to philosophy and/or theology. It seems as though consciousness fits precisely into this mold, unless one accepts a reductive materialist explanation, as offered by Dawkins, Daniel Dennett, or Steve Pinker, who deny the existence of the self[100] and present a radically different view of consciousness (one that denies a first-person perspective opting for a third person perspective, while denying the unity of consciousness).[101] Pinker has stated in an interview shared with Dawkins

---

98. See section 7.4.

99. Russell, *Cosmology*, 251–52.

100. Menuge, *Agents under Fire*, 130.

101. Searle explains the incoherence of this view, particularly of Dennett's denial of consciousness: "To put it as clearly as I can: in his book, *Consciousness Explained*,

that "there's considerable evidence that the unified self is a fiction—that the mind is a congeries of parts operating asynchronously, and that it's only an illusion that there's a president in the Oval Office of the brain who oversees the activity of everything."[102]

It is striking to see how one uses consciousness and conscious activity to deny consciousness or that it is merely an illusion. So, from the onset we see a resistance from Russell to accommodating a model like DE, but are these restraints all necessary for CMI to work? I will argue that they are not. Perhaps it is this insistence on relying on methodological naturalism in every instance that is creating an impasse for the influence of theology upon the sciences. What about Clayton's concern with the CMI's ability to create a progressive problemshift from a Lakotosian perspective? Could this be where theology can make its largest impact? Interestingly, Russell has suggested:

> Later amplification could become relevant once the domain of the "classical," ordinary world has emerged from the proceeding domain where only quantum mechanics applies. Top-down causality in the form of divine action within the context of the mind/brain problem could be appropriated by God once the evolution of creatures capable of even primitive sentience has occurred. Divine causality as viewed by neo-Thomism and by process theology also applies throughout the entire history of the universe.[103]

Perhaps other singular events would require a top-down causality as well, i.e., the origin of life/information and consciousness (self-consciousness).

Finally, I believe that his notion of FINLON, despite Russell's argumentation otherwise, could betray NIODA, unless somehow new laws of physics pop up in the future of the universe, at a specific designated time

---

Dennett denies the existence of consciousness. He continues to use the word, but he means something different by it. For him, it refers only to third-person phenomena, not to the first-person conscious feelings and experiences we all have. For Dennett there is no difference between us humans and complex zombies who lack any inner feelings, because we are all just complex zombies. [. . .] I regard his view as self-refuting because it denies the existence of the data which a theory of consciousness is supposed to explain . . . Here is the paradox of this exchange: I am a conscious reviewer consciously answering the objections of an author who gives every indication of being consciously and puzzlingly angry. I do this for a readership that I assume is conscious. How then can I take seriously his claim that consciousness does not really exist?" See Searle and Dennett, "'The Mystery of Consciousness': An Exchange."

102. Menuge, *Agents under Fire*, 130. Quote originally taken from Dawkins, in an interview with Pinker, "Is Science Killing the Soul?"

103. Russell, *Cosmology*, 252.

ordained by God in the initial conditions of the universe. However, this would lead us down the same problematic path of whether the laws of physics can contain such prescriptions as informational content. FINLON seems to be able to operate with the three broad models of TE. It seems that DE offers the most flexibility in following the evidence wherever it leads, as God is not restricted in his action. This view of TE affirms UCD while being open to God's action in finite singular events that can be philosophically and/or scientifically adduced, not in how it is carried forth, but that it indeed did occur. Otherwise, perhaps a combinational approach of one or more versions of TE may be viable. But I will explore such arguments in a subsequent section on the application of CMI and the significant role it will play in understanding the origins and emergence of consciousness. In chapter 7, we will discuss the legitimacy of NIODA in lieu of Plantinga's critique.[104] I will also consider another option where God could interact through informational structures without suspending or breaking the laws of nature, a view expounded by mathematician and philosopher William Dembski.[105] For now, let us keep a very important question in mind that we will return to later: What is really meant by intervention? Understanding what intervention entails will be the key to the apparent impasse in the acceptance of theology influencing the sciences (and perhaps Clayton's concern about the CMI fulfilling a research program). Now we can examine Teilhard de Chardin's "scientific theology" and how it applies to questions about God, creation, evolution, panpsychism, complexity and consciousness.

104. See section 7.4.

105. This will also be connected to the Trinitarian Mode of Creation in chapter 6.

Chapter 4

A Test Case: Teilhard's
"Scientific Theology"

4.1 Introduction

I WILL TREAT THIS chapter as a test case for the first prong of this book: to ascertain the role and fruitfulness that the Christian conception of God can provide in understanding the origin of consciousness. Why a test case? The simple reason is to explore how far Teilhard can help in the endeavor of this book, given the subject matter of his work on God, creation, evolution, complexity, and consciousness. Teilhard's work has the potential to shed some light on the Christian conception of God and creation in understanding the origin of consciousness.

Teilhard was born on May 1, 1881, in a chateau near the village of Orcines in France.[1] He died on Easter Sunday in 1955 in New York City. His writings came during an interesting period. He was almost an exact contemporary of Albert Einstein (1879–1955) who played a fundamental role in the development of modern cosmology with his theories of general and special relativity. Remarkably, both Einstein and Teilhard have come to have lasting impacts in their respective scientific fields as well as a deep and lasting influence in popular consciousness. Einstein also, though indirectly, played an important part in the development of big bang cosmology,[2] a theory which will be essential to the development of part of our argumentation for a Christian conception of creation. In the realm of biological evolution, Darwin and Wallace had proposed their theory of evolution by natural selection in 1859. It had begun to gain favor among many naturalists, mostly in the Anglo-American realm. The modern synthesis was

1. Aczel, *The Jesuit and the Skull*, 71.

2. Independently, Alexander Friedmann and George Lemaître provided solutions to Einstein's field equations, which were fundamental to demonstrating the expansion of the universe.

developed between 1936 and 1947.[3] In France, there was a large resistance to Darwinism. Neo-Lamarckism and orthogenesis were considered by French philosophers and biologists to be mechanistically superior in their explanatory scope and power to the conjoint of natural selection and random variation. Teilhard held to these views with a strong teleological impetus, which shaped his understanding of evolutionary biology. This has also helped our understanding of convergence. It was not until years later in France, partially due to cultural factors, that Neo-Darwinism gained greater acceptance. Nonetheless, in the ensuing years, Teilhard's ideas became increasingly well received by theologians.

4.2 Exploring Teilhard's General Conception of God

In order to ascertain Teilhard's views on the Christian conception of God and creation in understanding the origins, it will be important to look primarily at the following works: *Christianity and Evolution, The Divine Milieu, Human Energy, The Heart of Matter,* and *The Phenomenon of Man.* Throughout his various works Teilhard unpacks a series of terms that are relevant to understanding his position on consciousness. Teilhard does not delve into a discussion of the divine attributes, as he seems to disregard scholasticism, but one can ascertain his general conception of God through his understanding of God's relationship to the world. This section will seek to answer the following question: What sort of God did Teilhard believe there existed—a personal God or one of another kind?

A personal God is a God that can be identified as a person[4] as opposed to an impersonal force or one that is equated with physical reality (universe), as with pantheism. Furthermore, a personal God is not solely a "Prime Mover" or a transcendent cause, that has no vested interested in His creation, as understood with deism. Rather a personal God is a God who answers prayers and is involved in a profound relationship with His creation, including humans who worship such a God. In Christianity, God is tri-personal, as revealed through the salvific designations of God the Father, God the Son, and God the Holy Spirit. This God is also considered to be a

---

3. See Bock, "Reviewed Work: The Evolutionary Synthesis. Perspectives on the Unification of Biology," 644–66.

4. See Wainright, "Concepts of God."

maximally great being[5] in classical Christian theism, and has the attributes of omniscience, omnipotence, omnipresence, and omnibenevolence.[6]

Part of the task of this book is not only to uphold a classical Christian conception of God as revealed through Scripture, but the God of classical theism, which has been fundamental to the Christian tradition from its commencement up until the twentieth century.[7] According to the philosophical theologian John W. Cooper, classical theism maintains that God is "transcendent, self-sufficient, eternal, and immutable in relation to the world; thus he does not change through time and is not affected by his relation to his creatures."[8]

Although Teilhard does not explicitly deny any of the historical creedal statements regarding orthodox Christian faith, his thought implies that his idea of God is significantly distinct from that of orthodox Christianity.[9] As is the case with most thinkers, one can witness an evolution in Teilhard's thought, which includes his "faith"[10] in the world, spirit, and immortality.[11] Throughout his many writings, his views about God appear to be ambiguous and often contradictory since on the one hand he affirms a transcendent and self-sufficient God, but then on the other hand expresses seemingly deep pantheistic inclinations. This indeed presents a difficulty in ascertaining his true position on the matter. Some Teilhardian commentators have offered strikingly different views regarding Teilhard's conception of God; these will be worth exploring in detail.

---

5. Wainright, "Two (or Maybe One and a Half) Cheers for Perfect Being Theology," 228–51.

6. This is something we will return to when we look at the concept of Divine Simplicity or God's Simplicity, since such a doctrine holds there are no distinctions in God, so God cannot possess different metaphysical parts, such as these attributes.

7. Cooper, *Panentheism, the Other God of the Philosophers*, 14.

8. Ibid., 14.

9. McCarty, *Makers of the Modern Theological Mind*, 134.

10. Teilhard, *How I Believe*, 13. In this context Teilhard uses the word "faith" to signify the use of our intelligence in understanding the universe. This should be contrasted with a biblical understanding of faith signifying something closer to trust, particularly in God and others.

11. McCarty, *Teilhard de Chardin*, 25, 28–30. McCarty speaks of a text that Teilhard was asked to write by Msgr. Bruno de Solages, entitled *How I Believe*. The author goes on to explain the evolutions of Teilhard's faith, which include faith in the world, spirit, immortality, and personality.

4.2.1 Christian Pantheism or Christocentric Panentheism?

Teilhard declares that his understanding of God and the cosmos is indeed pantheistic. In his concluding remarks to the introduction of *Christianity and Evolution*, Teilhard suggests that:

> The whole of the foregoing exposition makes it clear that Christianity is pre-eminently a faith in the progressive unification of the world in God; it is essentially universalist, organic and 'monist'.
>
> There is obviously some special quality in this 'pan-Christic' monism . . . It is only in fact 'pantheism' of love or Christian 'pantheism' (that in which each being is super-personalized, super centred, by union with Christ, the divine super-center)—it is only that pantheism which correctly interprets and fully satisfies religious aspirations of man, whose dream is ultimately to lose self-consciousness in unity.[12]

Teilhard, in his writings on pantheism makes a distinction between pagan/scientific pantheisms and Christian pantheism.[13] Teilhard enlists these understandings in the following way:

a. Those for which the unity of the whole is born from the fusion of elements—as the former appears, so the latter disappears. Despite these distinctions and the use of language.

b. Those for which the elements are fulfilled by entering a deeper centre which dominates them and super-centres them in itself.[14]

Teilhard rejects the first and opts for the latter (pantheism), claiming that it is the only "intellectually justifiable and mystically satisfying" option and that is what is expressed in the "Christian attitude."[15] It seems that Teilhard is appealing to historical contingencies, namely that believers on the one hand are influenced by modern science and feel that the concepts of the incarnation and divinity of Christ contradict such notions, but on the other hand want a way of believing in such things without contradicting modern science (and without being too anthropocentric and anthropomorphic for

---

12. Teilhard, *Christianity and Evolution*, 171.

13. See Bruteau, *Evolution Toward Divinity*, for an interesting treatment of Teilhard's pantheistic inclinations and how they relate to the Hindu traditions. Though much resistance in his earlier writings suggests an aversion to Eastern pantheism, it bears some significant similarities as his evolutionary theology developed.

14. Teilhard, *Christianity and Evolution*, 136–37.

15. Ibid.

the twentieth-century mind). But why is this so? Teilhard's corrective to the climate of thought in his times is to suggest a "Christian pantheism." The logic follows that if Christ needs to be saved by the process he brought into being, then he was not at all responsible for its existence. Christ goes from evolver to that which has evolved.[16] Physicist Wolfgang Smith has been a proponent of the idea that Teilhard had an agenda to reconstruct the classical Christian conception of God, in which eventually, even He must bow down to the process of evolution and go from being the evolver to part of the evolved.[17] Although Smith's concerns are certainly understandable, it seems that, the broader context of Teilhard's belief has not been fully examined. To understand what Teilhard envisions with respect to God and Christ, the following passage may be helpful: "a Christ whose features do not adapt themselves to the requirements of a world that is evolutive in structure will tend more and more to be eliminated out of hand."[18] This is suggestive of a further conception, one that Joseph Ratzinger (Pope Benedict XVI) has been fond of: the cosmic Christ. Ilia Delio illustrates this notion:

> When the adjective "cosmic" is used to describe Christ, it means that Christ is the instrument in God's creative activity, the source and goal of all things, the bond and sustaining power of the whole creation; the head and the ruler of the universe. Basically the term relates Christ to the entire created order, emphasizing that Christ's relationship to creation extends beyond the compass of earthly humans and includes the whole cosmos.[19]

What is essential in order to understand Teilhard is the centrality of his evolutionary view of the world. For someone like Smith who rejects evolution a priori due to certain commitments, it is impossible to fuse evolutionary notions into such a worldview (especially considering that the scientific criticisms that come to light under such presuppositions—even though such criticisms must be assessed on their own merit). Evolution is vitally significant in its many manifestations and definitions to this book, not in the exact same way it was for Teilhard, but it remains nonetheless an indispensable component to understanding God's creation and creative

16. Although not explicitly stated in such terms, this is the logical deduction of such a question. Teilhard, *The Heart of Matter*, 92. An interesting diagram can be found on page 134 of *Christianity and Evolution*, which can help visualize what Teilhard has in mind concerning the Universal or Cosmic Christ, Historic (Jesus) Christ and The Divine (Trinitarian Godhead which includes the second person of the Trinity—the Son of God).

17. Smith, *Theistic Evolution*, 133.

18. Teilhard, *Christianity and Evolution*, 74.

19. Delio, *Christ in Evolution*, 50.

action. Smith does not delineate evolution carefully; therefore, his critique misses the mark in many instances. Smith focuses on Christ's role in human salvation but not Christ's role (in a total sense; historic vs. universal Christ vs. Divine Godhead)[20] as demonstrated by Teilhard, extends to the totality of the universe as exemplified also through Delio's reasoning. This is an important point to be made in light of Smith's criticisms.

Despite the interesting propositions regarding a cosmic Christ, who extends beyond solely human salvation, but is intimately involved in the future transformation of the whole cosmos, there are still some rather looming problems in Teilhard's scientific theology that have been swept under the rug. For example, Teilhard has a peculiar vision of Christ in lieu of his views on evolution. He sees Christ as an evolving Christ,[21] much as his vision of God becoming part of the evolutionary process. Christ is dependent upon the cosmogenetic process,[22] as Teilhard intimates himself a month before his own death: "It is Christ, in very truth, who saves—but should we not immediately add that, at the same time, it is Christ who is saved by Evolution?"[23] No matter how you frame it, anything that suggests that an eternal God needs to be saved by a created process is pushing the frontiers of radicalness and heterodoxy. According to Smith, Teilhard's views in fact have no place for the incarnation in the traditional Christian sense; nothing can ultimately enter into the universe except through a process of evolution, since all is reducible to a cosmic evolution.[24] One may think this is a misreading of Teilhard. Teilhard suggests that creation "can be effected only by an *evolutive process* (of personalizing synthesis) and that it can come into action *only once*: when absolute multiple is reduced, nothing is left to be united either in God or 'outside' God." What is outside of God for a Christian pantheist or a Christocentric panentheist? Nothing, as the world is in God and God is in the world.[25]

Teilhard left his writings open to speculative interpretation. What is clear is that Teilhard's conception of the Christian God is not classical, but instead a sort of hylomorphism between God and the world. Given this, it seems that the panentheistic position is the one most consistent with Teilhard's views from his early to later writings. Nonetheless, the best corrective to these slippery inclinations is to present a robust defense of the Christian

20. Teilhard, *Christianity and Evolution*, 134.

21. Smith, *Theistic Evolution*, 133.

22. Ibid.

23. Teilhard, *The Heart of Matter*, 92.

24. Smith, *Theistic Evolution*, 138.

25. John Culp, "Panentheism."

God and the concept of creation through erudite philosophy, theology, and modern science. This will be demonstrated in chapter 5 of this book.

What about Christocentric panentheism? John Cooper has laid out a case that Teilhard affirmed both God's transcendence and immanence.[26] He has provided many of the same texts we have examined in support of this. Cooper adds a helpful insight to differentiate a classical interpretation of transcendence and immanence to Teilhard's vision:

> Teilhard is aware that his understanding of God's transcendence and immanence is different than in the tradition of Anselm and Aquinas. His aim is to combine the transcendent God of classical orthodoxy with the God immanent in cosmic evolution: "An exact conjunction is produced between the old God of the Above and the God of the Ahead."[27]

Cooper classifies Teilhard's self-identification as a "Christian pantheist" with a more accurate depiction: "Teilhard is a panentheist precisely because his 'pantheism of differentiation' includes a sufficient ontology of the many within the One. Creatures are distinct from God because, according to his metaphysics of union, for creatures, 'to be is to be unified.' Thus they are distinct from God, the Unifier . . . From Alpha to Omega, God as Christ is the One in whom All exist."[28] From this elucidation of Teilhard's understanding of God and His relation to the creative order, it seems that Teilhard is extolling a panentheistic position over that of a pantheistic one, even though he used the latter term.[29]

While a panentheistic position is not as heterodox as a pantheistic one, as Smith has indicated in his overall criticisms of Teilhard,[30] it still cannot be accepted for reasons that will be clarified in the conclusion.

---

26. Cooper, *Panentheism*, 156–57.

27. Ibid., 157.

28. Ibid., 161.

29. Ibid., 161; King, *Spirit of Fire*, 59, 86; Grenz and Olson, *Twentieth-Century Theology*, 142.

30. Smith would lead one to believe that Teilhard is in fact a pantheist, but a deeper study demonstrates that the accurate position would be panentheism despite some of Teilhard's ambiguities concerning God's nature and attributes. See the following works for the recent conflation and distinction concerning panentheism and pantheism in the works of prominent philosopher/theologians such as Shults, Clayton, and Pannenberg: see Craig, "Pantheists in Spite of Themselves" in *For Faith and Clarity*, 135–56; Rowe, "Does Panentheism Reduce to Pantheism? A Response to Craig," 65–67.

4.3 Teilhard's Conception of Creation—Evolution as Creation: Making Things Make Themselves

Early on in his career as a paleontologist, Teilhard had already incorporated evolutionary thought into his understanding of paleontology. In his 1915 to 1919 journal, he made the following comment: "The adoption of the evolutionary model to explain the formation of the World entails a certain way of coming to be 'in the absence of any prior subject matter', and implies there is a deep ontological reason for the world."[31] This demonstrates that from the onset, evolutionary notions are deeply embedded into Teilhard's understanding of the interactivity between science, theology, and metaphysics.

It must be said that Teilhard's vision of evolution is far more comprehensive, because it embodies a cosmology rather than a theory solely concerned with biological origins, like Darwin and previous thinkers had envisioned. John Haught, who has spent many years studying Teilhard, explicates the structure of Teilhard's view of evolution:

> For Teilhard the whole universe is in evolution and there is a clear direction to the cosmic story. He consciously extended the term evolution beyond its biological meaning and applied it also to cosmic process. In spite of the obvious meandering or branching character of biological evolution, he observed, the universe as a whole has clearly moved in the direction of increasing organized complexity. The cosmic process has gone through the preatomic, atomic, molecular, unicellular, multicellular, vertebrate, primate, and human phases of evolution. During this journey the universe has manifested a measurable growth in instances of organized complexity.[32]

Teilhard's vision and understanding of evolution can be seen as an overarching metaphysical narrative, not something restricted solely to biological origins. In Teilhard's view, evolution is pushing toward life, then from life toward consciousness, which then eventually leads to a collective consciousness amongst humanity, which eventually connects with the cosmic Christ.[33] This linear development aligns well with either PE or DE understandings of TE. Teilhard articulates this as: "Cosmogenesis reveals itself . . . first as Biogenesis and then Noogenesis [emergence of mind], and finally

31. Teilhard, *Journal* [26 août 1915–4 janvier 1919], 264. As quoted in Galleni and van Dyck, "A Model of Interaction Between Science and Theology Based on the Scientific Paper of Pierre Teilhard de Chardin," 59.

32. Haught, "In Search of a God for Evolution: Paul Tillich and Pierre Teilhard de Chardin," 541.

33. Cooper, *Panentheism*, 149.

culminates in the Christogenesis which every Christian venerates . . . The Christ of Revelation is none other than the *Omega of Evolution*."[34] Moreover, the concept of convergence is important to Teilhard's view of evolution. Mark McMenamin writes, "Convergent evolution is the process by which similar morphological or behavioral traits are acquired by unrelated lineages of organisms."[35] These are statistical anomalies that occur throughout the history of life on Earth. These are best explained by PE or DE[36] rather than NTE or naturalistic evolution ([NE] an overall evolutionary process understood to be purposeless and undirected as many secular biologists hold). Teilhard is one of the first biologists to give a proper interpretation of convergence as later revealed.[37]

Louis M. Savary, in his book *Teilhard de Chardin—The Divine Milieu Explained: A Spirituality for the 21st Century,* illuminates that though historically, many within the church have found notions of evolution threatening, Teilhard took an opposite approach:

> Teilhard, who understood evolution better than most and had more deeply explored it, saw that it offered no threat to Christian theology, but rather confirmed what St. Paul envisioned as the growth and development of the total Body of Christ. [Similarly, t]oday the church has come to recognize that evolutionary theories offer no threat to Christian living, but can even be a helpful guide.[38]

The late eminent Ukrainian born-American geneticist, Theodosius Dobzhansky, echoed these sentiments when he stated: "I believe with the great Teilhard de Chardin that evolution is God's method of creation."[39] Indeed, Teilhard emphasizes that "God does not make: He makes things

---

34. Teilhard, *The Heart of Matter*, 94, 92.

35. McMenamin, "Teilhard's Legacy in Science," 34.

36. Several important texts in recent years of thinkers who hold to PE or DE have argued for convergent evolution. See Conway Morris, *Life's Solution*; Denton, *Nature's Destiny*.

37. See McMenamin, *The Garden of Ediacara*. McMenamin's text argues for convergent evolution as well.

38. Savary, *Teilhard de Chardin—The Divine Milieu Explained*, 195.

39. Dobzhansky. "Nothing in Biology Makes Sense Except in the Light of Evolution," 125. The title and sentiment of this article has been taken to task by various thinkers. Although evolution is an important concept, it is not necessary to all of the biological and bio-medical sciences. For example, see Wells, *Icons of Evolution: Science or Myth*, 245–48.

make themselves."[40] This is a simple summary of how Teilhard envisions God's action.

Recall that in our previous chapter on creation and evolution we examined three different views concerning TE. It seems reasonable to suggest that Teilhard's view of evolution conforms most to PE with hints of DE.[41] Indeed, like proponents of NTE and PE, Teilhard favors a view in which God permits autonomy for creation. The laws of physics are seen in PE as inciting the creation of novel features, structures, and organisms throughout the cosmos, a view consonant with Teilhard's. PE also sees an increase in complexity and so a directionality toward evolutionary development. As was seen with Haught's observation, Teilhard envisions a cosmic evolution, which extends far beyond mere biological evolution, to which discussions of Darwinism and even Lamarckism are typically limited to. What is of note is Teilhard envisions that consciousness is an emergent property of the evolutionary process. Teilhard developed an explanation of how this could come about long before Neo-Darwinists began to, in relatively recent years. Darwin looked solely at the differences between humans and the lower primates and argued it was in degree, not kind.[42] However, scientists in recent years have suggested this to be "Darwin's mistake." Indeed, there is a significant gap between human and animal consciousness. He also suggested that the similarities we see among the apes and human behavior, including emotions and even anatomy, indicated a gradual leading up to the higher degree of consciousness, but he failed to propose an actual mechanism. In so doing, he made the assumption that natural selection was responsible, while acting on random variation as natural phenomena, with regard to how such a thing could come about. Teilhard, on the other hand, developed his notion of complexification and consciousness, which will be the focus of the next section. It is important to mention that Teilhard's understanding of evolution is intimately connected to his notion

---

40. Teilhard, *Christianity and Evolution*, 28.

41. See North, *Teilhard and the Creation of the Soul*, 82. An interesting quote by Robert North exemplifies Teilhard's incessant attempt to reconcile theology with science: "But to maintain that evolution proceeds altogether without a plan is ultimately to deny a creating God. Conversely, to cling relentlessly to "Lamarckian orthogenesis" in face of his colleagues' opposition was Teilhard's scientific jargon way of affirming a creating God as known even to science." Orthogenesis is a teleological view of evolution which proceeds towards a particular goal through increasing in complexity. It could be considered a "driving force." Aside from Teilhard, Jean Baptiste Lamarck and Henri Bergson held to such a view of evolution.

42. Penn et al., "Darwin's mistake: explaining the discontinuity between human and nonhuman minds."

of complexification/consciousness, so the discussion regarding evolution will entail a discussion of those elements as well.

4.4 The Law of Complexity-Consciousness

Teilhard provides us with a first glimpse in his law of complexity-consciousness when he states: "The stuff of the universe, woven in a single piece according to one and the same system, but never repeating itself from one point to another, represents a single figure. Structurally it forms a Whole."[43] Teilhard observes a tendency inherent within matter; one of increasing complexity. This increasing complexity develops from the geosphere (barysphere, lithosphere, hydrosphere, atmosphere, and stratosphere), to the biosphere, to the noosphere (the sphere of mind [consciousness] represented by persons, in the case of the Earth, human persons).

This is what is witnessed throughout the Earth's history, i.e., that matter increases complexity from inorganic to organic matter, then to plant, then to the diversity of animal organisms we see, until finally evolution of human consciousness is reached, and from there cultures and technologies evolve. This culmination of evolutionary development meets an ultimate point of collective consciousness, a Superperson (Omega Point/cosmic Christ), in communion with all individual persons in which the source of bonding is love (this will be explored further below).

Just as Teilhard sees consciousness in different degrees throughout the cosmos and most basic elements of matter, he also sees love itself in different degrees as binding the fabric of reality together.

The law of complexity-consciousness is the beating heart of Teilhard's "scientific theology." It is the *raison d'*être for his understanding of the process of evolution. This is the mechanism, if you will, of his evolutionary theory. Darwin had his mechanisms of natural selection and random variation; natural selection encompasses the capacity of organisms to adapt, while random variation is the innovative change that biological structures and organisms overall endure, which are weeded out or preserved by natural selection. The reason why Teilhard's notion of evolution is of particular interest for this component of this book, regarding the origins and emergence of consciousness, lies with the fruitfulness if any, that can be derived from his law of complexity-consciousness. Teilhard's overall contribution to the broader question will be assessed at the conclusion of this chapter.

---

43. Teilhard, *The Phenomenon of Man*, 45.

4.4.1 Some Preliminaries

Before we immerse ourselves into the heart of his law of complexity-consciousness, it is useful to make a few delineations.

First, how does Teilhard understand the soul?[44] A first thing to note is that one would be extremely hard pressed to find a definition of soul throughout Teilhard's works. Teilhard commentator and theologian Robert North curiously never provides us with a definition of Teilhard's view of the soul, but offers remarks associated with consciousness, continuity, and psyche.[45] Having sifted through the major works of Teilhard, this seems to be absent. He often writes of the soul in conjunction to spirit, psyche, and consciousness. It would be difficult to say that he sees these terms as synonymous, but as we shall see, he does indeed use them in synonymous fashions at times. Teilhard rejects any Cartesian substance/dualism as an explanation for the soul. Teilhard's "scientific phenomenology" or "scientific theology" rejects such dualism since it does not entail a holistic view of the universe. But Teilhard does allow for the separation of the body and soul at death, affirming the soul's autonomy.[46] Nevertheless, Teilhard sees a substantial connection between body and soul, not a disjunction, much like his notions of the connection between matter and spirit. This allows Teilhard to make a strong link between humanity and the physical world, one which he saw lacking at the time of his writings, as we saw with his criticism of materialists and spiritualists alike. Teilhard understands the soul as being the "form of the body."[47] Teilhard also suggests that from a psychological standpoint, the soul is "incredibly subtle and complex."[48] It is worth mentioning that the dialectic between the scientific materialists and the Christian spiritualists plays a fundamental role in Teilhard's

---

44. It is interesting to note that throughout the index of *The Phenomenon of Man*, whenever one looks up the individual terms consciousness, intelligence, mind, psyche, radial (internal) energy, soul, or spirit, along with the page references it says to see also see all the other associated terms. It is as though the translator sees not only a strong affinity with these terms but a deep synonymy as well. See index of Teilhard, *The Phenomenon of Man*, 315–20.

45. North, *Teilhard and the Creation of the Soul*, 307. One can see in the index that under soul one is referenced to look at other terms such as continuity, consciousness, inner face, and psyche. Keep in mind that this is in a book that focuses on Teilhard's conception of soul and its creation. This should send a strong signal that Teilhard himself associated such a term with these aforementioned ones and spoke of them in conjunction.

46. Teilhard, *The Phenomenon of Man*, 272.

47. Rideau, *Teilhard de Chardin*, 429.

48. Teilhard, *The Phenomenon of Man*, 281.

phenomenology. It is a holistic approach that forms the basis for Teilhard's phenomenology, which can be deconstructed into five distinct layers: cosmology, anthropology, metaphysics, ontology, and theology.[49]

So, how does Teilhard see the connection between the soul and consciousness? It does not seem that it is an explicit connection, but more of an implicit one. This is particularly true when it comes to speaking of its origins and emergence. Teilhard understands the origin of the human soul with the ability for reflection. He states:

> I confine myself here to the phenomena, i.e., to the experimental relations between consciousness and complexity, without prejudging the deeper causes which govern the whole issue? In virtue of the limitations imposed on our sensory knowledge by the play of the temporo-spatial series, it is only it seems, under the appearances of a critical point that we can grasp experimentally the 'hominising' (spiritualising) step to reflection. But, with that said, there is nothing to prevent the thinker who adopts a spiritual explanation from positing (for reasons of a higher order and at a later stage of his dialectic), under the phenomenal veil of revolutionary transformation whatever 'creative' operation or 'special intervention' he likes (see Prefatory Note). Is it not a principle universally accepted by Christian thought in its theological interpretation of reality that for our minds there are different and successive planes of knowledge?[50]

This quote is in reference to the self-reflective ability of consciousness reached in the hominization of man. Teilhard can be taken to speak synonymously of the origin of consciousness and the soul[51] as being created out of nothing by God (this is an "intervention" that he iterates can be taken without contradiction to his system).[52] Smith, in a criticism of Teilhard's position on the soul and consciousness, suggests that Teilhard understands the soul to be produced by space-time alone and the process of complexification.[53]

---

49. Rideau, *Teilhard de Chardin: A Guide to his Thought*, 40–41.

50. Teilhard, *The Phenomenon of Man*, 169n1.

51. Teilhard, *Human Energy*, 13, 24n, 143.

52. North, *Teilhard and the Creation of the Soul*, 62–63. As we will explore below, North disagrees with the intervention of the creation of the soul and chastises Teilhard for its inclusion, as it is not necessary to his own understanding. We saw a similar claim with Lamoureux's *Evolutionary Creation*. I have classified both Teilhard's evolutionary system, as well as Lamoureux's, predominantly under PE, but are they instead interventions consistent with such TE models? We have argued that the distinction is not made by virtue of limitations or definitional structure.

53. Smith, *Theistic Evolution*, 58.

Based on my careful reading of Teilhard, I see his position on the soul and consciousness as being left a rather open-ended question.

Robert North comments on Teilhard's understanding of consciousness and the soul and implies the two are synonymous in Teilhard's thought. North sees the soul as the "form" of the body and following Karl Rahner, does not hold to a creationist view of the soul, but a traducian one.[54] Moreover, North follows Rahner more closely than Teilhard with respect to the origin of the soul. The main distinction lies in their methodologies.[55] Rahner and North rely on understanding God's action in a metaphysical sense, rather than a physical-psychical sense as does Teilhard.[56] Rahner's and North's approaches are not open to scientific investigation.[57] They are not aiming to integrate science and theology as Teilhard did or I seek to do. Instead they remain at the level of independence; non-overlapping magisterium—science and theology occupying distinct domains of knowledge. Additionally, they are not seriously entertaining the problem that origins and emergence of the soul and consciousness pose for methodological naturalism/materialism. As we have seen, a different science is required to explain such phenomena; hence it is appropriate to emphasize that they ignore this difficulty and proceed to focusing their investigation solely on a metaphysical understanding. This approach is wholly unsatisfying as previously stated, since metaphysics, theology, and science inevitably overlap and are deeply intertwined. It is ultimately one reality and one world that are to be understood.

Second, for Teilhard, taking note from Henri Bergson, matter and spirit were not two separate things "but two states or two aspects of one and the same cosmic Stuff."[58] Teilhard's view of consciousness is panpsychism[59] since he interprets "[a]ll energy as essentially psychic."[60]

Teilhard assures that "all consciousness" is derived from spirit.[61] At times we witness Teilhard using soul synonymously with spirit, for

54. North, *Teilhard and the Creation of the Soul*, 208, 213–23; 257–59.

55. Rahner, "Christology with an Evolutionary View of the World, 159–60; Rahner, "Das Selbstverstandnis der Theologie vor dem Anspruch der Naturwissenschaft, 5, 21.

56. North, *Teilhard and the Creation of the Soul*, x–xi, 233–36, 242–44; Edwards, "Teilhard's Vision as Agenda for Rahner's Christology," 58.

57. See Rahner, *Hominisation*; North, *Teilhard and the Creation of the Soul*, 228–39 (especially 233–36).

58. Teilhard, *The Heart of Matter*, 26.

59. McCarty, *Teilhard de Chardin*, 49–50.

60. Teilhard, *The Phenomenon of Man*, 64–65.

61. Teilhard, Letter of May 4, 1931: "He Doesn't See That the Cosmos Holds Together Not by Matter But by Spirit" (Letters from a Traveller, 177).

instance, in reference to the illusion of materialism: "the sole stability is imported to them by their synthetic element, that is, by that which is their soul or spirit to a more or less perfect degree."[62] Through quoting theologian and Teilhardian scholar Henri de Lubac, we see the interchangeability between spirit and soul:

> Hence, Teilhard duplicates the classic idea of the immortality of each spiritual soul by that of a collective immortality. He duplicates it, but, we should note, he does not replace it. For "the spirit of the earth" has nothing about it of an undifferentiated collective reality: it is composed of personal spirits. The process of spiritualization is in effect identically a process of personalization; it terminates in "the incommunicable uniqueness of each reflective element" and this is one of the ways in which the Teilhardian expression of "personal universe" must be understood. The irreversibility of the cosmos is thus in the final analysis the personal immortality of all the souls that compose it. Indeed, at its terminus, the cosmos in its very unity is essentially a "world of souls."[63]

There are two instances where we witness this affinity and synonymy of soul and spirit in Teilhard: "what binds the monads together is not, properly speaking, the body, but the soul," and when he states: "[The] only consistence beings have come to them from their synthetic element, in other words from what, at a more perfect or less perfect degree, is their soul, their spirit."[64] Spirit, like soul, is always embodied in unity for Teilhard[65] until the moment of death.[66]

In an effort to avoid dualism, which he deems as impossible and anti-scientific, Teilhard proposes two different components to fundamental energy: "a *tangential energy* which links the element with all others of the same order (that is to say, of the same complexity and the same centricity) as itself in the universe; and a *radial energy* which draws it toward ever greater complexity and centricity—in other words forwards."[67] What is important to

---

62. Teilhard, *The Phenomenon of Man*, 43.

63. de Lubac, *Teilhard Explained*, 48.

64. Teilhard, *Science and Christ*, 29. This second quote is almost identical to the one found in *The Phenomenon of Man* a few lines above.

65. Teilhard, *Science and Christ*, 50.

66. See de Lubac, *Teilhard Explained*, 88. In defining spirit and matter, de Lubac provides an interesting definition: "Distinct but like two faces of one same energy. The spirit of man possesses a constitution that enables it to subsist after being detached from matter."

67. Teilhard, *The Phenomenon of Man*, 64–65.

note with respect to our study on the origins and emergence of consciousness when taking Teilhard's view into account is that although Teilhard sees psyche (consciousness) at the most rudimentary aspects of matter,[68] .i.e., subatomic particles, he nonetheless makes a profound distinction between this, its existence in animals (simple ability of perception), and consciousness when reached at the human level.[69] Human consciousness, according to Teilhard, is the capacity for reflective thought (noogenesis)[70] which can turn back on itself (self-awareness). This is what Teilhard refers to as the process of hominization.[71] As philosopher and theologian Émile Rideau notes with respect to what Teilhard understands of human consciousness:

> Though rooted in animality, the phenomenon of man is not comparable with it and transcends it: in spite of many analogies with animal . . . Man is not a fortuitous or accidental phenomenon, but one obviously prepared and, in a sense willed—evolution's crowning success.[72]

Thus, we can give a threefold distinction; consciousness understood at the fundamental unifying level of matter, also understood synonymously with spirit, is psyche; basic animal perception is taken as a lower level of consciousness as well; thirdly, reflective human self-consciousness is taken as the highest point.

When Teilhard speaks of the "within of things," he is referring to a spiritual/psychical ("mind") dimension, whereas when he speaks of a "without of things," he is speaking of a physical dimension (matter).[73] Teilhard speaks of the dichotomy created between the materialists and spiritualists, calling for a union between the two, in order to be congruent with his panentheism. He suggests:

> that the two points of view require to be brought into union, and that they soon will unite in a kind of phenomenology or generalised psychic in which the internal aspect of the world will be taken into account. Otherwise, so it seems to me, it is impossible to cover the totality of the cosmic phenomenon by one coherent explanation such as science must construct.[74]

68. Ibid., 301–2.

69. See three distinct levels of explanation of consciousness: de Lubac, *Teilhard Explained*, 84.

70. Teilhard, *The Phenomenon of Man*, 181–82.

71. Ibid., 164–65.

72. Rideau, *Teilhard de Chardin*, 53.

73. Teilhard, *The Phenomenon of Man*, 53–66.

74. Ibid., 53.

This is a very important insight. It is one which involves questions of the methodology and nature of science (e.g., methodological naturalism). It involves a broader theme than science in the aforementioned sense, since science as such only examines physical phenomena. This is crucial to the question of how theology can influence science, but it broaches the limits and demarcations of science. This is why a modern understanding of science is lacking. Teilhard's statement (at the beginning of *The Phenomenon of Man*), which iterates a different a view of science, one that I believe is more properly understood as a "scientific theology" or even a "scientific phenomenology," is indispensable. Here is one of the fruits we can take away from Teilhard's thought, i.e., the importance of studying psychical and spiritual realities in a rational[75] and scientific manner. It is a holistic approach to Teilhard's science and theology (particularly modern science and Catholic theology). Whether the details are correct or right, this approach seems to be absent up until recent history.

We now return to Teilhard's two types of energies: tangential and radial. It is the interplay of these two energies that is vital to understanding Teilhard's law of complexity-consciousness. Tangential is responsible for the law-like characteristics found in individual entities and their functionality, whether it is physical, chemical, or biological. Radial energy and its effects, on the other hand, as previously noted, is what drives things forward, an impetus for the emergence of life from chemical arrangements and consciousness (in its different levels), ultimately from the evolution of life.

One last point before proceeding to a section devoted to Teilhard's law of complexity-consciousness is his emphasis on the concept of love and how it is essential to his understanding of God and evolution. De Lubac states what is of primary significance to Teilhard:

> The concrete Presence at the heart of the Universe, dominating it, animating it, and drawing it to him—the presence of a personal God—super personal, i.e., ultra-personal—of a loving and provident God of a God who can reveal himself, and has in fact revealed himself—of a God who is all Love—this was for Teilhard the supreme truth.[76]

Rideau indicates that for Teilhard, such a love is not a blind process, nor is it unnamed. It is a love identified in Christ (Omega Point), as Teilhard states himself:

---

75. I take that to mean in a philosophical manner, not one confined to the limits of the scientific method.

76. de Lubac, *Teilhard de Chardin*, 16

> For a Christian believer, it is interesting to note that the final suc-
> cess of hominization (and thus cosmic involution) is positively
> guaranteed by the 'redeeming virtue' of the God incarnate in his
> creation. But this takes us beyond the plan of phenomenology.[77]

Thus, the culmination of evolution/involution and complexity-consciousness at its height is in line with the pinnacle of love: God/Christ (Omega Point).

Teilhard also speaks of a love that is fundamental to all existence, from being to being, and intrinsic to the processes that govern matter and the entire universe:

> Considered in its full biological reality, love—that is to say, the
> affinity of being with being—is not peculiar to man. It is a gener-
> al property of all life and as such it embraces, in its varieties and
> degrees, all the forms successively adopted by organised mat-
> ter. In mammals, so close to ourselves, it is easily recognized in
> its different modalities: sexual passion, parental instinct, social
> solidarity, etc. Farther off, that is to say lower down on the tree
> of life, analogies are more obscure until they become so faint as
> to be imperceptible. But this is the place to repeat what I said
> earlier when we were discussing the 'within of things'. If there
> were no real internal level—indeed in the molecule itself—it
> would be physically impossible for love to appear higher up,
> with us, in 'hominised' form.[78]

Thus, Teilhard sees that in the very self-organizational capacities of matter, the affinities that exist between beings is summed up by an intrinsic love, which is the explanation for the organization and symmetry in the created order; without it, none of this evolutionary development would be possible. Whether one accepts this explanation of love is another matter, but it is fundamental to Teilhard's whole understanding of evolutionary development and the very fabric of the cosmos.

4.4.2 Complexity to Consciousness: The Arrow of Time

Essential to Teilhard's law of complexity-consciousness is the arrow of time; whereby complexity eventually leads to consciousness through ever-developing evolutionary changes.[79] Modern cosmology indicates that the universe is roughly 13.7 billion years old, and that it expanded from a sin-

---

77. Teilhard, *The Phenomenon of Man*, 308n2.

78. Ibid., 264.

79. Ibid., 300–2.

gularity. So, a good place to start, which is not typically discussed in regard to Teilhard's law of complexity-consciousness, is the origin of the universe.[80] The law of complexity-consciousness is predicated on change and a forward direction of time. It would seem that Teilhard would embrace what big bang cosmology entails; however, it is difficult to ascertain precisely what he believed in this regard. Though astronomer and Catholic priest Georges Lemaître proposed his hypothesis of the "primeval atom," which later through various developments became known as the big bang theory in 1927, Teilhard seemed in many ways oblivious to much of the science that accompanied that cosmology. Expansion of the universe characterizes the standard big bang model. The revolutionary independent discoveries of Russian mathematician Alexander Friedmann (1922) and Lemaître (1927) provided the solutions to Einstein's field equations, predicting the expansion of the universe.[81] Thus, evidence for the commencement of the universe, the workings, and the beginnings were at play throughout the period of Teilhard's writings. Though the scientific discoveries of his time were not at their height until 1964, with the discovery of cosmic microwave background radiation, Teilhard was surely aware of them. Accordingly, Teilhard does offer an acknowledgment of Lemaître's ideas in a note dated October 7, 1948:

> Nobody dreams of blaming Canon Lemaître for speaking of an 'expanding Universe' (spatially). For my part, I am doing no more than putting forward the complementary picture of a Universe 'that folds (organically, that is physic-chemically and psychically) upon itself'. Neither of us introduces philosophy or theology. But what we have here, as Péguy would have said, is a 'porch' which for many of our contemporaries, I believe, provides a way into the Church.[82]

Teilhard's closing words are an interesting choice, seeming to indicate his intuition regarding a finite past, with a telic understanding of evolutionary development. That incipient point is central to the argument of this book for the origins and emergence of consciousness. Moreover, in the postscript of *The Phenomenon of Man,* Teilhard does indeed make reference to the expansion of the universe:

---

80. Delio, *The Emergent Christ,* 15–17; although an important work in Teilhardian scholarship, Delio does not discuss Teilhard's evolutionary understanding in light of her section on big bang cosmology.

81 Shu, "Friedmann-Lemaitre Models"; Kragh and Smith, "Who Discovered the Expanding Universe? *History of Science*," 145–48.

82. Teilhard, "The Basis of My Attitude" dated in *The Heart of Matter,* 148.

That if the universe, regarded sidereally, is in process of spatial expansion (from the infinitesimal to the immense), in the same way and still more clearly it presents itself to us, physico-chemically, as in the process of organic *involution* upon itself (from the extremely simple to the extremely complex) and, moreover, this particular involution 'of complexity' is experimentally bound up with a correlative increase in interiorisation, that is to say in the psyche or consciousness.[83]

Teilhard uses the term "transformism" to speak of changes occurring at fundamental stages in his law of complexity-consciousness, which seems to correspond with the term "emergence." Transformism explains the emergence of new entities, or kinds of "being."[84] This leads to the formation of "the barysphere, lithosphere, hydrosphere, atmosphere and stratosphere."[85] This interplay between tangential and radial energy came to formulate life-sustaining environments in two directions: crystallizing and polymerizing worlds.[86] Then, eventually life emerges from these necessary life-sustaining components. Teilhard recognizes that at the origin of life, which he refers to as the cellular revolution, there is both an external and internal revolution. Teilhard recognizes that in the cell:

> is really the stuff of the universe reappearing once again with all its characteristics—only this time it has reached a higher rung of complexity and thus, by the same stroke (if our hypothesis be well founded), advanced still further in *interiority*, i.e. in consciousness . . . I assume a decisive step in the progress of consciousness on Earth to have taken place at this particular stage of evolution [at the origin of life].[87]

Here we can witness Teilhard's panpsychism at play. We can also see that Teilhard has a deep appreciation for life being a remarkably different type of being than material constituents alone, i.e., that there is an organized complexity. In light of this intertwinement between tangential and radial energies at the origin of life, Teilhard indicates that:

> it is incumbent on me to explain in what specific way the internal ('radial') energy is modified to correspond with the

83. Teilhard, *The Phenomenon of Man*, 301.

84. See Teilhard, "Notes on the Essence of Transformism," in *Heart of Matter*, 107–14.

85. Teilhard, *The Phenomenon of Man*, 68.

86. Ibid., 68–71.

87. Ibid., 87–88.

external ('tangential') constitution of the cellular unit. If we have already endowed the long chain of atoms, then molecules, then mega-molecules, with the obscure and remote sources of rudimentary free activity, it is not by totally new beginning but by a *metamorphosis* that the cellular revolution should express itself physically. But how? How are we to envisage the change-over (how are we even to find room for a change-over) from the pre-consciousness inherent in pre-life to the consciousness, however elementary, of the first true living creature? Are there several ways for a creature to have a within?[88]

In this remarkable passage we witness Teilhard struggling to provide an articulation of the essence of the first self-replicating organism. Teilhard lacked the scientific language to articulate precisely how this first organism was fundamentally different from basic proteins arranged in different ways. James Watson and Francis Crick (1916–2004) elucidated the double helical structure of the deoxyribonucleic acid (DNA molecule) in 1953.[89] This was essential to realizing the degree of functional complexity necessary for the existence of a modern cell. Unfortunately, it seems Teilhard was expressing some intuition of this functional complexity through his musings with interiority and psychical capacities within the cell, but he simply lacked the means necessary to understand this at the time. But how could he? The origin of life is not only a radicalization or a revolution in matter; it is the birth of informational complexity. Scientific materialists are still not coming to grips with this in our present scientific era. They are retaining the great barriers of materialistic understanding of how life arose and the associated information processing system. There are a host of problems in explaining the origin of life through self-organizational processes and materialistic scenarios.[90]

The evolutionary progression from simple organisms to the ever-expanding diversity of life until reaching the radial energy within humanity, which is transformed into consciousness, has led to the ability of reflection and thought and its direct association with self-consciousness. It is what we can call personhood, something that animals do not ultimately share with humanity, despite their own interiorization and "soulful" capacities. It is here that Teilhard shares a profound insight regarding the evolution of consciousness and distinguishes it from physical capacities. This includes the structure

88. Ibid., 88

89. Watson and Crick, "A Structure for Deoxyribose Nucleic Acid," 737–38.

90. For an exposé of the problems with materialistic origin of life scenarios, see Meyer, *Signature in the Cell*, 229–52; Davies, *The Fifth Miracle*; Johnson, *The Programming of Life*.

of a brain, i.e., the physiological inner workings of the brain are insufficient to indicate the degree of consciousness possessed by an organism. Teilhard in his own words expresses this phenomenon:

> What was previously only a centred surface became a centre. By a tiny 'tangential' increase, the 'radial' was turned back on itself and so to speak took an infinite leap forward. Outwardly, almost nothing in the organs had changed. But in depth, a great revolution had taken place: consciousness was now leaping and boiling in a space of super-sensory relationships and representations; and simultaneously consciousness was capable of perceiving itself in the concentrated simplicity of its faculties. And all this happened for the first time.[91]

What is intriguing about this passage is that it demonstrates that Teilhard had a distinct understanding of evolution than that of Darwin, who saw the difference in human consciousness as being one of degree, not kind, from the lower mammals.

It is interesting to note that Wallace's position (explored in the introduction) regarding the uniqueness of a human person seemed to be more congruent with Teilhard.[92] Teilhard does not agree with any mode of intervention, but leads one to believe there is a definite direction to evolution. One of the graces of Teilhard's vision of evolution and his associated law of complexity-consciousness was that it contained elements that made it more consonant with how reality seems to be, i.e., that mind is a prime-essential component of reality, unlike the metaphysical Darwinists such as Dennett, Coyne, and Dawkins, who assert the converse, that mind is solely the by-product of the evolutionary process. Wallace shared Teilhard's vision of evolution in that it is tending toward more complexity and hence higher states of consciousness, as Michael Shermer writes: "Commingling his teleological thinking about the directional nature of evolution with the spiritual phenomenon he was observing, Wallace understood the ultimate purpose of nature to be the development of the spirit—the final end of an

91. Teilhard, *The Phenomenon of Man*, 169.

92. Wallace argues in ways similar to Teilhard, i.e., that there is a profound distinction between the inorganic and organic world (origin of life); primitive life and creatures like insects and sentient beings (exhibiting qualia) like in animals such as birds, dogs, cats, and monkeys etc.; and finally the level of consciousness between sentient animals and human consciousness (which display high levels of self-consciousness/awareness comprising the intellect and will). See Flannery, *Alfred Russell Wallace's Theory of Intelligent Evolution*; Flannery, *Nature's Prophet: Alfred Russel Wallace's Evolution from Natural Selection to Natural Theology*, 84, 187–95.

immeasurably long evolutionary process."[93] This sounds awfully similar to Teilhard's noosphere and Omega Point.

Teilhard stated earlier that "It is not merely a matter of change of degree, but of a change of nature, resulting from a change of state."[94] This passage demonstrates that Teilhard, although reinforcing a correlation between increasing complexity and consciousness, is unsure of the precise correlation between the two, since it is not just a matter of degree but a radical transformation.

According to North, who explains that increasing complexity in a general sense may indicate an increase in consciousness, but this is not necessarily true in all instances:

> The only part which we really observe is this: The reactions exhibited by more complex structures approximate progressively to those prompted by human consciousness. This holds even for inorganic and plant units. On higher levels, concretely, behavior comes more like human conscious behavior in measurable proportion as the complexity of the nervous system and eventually the size of the brain approach closer to those of man. This is verifiable only in a general way, regarding certain key species. Moreover it in no way applies to individual specimens. Not every human with a larger brainpan is more intelligent than other humans. We are comparing merely the overall size of molecular structure within contrasted groups. There are doubtless samples like the beaver or bee which do not fit this rule of thumb.[95]

North also suggests that some species may increase in structural growth, but not exhibit higher levels of consciousness,[96] which would indicate an exception to Teilhard's law. For instance, one can think of how insects may increase organization and behavior due to complexification, but this does not necessarily signify an increase in consciousness. Teilhard of course would reply that this does not violate the overall tendency and direction of increasing complexity/consciousness because the trend would continue with the majority, even though individual species may fail to "follow."[97]

93. Shermer, *In Darwin's Shadow*, 176.

94. Teilhard, *The Phenomenon of Man*, 166.

95. North, *Teilhard and the Creation of the Soul*, 11. This work contains many interesting insights on complexity, consciousness, creation, evolution, and the soul. It takes into account some of Karl Rahner's thought on the creation of the soul and hominization. Rahner wrote the introduction to this text.

96. North, *Teilhard and the Creation of the Soul*, 12.

97. A position that can be contrasted with this is the late paleontologist Stephen J. Gould's view. He held that the history of life on earth is marked by a series of

Nonetheless, to return to Teilhard's observations on human consciousness, he suggests that "outwardly, almost nothing in the organs had changed."[98] One could take that to mean that physiologically speaking, one cannot see a major difference between, for example, a minor increase in complexity and an extreme increase in consciousness. The moment of higher consciousness accompanied by the ability of self-reflection can be taken as a singular event in the evolution of the biosphere. So, the origin of consciousness is not recognizable through anything physiological. When comparing two brains, one of a prototypic human compared to that of a true human, for example, they might show the same identical complexity, but not the same type of rational mental/cognitive capacities. Here it may be that we realize that there is not a 1 to 1 correspondence (matching correlation) with Teilhard's notion of complexity and consciousness. Teilhard states this in support of the correspondence between complexity and consciousness: "It is true that in the end, from the organic point of view, the whole metamorphosis leading to man depends on the question of a better brain. But how was this cerebral perfecting to be carried out—how could it have worked—if there had not been a whole series of other conditions realised at just the same time?"[99] We are left in the dark about the exact relationship between consciousness and increasing complexity, since a physiological state, such as a more complex (larger) brain is not necessarily equivalent to higher consciousness. Teilhard seems to acknowledge this problematic even further when he reiterates this mystery in an implicit way regarding the irreducibility of the mind to the brain:

> Dearly would we love to know what those first parents of ours looked like, the ones that stood just this side of the threshold of reflection. As I have already said, that threshold had to be crossed in a single stride. Imagine the past to have been photographed section by section: at that critical moment of initial hominisation, what should we see when we developed our film? If we have understood the limits of enlargement imposed by nature on the instrument which helps us to study the landscape of the past, we shall be prepared to forgo the satisfaction of this futile curiosity. No photograph could record upon the human phylum this passage to reflection which so naturally intrigues us, for the simple reason that the phenomenon took place inside

---

contingencies without a linear trend towards complexity. See Gould, *Wonderful Life*, 48.

98. Teilhard, *The Phenomenon of Man*, 169.

99. Ibid., 170.

that which is always lacking in a reconstructed phylum—the peduncle of its original forms.[100]

What Teilhard described in the above quote is precisely a significant change, i.e., the origin of human consciousness. However, Teilhard's overall view of evolution and his conception of God cannot ultimately account for its origin, as I will argue in the conclusion. The purpose of this book is to seek a corrective or a better explanation for this phenomenon and singular event in our Earth's history. Having said that, Teilhard is attentively aware of the problem of the "within of things" regarding the origin of consciousness when comes to its physical correlates.

North provides some valuable insights for further thought, regarding the various discontinuities that nature exhibits and the difficulties it poses for our possession of knowledge regarding consciousness:

> There is a "threshold" or gulf which *severs* man from the pos-
> sessors of various other degrees of approach toward conscious-
> ness. It severs also animal from plant, life from inorganic
> matter. Ormea [an Italian commentator on Teilhard's work]
> notes that *every* birth, not only every species change, is a dis-
> continuity as well as continuity. As a maximum defense of the
> uniqueness of man's soul, post-Cartesian Catholics have loved
> to dogmatize that every such threshold, and especially the gulf
> between nonlife and life, requires a uniquely immediate in-
> tervention of the Creator. This assertion is simply unproved:
> whether or not (as seems likely) its contrary is at present of
> course of being shown experimentally.[101]

North then argues that the origin of life cannot be proven spontaneously, nor can divine intervention,[102] but as I will argue, this misses the point since we must follow the evidence and better argumentation wherever it leads. Nonetheless, North admits discontinuity is real and an interesting feature of nature. Discontinuity is not a given; alternatively we could observe pure continuity without any breaks. Thus, this does not necessarily mean it is a figment of our imagination but perhaps a *real* discontinuity, unless our understanding is completely off. Nonetheless, North indicates that we must be careful in how we express continuity and discontinuity within the created order and the relation to God's action. There are several points he makes that are worth examining. Through a series of what he calls the surety of

---

100. Ibid., 186–87.
101. North, *Teilhard and the Creation of the Soul*, 12.
102. Ibid.

"cherished" ideals or slogans such as "Matter cannot become spirit, and matter cannot produce spirit,"[103] he demonstrates an interesting lesson when we work from the converse (spirit becoming matter), though there is this seemingly irreducible discontinuity between matter and spirit.[104] Then North rightly acknowledges that the complete opposite is true from the Christian perspective:

> "Spirit can produce matter." (God created the world.) "Spirit can become matter." To omit from our present perspective the mystery of God becoming man, we allude rather to the more accessible fact that "the soul is the form of the body." [. . .] The soul is not held to "produce" this matter after the fashion of an efficient cause, but nevertheless this body which I actually possess is determined by the form and not by the *materia prima*.[105]

Continuing with his reasoning, North states:

> If all the matter which there is was produced by spirit; if much of the matter is concretely determined to its individual existing reality by spirit here and now: then it would seem unwarrantable to extend the slogan "matter cannot produce spirit" to imply unwarrantably "spirit cannot, immediately, produce spirit . . . Is it in fact true that spirit (except God) cannot produce spirit? It may be. But if so, it is not the slogan we started from."[106]

Carrying forward, an interesting insight is revealed: opposing the materialistic presupposition that causation is always bottom-up (or as North puts it "the superior by the inferior"), where "thought is by life, life is by matter." Teilhard spins it around to where it is top-down causation, where the superior explains the inferior "matter and life by the thought to which they are ordered, thought itself by the final collective regrouping of humans persons about a super-personal transcendent center."[107] What is revealed here is the understanding North has of Teilhard's view of panspychism, namely that psyche is conjoined to matter at its fundamental components, so that there is a unity between the two, and as complexity develops, so does the correlate of consciousness. Yet, as we have previously witnessed, Teilhard does not think that complexity explains away the origin of human consciousness.

---

103. Ibid., 31.
104. Ibid.
105. Ibid.
106. Ibid., 32.
107. Ibid.

North indicates that what theologians suggest by "matter [not produc-ing] spirit" really means that "spirit cannot produce spirit; only God can."[108] Perhaps some would affirm this, based on their beliefs and presupposi-tions. But does the logic follow that since spirit can produce matter, that the converse is true? Could this assume that spirit left potency for matter to become spirit or that matter has such inherent potency? This would require orthogenesis in some way to be true. Do we have sufficient evidence of this? I'm not sure if this is logically possible. Even if it is logically possible, it does not mean that it is the actual state of affairs we find ourselves in, in this particular universe or reality.

Teilhard postulates an "inner spiritual energy," which would be in line with orthogenesis, which can be found in its most minimal form, in inorganic matter, which combines and recombines, complexifying more and more in consciousness until a human person is eventually derived from the evolutionary process.[109] This is how North states Teilhard's view, which is in line with the suggestion that Teilhard is seeing an increasing complexity resulting in a human person with a soul; hence, complexity-consciousness leads to the soul, which distinguishes humans from animals. Teilhard has admitted that the traditional position—that the human soul was created out of nothing—is not incompatible with his "hypothesis."[110] This also attests to the reality that the soul is a creature and not divine.[111] However, Teilhard has suggested that he affirms a position that would not require any sort of intervention:

> First of all, it appears contradictory (to the nature of participat-ed being) to imagine God creating an *isolated* thing. Only one being can exist in isolation: Ens *a se* (being which exists only in itself). Everything which is not God is essentially multitude or-ganized in itself, and multitude organizing around itself. If God, then, is to *make a soul*, there is only one way open to his power: *to create a world*. In consequence, man includes among his fully realized conditions of possibility more than just 'animality and rationality'; the notion of man implies also 'mankind, earth, universe . . . ' This takes us a long way from the facile 'possibility' which the logicians imagine for things.[112]

---

108. Ibid. North also states that "Obviously if finite spirit exists, it has been pro-duced therefore it can be produced. But it could have been produced by God rather than by spirit. This cannot just be assumed; it must be proved. We will examine the proof in due time." Proof must be used in a very loose sense in this context.

109. Ibid., 204.

110. Ibid.

111. Ibid., 214.

112. Teilhard, *Christianity and Evolution*, 32.

Teilhard sidesteps from PE into DE for suggesting that the creation of the soul is not incompatible with his "hypothesis." Recall that PE suggests that God can intervene but that God's creation is without flaw from the incipient moment (as is implied in Teilhard's quote). This is what is meant by hints of DE with a predominant focus on PE for Teilhard's view of TE.

North devotes a chapter to church teaching on the creation of the soul and notes that: "Only some of the declarations on soul-creation add the term 'immediately'; and others add 'out of nothing.'"[113]

Relying on Karl Rahner, North gives an account for the origin of the soul and life as being created by God tying the soul to the body, reflective of a human person, not as two separate entities. North states:

> Rahner's solution is that God's creative power does not appear in nature as one cause ranged in its place alongside various others, but God's causality is equally operative in all emergence of new beings. This is revitalized doctrine of concursus. Every production of a new being means that the cause outdid itself, or "the less produced the greater." This is accounted for by the fact that God as co-producer furnishes the Being, the new Being, the plus . . . Human parents do not really produce a human soul, but no one else does either. The soul is not a separate reality, a bird to be put into a cage as Plato thought. There is no soul unless there is being.[114]

Does this resolve the problem of the origin and emergence of consciousness which would entail the same discussion as the soul? North affirms that no intervention of God is necessary throughout evolution. He also states that the only criticism of Teilhard that should be made was for the insertion of footnotes that suggest an accommodation to notions of the compatibility of God's intervention for the creation of the soul.[115]

Bear in mind that in chapter 3 we discussed the problematics involved with the different positions involved in TE (NTE, PE, and DE) regarding God's action. The issue of PE being able to encompass all of the universe's phenomena is an open-ended question, but PE has its difficulties as were outlined in the previous chapter.

In light of this, several problems arise with the notion of God's action with respect to the origins and emergence of consciousness (which implies the creation of the soul). Is the discontinuity real or mere illusion? Was God's intervention necessary because of the discontinuity observed in nature, or

113. Ibid., 227.
114. Ibid., 239.
115. Ibid., 238.

is it just our perception of these gaps, that we are creating a god-of-the-gaps issue here? Or is reality such that this discontinuity, which points one in the direction of a divine intervention, is like a signpost to transcendence? As interesting as his ventures into Teilhard and the creation of the soul are, I'm not sure that North has made his case. Must we resist this inclination lest we are shown to be wrong in the future? I suggest that in this instance we require positive argumentation as to why there is not only discontinuity, but as to why God would serve as a plausible explanation. An inference to the best explanation avoids a god-of-the-gaps trap. The other problematic would be if such is the case, then what do we mean by intervention? More-over, as North notes, Aquinas, in reference to "form" or "creation," regards the soul as a concept relegated primarily to the domains of science and phi-losophy.[116] Science and philosophical understanding based on innovations of science would not make the situation as neat and tidy as North suggests. One would need to know the best explanation for such emergent properties and whether or not it occurred through nature's endowed creative capaci-ties. This is precisely the point Meyer has made with Lamoureux's program concerning whether the laws of physics can produce information or not. Science takes a step further for philosophic and theological reflection. Yes, we can affirm as North and Rahner do that God is the Creator of all, but to have significance we want our reasoning to not only be influenced by science but to influence science, as we set out to do with the CMI. Never-theless, this is a difficult question that cannot be explored here, but will be given the deserved reflection in later chapters.[117]

Teilhard also focuses on elements of self-consciousness that are rel-evant to the main subject driving this book. In *The Phenomenon of Man* he makes an intriguing point about the emergence of consciousness in the realization of humanity's place in the created order. This is something that occurs in the history of the noosphere namely the self-realization that human beings are products of the evolutionary process. Teilhard sees the ultimate self-awareness in precisely just that, the discovery of evolution. Teilhard explains this point in human consciousness:

> we see not only thought as participating in evolution as an anomaly or as an epiphenomenon; but evolution as so reduc-ible to and identifiable with a progress toward thought that movement of our souls expresses and measures the very stages of progress of evolution itself. Man discovers that he is nothing

116. Ibid., 227.

117. We will return to this issue in the section dealing with how theology can influ-ence the sciences. See chapter 7.3.1.

else than evolution become conscious of itself to borrow Julian
Huxley's striking expression.[118]

Teilhard goes on to emphasize that "the consciousness of each of us is evolution looking at itself and reflecting upon itself."[119] This is no doubt a profound
realization about humanity's own self-awareness. It is the birth of the notion
of humanity's discovery of its place in the grand scheme of the history of the
cosmos. Notice that such a realization would tie nicely with any of the three
TE models (which encompass UCD).

Questions arise as to what binds and grounds this process of complexification? A much-neglected part of Teilhard's evolutionary understanding
of the cosmos and complexity/consciousness is its dependence upon God.
In light of his Omega Point, Teilhard has some interesting insights that are
brought forth by the interpretative frameworks of others. Cooper discerns
two arguments that Teilhard provides with respect to the existence of Omega Point.[120] First, Teilhard centers the concept of love on the Omega Point.
He argues that this capacity to attract presents throughout the cosmos and
is grounded in the Omega: "To be supremely attractive, Omega must be
already supremely present."[121] Second, Teilhard seems to provide a sort of
"unmoved mover" or principle of sufficient reason argument, whereby the
evolutionary process is wholly dependent on a being not subject to cessa-
tion from existence. Teilhard explains: "Omega must be independent of the
collapse of the powers with which evolution is woven . . . In its evolutionary
aspects Omega still only shows *half* of itself. At the same time that it is the
term of the series, it is also *outside* all series."[122] Teilhard is expounding some
natural theology, presenting an argument on the dependency of the evolutionary process upon God in God's transcendent capacity. This serves well
for some of the arguments that will be presented with respect to theology
influencing science in terms of the origins and emergence of consciousness.
One could of course ask the question, why is it that matter and life have the
inherent capacity to complexify more and more? Alongside this ability to
complexify comes a high level of functionally integrated complexity, which
eventually leads to an ultimate collective transcendence culminating in the
Omega Point. The answer will not come from autonomous nature; therefore
it seems NTE is not wholly accurate but PE or DE is, in order to describe
Teilhard's evolutionary theology through his law of complexity-conscious-

118. Teilhard, *The Phenomenon of Man*, 221.

119. Ibid., 221.

120. Cooper, *Panentheism*, 154.

121. Teilhard, *The Phenomenon of Man*, 269.

122. Ibid., 270.

ness. It would seem reasonable to suggest that Teilhard views this capacity as conferred onto nature by God who is both transcendent to nature and immanent within it.

Despite Cooper's discernment of Teilhard's twofold argument, which grounds the evolutionary process as somehow dependent upon God, it seems to contradict what Teilhard iterates in *Christianity and Evolution* regarding repulsion for any such "unmoved mover" or "prime mover" arguments. He demonstrates a clear aversion to Aristotelian and scholastic philosophy.[123] Admittedly, the argument that Cooper discerns in Teilhard is somewhat different; it bears some similarity in affirming God's existence, necessity, and grounding for all of reality (including evolutionary processes). Thus, in Teilhard's view there is a denial of the world being contingent and dependent upon God through either *creation ex nihilo* or *creation ex vetera* (in sustaining the universe). Rather, Teilhard sees an interdependence of God, the created order, and evolution. As Ilia Delio points out:

> Teilhard opposed the idea of an absolutely gratuitous creation which makes creation independent of God or merely contingent on God. For Thomas Aquinas, creation is the outflow of the divine will. God freely chooses to create. Teilhard felt, however, that this type of radical dependency between God and creation diminishes the significance of the world in relation to God.[124]

Teilhard drives home the point of interdependence between God and the universe: "In truth it is not the sense of contingence of the created but the sense of mutual completion of the world and God which gives life to Christianity."[125] On one hand, it seems that a case can be made as Cooper suggests that Teilhard views evolutionary processes as dependent on God, and on the other hand it seems we can find Teilhard's words to be challenging God's sovereignty, aseity, and freedom from the world (the created order). It seems the answer lies in Teilhard's view of God and God's relationship to the world. Teilhard's Christocentric panentheism indicates a co-dependence of God and the world, as opposed to a more classical Christian theistic approach as evident with Augustine, Anselm, and Aquinas, whereby the world and all of its processes are utterly dependent upon God's creative and sustaining action. The world would not exist without God.

Some problems do arise with Teilhard's law of complexity-consciousness. For instance, Teilhard theorizes that all matter is in the process of becoming spirit through progressive complexification, which entails "matter

---

123. Teilhard, *Christianity and Evolution*, 239–40.

124. Delio "Evolution and the Rise of the Secular God," 45.

125. Teilhard, *Christianity and Evolution*, 227.

[giving] birth to life, consciousness and thought—in a word, gives birth to 'spirit'"[126] and that it is "experimentally as the specific effect of organized complexity."[127] An important objection is that consciousness is not observable in an empirical sense, like bodies and behaviors are.[128] This is something that Teilhard acknowledges, but he draws confusion when speaking as though we can perform an experiment in the normative scientific sense. Consciousness is solely observable in a subjective sense. We are conscious of ourselves, others, and the world around us, but we are not "conscious of someone else's consciousness."[129] Although we may postulate through our empathetic nature what may be going on in someone else's mind, a significant difficulty for Teilhard is raised when it comes to defining it "experimentally."[130] Similarly, as North observes:

> the only "consciousness" anyone really knows by experience is his own. What man observes in other realities, even other men, is simply to the reactions which he sees prompted in himself by his consciousness. If we are careful to keep remembering this, then we may warrantably extend the same observations to plant and mineral structure . . . [s]carcely anyone will deny that a puppy's reaction to kindness merits the name of both "knowledge" and "love" to a greater extent than some other chemical reactions in the universe.[131]

There is something indeed observable, but to quantify it experimentally seems to be another matter altogether. Nonetheless, complexity as used by Teilhard is not a "well defined parameter."[132]

There is no way of accounting for consciousness being proportional to the complexity of an organism. Teilhard admits this, but for dubious reasons such as the enormity of the calculations[133]: "once we are past molecules . . . the very hugeness of the values we meet makes any numerical calculation of complexities impossible."[134] Smith questions Teilhard's panpsychism, or as he frames it: "that some kind of rudimentary consciousness exists even in the

126. Teilhard, *The Phenomenon of Man*, 301.

127. Ibid.

128. Smith, *Theistic Evolution*, 54.

129. Ibid.

130. Ibid.

131 North, *Teilhard and the Creation of the Soul*, 13.

132. Smith, *Theistic Evolution*, 54.

133. Ibid., 55.

134. Teilhard, *Man's Place in Nature*, 47.

simplest of corpuscles."[135] One could ask Teilhard, where is the evidence that consciousness exists in rocks or protons? It seems as though part of the difficulty lies with Teilhard's understanding of consciousness. He does not carefully distinguish between complexity and consciousness. Yet, this seems to be an inevitable part and parcel of the metaphysical approach Teilhard embraces regarding consciousness (i.e., panpsychism). Part of the problem lies in the use of consciousness to encompass three distinct definitions, where it would have been useful for Teilhard to distinguish between complexity/specified complexity, information (functional), and consciousness. As was acknowledged, Teilhard lacked the language and science to understand functional information, since the structure of the double helical DNA molecule was discovered a year after his death. The science of information has exploded since then. Thus much of the ambiguity and confusion lies in using terms synonymously or extending them so far that they lose their distinguishing significance. Be that as it may, it should be noted that information—whether specified or redundant—is what exists in inorganic matter for Teilhard (and for that matter, organic matter that composes living organisms including humans), as opposed to consciousness (in terms of a panpsychist understanding), but rather from understanding information and complexity.[136]

4.5 Teilhard's Concept of Ultra-Physics

Teilhard's concept of "ultra-physics" is one that has not been explored with great depth by his interlocutors, nor was it one that was developed at great length by Teilhard. I contend that it is a concept that can aid in understanding the origin of consciousness. It sits at the boundary of science and philosophy. It seeks to understand the psychophysical in relationship to one another, which is something that Teilhard had observed as sorely lacking in Western science.[137] His critics have dismissed this too soon. The main problem is that Teilhard had not fully developed this science of "ultra-physics."[138]

135. Smith, *Theistic Evolution*, 61.

136. See note on specified complexity in the introduction.

137. Conversely, in Eastern philosophy where consciousness and mind play a primary role over the material, it could be said to be true, that the material is considered to be even a delusion.

138. de Lubac, *Teilhard de Chardin: The Man and His Meaning*, 100. De Lubac suggests that this is where Teilhard's originality lies, but also where a twofold limitation arises because of lack of clarity and a lack of "methodical consideration." De Lubac, *Teilhard Explained*, 88. Here de Lubac, in his definition, explains that the "ultra-physics" is a science that has "yet to be elaborated"; In Rideau, *Teilhard de Chardin: a Guide to his Thought*, 43, 341, Rideau explains that "the term ultra-physics, contradictory in

An intriguing Teilhard quote given by de Lubac reveals this program of 'ultra-physics' he spent such a significant amount of time reflecting on:

> It seems to me [he wrote] that I have almost succeeded in for-
> mulating a sort of "Physics of the Spirit," which expresses more
> completely the suggestions sketched out in my note on the
> Phenomenon of Man. It is a sort of reduction of the Universe
> to the spiritual, on the physical plane . . . that has for me the
> fortunately corollary of legitimizing the retention of person (i.e.
> the "immortality of souls") in the Universe. I shall try, in this
> paper, to pin down this prospect of a World whose equilibrium
> consists in painfully resting on a Consciousness and a Personal-
> ization that is continually growing greater—an exact reversal of
> the World of modern Science.[139]

As has been mentioned before, and proven through this quote, this is something that Teilhard recognized well before contemporary scientists and philosophers, who are now involved with the study of consciousness, and are arguing for the need of a new mode of explanation or "science" for the phenomenon of psyche/consciousness. Sadly, the fact remains that many still do not see an issue (as is the case with reductive materialists). Other intriguing possibilities are raised from the notion of Teilhard's "ultra-physics": is it something that can shed light not only on the origins and emergence of consciousness, but on God's action in the world? Could it bring any further knowledge, in discerning how the psychical can interact with the physical and by extension the immaterial with the material? As difficult as these issues are to conceptualize, they do indeed raise intriguing questions about such scientific, philosophical, and theological notions.

---

appearance but dialectical in fact, indicates in the first place fidelity to positive and scientific experience, the indissoluble adherence of philosophical reflection to facts, concern for rationality, and the desire to express the laws of the real and the necessity of the order of things. It implies also a negation, by which thought goes beyond the order of verifiable evidence, the measurable relations of phenomena, to express the secret of their being and the goal to which they are directed, the law of their essence and of their movement."; Teilhard, *Science and Christ*, 96–97. Teilhard explains two important points of the new physics or "ultra-physics"; Teilhard, *Human Energy*, 70, 90–91.

139. de Lubac, *Teilhard de Chardin: The Man and His Meaning*, 153. Again, here de Lubac recognizes the profundity of what Teilhard is setting out to do but acknowledges that it is not fully realized or as he puts it "not yet elaborated." See de Lubac, *Teilhard Explained*, 88.

4.6 Conclusion

Teilhard's pioneering work, and his legacy as well as the accessibility of his works are what in my estimation have played an important role in the vitalization of the science-theology dialogue in the twentieth century. Russell's CMI in an indirect and perhaps subtle way has been possible because of Teilhard's ground-breaking work in the intersection of philosophy, science, and theology. Unfortunately, Teilhard did not have the language or the understanding of contemporary science to make proper judgments in such domains, despite some interesting notions about tangential and radial energies, which are hard to quantify from a scientific perspective.

I cannot accept his view of panentheism for a number of reasons. I do not accept interdependence between God and the world. I see the world as utterly dependent on God for scientific, philosophical, and theological reasoning. The finitude of the past as argued through the expansion of the universe and the second law of thermodynamics points to a transcendent cause. Philosophical arguments that demonstrate the impossibility of traversing an infinite series of past events corroborate these scientific reasons. I will not delve into this argument further here, but will examine this in my brief presentation of the Kalam Cosmological Argument[140] in the following section of this book. Theologically, Teilhard's radical notion of interdependence of God and the world cannot be affirmed scripturally, reasonably, or consistently through Christian doctrine.[141] In addition, it contradicts our understanding of creation as outlined in chapter 3. Divine simplicity serves as a corrective to this notion.[142]

Having said all that, Teilhard has brought some fruits. I will highlight these valuable points as I close this chapter. He was the first to integrate a Christian vision of the world (albeit somewhat radical) with a scientific perspective on an evolving universe. Second, he opened the gateway to the science-Christian theology dialogue we find ourselves in today. Third, he has provided a holistic approach to examining not just physical, but also psychical and spiritual realities. This method of inquiry, despite the flaws in Teilhard's specific approach, is important for Russell's CMI, in finding a way that theology can potentially influence the sciences and move forward

---

140. See Nowacki, *The Kalam Cosmological Argument for God*; Craig, *The Kalam Cosmological Argument*; Davidson, *Proofs for Eternity, Creation and the Existence of God in Medieval Islamic and Jewish Philosophy*.

141. See Copan and Craig, *Creation Out of Nothing*; Copan, "Is Creatio Ex Nihilo A Post-Biblical Invention? An Examination of Gerhard May's Proposal," 77–93; Cooper, *Panentheism*, 319–46.

142. See section 5.4.

from a regulative ideal, to making an actual impact. This is where I think the Teilhardian concept of "ultra-physics" can be utilized as a springboard (since it was not fully developed in his writings) and taken further with insights from contemporary science, philosophy, and theology regarding consciousness. This approach will be used in chapter 7 to explore a potential research guideline. Fourth, Teilhard was the first to seriously look at the importance of the origin of consciousness and attempt to integrate it in an ongoing process with respect to physical evolution and his law of complexity-consciousness. Fifth, what Teilhard was able to accomplish in spite of his critics was remarkable. He was able to demonstrate through his understanding of evolution that humanity is exceptional and unique with respect to the rest of creation, precisely because of the abilities for thought, reflection, a sense of morality, and love, which are possible because of embodied consciousness. All the while he managed to stay in line with modern scientific understanding, which remains relevant today (UCD) in that we are recent spinoffs from the primate family. Teilhard sees human origins and consciousness as a discrete/singular event that creates a sharp disjunction in the animal kingdom, as opposed to Darwin's gradualism in order to encompass all phenomena (including morality, consciousness, love etc.). This would be in line with the scriptural interpretation of Gen 1:27 in reference to humanity being created in the image and likeness of God. Sixth, that there is not a 1 to 1 correspondence with complexity and consciousness; the mind is not irreducible to the brain—we must seek an alternative explanation. Seventh, Teilhard elucidated the usual vagueness that consciousness, thought, reflection, psyche, mind, the soul, and such related concepts are usually met with, so that they cannot be examined by the standard scientific tools in the effort to understand their origins and emergence. This is a profound insight that will play a role in the direction of this book. Though it seems Teilhard's overall understanding of evolution is not viable, it offers crucial insight for contemporary discussions. It is one that repudiates not only metaphysical naturalism but methodological naturalism as well, when it comes to examining the origin of consciousness. Eighth, Teilhard's take on evolution in relating God's action is fascinating but remains nonetheless problematic. His overall view of evolution is PE and even includes elements of DE. Both of these will be of use for further exploration on the origin of consciousness. Nonetheless, we have outlined reasons as to why absolute views of PE lack explanatory scope and power (even though we see hints of Teilhard assimilating DE to explain the origin of the soul and consciousness). Therefore, we will utilize these fruits for the purpose of this book as best we can, while weeding out the components that make it incompatible with a classical and personal Christian conception of God and creation.

Chapter 5

Arguments from Natural
Theology & Philosophical Theology

CENTAC & Divine Simplicity

5.1 Introduction

THE SUBSEQUENT SIX ARGUMENTS are meant to build the ground for this book, namely understanding the origin of consciousness through the Christian conception of God and creation. These also provide arguments in support of theological research programs, which are meant to influence scientific research programs, through providing justification for some of the guidelines in chapter 7, from our transformation of Russell's CMI in its application to the origin of consciousness. The first five arguments seek to build a cumulative case for God as Creator, through several lines of evidence as demonstrated through the sciences when coupled with philosophical reasoning.

The arguments are as follows: a cosmological argument based on the principle of determination: 1) The Kalam Cosmological Argument; The Teleological Argument is a collective of the next four arguments; 2) Fine-tuning of the laws of physics; 3) Fine-tuning of the laws of biology; 4) Origin of life—origin of information—specified complexity; a final cause argument: 5) FINLON—Convergent Evolution, Complexity and Consciousness; and finally, an argument from philosophical theology concerning the nature of God: 6) The Christian conception of God: divine simplicity (God's Simplicity).

Before proceeding further, it is worth noting that each of these arguments have been the subject of much intense debate amongst philosophers of religion, philosophers of science, theologians, and scientists. There are voluminous treatments as well as a plethora of articles devoted to these arguments, so I will only be able to scratch the surface and provide an explanation for why they support the Christian conception of God and creation as the source of understanding the origin of consciousness. Likewise, it would be impossible to give an extensive treatment on each argument given the space in this book. The following arguments of natural theology that will be examined include the Kalam Cosmological Argument, the fine-tuning of the laws of physics and biology, the origin of life, and convergent evolution (related to the FINLON for consciousness) all of which function to produce what I have dubbed "The Cumulative Evolutionary Natural Theological Argument from Consciousness (CENTAC)."[1] Each of the arguments in CENTAC provides one sequential layering after another for God as undergirding the very existence of the universe and the process of cosmic evolution. I believe that CENTAC is compatible with the different models of creation and evolution, although the scientific creationist models would argue for many interventions from God throughout the history of the universe. The closest approximation would be either PE or DE in order to understand CENTAC from a creationist perspective. These arguments function powerfully together to demonstrate that God is the Creator of the universe via *creation ex nihilo* and that He is also responsible for the structure of the universe in terms of the laws of physics that permit the existence of matter and the creation of galaxies and planets. God is also responsible for the laws of biology, which reveal purpose and undergird the telic component of biological evolution. Each of these components is necessary for consciousness to eventually originate in the history of cosmic evolution. The origin of information necessary for the first replicating system, which is presupposed in all of evolutionary biology, also points persuasively toward mind and consciousness (God) being the reason for these realities. Another argument that will be examined is one in the domain of philosophical theology, God's Simplicity. The arguments from the CENTAC model support not only the existence of God, but point toward His simple essence.

5.2 God as Creator—the Kalam Cosmological Argument (KCA)

The KCA comes under a family of arguments known broadly as the cosmological argument. In an extensive historical examination, laid out in his 1980 book, *The Cosmological Argument: From Plato to Leibniz*, William Lane Craig develops a tremendously useful distinction between the three

---

1. See chapter 7.3.1, guideline 2b for an explanation of the application of the argument to Russell's CMI. Another component regarding the intelligibility of the cosmos is examined in the Lonergan-Helminiak understanding of consciousness in chapter 8.

main types of cosmological arguments: "[first], the arguments based on the principle of determination, [second], arguments based on the principle of causality and [third,] arguments based on the principle of sufficient reason."[2] The KCA is an example of the first type. Its roots can be traced back to John Philoponus in the sixth century.[3] This argument finds itself at the interface of philosophy, science, and theology. It sits well with any of paths 6 to 8 where TRP influence SRP (topics that will be fully clarified in chapter 7). The KCA also aligns well with the concept of *creation ex nihilo*, which allows us to identify philosophical assumptions underlying cosmology regarding the finitude of the past. The KCA provides philosophical warrant for assumptions like these which will appear as (path 6). This in turn provides arguments that suggest that finite embodied consciousness cannot have always existed. For this purpose, it is necessary to incorporate this line of argument in relation to the origin of consciousness. The KCA acts as a terminator to any sort of infinite regression. The concept of *creation ex nihilo* can also act as a source of inspiration/motivation for new theories in cosmology related to the expanse of the universe (see path 7 in chapter 7), which in turn can lead to "selection rules" for choosing scientific theories (see path 8 in chapter 7). Most importantly, the KCA provides a route to understanding how consciousness could originate in the first place. Since an infinite number of past events are said to be impossible in a universe with a finite past, our evolutionary history would neither allow consciousness to arrive at the present moment, nor any moment at all.

Although I believe that the Thomistic arguments based on the principle of causality are still cogent in and of themselves, I do not think they are as forceful as the KCA. In this area, I favor the approach of Bonaventure, who disagreed with Aquinas when arguing for the finitude of the past. Aquinas, as I understand him, believed by scriptural faith (it must be emphatically clarified that this is not a form of fideism) that the world was created by God *ex nihilo* with a finite beginning because of his interpretation of Gen 1. Yet, he thought that reason alone could not permit us to make a conclusion either way, since the antonymic nature of the arguments for the infinite past as opposed to those for the finite past had no bearing on God as Creator. Nonetheless, in spite of this, he was persuaded by the science of his time,

---

2. Craig, *The Cosmological Argument*, 283; See, 282–95, where Craig provides an in-depth discussion and examples of these conflations and "blurring/amalgamations" between the three different cosmological arguments. See also Ventureyra, "The Cosmological Argument & the Place of Contestation in Philosophical Discourse: From Plato & Aristotle to Contemporary Debates," 53–54.

3. See introduction for section on Philoponus in the history of the science-theology dialogue.

which affirmed the eternality of the past.[4] Given contemporary discoveries in modern physics and cosmology, I disagree with that position.

The debates that were ignited by Philoponus have continued throughout the ages with al-Ghazali versus Averroes, Saadia versus Maimonides, and Bonaventure versus Aquinas. Immanuel Kant even took a deep interest in the argument with his First Antinomy.[5] Much ink has continued to be spilled over this argument in the past fifty years.[6]

The KCA's modern formulation can be best described with the following deductive argument:

1. Everything that begins to exist has a cause of its existence.

2. The universe began to exist.

3. Therefore, the universe has a cause of its existence.[7]

The first premise of this argument seems certainly more plausible than its denial.[8] The burden of proof is on the objector of such a prin-

---

4. See Aquinas, *De Aeternitate Mundi.*

5. Craig explores the antinomy; he finds solid argumentation on behalf of the book but weak on behalf of the antithesis. See, Craig, *The Kalam Cosmological Argument*, Appendix 2: The Kalam Cosmological Argument and the book of Kant's First Antinomy, 189–205.

6. See Hackett, in his book *The Resurrection of Theism: Prolegomena to Christian Theism.* Originally published in 1957, it had a version of the KCA which came to heavily influence William Lane Craig. So much so that he wanted to pursue his doctoral studies on the KCA, in order to revive the argument in modern philosophy. This testimony can be found on the Evangelical Philosophical Society website: http://www.epsociety. org/library/articles.asp?pid=140; Nowacki, *The Kalam Cosmological Argument for God.* Nowacki provides a useful taxonomy of objections and replies regarding the KCA, he then describes the modal requirements for the KCA, and tries to develop a substantial modality with respect to the thought experiments used to support the KCA; Moreland, *Scaling the Secular City*, 18–42; See also Moreland, "A Response to a Platonistic and a Set-Theoretic Objection to the Kalam Cosmological Argument," 373–90. For a list of published books and articles including defenses and objections up until May 2009, see Muehlhauser, "The Kalam Cosmological Argument: Bibliography," no pages, http:// commonsenseatheism.com/?p=1637.

7. Craig, *The Kalam Cosmological Argument*, 63. The warrant I provide for the first two premises of this argument are quite brief in comparison to the treatments provided by Craig and many of the supporters of the KCA. My intention is to very briefly outline strong reasons to support this argument in lieu of Philoponus' reasoning in the sixth century. I will not engage in all the criticisms and objections to these premises since that would extend far beyond the objective of this paper.

8. Nowacki has sought to examine the first premise and attempt to fortify it beyond logically possibility, in regard to this he states:
For my own part, Craig's curious lack of persuasive power on this subject was one of the factors that motivated development of the theory of substantial possibility presented

ciple. Hume reasoned that since it is possible to conceive the beginning of some uncaused object; and that this demonstrated that such a thing is not necessarily impossible.[9] But this objection seems odd because to merely imagine something coming into being uncaused is mere speculation with neither evidential nor experiential backing. The point is that many things we can imagine do not correspond with reality. One can imagine that rocks can reflect upon the nature of reality, but of course such a thing is impossible given what we know about the capacities of inorganic matter. Much in the same way, I can imagine a Tyrannosaurus rex appearing right before me, but causal mechanisms do not permit such a thing, and so it is for Hume's conceptualization of things popping into being uncaused. It does not add anything to the plausibility of such a thing actually occurring in reality. Mere conceptualization is just that and cannot be held as an objection to causality. Similarly, at the subatomic level there is confusion. Because of the infinitesimal size of particles at that level, the notion that they may come into being uncaused, from nothing, is a misconception. Quantum-mechanical events may not have causally deterministic explanations through classical mechanics, but this in no way suggests that they are uncaused or a-causal.[10]

In defense of the second premise of the argument, two lines of scientific evidence will be presented. The first is the expansion of the universe, which is intimately connected with big bang cosmology. In fact, the expansion of the universe essentially defines the standard big bang model. The Friedmann-Lemaître model, which corresponds with the standard big bang model, describes the increasing distances between galactic bodies as time progresses.[11] What is of note is that this represents the expansion of space-time itself, not pre-existing space.[12] Consequently, in 1929 Edwin Hubble corroborated Friedmann's and Lemaître's calculations, predicting isotropic expansion through the discovery that distant galaxies are receding from our

---

in chapters 3 and 4 of [his book on the KCA]. Craig's underdetermined and somewhat quirky views on causation make it difficult for him to respond to critics who base their objections to the KCA on the mere logical possibility of instantiating an actual infinite. Although Craig himself is aware of the differences between logical possibility and stronger notions of possibility—he firmly asserts that the KCA must be situated within a modal context richer than that of logical possibility—just what Craig means by his frequent invocations to stronger notions of possibility is unacceptably vague.

Nowacki, *The Kalam Cosmological Argument for God,* 28.

9. As argued in Mackie, *The Miracle of Theism,* 94; originates in Hume, *A Treatise on Human Nature,* Book I, Section III, Part III.

10. Davis, *Frontiers of Science and Faith,* 55–56.

11. Ibid.

12. Ibid.

vantage point, reinforcing the idea that this must have been the result of an astounding "explosion."[13] Hubble's deductions were based on the fact that light withdrawing from objects traveling at high velocities is red-shifted.[14] The expansion of the universe indicates less and less dense states. This implies that if one reverses the process and extrapolates back in time, it leads to the conclusion that the universe must have been in an extremely dense state in the finite past.[15] This is known as the singularity whereby all matter, energy, space, and time came into being. A recent critical essay, written by Alex Vilenkin, a leading cosmologist, published at the end of October 2015 in *Inference: International Review of Science* argues that the universe had a beginning and that a "singularity appears to be unavoidable." He co-posited along with two others "The Borde-Guth-Vilenkin theorem." This theorem according to Vilenkin intimates that "if the universe is expanding at an average rate, then its history cannot be indefinitely continued into the past."[16]

The second scientific argument involves the second law of thermodynamics. This argument suggests that given a sufficient amount of time, the universe and all its processes will run down and reach a state of equilibrium or maximum entropy. For instance, the sun cannot burn and produce light ad infinitum; due to this fact, the question arises as to why it hasn't burned out already, if it has existed from an eternal past.

In addition to scientific evidence, two philosophical arguments with intriguing examples will be provided. First, the impossibility of the occurrence of an actual infinite number of past events, which demonstrates that the past, in order to arrive at the present moment, must have had a finite number of events. "Hilbert's Hotel"[17] is used as a "thought experiment" to

13. Hubble, "A Relation between Distance and Radial Velocity among Extra-Galactic Nebulae," 168–73.

14. Ibid.

15. Davies, "The Mind of God," 48.

16. Vilenkin, "The Beginning of the Universe." Vilenkin does not believe one can infer God's existence because of the finitude of the past, but according to his writings he has not really looked at the KCA in depth, though he does deny the first premise for seemingly scientific reasons. See Borde et al., "Inflationary Spacetimes Are Not Past-Complete," 3.

17. See Craig, *The Kalam Cosmological Argument*, 84–86. A good illustration of the incoherence of an infinite number of things existing in reality is David Hilbert's Hotel. This peculiar hotel begins with a finite number of rooms without any vacancies, so that a new guest is turned away. But then the hotel is transformed into one with an infinite number of rooms which are all filled up. Now when a new guest arrives, he or she can go to the first room while the manager shifts every other guest from room 2 to 3, 3 to 4, and so on unto infinity. Things get stranger when an infinite number of guests show up, and each customer is shifted into a room number twice number of the previous room, leaving all the odd-numbered rooms vacant. Thus, accommodating all

illustrate the various absurdities that arise in envisioning the existence of an actual infinite.[18] The second philosophical argument, offered in support of the second premise, states that it is impossible to form an actual infinite by "successive addition." The thought experiment of Tristram Shandy,[19] who takes a year to write a day of his life, is offered as an example to illustrate the various absurdities that arise with the formation of an actual infinite via successive addition. By comparison with development of the KCA over previous historical periods, the two scientific lines of evidence coupled with the two philosophical arguments in more recent years, have indeed positioned the KCA as empirically robust. Thus, the KCA demonstrates through both scientific and philosophical argumentation that the notion of an infinite number of past events leads to absurdities and to the impossibility of any event transpiring within the universe, including the origin of consciousness.

5.3 God as Creator: Teleological

We now shift our attention from the KCA to four teleological arguments. The first is the fine-tuning of the laws of physics as defended by Robin Collins, who has a background in physics and a doctorate in philosophy. The second is built by biochemist and medical doctor Michael Denton on the fine-tuning of the laws of biology. The third argument deals with

---

the infinite number of guests into the odd-numbered vacant rooms and again having an infinite number of rooms filled, even though an infinite number of rooms were previously occupied with zero vacancies. Things can get even more bizarre than this if all the people in the odd-numbered rooms check out. Even though an infinite number of guests would have been checked out, an infinite number of rooms would still remain. See Hilbert, "On the Infinite," 183–201.

18. For an example of a common objection, see Craig's response to Richard Swinburne's objection against an actual infinite existing in time: http://www.reasonablefaith.org/swinburne-on-the-kalam-cosmological-argument.

19. Copan and Craig, *Creation out of Nothing*, 213–16. One can argue that an infinite collection could never be made by beginning at a certain point and just adding members. In essence, one cannot count from one to infinity, nor from infinity to one. This dilemma is known as the impossibility of traversing the infinite. A helpful illustration is the paradox of Tristram Shandy. This paradox, as developed by Craig, shows the impossibility of forming an actually infinite collection of things by adding one member after another. Shandy writes his autobiography at an incredibly slow pace, whereby it takes him a year to record one day of his life. The paradox can be ultimately summed up with this statement: "If Tristram Shandy would have finished his book by today, then he would have finished it yesterday." (Copan and Craig, *Creation out of Nothing*, 216.) So, we can ultimately argue that if the universe does not have a point of beginning, then we have no reason for the present moment to have arrived, but from a common-sense point of view, it has, therefore we know that the events of the physical past are not without beginning.

Stephen Meyer's development of the origin of information for the first self-replicating organism. The fourth and final teleological argument, involves Russell's concept of FINLON with respect to the advent of human consciousness (self-consciousness). This is demonstrated through convergent evolution. As organisms increase in complexity, so begins this groaning towards phenomenal consciousness and finally toward the human capacity for a high level of self-awareness. The order chosen reflects chronological layering in cosmic and biological evolution; each previous step is presupposed for the existence of the next. These arguments which I have provided, combined, and dubbed CENTAC serve not only to demonstrate God's existence but also to ground the origin of consciousness in God, since each are necessary steps in the evolutionary history of the universe, for the advent of self-consciousness.

5.3.1 The Fine-Tuning of the Laws of Physics[20]

In order for cosmic, chemical, and biological evolution to transpire in the first place, the universe must not only have had a beginning, but also must be finely tuned. The fine-tuning refers to the surprisingly precise calibrations of the laws of nature, the initial conditions, and fundamental constants of the cosmos, which permit life to exist. Without the fine-tuning of the universe, neither matter nor motion could exist, and therefore no process of evolutionary change could exist either. Evolution presupposes the fine-tuning of the universe. As we can see, each step of these natural theological arguments plays a role in the possibility and existence of embodied consciousness. God's creative action is necessary, all the way through each step for consciousness to originate.

Collins is considered to be the most rigorous defender of the Teleological Argument as it applies to physics. He has written extensively defending the fine-tuning argument for God's existence,[21] against the alternatives of natural/physical necessity and chance (the multiverse hypothesis). Collins suggests that the universe must be "precisely set" for the existence of

20. Two groundbreaking books that explore the fine-tuning argument include: Barrow and Tipler, *The Anthropic Cosmological Principle*; Leslie, *Universes*.

21. Collins, "A Scientific Argument for the Existence of God: The Fine-Tuning Design Argument," 47–75; Collins, "God, Design, and Fine-Tuning," 54–65; Collins, "The Many-Worlds Hypothesis as an Explanation of Cosmic Fine-Tuning: An Alternative to Design?" 654–66; Collins, "The Teleological Argument: An Exploration of the Fine-Tuning of the Universe," 202–81; Collins, "The Fine-Tuning of the Cosmos: A Fresh Look at its Implications," 207–20.

embodied conscious beings, dubbed embodied conscious agents (ECA—agents for delineating beings with rationality and volition).[22]

The claim made by this version of the Teleological Argument is that the laws, constants, and initial conditions of the universe are balanced on a razor's edge. Each of the laws, constants, and initial conditions are calibrated to an extremely precise degree, to such an extent that they are necessary for the building blocks of self-replicating systems to function. DNA and RNA are fundamental to life; singled-celled organisms and complex sentient beings such as ourselves who possess embodied self-consciousness all have one thing in common: they are intricately designed systems. If these laws and principles were not so finely calibrated, embodied self-consciousness would be impossible. Thus far, we have only begun to scratch the surface of fine-tuning of the laws of nature, having explored neither the fine-tuning of the initial conditions nor the fundamental constants/parameters of physics. We do not have space to examine all, but I will provide one example. It is important to keep in mind that there are many other of these parameters that must be calibrated in a very precise fashion and in line with one another in order to produce life permitting universes, these include (and are not limited to): strong nuclear force constant; weak nuclear force constant; gravitational force constant; electromagnetic force constant; ratio of electromagnetic force constant to gravitational force constant; expansion rate of the universe; entropy level of the universe; velocity of light; age of the universe; uncertainty magnitude in the Heisenberg uncertainty principle; and there are many more (this is just to name a few). Without these and many other parameters being calibrated and tuned with one another, life would not exist, and matter would not even be able to coalesce into stars.[23]

One of the astonishingly precise calibrations required of an initial condition is that of the distribution of mass-energy. Roger Penrose has suggested that "In order to produce a universe resembling the one in which we live, the Creator would have to aim for an absurdly tiny volume of the phase space of possible universes."[24] Penrose's calculations indicate that this volume is $1/10^{10^{123}}$—keep in mind that within the known universe there are 10^{80} atoms (in other words, ten quadrillion vigintillion and one-hundred thousand quadrillion vigintillion atoms). This calculation of Penrose is enormously larger than that! The mind reels and reels at such numbers.[25]

22. Collins, "The Fine-Tuning Evidence if Convincing," 35.

23. See Simon Friederich, "Fine-Tuning," no pages.

24. As quoted in Collins, "The Fine-Tuning Evidence is Convincing," 39. See Penrose, *The Emperor's New Mind*, 343.

25. Penrose, *The Emperor's New Mind*, 343.

To demonstrate how infinitesimally small the probability of reaching such a phase space is, as Collins states, "is much, much greater than the precision that would be required to hit an individual proton given the entire visible universe were a dart board!"[26]

For the sake of simplicity, similar to the KCA, the fine-tuning argument can be summarized with the following syllogism:

1. The fine-tuning of the universe is due either to physical necessity, chance, or design.

2. It is not due to physical necessity or chance.

3. Therefore, it is due to design.[27]

I will provide one reason each as to why it cannot be due to physical necessity or chance. There is no reason to think that the constants, initial conditions, and laws of nature *had* to be the way they are, and that life is inevitable. Did the universe *have* to be the way that it is? This claim makes the suggestion that a life prohibiting universe would be impossible but there is no evidence of this, given the fact that these parameters can take on a large number of differing values without direct dependence on one another.

The other explanation, namely of chance, has a series of objections. Much of Collins's work deals with a single universe, but he also addresses the multiverse.[28] It should be noted that the multiverse could function as a grander design of God. Design and the multiverse are not mutually exclusive options. The multi-world hypothesis is typically set as an alternative to design as an explanation of the fine-tuning of the universe. The multiverse suggests that a large number of combinations of calibrations between the initial conditions, laws of nature, and constants could take place, the majority of which are non-life permitting, but some of which are life permitting. The problem with this view is that there has not been a plausible mechanism

26. Collins, "The Fine-Tuning Evidence is Convincing," 39.

27. Craig is known for summarizing complex arguments in the form of syllogisms for the sake of neatly organizing the major premises in a logically well-structured manner. See, Craig, "Theism Defended," 909; see also whole article, 901–19. Craig also deals with the objection as to the possibility that these three alternatives are not exhaustive, see, Craig, *Reasonable Faith*, 161. Craig does not directly address the combination of chance, physical necessity, and design or the combination of one with design. In my estimation, design would undercut either alternative so that if there are elements of chance or necessity that this is due overall to design.

28. Collins, "The Multiverse, Theism, and the Christian Faith." Invited presentation for Wheaton College Symposium, "String Theory and the Multiverse: Philosophical and Theological Implications," March 26–27, 2008; Collins, "The Multiverse Hypothesis: A Theistic Perspective." 459–80.

provided to explain what is generating, if anything, these universes into being along with their tuning or fine-tuning.[29]

Thus, the laws of nature, the initial conditions, and the constants of physics are best explained by a designing mind of pure self-consciousness transcending the universe. These parameters are fundamental to the existence of embodied beings which possess self-consciousness.

5.3.2 The Fine-Tuning of the Laws of Biology

Before we proceed to the argument concerning the origin of life (origin of specified complex information), it is worth mentioning even if briefly that there is another level of fine-tuning beyond the one previously discussed. This has been extensively explored by Michael Denton. He discusses some unique properties of carbon, oxygen, and water.[30] Denton also discusses the fitness and vitality of the following components that permit a life sustaining universe, such as vital fluids; the fitness of light; the fitness of the elements and the Earth; the fitness of carbon; vital gases; the fitness of the metals; and the fitness of the cell.[31] He suggests that these unique properties seem to be calibrated for complex biochemical systems. For instance, water has a low viscosity, one that is essential for sustaining life. If the viscosity was any lower, it would not permit the microscopic structures of our cells to survive interactions with outside forces. If it was slightly thicker, it would be problematic for pumping blood through our bodies and many of the functions of our circulatory system. Denton explains:

> In the case of higher organisms, it must be low enough [the viscosity of water] to permit perfusion of the tissues via a system of capillaries down to 3 to 5 microns in diameter, which are sufficiently small to bring within the diffusional distance all the tissue cells of the body without their occupying a large proportion of the volume of the tissues. If it was much higher, diffusion would be prohibitively slow, and while very simple cell systems might be possible, large, complex, metabolically active organisms would not. No conceivable, set of compensatory changes—increasing the number of diameter of the capillaries, increasing

29. For other arguments against the multiverse (multiple worlds hypothesis), see Craig, "Theism Defended," 911–12; Collins, "The Fine-Tuning Evidence is Convincing," 36; Collins, "The Anthropic Principle: A Fresh Look at its Implications."

30. See Denton, *Nature's Destiny*, chapters 3 to 6.

31. Ibid., chapters 2–6; 9–10.

the flow rate, or decreasing average cell size, etc.—could be engineered to make mammalian life possible.[32]

These complex biochemical systems provide the necessary conditions for life to originate, exist, and proliferate. Indeed, the evolution of beings with embodied self-consciousness is dependent on many of the parameters that Denton discusses. As Teilhard has argued, there is a deep connection between our complexity and consciousness. Denton's line of reasoning certainly does not contradict such a view.[33]

Both Denton and Kauffman hold notions regarding the origin of life and consciousness very similar to those of this book. Yet, they do not embrace a classical theistic perspective, even though they do seem to indicate there is a deep purposiveness within nature and that this may be the result of a planned order derived ultimately from pure consciousness (whatever that might look like).[34]

Collins suggests that this level of biochemical/biological tuning is dependent upon the fine-tuning at the level of physics.[35] This helps illustrate a cumulative case for God as the ground of all being but as being intimately involved in His creation.

5.3.3 The Birth of Life, the Origin of Information, and Specified Complexity[36]

Fundamental to our discussion on the origin of consciousness is the origin of information for building the first replicating system/organism. This it seems is the first major influx of an information-rich system.[37] Information, as we have seen, is also a vital component to understand the nature and origin of consciousness (as will be discussed on our proposed guidelines regarding scientific theories of consciousness—in chapter 7).

32. Ibid., 36–37.

33. See section 3.6.2.

34. For a treatment of the relationship between biological evolution and Christian spirituality, where I discuss Denton and Kauffman's ideas in greater depth, see Ventureyra, "Science & Christian Spirituality: The Relationship between Christian Spirituality and Biological Evolution," 1–20.

35. Collins, "The Teleological Argument: An Exploration of the Fine-Tuning of the Universe," 225.

36. See footnote 1 of the introduction.

37. Recall our definition of specified complexity in the introduction.

Philosopher of science Stephen C. Meyer[38] has provided the most up-to-date version of the Teleological Argument as applied to the origin of life.[39] It could be called a design-information-theoretic argument. It is worth mentioning that Meyer's work uses standard lines of scientific reasoning like IBE, which do not depend on IDT.

In chapter 7, we will discuss the possibility of God's action through QM and an informationally porous universe. The origin of life, which possesses a high degree of specified complexity (an information-rich system), whether it occurred singularly on Earth or elsewhere in the universe or multiple times, seems like the sort of thing one would expect to originate or emerge at a specific point in the history of the evolution of the universe. It is a necessary component, leading up to consciousness of all stripes and eventually to self-conscious beings such as humans. This

38. Meyer has been working on the problem of the origin of information for many years. This was the subject of his graduate studies at Cambridge University. See Meyer, "An Interdisciplinary History of Scientific Ideas about the Origin of Life"; Meyer, "Of Clues and Causes: A Methodological Interpretation of Origin of Life Studies." Meyer, because of his ties to ID, leaves the identification of the designer unnamed unless asked about his personal beliefs. He then identifies the designer with the Judeo-Christian God. Thomas Nagel has endorsed Meyer's work in his text *Mind & Cosmos*. Nagel acknowledges that he has been deeply stimulated by the arguments articulated by proponents of Intelligent Design (ID) such as Michael Behe and Stephen Meyer. He believes that although they may be partly motivated by their religious perspectives, they "should be taken seriously" and "do not deserve the scorn with which they are commonly met. It is manifestly unfair" (p. 10). Although Nagel recognizes the strong force in much of their argumentation, he still resists the conclusion offered up by exponents of ID in positing a designer: "So my speculations about an alternative to physics as a theory of everything do not invoke a transcendent being but tend toward complications to the immanent character of the natural order. That would also be a more unifying explanation than the design hypothesis" (p. 12). He never fully expresses this more unifying explanation he conceives of; rather, he suggests that "his aim is not so much to argue against reductionism as to investigate the consequences of rejecting it—to present the problem rather than to propose a solution" (p.15).

39. Meyer sees his program with ID as a scientific one, so he would not use the argument in the same manner nor have the same interpretation that I have and its purposes for this book. For instance, in this book I endorse a teleological evolution of sorts, but Meyer rejects any sort of theistic or teleological evolution. See, Meyer, "Teleological Evolution: The Difference It Doesn't Make," 89–100. This is not to say that Meyer does not have legitimate concerns (i.e., information being stored in the laws of nature/constants of physics) but theistic evolution accounts for the evidence better than does his own preference of OEC. Look at chapter 3, for my criticism of OEC when it comes to evolution and the origin of consciousness. As with all ID proponents who want their research to be recognized eventually by other scientists, philosophers, and theologians, they are very careful to distinguish their belief from what they call the "scientific" theory of ID. Meyer has argued for God though; see Meyer, "The Return of the God Hypothesis," 1–38.

presents an extreme influx of information at a given moment, an event like no other when it first occurred throughout the cosmos. This would indeed be classified as a FINLON. Meyer's work is of interest to this book not because of its support of ID, which is a debate that has stirred a wide range of political controversy with much emotion, but because of the rigor and documentation put into his book *Signature in the Cell*. It seems that there is the signature of a mind on the origin of information and the first self-replicating system (the cell).[40] It is important to note that by taking Meyer's work seriously, we do not have to endorse ID, but we must take seriously the implications presented by this massive influx of specified information roughly 3.5 billion years ago on the Earth. The case that a mind is behind this influx in no way supports ID, particularly in an interventionist mode (as those who partake in DAP[41] [will also be explained in chapter 7] might fear). But rather it can be embraced for its fruitfulness to the overall endeavor of this book, namely, understanding the origin of consciousness through the Christian conception of God and creation. The transcendent nature of information is what provides an intuitive clue to its origins. As we have also explored, information not only possesses a transcendent nature, it also seems to play a vital role in understanding the degree of consciousness we possess, including self-consciousness. The fact that the science of consciousness is developing is proven out by the use of theories of consciousness which have given rise to IIT and PSII.

Meyer builds a case for agent causation using standard scientific modes of reasoning. He uses abductive reasoning, which is standard to the historical sciences.[42] This involves making an inference to the best explanation among competing hypotheses.[43] Meyer employs this method in order to explain by what means the origin of life came about. Meyer emphatically states that:

40. Meyer's work on the origin of information subsequent to his graduate studies has been quite lengthy. Some works include: Meyer, "Evidence of Design in Physics and Biology: From the Origin of the Universe to the Origin of Life," vol 9, 53–111; Meyer, "DNA and the Origin of Life: Information, Specification and Explanation," 223–85; Meyer, "The Origin of Biological Information and the Higher Taxonomic Categories," 174–213; Meyer, "DNA: The Signature in the Cell," 293–345.

41. An explanation of DAP: Divine Action Project (DAP) is a project which examines how God interacts with the world.

42. See chapter 2. It was used by both Charles Darwin and Charles Lyell. Charles Lyell mentored Darwin and used abductive reasoning in his *Principles of Geology* wherein he argued if you want to explain events of the past, you should utilize presently acting causes instead of devising exotic explanations. Darwin employed similar reasoning in his *On the Origin of Species*.

43. See Lipton, *Inference to the Best Explanation*.

The inability of genetic algorithms, ribozyme engineering, and prebiotic simulations to generate information without intelligence reinforced what I had discovered in my study of other origin-of-life theories. Undirected materialistic causes have not demonstrated the capacity to generate significant amounts of specified information. At the same time, conscious intelligence has repeatedly shown itself capable of producing such information. It follows that mind—conscious, rational intelligent agency—what philosophers call "agent causation," now stands as the only cause known to be capable of generating large amounts of specified information starting from a nonliving state . . . If there are no other known causes—if there is only one known cause—of a given effect, then the presence of the effect points unambiguously back to the (uniquely adequate) cause.[44]

We can summarize Meyer's findings with the following argument:

1. The origin of information needed to build the first replicating system is due either to natural law, chance, a combination of chance and natural law or design.

2. It is neither due to natural law or chance, nor to a combination of the two.

3. Therefore, it is due to design.[45]

This summarizes the argument for the origin of information needed to build the first self-replicating system. Natural law is clear that self-organizational processes have an inherent incapacity to generate specified information.[46] Chance is not taken seriously by any of the origin of life researchers, since it goes far beyond the probabilistic resources available, since the beginning of the universe.[47] The combination of chance and natural law does not work either; this is demonstrated by computer simulations that attempt to produce plausible naturalistic scenarios:

44. Meyer, *Signature in the Cell*, 341. Since intelligence is the only known cause of specified information, the presence of specified information-rich sequences in even the simplest living systems points definitely to the past existence and activity of a designing intelligence.

45. I am presenting a syllogistic deductive argument to demonstrate that the origin of life is due to design, which is not how Meyer presents the argument in *Signature in the Cell*. He presents it as an IBE.

46. For a thorough investigation of all different self-organizational processes as an explanation for the origin of life, and the RNA world hypothesis, see Meyer, *Signature in the Cell*, chapters 11, 12, and 14.

47. See, Meyer, *Signature in the Cell*, chapter 10.

The failure of genetic algorithms to simulate the production of the specified information within the obviously artificial domain of a computer only provided another illustration of this apparently ubiquitous problem. These attempts to simulate how purely undirected processes might have produced information only pushed the information problem back to a decidedly directing entity—the human mind.[48]

Thus, we are left with one plausible alternative: design, i.e., a mind, a pure self-conscious being outside of the created order.

5.3.4 FINLON—Convergent Evolution, Complexity, and Consciousness

The final step of CENTAC is an argument that seeks to demonstrate that the advent of self-consciousness is through convergent evolution, and through the ubiquitous nature of the organismal development of complexity, leading to higher levels of consciousness, which finds its pinnacle in humanity. The advent of human self-consciousness represents a FINLON in the history of the universe. This FINLON was possible through the planned/directed evolution of organisms throughout our planet's history, initially spawned by the origin of functional information (which also marks a previous FINLON), from which all life was derived. Throughout the animal kingdom we witness the ubiquity of convergence. Animals with different evolutionary lineages produce similar structures. One can think of the nature and function of wings since bats, birds, insects, and pterosaurs all evolved wings for the purpose of flying, even though their last common ancestor would have been wingless. This highlights an analogous structure, as opposed to a homologous structure, which indicates that they share a common origin for a particular structure (in terms of their last common ancestor).

Through the law of complexity/consciousness offered by Teilhard, we see the ultimate progression toward consciousness, through chemical evolution, then onto biological evolution, from which organisms complexify and increase in consciousness. Depending on how we view consciousness, we see a deep correlation between the increasing of complexity and higher levels of consciousness. One need only think of the complexity of the human brain, which is the most complex structure in the known universe. The higher levels of consciousness through which self-consciousness is possible permit not only the realization of self, but of the world around

---

48. Ibid., 294.

us, including the structure of language, logic, science, mathematics, and philosophical and theological reflection. For Teilhard, matter is intimately connected to consciousness, as he espoused with his understanding of panpsychism, designated as one possible explanation, but one which will require further development in terms of precisely *how* it occurs. Though it seems logically possible to embrace panpsychism, I propose instead a complex interaction of God through QM and informational structures, which will be explored in greater detail in chapters 6 and 7.

In reflection on evolution and convergence in the thought of Teilhard, Ilia Delio states:

> The human person is not a ready-made fact but the outflow of billions of years of evolution, beginning with cosmogenesis and the billions of years that led to biogenesis. He [Teilhard] saw evolution of the human person as part of the whole natural process of creativity and generativity. Evolution is not a background to the human story; it is the human story. The human person is not the great exception to evolution but its recapitulation. Convergent evolution is directed toward a projected point of maximum human organization and consciousness. Through the meandering process of evolution consciousness unfolds through the activities of complexification and convergence. Elements are drawn together and, as they are, new levels of relationships are formed. Consciousness is, in a basic sense, the flow of information across complex levels of informational flow. Hence, convergence is the ongoing process of complexification, and the process of convergence and complexity form the necessary conditions for the rise of consciousness in evolution.[49]

Thus, as we see in Delio's observation of the Teilhardian law of complexity/consciousness and evolutionary natural theology, the vitality of convergence for the increases in complexity and consciousness throughout the history of the universe. This raises the issue of diachronic versus synchronic with respect to the origin and evolution of certain phenomena including consciousness. Evolution as we understand it, is largely a diachronic process. Consciousness as we see in phenomenal consciousness (qualia) exists in different degrees throughout the whole of the animal kingdom. Invertebrates for instance, such as coleoid cephalopods—octopuses, squid, and cuttlefish—evolved larger brains and have higher consciousness than many other invertebrates. Animals of different sorts and in varying degrees

---

49. Delio, "Evolution Toward Personhood," 110. See also Teilhard, *Christianity and Evolution*, 87.

possess phenomenal consciousness, but this is precisely the difficult question: how to assess what it's like to be a particular organism.[50] As human observers devoid of the actual experience, we can only empathize based on our own subjective experience what it is like to be another species. As far as we know, humans are the only species that possess the cognitive capacities for higher thought and awareness. This is part of the difficulty with the various theistic evolutionary models and ways of explaining divine action. This is directly related to a FINLON, but the origin of phenomenal consciousness (which many animals possess to varying degrees) is distinct from self-consciousness as exhibited by humans with profound capacities for reflection and thought. To be sure, it is possible that the origin of phenomenal consciousness could also be a FINLON, which eventually led to human self-consciousness, the main FINLON this book is concerned with.

Since a science of consciousness should explain the precise relationship between subjective mental states and brain states, this is where the work of Phillippe Rochat is of extreme interest.[51] Can we measure self-consciousness among humans? Rochat outlines six different levels of self-awareness and how they unfold through the use of recognizing one's self through a mirror, including:

> Level 0: confusion—this is a level of no self-awareness—they are unaware of the mirror reflection or the mirror itself.

> Level 1: differentiation—when looking into a mirror, they realize the mirror reflects things and they can distinguish between their own movement as seen through the mirror and the surrounding environment.

> Level 2: situation—they can make the connection between movements in a mirror with their own body—what is portrayed in the mirror is linked to the self.

> Level 3: identification—they recognize that they can see themselves in the mirror and that it isn't somebody or something else.

> Level 4: permanence—a permanent self is experienced beyond mirror imagery.

50. Thomas Nagel was the first to fully articulate the "what it is like," i.e., the subjective experience of being a particular organism with particular mental states and a conscious life, see Nagel, "What Is It Like to Be a Bat?" 435–50.

51. See Rochat, "Five Levels of Awareness as They Unfold Early in Life," 717–31; Rochat, "Layers of awareness in development," 122–145.

Level 5: self-consciousness or meta-self-awareness—at this stage they not only recognize themselves but recognize that others recognize them.[52]

Rochat's research demonstrates that such things can be measured in infants and toddlers, but this would require a cognitive neuroscience of self-awareness. In turn, it would require a study which deals with the neural correlates of consciousness—this will provide some sort of quantifiable and measurable knowledge.[53] The question also remains as to how this is transferable to our evolutionary history at the moment of "first" consciousness. Several studies have been done on other mammals.

In its application to non-human animals, a test was developed by Gordon Gallup Jr., known as the mirror self-recognition test (MSRT) in which animals are observed to determine whether they possess the ability to recognize themselves in the mirror, as a criterion for self-consciousness (awareness). Mammals, reptiles, birds, and other animals experience qualia to varying degrees, but the question of self-consciousness, and the degree to which it is connected to qualia, seems to require further reflection/analyses.[54] As discussed in the introduction, this is not to say they are not connected; indeed they clearly are, but I'm not sure we can go so far as Damasio and say phenomenal consciousness is dependent on self-consciousness.[55] The MSRT was initially tested on chimpanzees but has been used on a number of animals including other primates (bonobo,[56] Bornean orangutan,[57]) bottlenose dolphin,[58] killer whale,[59] and birds (Eur-

52. Ibid., 718–22.

53. See Lou et al., "Towards a cognitive neuroscience of self-awareness," 765–773; Johnson et al., "Neural correlates of self-reflection," 1808–1814; Keenan et al., "An Overview of Self-Awareness and the Brain." In order to gain accurate results to measure the neural correlates of self-awareness, as they develop through childhood, fMRI and other empirical tests would have to be administered through Rochat's 5 levels but for obvious reasons there may be ethical obstacles to such a thing. The listed experiments use adult subjects.

54. Gallup Jr., "Chimpanzees: Self-Recognition," 86–87.

55. See introduction; Damasio, *Self Comes to Mind*, 181.

56. See Westergaard and Hyatt, "The Responses of Bonobos (Pan paniscus) to Their Mirror Images: Evidence of Self-Recognition," 273–79

57. See Suárez and Gallup, "Self-Recognition in Chimpanzees and Orangutans, But Not Gorillas," 175–88.

58. See Marten and Psarakos, "Evidence of Self-Awareness in the Bottlenose Dolphin (Tursiops truncatus)," 361–79; Reiss and Marino, "Mirror Self-Recognition in the Bottlenose Dolphin: A Case of Cognitive Convergence," 5937–42

59. See Delfour and Marten, "Mirror Image Processing in Three Marine Mammal Species: Killer Whales (Orcinus orca), False Killer Whales (Pseudorca crassidens) and

asian magpie).[60] These animals passed the MSRT with varying degrees of success. There are many other animals that failed the MSRT but have shown other evidence of self-recognition. There are also a series of criticisms and potential methodological flaws concerning the MSRT—one major concern is whether mirror self-recognition truly implies self-consciousness.[61] Studies with non-human animals concerning self-consciousness demonstrate that although some animals may demonstrate prototypic self-consciousness or a lesser degree of self-consciousness, there is still a huge gap between human self-consciousness and the rest of the animal kingdom. In a study where one elephant was able to pass the MSRT, primatologist Frans de Waal and his team observed the convergent relationship with respect to cognitive capacities (i.e., self-consciousness):

> Considered an indicator of self-awareness, mirror self-recognition (MSR) has long seemed limited to humans and apes. In both phylogeny and human ontogeny, MSR is thought to correlate with higher forms of empathy and altruistic behavior. Apart from humans and apes, dolphins and elephants are also known for such capacities. After the recent discovery of MSR in dolphins (Tursiops truncatus), elephants thus were the next logical candidate species. We exposed three Asian elephants (Elephas maximus) to a large mirror to investigate their responses. Animals that possess MSR typically progress through four stages of behavior when facing a mirror: (i) social responses, (ii) physical inspection (e.g., looking behind the mirror), (iii) repetitive mirror-testing behavior, and (iv) realization of seeing themselves. Visible marks and invisible sham-marks were applied to the elephants' heads to test whether they would pass the litmus "mark test" for MSR in which an individual spontaneously uses a mirror to touch an otherwise imperceptible mark on its own body. Here, we report a successful MSR elephant study and report striking parallels in the progression of responses to mirrors among apes, dolphins, and elephants. These parallels suggest convergent cognitive evolution most likely related to complex sociality and cooperation.[62]

California Sea Lions (Zalophus californianus)," 181–90.

60. See Prior, Schwarz and Güntürkün, "Mirror-Induced Behavior in the Magpie (Pica pica): Evidence of Self-Recognition," e202

61. See Suddendorf and Collier-Baker, "The Evolution of Primate Visual Self-Recognition: Evidence of Absence in Lesser Apes," 1671–77; Asendorpf, et al., "Self-Awareness and Other-Awareness II: Mirror Self-Recognition, Social Contingency Awareness, and Synchronic Imitation," 313–21.

62. Plotnik, de Wall, and Reiss, "Self-Recognition in an Asian Elephant,"

Nonetheless, this may be the sort of thing one might expect through a transformative process such as evolution, where there is an increase in complexity and consciousness throughout the passage of time. Simon Conway Morris, in his excellent book, *Life's Solution: Inevitable Humans in a Lonely Universe,* which focuses "on the realities of evolutionary convergence: the recurrent tendency of biological organization to arrive at the same 'solution' to a particular 'need,'"[63] discusses a great many examples of convergence. On a discussion concerning intelligence, he focuses on the bottlenose dolphin:

> In the case of dolphins and humans it will be apparent that despite both are mammals their brains, as Lori Marino stresses, 'represent two fundamentally different cortical organizational themes . . . and thus compels the conclusion that any similar complex cognitive processes between primates and cetaceans are convergent.' The evolution of the brain cannot therefore be divorced from its adaptational requirements and a corresponding moulding of function to those needs. This is important, not only because it confers a predictability to the evolution of the brain structure (see pp. 266–67), but because it also suggests that while the routes to adaptive success, of which one is higher intelligence, may be quite strikingly different (as in dolphins and humans) the end-points converge again and again.
>
> It remains the case that in some ways the dolphin brain is a curious amalgam of a rather archaic brain, reminiscent of the relatively primitive condition seen in such mammals as the hedgehog and the bat, combined with the massive enlargement of the deeply convoluted lobes that gives in an uncanny similarity to our own brains [. . .]. Even so, the complexity of the dolphins' social life, sophisticated and specific communication, and ability to mimic and learn clearly indicate that complex intelligence is not the unique preserve of humans, and that in some respects the convergence seen in dolphins is more compelling than the classical comparisons with apes. To this list should, of course, be added the playfulness of dolphins, perhaps best exemplified by the blowing of bubble-rings [. . .] where both some degree of forethought in their production and an ability to manipulate ascending circle of air are again consistent with some degree of cognition.[64]

17053–057.

63. Conway Morris, "Life's Solution: Inevitable Humans in a Lonely Universe," xii.

64. Ibid., 256–58.

One may ask, if one were a naturalist, as to why these higher degrees of self-consciousness as found in humans and even in dolphins have
eventually manifested themselves throughout the course of evolution?
Dolphins seem to possess a great affinity with human consciousness in
their complex interactions and even self-recognition. As truly remarkable
as this is, why is it possible that humans are the only ones able to possess the degree of self-consciousness that we do? Why can we fathom our
impending death and realize our finitude? Why can we deeply introspect
and contemplate our own nature, the cosmos, God? To be sure, this is
not to take away from the remarkableness of the bottlenose dolphin and
its cognitive capacity, nor to suggest that in thousands of years from now
such self-consciousness may not develop even beyond us, but aside from
mere speculation we cannot place such animals on par with humans despite the convergence in intelligence.[65] Denton lists a series of key adapta-
tions that have been crucial to the success and uniqueness of our species,
including: "(1) high intelligence, (2) linguistic communication, (3) highly
developed visual ability, (4) possession of a superb manipulative tool—the
hand, (5) our upright stance, and (6) our being a highly social species."[66]
In addition, Denton lists the ability to harness fire, which has given us the
ability to advance our technology "through the use of metals, to scientific and technological knowledge."[67] Denton acknowledges that although
"dolphins, parrots, seals, and apes" possess high cognitive capacities, they
pale in comparison to humankind.[68] Physicist Paul C. W. Davies, continuing with this thought, wonders about how we can even comprehend the
rationality and structure of reality—why should it be comprehensible to
us especially from an evolutionary survival standpoint?

> What is remarkable is that human beings are actually able to
> carry out this code-breaking operation, that the human mind
> has necessary intellectual equipment for us to "unlock the
> secrets of nature" and make a passable attempt at completing
> nature's "cryptic crossword." It would be easy to imagine a world
> in which the regularities of nature were transparent and obvious
> to all at a glance. We can also imagine another world in which
> either there were no regularities, or the regularities were so well
> hidden, so subtle, that the cosmic code would require vastly

65. See Penn et al., "Darwin's mistake: Explaining the discontinuity between human
and nonhuman minds"; Sara J. Shettleworth, "Modularity, comparative cognition and
human uniqueness." These articles provide arguments for human cognitive uniqueness.

66. Denton, *Nature's Destiny,* 238.

67. Ibid., 239.

68. Ibid.

more brainpower than humans possess. But instead, we find a situation in which the difficulty of the cosmic code seems almost to be attuned to human capabilities. To be sure, we have a pretty tough struggle decoding nature, but so far we have had a good deal of success. The challenge is just hard enough to attract some of the best brains available, but not so hard as to defeat their combined efforts and deflect them onto easier tasks.

The mystery in all this is that human intellectual powers are presumably determined by biological evolution, and have absolutely no connection with doing science. Our brains have evolved in response to environmental pressures, such as the ability to hunt, avoid predators, dodge falling objects, etc. What has this got to do with discovering the laws of electromagnetism or the structure of the atom? John Barrow is also mystified: "Why should our cognitive processes have tuned themselves to such an extravagant quest as the understanding of the entire Universe?" he asks. "Why should it be us? None of the sophisticated ideas involved appear to offer any selective advantage to be exploited during the pre-conscious period of our evolution . . . . How fortuitous that our minds (or at least the minds of some) should be poised to fathom the depths of Nature's secrets."[69]

Thus, we can see a deep consonance with the issue Davies raises with respect to the universe's comprehensibility and Lonergan's notion of intelligibility.[70] It is also related to the argument of Richard and Gonzalez in *The Privileged Planet* with respect to the correlation between humans living in a habitable zone, which allows them to carry out scientific understanding such as measurability.[71]

Although there is a certain ubiquity to consciousness, as phenomenal consciousness and lower degrees of self-consciousness, none are found like they are in human capacities. Indeed, given the reality of human self-consciousness, this is clearly an instance of a FINLON. The beginning of the universe, the fine-tuning of the laws of nature, initial conditions, constants of physics, the unique properties of carbon, oxygen, and water necessary for complex biochemical interactions, and the necessity of information-rich systems for life and its reproduction, suggest a strong dependence on mind, but all of these are necessary for the advent of embodied consciousness. All of this evidence seems to point persuasively in the same direction; namely toward God. But what are we to make of such a

69. Davies, *The Mind of God*, 149.

70. See chapter 8.3.

71. Ibid.

God? How are we to reflect on such a being? We have now seen five layers of the natural theological arguments supporting God as the source of the origin of human self-consciousness.

5.4 Christian Conception of God: Divine Simplicity (God's Simplicity)

What sort of conception of God serves as a plausible explanation for such phenomena, that is, for the origin of the universe and origin of consciousness? It is worth mentioning that the causal efficacy of God as a transcendent source of being, as a first and final cause, could explain both the origin of the universe and consciousness. Still, the idea of divine simplicity highlights the true nature of God from which all other theological and philosophical notions of God proceed, and is rooted in the classical tradition of Augustine, Anselm, and Aquinas. God's being is His essence/nature. As Peter Weigel observes, divine simplicity functions as a kind of shorthand for the basic ontology of a first cause.[72]

In order to explain the fine-tuning of the laws of nature, the initial conditions, and the constants of physics, the fine-tuning of biochemical systems that life is dependent upon, and the information necessary to produce the first replicating system (the origin of life), one must appeal to something or someone that can ground such phenomena in reality. As will be explored and developed in this argument, such a transcendent being must be absolutely simple. The doctrine of God's simplicity will be fruitful at this juncture.

James E. Dolezal, in exploring the patristic witness to a prototypic understanding of divine simplicity, explains Wolfhart Pannenberg's assessment of the influence of Plato and Aristotle on simplicity: "everything composite can be divided again, and consequently is mutable . . . Everything composite necessarily has a ground of its composition outside of itself, and therefore cannot be the ultimate origin. This origin must therefore be simple."[73]

Dolezal further observes that:

> The Greeks never truly arrived at the notion of a simple God because they were committed to a dualistic conception of reality. The early Christians recognized that if one posited the two first principles, such as God and matter, then neither principle

72. Weigel, *Aquinas on Simplicity*, 38.

73. As quoted in James E. Dolezal, *God without Parts*, 3. See also Pannenberg, *Basic Questions in Theology: Collected Essays*, II:131; Plato, *Republic* 382e; *Timaeus* 41a, b; Aristotle, *Metaphysics* 1074a33–38; 1071b20f.; 1072a32f.; 1072b5–13; and 1015b11f.

could be *absolutely* simple or suffice as the absolute explanation of the universe.[74]

Dolezal's observation illustrates why the sixth-century arguments of Philoponus (which later developed into the KCA) against an infinite past, exemplify the logical inferencing for distinguishing between God and all finite and contingent reality. It offers support to the doctrine of *creation ex nihilo*.

Although both Augustine and Anselm provided their own formulations,[75] Thomas Aquinas[76] was the first to expound a rigorous defense of the doctrine of divine simplicity.[77] In the *Summa Theologiae* he gives the doctrine precedence over all other divine attributes and perfections.[78] This is because the doctrine of divine simplicity delineates the true nature of God from which all other theological and philosophical notions of God proceed. Thomistic philosopher Eleonore Stump indicates that it is "fundamental to the Thomistic worldview [and that, it] is foundational for everything in Aquinas's thought from his metaphysics to his ethics."[79] From a Christian understanding, reality consists of both spiritual and material substances and also what are known as abstract objects. Spiritual beings include God and angels while material beings comprise anything consisting of physical reality, which includes subatomic particles to celestial bodies and abstract objects include things like numbers, propositions, and logic. The understanding Aquinas held of physical beings, follows an Aristotelian framework for matter and form. God's simplicity excludes God from such delineations.

According to Stump, the doctrine as is understood by Aquinas, can be distinguished by three main contentions[80]: i) the impossibility that God possesses any spatial or temporal parts, thus God cannot be a physical entity;

---

74. Dolezal, *God without Parts*, 3n4. For an in-depth treatment of Plato and Aristotle thought in relation to divine simplicity, see Immink, *Divine Simplicity*, 51–73. Some would disagree with this statement as a post-Christian "projection" of the Greek.

75. See Augustine, *De trinitate* VI, 7–8; Anselm, *Monologion* chapter 17.

76. See "Questiones disputatae de potentia," 7.1; "Summa contra gentiles," I.18, I.21–23, I.31; "Summa theologiae," Ia. 3 for the treatment of divine simplicity St. Thomas Aquinas.

77. See Richards, *The Untamed God*, 213.

78. Richards refers to divine simplicity as the first of all divine attributes treated by St. Thomas Aquinas in "Summa theologiae,"

79. Stump, *Aquinas*, 92.

80. Stump suggests that the understanding Aquinas held of the doctrine of simplicity can be explained through three specific theses. See Stump, *Aquinas*, 96.

ii) the impossibility that God possesses any intrinsic accidental properties; and lastly, iii) the only thing attributable to God is His essence or nature.[81]

The first contention affirms a distinction between God and material reality. As Aquinas states:

> It is impossible that matter should exist in God. First, because matter is in potentiality. Hence it is impossible that God should be composed of matter and form. Secondly, because everything composed of matter and form owes its perfection and goodness to its form; therefore its goodness is participated inasmuch as matter participates in form . . . Thirdly, because every agent acts by its form; hence the manner in which it has its form is the manner in which it is an agent. Therefore whatever is primarily and essentially form. Now God is the first agent, since He is the first efficient cause. He is therefore of His essence of a form; and not composed of matter and form. (ST Ia. 3.2.).[82]

Thus, God cannot be a physical being. Moreover, God is simple in the strongest sense since God does not have any parts at all, whether physical, temporal, spatial, or metaphysical. Moreover, no distinctions between property, essence and existence, actuality and potentiality, exist in God. Complementary to this, Aquinas develops God's eternality which includes His being outside of time; hence, no temporal parts.[83] This is derived from the development of divine immutability by Aquinas but ultimately from divine simplicity.[84]

---

81. Stump, "God's Simplicity," 135; Stump, *Aquinas*, 96–98. Stump combines lack of spatial and temporal parts in God because this is crucial for material composition thus in the thought of Aquinas there is a distinction between God and such parts.

82. Aquinas, "Summa theologiae," in Sancti Thomae de Aquino Opera Omnia Iussu Leonis XIII. Vols. 4–12 of 50 vols.

83. Stump, *Aquinas*, 96.

84. Ibid. It is worth mentioning that in relatively recent years, there have been several erudite defenses of divine simplicity. These include a 1989 article by the late Fr. Dewan, entitled "Saint Thomas, Alvin Plantinga and the Divine Simplicity" published in *the Modern Schoolman,* which is a response to Plantinga's Aquinas lecture of 1980 entitled: *Does God Have a Nature?* Other defenses include Peter Weigel's book-long treatment, *Aquinas on Simplicity,* and most recently Dolezal's *God without Parts,* another full-length treatment of the subject. See also Stump and Kretzmann, "Absolute Simplicity," 353–91. The most comprehensive critique of divine simplicity is found in Christopher Hughe's *A Complex Theory of a Simple God.* Nonetheless, despite the many criticisms and detractions, the doctrine is alive and well in contemporary philosophical and theological discussions.

The transcendence of God beyond space and time is derived from Aquinas in his development of divine immutability, but ultimately from divine simplicity.[85]

The second contention is exemplified when Aquinas states: "There can be no accident in God. First, because a subject is related to an accident as potentiality not actuality, for with regard to an accident a subject is in actuality in a certain respect. But being in potentiality is entirely removed from God" (ST Ia.3.6.).

The important discrepancy to note here is that an extrinsic change to the properties of a particular entity will not change the entity, whereas an intrinsic change will. Yet as Stump notes, "no entity, not even a mathematical or divine entity, can be exempted from having extrinsic accidental properties," even though they lack intrinsic accidental properties.[86]

The third contention regarding divine simplicity in Aquinas's thought is that God is His own nature or essence.[87] There cannot be any distinction between properties in God. All created things possess differences between their essence and existence but not so for God. According to the doctrine of divine simplicity, God is equivalent to His existence.

We can now explore some basic implications of the KCA for the first contention of divine simplicity. The absence of properties can be deduced through an apophatic theology. As the cause of space and time, this cause must transcend space and time, rendering the cause to exist timelessly and non-spatially.[88] This would also imply that the cause is immutable and immaterial, since timelessness implies immutability and immutability, immateriality. The cause must also be without beginning and uncaused. Reexamining a summary of the understanding Aquinas gives us of divine simplicity echoes this since, as Stump has noted: "It is impossible that God have any spatial or temporal parts that can be distinguished from one another as here rather than there or as now rather than then, and so God cannot be a physical entity."[89]

---

85. Stump, *Aquinas*, 96. In a justification for combining the lack of spatial and temporal parts, "Aquinas denies that there is any matter in God or that God has any dimensions, and so he rules out spatial parts in God. In addition, Aquinas derives eternality, which includes God's being outside of time, from divine immutability, which he derives in turn from divine simplicity. On Aquinas's view, then, the doctrine of simplicity also has the implication that God has no temporal parts." The key is that it has the implication. See *ST* Ia.3.1–2.; *ST* Ia.10.1; *ST* Ia.9.1.

86. Stump, *Aquinas*, 97.

87. Ibid.

88. Craig, *Reasonable Faith*, 152.

89. Stump, *Aquinas*, 96.

Thus, the implications the KCA derives of a transcendent cause bear a resemblance to the first contention of Aquinas of the simplicity of God since immateriality, timelessness, non-spatiality, and immutability are established. This is in line with Weigel's observation that:

> [T]he claims of simplicity function as a kind of shorthand for the basic ontology of a first cause, then it is natural to place simplicity right after the arguments for the existence of a first cause. Aquinas, moreover, realized that the claims of simplicity articulate an ontological situation that the other major predicates presuppose in the state of affairs that they each describe as true of the first cause.[90]

This method of establishing an apophatic description of God through the KCA is evidentially based through use of the best science and philosophy at hand. For this reason, it can be deemed superior to arguments based on the principle of causality for deriving the simplicity of God, though cosmological arguments based on the principle of causality are nonetheless powerful for establishing a God who sustains the universe. But what exactly does God's simplicity entail?

Since Aquinas anticipated an objection being raised to this when he expounded his argument for a first cause, which is central to establishing the transcendence of God beyond physical reality, a crucial distinction must be made before we proceed. The objection lay in bringing attention to an apparent confusion between essences with existence. This illustrates the distinction between God's nature and the fact that God exists.[91] One may

90. Weigel, *Aquinas on Simplicity*, 38.

91. See Weigel, Aquinas on Simplicity, 74. Weigel points out:

'Does God exist?' is a separate issue from the question 'What (essentially) is God?' Thus, to identify essence and existence is to focus these two separate matters since we do not know God's essence but we know that God exists. (One could go in the reverse direction. To know that God's essence is somehow 'just to exist' does not guarantee there is in fact a God.) This manner of objection confuses the character of the divine essence with an inquiry into its existential status." See Aquinas, De potential q.7 ad.2 ad 1. The following quote "In reply to [this objection] it must be said that 'being' (ens) and 'is' (esse) is said in two ways, as in Metaphysics V. Sometimes [they] signify the essence of a thing or the act of existing; at other times they signify the truth of a proposition, even in things which have no being: just as we say 'blindness is' because it is true that a man is blind. Accordingly, when John Damascene says that the being of God is evident to us, the being of God is understood as in the second way but not in the first. For in the first way God's existence is the same as his substance, and so just as his essence is not known neither in his esse [act of his existence]. In the second way we know that God is because we conceive this proposition in our mind [reasoning] from his effects."

want to know what kind of God exists, but the question of God existing is a separate one. Having said that, one can make certain deductions about a cause after one legitimizes the existence of the cause.

It is important to note at this juncture that Aquinas is not convinced by arguments made a priori as is the case with the ontological argument from Anselm. It would be quite conceivable to perceive an association between essence and existence in God, as formulating some sort of ontological argument; by just affirming the essence of God, we would know His existence. [92]

Thus, by ruling out any *intrinsic* composition within God, whether metaphysical or physical, we separate God from all contingent beings (everything that is not God which includes *all* things, whether concrete or abstract objects), this doctrine also serves to refute any pantheistic or panentheistic tendencies. Some thinkers including Teilhard and Clayton (if we interpret him correctly), see panentheism as encompassing a 'world spirit' immanent in the created order, so that God's body, i.e., the created order, is also occupied by His spirit and is unfolding through the evolution of the cosmos. A thinker like the physicist Frank Tipler sees God as being represented by the singularity, where God as first cause encompasses all the laws of physics and matter. The point is, as Weigel reinforces, the understanding Aquinas gives us of divine simplicity rules out any such notions and reveals a strict and absolute distinction between the simplicity of God and the complexity of the universe (or that of matter).[93]

5.5 Conclusion

Although we see the importance of convergence, when it comes to self-consciousness and higher capacities for consciousness and cognition, it begs for a reasonable response. Given the multiple lines of argumentation we have dubbed CENTAC, we observe that not only do we find ourselves in a finite universe as demonstrated by the scientific and philosophical evidences of the KCA, which give us reasonable grounds to infer *creation ex nihilo*, we also see a series of finely-tuned calibrations of the laws of both biology and physics, that allow for the existence of matter, eventually

---

Maritain, "Toward a Thomistic Idea of Evolution," 87: "It is to God that the ultimate perfection of life belongs, for in Him intellection is not something other than existence, (God has the idea of Himself, and this idea is His being)."

92. Weigel, *Aquinas on Simplicity*, 74.

93. See Weigel, *Aquinas on Simplicity*, 174–75. I will return to the linkage between God's simplicity and the similarity between human's immaterial aspects briefly in the conclusion.

life, and ECAs. These conditions permit information and self-replicating systems to survive in such an environment. We also witness the ubiquity of consciousness in the form of both phenomenal and self-consciousness in variant degrees throughout the animal kingdom, with a culmination in humankind. The origin of life indeed represents a FINLON where life has become a regular and consistent feature of the universe since its first presentation, the same is true for both phenomenal and self-conscious existence, which as we also witnessed are bound up with one another. Despite the great similarities with other animals such as dolphins, we also see the uniqueness of humanity still (this is not to preclude the evolution of other beings with higher conscious life, elsewhere in the universe or in the future). Nonetheless, convergence is indeed ubiquitous throughout biological evolution. This is best explained by PE or DE. It is not the result of a merely naturalistic and undirected universe without purpose. There is collusion, so to speak, to CENTAC, which is undergirded by the action of God, as explained through the doctrine of divine simplicity, which transcends matter, space, time, and all metaphysical categories. Extreme levels of complexity are founded upon absolute simplicity, as founded in God's simplicity. We now turn to arguments from systematic theology, which piggyback on CENTAC and God's simplicity to explain the image-likeness stamp of humans, moral consciousness, and the Trinitarian Mode of Creation, by which God acts within the created order to bring about his desired plan. We may end with an eloquent paraphrasing of Darwin by Denton, which illustrates the wonder of creation because of the majesty of God:

> In the context of a teleological view of the cosmos, even if much of the overall order of organic nature was determined from the beginning, it is surely conceivable that the Creator, to paraphrase Darwin in the last paragraph of the *Origin of Species*, could have gifted organisms not only with the capacity of growth, reproduction, inheritance, and variability, but also with a limited degree of genuine autonomous creativity so that the world of life might reflect and mirror in small measure the creativity of God.[94]

---

94. Denton, *Nature's Destiny*, 365.

Chapter 6

Arguments from Systematic Theology

6.1 Introduction

THE FOLLOWING ARGUMENTS ARE inspired through the writings found in the Old and New Testaments, which support the origin of consciousness (as manifested in the origin of moral consciousness, which is a subsequent development of self-consciousness) being grounded in the Christian conception of God and creation. The method I propose in this chapter is one of analyzing the concept of the origin of consciousness through certain biblical texts, namely those which exemplify our creation in the image-likeness of God, our capacity for moral consciousness, and the involvement of the Holy Trinity in creation. I presuppose an intimate connection between the understanding of consciousness within this book and the biblical texts being utilized. This is not to argue that the original authors had an understanding of consciousness even remotely the same, but that given modern perspectives, we can see how these texts can still compliment an understanding of God's intimate relation with humans and our inner conscious life. I also presuppose that our moral awareness is intimately connected with our ability to discern between good and evil, and that this has been bestowed on us by our Creator (regardless of the method, i.e., different models of creation and evolution).[1] I also argue that the three persons of the Trinity each have a role in our creation. The authors of the holy texts were not cognizant of our current science but there is a consonance between modern cosmology and the notion of *creation ex nihilo* and our ability to understand goodness and evil.

---

1. See chapter 3.

6.2 Image-Likeness of God

In our discussion regarding the image-likeness of God, I wish to maintain the link between the two terms, following biblical scholar C. John Collins, I take them as synonymous with no real distinction:

> Since about the time of the Reformation, scholars have recognized that this [the separation and distinction between image/likeness] does not suit the text itself. First, there is no "and" joining "in our image" with "after our likeness." Second, in Genesis 1:27 we find simply "in God's image"; and finally, in Genesis 5:1 God made man "in the likeness of God." The best explanation for these data is to say that "in the image" and "after the likeness" refer to the same thing, with each clarifying the other.[2]

Theologian Millard J. Erickson, in his extensive work of systematic theology, *Christian Theology*, indicates that in discussions regarding the image-likeness of God, there are typically three main views: the substantive, relational, and functional.[3]

He links the image-likeness of God to our experience of consciousness and God. The substantive view is the one that I think is most relevant to our study concerning the origin of embodied self-consciousness. Our capacity for reason, self-knowledge, creativity, moral awareness, etc., mirrors that of God. The relational view suggests that we only possess the image-likeness of God when we are in relationship with Him; the substantive denies even the need to recognize the existence of God to bear his image-likeness. Lastly, the functional role suggests that humans carry a certain role within the created order, such as being a king and having dominion over the Earth and other creatures.[4]

The mere suggestion that humanity shares in God's image-likeness is demonstrative of something unique that the biblical authors saw in human nature. The main text of such an understanding is found in Genesis 1:26–28:

> And God said: 'Let us make man in our image, after our likeness;
> and let them have dominion over the fish of the sea, and over the

---

2. Collins, *Genesis 1–4: A Linguistic, Literary, and Theological Commentary*, 62.

3. See Erickson, *Christian Theology*, 498–510; Erickson, *Introducing Christian Doctrine*, 172–75.

4. Ecological sensitivity, for some theologians, has led to a preference for this view over the substantive and relational, in order to inspire human action in correcting the ecological crisis. Ironically the same verses about subduing or having dominion over the earth in Gen 1:26–28 as opposed to using the term stewardship are used to justify biblical action against human intervention in the ecological crisis. See, Davis, *Scripture, Culture, and Agriculture: an Agrarian reading of the Bible*.

fowl of the air, and over the cattle, and over all the earth, and over every creeping thing that creepeth upon the earth.' And God created man in His image, in the image of God He created him, male and female created He them. And God blessed them; and God said to them: 'Be fruitful, and multiply, and fill the earth, and subdue it; and have dominion over the fish of the sea, and over the fowl of the air, and over every living thing that creepeth upon the earth.'

This image-likeness stamp, which humans receive from God, ties in well with our understanding of consciousness (i.e., embodied human self-consciousness). This self-consciousness is the first step in humanity's capacity to possess awareness of one's self and one's relation to God and the rest of the created order.[5] With such a realization, (i.e., self-consciousness) comes the eventual ability to fathom and understand our purpose and plan in relation to creation. Humans can interact in a manner with God's created order, which is potentially beneficial to other humans, organisms, and the environment. Unfortunately, the converse is also true and has manifested itself in such a way that communication and relations have been severed not only with God but with fellow humans, and also other organisms and the environment. Throughout the NT, the image of God is related to Christ: Heb 1:3; Col 1:13–15; 1 Cor 11:7; Rom 8:29; 2 Cor 3:18; and 2 Cor 4:4–7. These verses exemplify and associate the glory of God as manifested through Christ and the perfect demonstration of God's image through the incarnation. It is through the words and deeds of Christ that we can see the plan for creation, since Christ exemplifies how we should love one another. Part of this image-likeness is not only our self-consciousness, but it is our self-consciousness as the transcendent component of our existence, which is manifested in God and imparted to us. Also associated with this transcendent aspect of consciousness with which we are endowed is a capacity to love, even to the point of doing so selflessly. God's love for humanity is also manifested in the resurrection of Christ, which is promised to all humans at the end of this temporal creation. It is that we share the spirit given to us, as it was given to Christ (1 Cor 15:22; Rom 8:11).

Thus, when it comes to the origin of consciousness, the image-likeness of God is intimately linked through our evident capacities for higher cognitive functions, including self-knowledge and moral awareness, which mirror that of God. It is our experience of consciousness and the very being of God that reflects the plausibility of God as the Creator of consciousness (given

5. It is this realization of self which initiates further evolution of our consciousness, so that we are able to develop the capacities for understanding nature, mathematics, science, and ourselves with all of our creative capacities toward technology.

CENTAC and our human experience in the natural world). Bernard Lonergan explicates how our image-likeness to God is exemplified in creation:

> To say that God created the world for his glory is to say that he created it not for his sake but for ours. He made us in his image, for our authenticity consists in being like him, in self-transcending, in being origins of value, in true love.[6]

This quote is a nice segue into moral consciousness. Lonergan has stated that authenticity which associates us to God is also "our deepest need and most prized achievement."[7] This is accomplished through self-transcendence.[8]

6.3 Moral Consciousness: A Propensity Toward Love?

Although mentioned in passing throughout the book thus far, this element of self-consciousness, i.e., moral self-consciousness, is important to our experience of consciousness. Moral consciousness finding its grounding in God, in the classical Christian conception of God, will allow Christianity to interact with evolutionary psychology and sociobiology on the origins of morality. Recall as well from chapter 4 that crucial to Teilhard's law of complexity-consciousness was the concept of love.[9]

Our capacity for moral consciousness allows us to live alongside the rest of creation by providing grounding for our morality through God. Lonergan spoke of a moral self-transcendence[10] or moral self-consciousness, which we will refer to as a moral consciousness. For Lonergan, moral self-transcendence is predicated on the ability to assess and judge values.[11] Embedded within our human nature and embodied consciousness is the ability to discern good from evil (Gen 3:3, 22). This is indeed seen as an awakening in the creation narrative with respect to the human condition, which undoubtedly plays a component/role in the origin of human self-consciousness. I would argue that moral self-consciousness/consciousness in the recognition of objective moral values and duties is a step forward in

6. Lonergan, *Method in Theology*, 117.

7. Ibid., 254.

8. Ibid., 104.

9. See sections 4.3 and 4.4.1.

10. See Lonergan, *Method in Theology*, 38, 45, 104, 121–22, 233, 242, 252, 289, 338, 357–58.

11. Ibid., 38.

God's PE/DE. Without the existence of God as argued through CENTAC and the classic Christian conception of God, which includes the attribute of omnibenevolence, there would be no way of grounding objective moral values and duties. If left to a naturalistic universe without, at a minimum, a classic theist position, morality would be relegated to being a spinoff of the process of sociobiological evolution. Moral actions would not necessarily be good or evil, but relative to how species with higher consciousness evolved, so certain actions would become taboo, such as murder or rape, but they would not necessarily be objectively morally wrong.[12]

We are now progressing from the origin of self-consciousness to the origin of moral self-consciousness, which is a directly associated step forward in God's plan/direction for us. Not only does it symbolize an awakening and self-realization, predicated on human ability to deliberate freely and to consciously distinguish good and evil, but it indeed represents a deep anthropological truth, even if through allegorical form.

Moreover, this allegorical representation of a deep awakening in self-consciousness regarding moral truths must have occurred at a specific moment in the history of the cosmos. Just as the advent of self-consciousness, moral consciousness represents an evolution of self-consciousness and moral awareness. Its etiology lies in God just as the origin of consciousness does, in terms of crude self-awareness or consciousness (this is just one step toward its perfection as manifested in Christ). For instance, as a thought experiment, I suggest that we can still keep an evolutionary view since this would be an historical one, to approach the Genesis narrative of "the Fall," with respect to the advent of moral agency, to ask: when did "Adam and Eve" develop a moral conscience—inside or outside of the "garden of Eden?" They were segregated from natural evil at a particular point in their evolution, so that they were not yet "responsible" for their actions. In a sense, the two forms of consciousness can coincide, but whether the remnants of this "original selfishness"[13] could be said to still affect them, once they were

---

12. This revolves around the debate whether we can ground objective moral values and duties naturalistically without recourse to God. Most theists and atheists alike would agree that this would be impossible. It also involves debates between "moral epistemology" and "moral ontology." The debate between Paul Kurtz and William Lane Craig examine these ideas. See Garcia and King, eds. *Is Goodness without God Good Enough? A Debate on Faith, Secularism, and Ethics.* When pressed hard enough, atheists admit that there are no objective moral values and duties, this is if they are to be consistent with their worldview. Nihilists fit under such a category but secular humanists in general hold to objective moral values and duties without any true grounding for them.

13. See Domning and Hellwig, *Original Selfishness: Original Sin and Evil in the Light of Evolution*, 184. See next page for further details.

expulsed from the Garden of Eden, is a matter of further reflection. Could it be instead that they had become tainted by their sin of pride?

Without delving deeply into debates regarding free will, when presented with a choice or multiple choices in any venue—in this particular case, moral decisions—we deliberate one way or another to choose the good or the evil. Through this ability we partake in a freedom bestowed upon us by the Creator (Gen 3:3, 22), a manifestation of the ultimate eternal divine freedom to create beings which can choose to love Him or not. We ourselves participate in a finite freedom, albeit constrained by the laws of physics, our genetics and environment to emulate our Creator's goodness (Eph 3:19). Gen 3, even if taken to be an etiological myth, exemplifies this. It speaks great truths about our human condition and the predicament we find ourselves in. Humans are also given the capacity to reject a true relationship with God, by either outright rejecting or suppressing our spiritual and moral likeness to Him.

We are endowed with a capacity to distinguish goodness from evil (Gen 3:22), which comes from the recognition of our image-likeness being derived from the ultimate source of goodness. In response to knowing evil and always choosing to do good despite our proclivities or desires to do otherwise, Christ, as the true manifestation of God's image-likeness, always reminds us to center our desires and consciousness toward love. This is exemplified not only in the command to love God first and foremost above all, but also in the command to love our neighbor as ourselves (Matt 22:37–39). Jesus commands us to love one another as he has loved us (John 13:34–35). God's image-likeness stamp on our true human nature is through knowing God's love, through knowing ourselves through this ability of self-consciousness and deliberation, as is grounded in Jesus's words: "Dear friends, let us love one another, for love comes from God. Everyone who loves has been born of God and knows God. Whoever does not love does not know God, because God is love" (John 4:7–8). Lonergan would refer to love for God, love for others, as a mode of self-transcendence, which would be the fulfillment of our self-consciousness. Or as Lonergan would put it "being in love with God is the basic fulfillment of our conscious intentionality."[14]

Jesus asks us to love in a radical manner, to love those who are our enemies and who persecute us: "But I tell you, love your enemies and pray for those who persecute you, that you may be children of your Father in heaven. He causes his sun to rise on the evil and the good, and sends rain on the righteous and the unrighteous" (Matt 5:44–45). Jesus also asks us to love completely selflessly and in a radical form of perfect altruism,

---

14. Lonergan, *Method in Theology*, 105.

which will help us break free from the shackles of our selfishness and sinful desires, in the form of sacrificing ourselves for our neighbor but to ultimately also save ourselves from our sinful and selfish nature. "My command is this: Love each other as I have loved you. Greater love has no one than this: to lay down one's life for one's friends" (John 15:12–13). It is in this sense that we can freely partake in God's love to others, through being created in His image-likeness.

Catholic paleontologist Daryl Domning and the late theologian Monika Hellwig entertain an intriguing idea of perfect altruism that is only exemplified through Christ in the created order. It helps break us free from our evolutionary roots of selfishness, which before the advent of moral consciousness, was manifested in humans through a propensity and innate predisposition to do everything in our capacity (or that of any particular organism) to survive. All organisms are selfish in a non-pejorative sense, but merely because of the propensity to survive.[15] Domning calls this inherent selfishness "original selfishness," as a substitute to what is typically referred to as "original sin."[16] All organisms share this original selfishness, from the origin of life to all present organisms, including humans. The difference with humans is that we have a moral consciousness to choose evil through free will, whereby guilt can result. Moral evil, though largely passed on through cultural transmission from sinful societies, is not the root. Moral evil is not the result of a pre-historic Fall, so eventually moral evil evolves out of physical evil. However, perfect unselfishness cannot come from natural processes. We need supernatural grace transcending our original selfishness through Christ's salvation. Thus, Domning and Hellwig see our emulation of the perfect altruism of Jesus, as portrayed through his words and ultimate act of love, his sacrifice on the Cross, as the way we may overcome "selfishness" and mere reciprocal altruism, as is found through much of the animal kingdom.[17] Similarly, in reference to Christian authenticity, Lonergan expresses how this is truly manifested:

> Christian authenticity—which is a love of others that does not shrink from self-sacrifice and suffering—is the sovereign means for overcoming evil. Christians bring about the kingdom of God in the world not only by doing good but also by overcoming evil with good (Rom 12, 21).[18]

15. Domning and Hellwig, *Original Selfishness*, 184.

16. Ibid.

17. Ibid.

18. Lonergan, *Method in Theology*, 291.

All of these verses exemplify God's perfect image-likeness through Christ, who embodies the perfect moral consciousness which is geared toward love for one another. This is demonstrated through God's true love and purpose for His creation. Jesus through the ultimate act of love and humility (His sacrificing atonement) is the One who demonstrates the true image-likeness stamp of God. Similarly, as has been explored in our section on Teilhard, as Teilhard views the manifestation of self-moral-consciousness in terms of love: "the final success of hominization" which is identified not with blind natural process but with Christ (Omega Point)—we are trending toward this ultimate love through our evolution, or "involution," as Teilhard would say, toward a collective consciousness culminating in the *parousia*.[19]

6.4 A Trinitarian Mode of Creation

Theologian Jürgen Moltmann sees the Christian doctrine of creation as a development of the OT monotheism whereby "the Father created heaven and earth through the Son in the Spirit."[20] Christ is seen through the NT as "the mediator in creation." The basis for this according to Moltmann is found in the writings of St. Paul (1 Cor 8:6; Heb 1:2).[21] Christ is identified not only as God's Son but also as His Eternal Wisdom (Prov 8:22–31). The Holy Spirit is also a co-Creator. It is the Holy Spirit which is responsible for the continual sustaining of creation, preserving it against annihilation due to the eschatological dimension of the Holy Spirit's role in creation:

> The presence and the efficacy of the Spirit is the eschatological goal of creation and reconciliation. All the works of God end in the presence of the Spirit . . . "When though takest away their breath, they die and return to their dust. When thou sendest forth thy breath, they are created; and though renewest the face of the ground" (Ps 104:29–30). This means that the Spirit is the efficacious power of the Creator and the power that quickens created beings. It also means that this power itself is creative, not created, and that it has been 'breathed forth' by the Creator, that is to say, emanated. And this, in its turn, means that in the Spirit the Creator himself is present in his creation. Through the presence of his own being, God preserves his creation against the annihilating Nothingness.[22]

19. See Teilhard, *The Phenomenon of Man*, 308n1; chapter 7 research guideline 7c.

20. Moltmann, *God in Creation*, 94.

21. Ibid., 94–95.

22. Ibid., 96–97.

The Father sends out the Son and the Holy Spirit. All act as co-creators. The direct work of the Father involved in creation is exemplified (Gen 1:3, 6, 9, 11, 14, 20, 24, 26; Ps 148:5; Isa 44:24, 45:12; Heb 11:3). The work of the Son in Creation, the one who liberates and redeems it, is also the Word: (John 1:1–3) and throughout the NT (John 17:24; Rev 1:8; Col 1:16–17; Rom 11:36), the Holy Spirit is the One who provides life to the world and brings all of it into participation in God's eternality (Gen 1:2; Job 26:13, 33:4; Ps 33:6, 104:30; 1 Cor 6:13–20, 2 Cor 1:22, 5:5; Eph 1:14). The Trinitarian doctrine of creation provides for and demonstrates God's transcendence and immanence. For theologians like Moltmann[23] and others including Teilhard and Clayton this is suggestive of a panentheism. This is a possible, though not necessary interpretation, particularly if we take seriously the implications of the KCA through the doctrine of divine simplicity.

In recent years, Dembski has developed an interesting concept of the Trinitarian interpretation of creation, which he has dubbed "the Trinitarian Mode of Creation" [24] (please see appendix 2 below). Dembski demonstrates a deep correlation between this mode of creation and "the mathematical theory of information"[25] as developed by Claude Shannon in his 1949 book *The Mathematical Theory of Communication*. In a nutshell Dembski associates God the Father as the Information Source, God the Son, represents the message through Jesus who is the incarnation of the divine Logos and the "transmitter" represents God the Holy Spirit taking the message and empowering it.[26] From there the message is to be transmitted to its receiver and destination, via a component known as the "signal," which entails the "divine energy," which represents God's activity in creation.[27] From the perspective of biblical theology, it is God the Father who initiates and is the originator of creation. He is the One who is the transcendent cause of the universe, the laws of physics and the propensity for evolution (Gen 1:1) through informational processes through the Word ([John 1:1–3] the message [God the Son]) playing a fundamental role within information (processing units of life) and the origin of consciousness while the Holy Spirit is intimately transmitting and is involved in the breath and sustaining of life and consciousness (Gen 1:2; Job 26:13). Therefore, we have God intimately involved in a Trinitarian sense, with respect to the origin of consciousness

23. Ibid., 98.

24. Dembski, *The End of Christianity*, chapter 10—The Trinitarian Mode of Creation.

25. Ibid., 86.

26. Ibid., 87.

27. Ibid.

through his image-likeness, moral self-consciousness—revealed through Christ and guided by the Holy Spirit in acting with our self-consciousness throughout temporal existence.

A theologically significant aspect of this communication system is the component known as the "noise source," which Dembski explains as "the distorting effects of sin and the Fall, which attempt to frustrate the divine energy. Hence the Lord's Prayer, 'Thy will be done on earth as it is in heaven.'"[28]

Directly related to this transmission of information from the Holy Trinity to creation is the nature of information. Dembski makes the point that the material medium where information can be located can always be destroyed, but information itself is indestructible. He argues that the information by which God created us is indestructible despite the effects of sin to distort such information. The ultimate source of information is the divine Logos, which provides a reliable source for the intelligibility of the world. Despite this intelligibility much of our knowledge seems distorted, and this Dembski attributes to the effects of the Fall, as he states:

> At the heart of the Fall is alienation. Beings are no longer properly in communion with other beings. We lie to ourselves. We lie to others. And others lie to us. Appearance and reality, though not divorced, are out of sync. The problem of epistemology within the Judeo-Christian tradition isn't to establish that we have knowledge but instead to root out the distortions that try to overthrow our knowledge.[29]

According to this approach, sin is appropriately seen as a communication breakdown between the Creator and His creation. What's more is that we can sense this communication breakdown amongst ourselves, even though we are able to communicate and transfer information to a high degree. It is fascinating to ponder how much more accurately we could communicate with God and ourselves without such a distorting effect.

A key concept we have already discussed is the transcendent nature of information,[30] and the understanding Dembski gives us of divine action, that the universe is "informationally" open. Dembski argues that indeterministic models of the universe through quantum mechanics provide the possibility for "divine action [to] impart information into matter without disrupting ordinary physical causality."[31]

28. Ibid.
29. Ibid., 104.
30. Ibid., chapter 11—Information Transcending Matter.
31. Ibid., 117.

6.5 Conclusion

God is the ultimate source of all goodness. This led to the evolution of humans who have come to recognize the purity of such love. Thus, we can recognize an intimate connection between the origin of self-consciousness as manifested through our innate moral awareness, given to us from our Creator who has stamped us with his image-likeness. This original stamp has provided us with the capacity to come to know truth and love as illustrated through the deeds of Jesus (His radical altruism through his perfect sacrifice) and His words (to love one another in spite of enmity). Despite the distorting effects of sin, which evolved through our "original selfishness," and our proclivity for survival, we can come to rebel against these predispositions through God's grace and our capacity to recognize the source of our goodness (even if in a tainted state). In the following chapter (guidelines 6b–d), we explore potential avenues of research concerning these arguments from systematic theology under path 7 in Russell's CMI.[32] The biblical authors did not possess the same cosmology, nor did they possess the same scientific understanding as we do in modern times, but God's creative capacity and the doctrine of image-likeness is still affirmed, without the same scientific and philosophical understanding. Our theologies have evolved since then. Nonetheless, the purpose is to incite research through these notions, in systematic theology to provide inspiration and/ or motivation for new scientific theories, as will be exemplified by guidelines 6 b, c, and d in section 7.3.1.

32. See section 7.3.1.

Chapter 7

The Application of Russell's CMI to the Christian Conception of God and Creation in Understanding the Origin of Consciousness

7.1 Introduction

WE NOW HONE IN on applying Russell's methodology, which takes into account the most recent scientific knowledge and its possible interaction with modern Christian theology. We can attempt to incorporate the fruits (mentioned in the conclusion of chapter 4) of Teilhardian thought into our research guidelines. The importance of Teilhard's thought is that it was a historic springboard for incorporating scientific findings and shedding new light on theological doctrines in the twentieth century. Russell's methodology extends much further than that of Teilhard; in the Teilhardian method, science influences theological doctrines but leaves little room for the converse. With the advent of Russell's CMI we have a way of explicitly unraveling how the origin of consciousness relates to this interaction.

It is also worth mentioning that this book can work with a variety of positions on consciousness that are broadly compatible with a classic understanding of the Christian God and creation. We will now examine scientific research programs that influence theological research programs and vice versa with respect to the origin of consciousness. This is where Russell's CMI will be specifically applied to understanding the Christian concept of God and creation on the origin of consciousness.

7.2 Scientific Research Programs à Theological Research Programs (SRP à TRP)

There are far too many scientific theories of consciousness to examine here. There are also a great many approaches proposed in the sciences to understanding consciousness, even though not all focus on understanding the origin of consciousness. Understanding its origin will give us a clue to the level of organismal complexity, including brain physiology and genetics, necessary for a certain level of consciousness.[1] This book is attempting to discern the origin of self-reflection as experienced by humans and its theological relevance.[2]

There are certainly ways that science regarding consciousness can influence theology. Recall Stoeger's reformulation of Russell's paths of interaction between science and theology, which were specific to physics interacting with theology in a generic understanding of science. We will now apply these to consciousness.[3] Let us take a look briefly at the first of these five paths. The bulk of this book will look toward the last three paths (6 to 8), since these relate to theology influencing science.

> *Path 1: Theories in the sciences can act directly as data that place constraints on theology.*

In his excellent article, "Neuroscience, the Person, and God," Philip Clayton lists a number of relatively recent findings from the neurosciences, which can place constraints on theology. We do not have the space to list all of these, but one of the more pointed findings was yielded from studies involving patients with frontotemporal degeneration (FD) and Alzheimer's disease (AD). This has provided us with greater insights into the link between

---

1. Tye, "Qualia," no pages.

2. The origin and experience of self-consciousness is part of the subjective phenomenological human experience. This is not to suggest that animals lack a certain level of self-awareness, but the extent to which it exists in humans seems to be something rather radical by comparison with the rest of the animal kingdom. Panpsychists who see consciousness as being ubiquitous throughout nature, and particularly in the animal kingdom, will certainly disagree with such a statement. Nonetheless, I should also point out that I am not at all against the possibility that in the future, through further evolutionary development in other species, this same sort of consciousness, i.e., the ability to introspect deeply on one's own consciousness can arise. Nor am I against the possibility that other unknown intelligences throughout the universe may possess such capacities. These notions are closely related to debates regarding human uniqueness, divine election, and the imago dei. Though interesting, space does not permit us to enter into such debates. Our focus is human self-consciousness.

3. See chapter 1 section 5, as well as chapter 2, section 6 of this book.

brain function and language.[4] The purpose of mentioning these studies is to show the profound effect that alterations and damages to the physiology of the brain can have on the thought and behavior of human persons. It indeed affects conscious activity. One excellent example of this is the finding of a positive correlation between the brain's physical complexity and its functionality with respect to the origin of consciousness and self-reflection. If particular areas of the brain, known to give rise to deep introspective thought on the nature of one's self and one's own existence, the existence of other minds, or the ability to think critically and abstractly, are damaged or affected, this ability seems to be at least suspended temporarily if not lost indefinitely. One need only think of the effects of alcohol, drugs, or anesthetics to recognize this inescapable correlation. These conditions, among many others, indeed put a constraint on theological notions concerning consciousness; although consciousness is not reducible to the physical stratum of the brain, one must take these causal connections seriously. One can take the position that the findings of the neurosciences are significant to further understanding the human person. However, they are insufficient to explain away the human person, and incapable of reducing consciousness completely to a physical state.[5] This observation is perfectly compatible with the aims of this book. Other constraints would come from particular scientific theories in cosmology, evolutionary biology, and psychology, and would play a role in explaining the origin of consciousness. An example of this would be that if one were to hold a particular understanding of evolution, such as Neo-Darwinism, one would have to be limited by the mutation-selection mechanisms to explain the level of complexity reached by the brain. In that view, one would either have to suggest that consciousness is an illusion formulated by the complex inner workings of the brain, or that it somehow emerges from the nexus of causal connections; this would be assuming that there is no direction or plan adduced, as would be logically

---

4. These are listed in Clayton's article, "Neuroscience, the Person and God," 182–83. For further readings on each respective point (as cited in Clayton's article), see Hodos and Hutler, "Evolution of Sensory Pathways in Vertebrates," 189–97; Beardsley, "The Machinery of Thought," 78–83; Grossman, et al., "Language Comprehension and Regional Cerebral Defects in Frontotemporal Degeneration and Alzheimer's Disease," 157–63; Aylward, et al., "Frontal Lobe Volume in Patients with Huntington's Disease," 252–58.; Lenhoff, et al., "William's Syndrome and the Brain," 68–73; Tormos, et al., "Lateralized Effects of Self-Induced Sadness and Happiness on Corticospinal Excitability," 487–91.

5. For an explanation of the Sufficiency versus Insufficiency debate, see Clayton, "Neuroscience, the Person and God,"188–89. The Sufficiency thesis suggests that the neurosciences will be able to explain everything about the human person including consciousness. The Insufficiency thesis, which is defended by thinkers such as David Chalmers, Thomas Nagel, Colin McGinn, John Searle, and Philip Clayton, suggest that consciousness cannot be explained away by the neurosciences.

consistent. Another example would be in evolutionary psychology. The notion of self-consciousness would provide humans with a selective advantage over other primates for adaptation and survival. This will be explored as part of the evolutionary natural theological argument below.

> Path 2: Theories in the sciences can act directly as data either to be "explained" by theology or as the basis for a theological constructive argument.

Russell typically cites t=0, as understood in big bang cosmology, as it has been historically explained through *creation ex nihilo* in theology. The notion of t=0 is significant to the development of the cumulative evolutionary natural theological argument from consciousness, in order to suggest that the Christian conception of God and creation functions as a highly plausible explanation for the origin of consciousness. What sort of data for theology can convergence with respect to self-consciousness/phenomenal consciousness suggest? What is the connection between consciousness and the neural correlates of consciousness? Does this only imply correlation and not causation? Science can only provide the data (neural correlates) and philosophy/theology can examine the implications of such findings. Science cannot make a definitive conclusion on the matter unless coupled with some philosophical framework.

> Path 3: Theories in the sciences, after philosophical analysis, can act indirectly as data for theology.

In this pathway, Russell adopts the indeterminacy of quantum mechanics through his philosophical theology, in order to support his framework of NIODA. This is something we will explore in greater depth.[6] Indeed, the use of QM to understand God's action is important to the science-theology dialogue and functions as one possibility for the way God could act within creation. Under this pathway, I wish to explore Dembski's notion of an informationally porous universe, which can also operate in harmony with QM, but which often seems neglected by those who support NIODA and DAP (divine action project). Dembski's work on information can create a well-structured bridge between theology and science, with philosophy as a mediator. It will be vital to examine how God interacts with consciousness and closely associated theories, which take information seriously, to understand consciousness. This also will be explored in greater depth in this chapter. The Trinitarian Mode of Creation that Dembski provides also offers a possible model to demonstrate the Christian conception of God's interaction, i.e., through a Trinitarian understanding of the world. This model will also be explored later in this chapter. Plantinga's notion of DCC also offers a

6. See section 7.4.

plausible alternative to NIODA and DAP, whereby God is involved beyond creation and conservation. There are also a great number of exciting scientific theories of consciousness. It will be worthwhile to examine some of the more significant ones (in path 8).

> *Path 4: Theories in the sciences can also act indirectly as data for theology when they are incorporated into a fully articulated philosophy of nature (for example, the process philosophy of Whitehead).*

One could also think of the evolutionary natural theology of Teilhard, whereby data from cosmic and evolutionary biology influences the second coming of Christ, the *parousia* as articulated in his famous notion of the noosphere (sphere of mind), which leads to the ascension of human beings to a transhuman state. The origin of consciousness in such a view can fit into the Teilhardian system through his law of complexity-consciousness, where consciousness reaches a boiling point in the evolution of primates and finally erupts into self-consciousness.

> *Path 5: Theories in the sciences can function heuristically in theology by providing conceptual inspiration, experiential inspiration, practical/moral inspiration, or aesthetic inspiration.*

For Russell, an example of this is biological evolution, which he sees as providing a sense of God's immanence in nature, through His involvement with random mutations through QM-NIODA. Nevertheless, this is problematic since it would make God responsible not only for beneficial mutations that provide a fuel to positive evolutionary change, but also to deleterious mutations that would exacerbate the problem of natural evil and directly involve God, creating more problems for a coherent theodicy.

One could argue along these lines that God guides the process of evolution through random mutations or other means (the plethora of mechanisms and other possible ways of divine action) to bring about self-consciousness, perhaps through an influx of information applied to the brain. The transcendent component plays a role in the Teilhardian notion of "ultra-physics," of the human person (a nonreductive) understanding, without creating a separation of the human person through a mind-body dichotomy, but rather through a holistic approach.

One could also argue that the fine-tuning inspires a sense of awe, alongside conceptual and aesthetic inspiration to God's creation, since the laws, initial conditions, and constants of physics are so precisely tuned but can be explained so elegantly and simply through mathematical equations in physics. Most of the equations in physics can be summarized with a few simple equations, for example, $E=MC^2$ in Einstein's theory of special relativity. It demonstrates that there is an increase to the relativistic mass (m) of a body from energy, exemplified by the motion of the body (kinetic energy) multiplied by the speed of light squared. This demonstrates that both mass (matter) and energy are interchangeable and fundamentally the same physical entities.

7.3 Theological Research Programs à Scientific Research Programs (TRP à SRP)

This section will examine three paths where theological research programs can influence scientific ones. This will initiate dialogue and move forward into research guidelines for deepening the interaction between theology and science.

> Path 6: *Theology can provide some of the philosophical assumptions underlying the sciences.*

In terms of pathway 6, our focus will be on the philosophical argumentation revolving around divine simplicity. This will be explored further in the guidelines for further constructive research into theology influencing science.

> Path 7: *Theological theories can act as sources of inspiration or motivation for new scientific theories.*

For instance, a theological theory of God's action and God interacting with His creation can be best explained by a scientific theory of consciousness, which takes information seriously. This would leave the door open to research into QM, Dembski's informationally porous universe, and his Trinitarian Mode of Creation along the discernment of the information necessary to explain the origin of consciousness. Several scientific theories of consciousness are worth exploring to even begin to tackle this. This will be explored in the guidelines for future research.

> Path 8: *Theological theories can lead to "selection rules" within the criteria for choosing scientific theories.*

It will be worth examining various theories of consciousness with respect to this pathway. For instance, if the doctrine of divine simplicity has any semblance to the transcendent component of our human nature, such as the self, which is not reducible to the material substrate (our physical bodies), whether one assumes a dualist, strict monist, or a dual aspect monist position, it would nonetheless be true. As Russell states, "if one considers a theological theory as true, then one can delineate what conditions must [be obtained] with [science, in this case neuroscience or cognitive science] for the possibility of its [sic] being true. These conditions in turn can serve as motivations for an individual or research scientist or group of colleagues to choose to pursue a particular scientific theory."[7] For example, if we consider the doctrine or "theory" of divine simplicity as true, we will further develop the reasoning for affirming an apophatic understanding of God through the implications and derivations from the KCA (which will be further examined below), since it serves well to argue for the finitude of the past while being corroborated by the standard big bang model, the second law of thermodynamics and a series of renewed philosophical arguments. It will be important to search for a theory that takes seriously—or at least is open at the interpretational level to accommodate—the transcendent component of the human person, whether or not it is "separate" from the human person (dualist, monist, or dual aspect monism).

7.3.1 Research Guidelines for Constructive Work in Origin of Consciousness Research in Light of Arguments from Natural Theology, Philosophical Theology, and Systematic Theology

Let us examine some guidelines in considering TRP à SRP. These guidelines are exploratory in nature. In some cases, as with guideline 5, I will explain several important theories of consciousness that can be selected through theological criteria, namely, Teilhard's notion of "ultra-physics." In this section, I will examine nine broad guidelines with various subguidelines as well. The concepts particular to natural theology and philosophical theology were developed in chapter 5. The suggested guidelines aim to stimulate further interdisciplinary research between scientists, philosophers, and theologians. The purpose of these guidelines is to give some potential direction for further research in the science-theology interaction, including concepts such as God's simplicity, various components of cosmic and biological evolution, Teilhard's "ultra-physics," and panpsychism. The best way to describe such an endeavor is to use Russell's own metaphor of a needle in a haystack:

> A metaphor I like to use to illustrate the need for such guidelines is that of searching for a needle in a haystack—when one is confronted by an immense field of haystacks. Instead of just starting with the one closest hand we first need some way to decide which haystacks are more likely to have a needle and which ones less likely or even unlikely to have one. These guidelines are meant to help us at this metalevel in which we are first searching for candidate haystacks and leaving to the

---

7. Russell, *Cosmology*, 305.

future more detailed searches of individual haystacks which pass the test of the guidelines.[8]

This is precisely the purpose behind proposing the following guidelines; it is not meant to be conclusive nor comprehensive, but rather a first clue as to where to look for understanding the origin of consciousness through the use of the Christian conception of God and creation.

Guideline 1a (path 8). God's simplicity as the source of all being.[9] This doctrine affirms that God is without physical, temporal, or metaphysical parts. In turn, this forms a coherent picture for God acting as the source of all physical and temporal reality (the universe/multiverse). For instance, guideline 2, which explores an evolutionary natural theology, finds its grounding in ultimate simplicity, i.e., God's simplicity. As the cause of matter, energy, space, time—the cause who transcends such properties is without them, therefore, immaterial, spaceless, and timeless. This conception of God serves as an intelligible alternative to redefinitions of nothingness in quantum cosmology, which differ from a metaphysical understanding of nothingness such as "non-being." This would provide a better explanation for the universe's rationality and comprehensibility. If we take mind/consciousness as a primary candidate for grounding reality, we would expect information and consciousness to be vital aspects of reality. This is something that seems out of place in a completely naturalistic and closed universe.[10]

8. Russell, *Time in Eternity*, 76.

9. I develop this guideline and 2a and 2b, at significant length in terms of Maritain's ideas of evolution while relating it to God's simplicity. See Ventureyra, "God's Simplicity, Evolution and the Origin of Consciousness," 137–55.

10. Russell makes an important distinction between open and closed universes with respect to how they are understood scientifically and theologically—God can interact whether the universe is closed or open scientifically but this would change God's action from interventionist or non-interventionist depending on which scientific picture we are utilizing, as he states:

> 1) all physical systems, whether open or closed in a scientific sense, are open to, and dependent on, God's action as Creator for their very existence. 2) God's special divine action can affect a physical system that is either open or closed system in the scientific sense of these terms. It would take an interventionist form of divine action to affect a system if the system were a deterministic one, while it could take a non-interventionist form of divine action if the system was an indeterministic one. . . In both cases, God acts; it is only the form of that action which is crucial here. Russell, "What we've learned from quantum mechanics about non-interventionist objective divine action in nature—and what are its remaining challenges?", 25 (April 2017 conference draft set to be published in the near future). It is worth noting that Russell takes issue with Plantinga's idea of open and closed universes with respect to how it is understood scientifically and theologically. Russell in this forthcoming article argues that Plantinga has misunderstood QM-NIODA (pages 23–30). For my purposes I acknowledge

Guideline 1b (path 6). The metaphysical principle of synonymy provides a guarantor for the existence of consciousness, i.e., embodied human self-consciousness. Finite creatures such as humans who possess embodied consciousness capable of self-reflection are analogous to God's eternal unembodied consciousness. God's simplicity provides the reason and existence for embodied human consciousness. Consciousness begets consciousness but finds its ultimate source in a transcendent eternal consciousness, known as God. God as a disembodied consciousness exists immaterially, spacelessly, and eternally. However, consciousness, which is embodied, indeed exists alongside and operates from a material substrate that is causally connected to the space-time continuum, yet not reducible to material structures. This would be in line with dual aspect monism (John Polkinghorne) or an interactive dualism (Charles Taliaferro). This will help correct our thinking of the transcendent nature of consciousness against theories or philosophies of consciousness which seek to eliminate consciousness or reduce it to merely the physical workings of the brain. This argument is strictly a guideline for future research.[11]

Guideline 2a (path 7). Planned or directed evolution. A planned or directed evolution where the universe emanates from God makes better sense of the nonphysical components found within physical reality, as opposed to a purely naturalistic notion of evolution or even a non-teleological one. Could nature be both discontinuous and continuous simultaneously? Can strong emergence resolve the origin of singular phenomena such as life, complexified body plans and behavior, self-reflective consciousness, etc.? If Teilhard is correct about a linear evolution that follows the arrow of time through ever-complexifying processes, as revealed through his law of complexity-consciousness, it raises the notion of the inevitability of the advent of self-reflection/self-consciousness. What about his view of panpsychism? This seems consistent with the notion that consciousness is occurring through a gradual ascent. Under such a view, one would expect remnants or lesser-developed versions of consciousness as found in matter and less complex life. On the other hand, different degrees of consciousness, although consistent with panpsychism, are not the sole explanation. One would expect different degrees if there is a gradual ascent to higher states of consciousness. The link between information and consciousness is vital as well; for example,

---

that God can act regardless of the scientific picture but argue against a "completely naturalistic and closed universe." See section 7.4.3 of this book.

11. See the conclusion of this book, as the principle of synonymy is mentioned but it will have to be left for future more rigorous research as it is beyond the scope of this book.

self-replicating systems exhibit information-rich processing capacities but are not conscious in the same way an animal would be.

Guideline 2b. The Cumulative Evolutionary Natural Theological Argument from Consciousness (CENTAC). There are a series of emergent phenomena that are best explained by God as understood in classical theism. Without the existence and evolution of such phenomena, the origin of human consciousness would not be possible. A consciousness that is self-conscious, capable of introspection, realization of death, the existence of other minds, the capacity for philosophical, scientific, and theological reflection, is only possible through these cumulative steps. In order for embodied consciousness (human consciousness) to emerge, the following components, plausibly explained by a transcendent God (as revealed in guideline 1), are necessary: 1) a universe via *creation ex nihilo* (path 6); 2) finely calibrated physical laws and constants which permit matter to form; 3) life which must be presupposed by consciousness in a developed manner as found in humanity (self-consciousness); 4) the ubiquity of convergence with respect to phenomenal and self-consciousness, while still affirming humankind's unique self-consciousness; 5) an ascent of cultural evolution; and 6) the very intelligibility of the cosmos. This is a Lonerganian intelligibility argument conjoined with Richards and Gonzalez's measurability/habitability argument. A search for evidence of convergence would be indicative of a planned or directed evolution. Multiple origins of life may reflect such a thing as well.

Guideline 2c. This is consonant with t=0 and big bang cosmology. The universe had a finite beginning, which is demonstrated through the KCA.

Guideline 2d. Why is the universe finely tuned for life? The physical laws, constants, and initial conditions of the universe are precisely calibrated for matter and life to exist. In turn, it is consonant with Teilhard's Law of Complexity-Consciousness, which would not be able to function without these precise calibrations. Evolution is dependent and presupposes such finely tuned calibrations.

Guideline 2e. What is the source of functional information necessary for building the first replicating system? The origin of life, i.e., the emergence of the first replicating system, has presented seemingly insurmountable obstacles for naturalistic origin of life scenarios. There are staggering improbabilities for building the simplest assemblage of protein components that may be capable of self-replication. In addition, there is a transcendent aspect to information that is non-reducible to the physical building blocks and components of such self-replicating systems. The origin of life seems to embody an example of a strong emergent system, assuming that it is possible that such a system could emerge.

Guidelines 2f. This guideline is an in-depth examination of various mechanisms of evolution as proposed by the Extended Synthesis and scientists like Margulis, Shapiro and others—and how this plays into understanding the origin of consciousness. Does it facilitate any understanding?

Guidelines 2g. This guideline entails more research into convergence. Why do dolphins, birds, and other animals from separate evolutionary lineages show the differing degrees of self-consciousness and intelligence? Why are they not as developed as our own? Is more time required? Were dolphins not able to develop technology because of physical limitations, i.e., no hands/non-terrestrial/no upright position in order to harness things like fire, which Denton notes as vital to our development of technology? What does this suggest of extra-terrestrial intelligence? If they evolved by a similar way of PE/DE through a variety of mechanisms, what sort of theological, philosophical, and scientific implications does this have?

Guideline 3a. Teilhard and panpsychism. Teilhard's notion of panpsychism can be explored as a potential resolution to the problem of the origin of human consciousness. A look at IIT and PSII as scientific applications to Teilhard's panpsychism can reveal the problems and various fruits that stem out of such a metaphysical approach.

Guideline 3b. This guideline could lead to an in-depth exploration of neuroscientist Christof Koch's more developed understanding of panpsychism in modern science. The appeal of panpsychism, in relation to Koch's thought and some of the elements of this thesis, could be summarized in the following way: 1) the unity of creation (he does not use such a term but meaning all of reality)—all matter and organisms are interrelated—precursors of behavior found in other animals; 2) All physical systems possess an interior mental aspect; 3) If consciousness is ubiquitous and Teilhard is correct about a linear evolution that follows, the arrow of time through the ever-complexifying process of evolution as revealed through his law of complexity-consciousness would lead to the advent of self-reflection/self-consciousness. If consciousness happens through a gradual ascent, would one not expect remnants or lesser-developed versions of consciousness as found in matter and less complex life? Digital code found in DNA and RNA are replicating systems that embody functional information (which seems to serve well for a panpsychist explanation).

Guideline 3c. Teilhard's panpsychism can be compared to naturalistic understandings of panpsychism. Can a resolution be found to the combination problem if the process of evolution and an understanding of panpsychism are both grounded by the Christian conception of God and creation?

Guideline 3d. This guideline looks into definitions of consciousness, information, and complexity. This seems to be a source of confusion with respect to panpsychism. Distinctions and relationships between complexity, specified complexity, organized complexity, functional information, and different definitions of consciousness (phenomenal, intentional, and introspective [self-consciousness]) could be explored. How do all these relate to panpsychism? How do we make the distinction?

Guideline 4. Information and God's action. One of the major objections to God's action in the world is that God does not move particles. The naturalist story of the universe conveys an understanding of a seamless continuity of physical things interacting with one another and obeying physical law. Dembski's notion of an informationally porous universe could provide interesting fruits when combined with scientific theories of consciousness such as IIT, PSII, or Orch-OR.

Guideline 5 (path 8). Theology/philosophical theology providing a conceptual basis to select the best of scientific theories of consciousness. Teilhard's suggestion of an "ultra-physics" as a "physics of spirit" sits at the boundary of science, theology, and philosophy—which seem to hint at an explanation for the nonphysical components of reality such as consciousness without having to adhere to a form of substance dualism. It also avoids the pitfalls of philosophies/theories that tend to reduce consciousness to something purely physical. This could inspire further research into the origin of singular events such as life on Earth and embodied human self-consciousness. Teilhard recognized that physics (natural science) on its own could never resolve the problem of consciousness because of its transcendent nature. Teilhard indeed recognized that the materialist (physicalist) versus the substance dualist paradigm did not encompass all of the options of the body-soul problem/debate. This is why his notion of "ultra-physics" could provide us with a selection rule for carrying forward more research by scientist(s) interested in the science-theology dialogue into different scientific theories of consciousness, which we will explore below.

Consciousness, much like information, operates through the physical but transcends it. It is suggestive of the irreducibility of consciousness to the brain. Teilhard's holistic approach avoids such dichotomies between materialism (physicalism) and substance dualism. Christian debates about the nature of consciousness seem to be stuck in this paradigm (as has been discussed above).[12]

Guideline 6 (path 7) Systematic theological doctrines can act as inspiration for scientific research. These arguments (6b–d) were explored in chapter 6 on systematic theology arguments.

Guideline 6a. Creation ex nihilo. This doctrine can inspire research into the finitude of the past as was proposed by Philoponus in the sixth century with philosophical arguments to defend a theological doctrine. This can act as motivation to find corroboration of the standard big bang model, which is an important argument for underlying the origin of consciousness and avoiding an infinite regress of past events, which as will be shown, leads to a series of incoherencies.

Guideline 6b. The doctrine of the image-likeness of God. This doctrine can inspire research that intersects with philosophy, theology, and science in terms of selecting anthropological theories that value the human person and the uniqueness of self-consciousness without denying its future potentiality in other species. This can act as an inspiration to the debates regarding the origin of self-consciousness as being attributed to human uniqueness or divine election. Whatever the case may be within the tent of Christian theism, it denies the eliminative approaches to consciousness and human importance and value.

Guideline 6c. The origin of moral consciousness. Part of an important aspect of self-consciousness is moral consciousness. Jesus's radical altruism seems unlike much of what we see in nature and throughout the history of humanity. Is there a biological basis to explain this unique phenomenon in the history of anthropological evolution? Or is it something that transcends ordinary scientific explanation? Regardless of the response, this notion can inspire research on the origins of not merely altruism, but "perfect" or radical altruism. Research can be involved in biblical criticism to authenticate particular biblical verses concerning Jesus's words and deeds pertaining to the concept of radical/perfect altruism. This can inspire lines of research in sociobiological evolution, NT criticism, and comparative religions. It would also be useful to further research into Teilhard's notion of love, as Teilhard refers to the "final success of hominization" and how it unifies his law of

12. At the 2016 conference in Tucson, Arizona: *The Science of Consciousness*, I prepared a presentation arguing for the application of Russell's program (paths 6 to 8) in the CMI for the origin of consciousness through using Teilhard's thought and IIT. See Ventureyra, "The Origin of Consciousness: A Research Program for the Science-Theology Interaction," abstract 99 (2016): 94.

complexity-consciousness. This could be built as argumentation against purely naturalistic views of how moral values and that duties arise from an evolutionarily perspective. Perhaps future research into science supporting the theological/philosophical insight of how objective moral values and duties cannot arise without recourse to the classical Christian conception of God.

6d. *Trinitarian Mode of Creation.* The involvement of the Holy Trinity in creation can act to inspire research into the connection of information to the material world; how God interacts with physical systems. This can lead to research on the synonymy between divine agency and human agency.[13] This could also have an inspirational impact on personal prayer for everyone. This could illumine the relationship between wellbeing and spirituality, both for inner and physical wellbeing. Many modalities of future research could be inspired by gaining understanding of this mode of creation.

Guideline 7 (path 7). In what ways can the connection between the origin of life and the origin of consciousness be explored? God's action through QM and informational structures seems to be a strong link, but how? These two FINLONs represent an incredible affinity, but what precisely is this connection? Further research should be able to better clarify this connection.

Guideline 8 (path 7). Different Christian understandings of consciousness, such as Moreland's substance dualism, the Lonergan-Helminiak Tripartite Transcendent Model, and Clayton's emergent monism, provide three distinct frameworks for examining self-consciousness. These widely varied models can act as inspirations to incite further exploration into not only self-consciousness, but also its connection to phenomenal consciousness. An exploration of this sort can perhaps help both philosophers and scientists to see ways out of particular conundrums in understanding the origin of consciousness, while coupled with different understandings of evolution such as PE and DE. Moreover, these frameworks for understanding consciousness can be examined in light of the various theories of consciousness, including IIT, PSII, Orch-OR, and dualist notions with scientific implications, and perhaps others that were not examined here or may be discovered in the future.

Guideline 9 (path 6). The nature of FINLONs/FINLONCs. How many FINLONs are directly or indirectly related to the origin of consciousness? Is it only the instantiation of one new law of nature, or the coordination of

---

13. See section 8.4 on Clayton and agency. See also conclusion with Pambrun's use of analogy and Clayton's use of agency.

pre-existing laws with one new law or several new ones? How do we recognize the difference? How can we exclude or include these possibilities?

7.3.2 Different Scientific Theories of Consciousness

Application of Russell's CMI is of importance in understanding how theology can begin to potentially influence the sciences and move forward from a regulative ideal to making an actual impact. Here we can examine several promising theories/approaches to consciousness that will have significant implications for understanding the origin of consciousness.

In this section we will examine the potential fruitfulness of some of the theories of consciousness (beginning with those using notions of information), including IIT, PSII, Orch-OR, and dualist notions with scientific implications. To be sure there are many other theories of consciousness[14] but the ones discussed here seem to have the greatest potential for fruitfulness in advancing the research program proposed in this book, intended to gain understanding of the origin of consciousness through the Christian conception of God and creation.

7.3.2.1 *Integrated Information Theory (IIT)*

A more precise picture of the relationship between complexity, information, and consciousness could be found through a new theory of consciousness known as IIT. This theory was proposed initially by neuroscientist and psychiatrist Guilio Tononi.[15] If successful it can provide a minimal threshold for informational content, necessary for performing certain functions and possessing particular conscious states including self-consciousness. One conceivable option would be to measure the informational content of the

14. Other competing theories of consciousness include: Global Neuronal Workspace Theory (GNWS); Higher Order Thought Theory (HOT); Prediction Error Minimization (PEM); Metacognitive Theories (MetaCog); Higher Order Certainty Index Theory (HOCert); Radical Plasticity Thesis (RPT); Recurrent Processing (Loop); Attended Intermediate-Level Representation Theory (AIR); First Order Theories (FOT); Virtual Reality Theory (VR); Consciousness is for Other People (Soc), and The Quasicrystalline Nature of Consciousness. For a treatment of the Quasicrystalline Nature of Consciousness, which presents some interesting and seemingly paradoxical ideas for retroactive creation, time, information, and consciousness whereby the whole and the constituent parts reflect back on one another, see Irwin, "A New Approach to the Hard Problem of Consciousness: A Quasicrystalline Language of 'Primitive Units of Consciousness' in Quantized Spacetime (Part I)," 483–97.

15. See Tononi, *Phi: A Voyage from the Brain to the Soul;* Tononi and Koch, "Consciousness: here, there and everywhere?"; Koch, *Consciousness: Confessions of a Romantic Reductionist,* 113–36.

brain of an infant or toddler, at the brink of becoming self-conscious.[16] Another way of measuring self-consciousness may arise through measuring the substratum of information embedded for artificial intelligence purposes, whether robotic or computerized in some way. If we are capable of measuring the informational content of conscious states in this way, then it would vindicate a sort of functionalism.[17] To circumvent the "hard problem" of consciousness, IIT begins by assuming the existence of consciousness and then finds evidence for it through the physical substrate, where consciousness is embodied (i.e., the brain). One of the main assumptions regarding IIT lies in asserting that conscious experience can be fully explained by the physical system in which it is embedded, whereby the properties of the experience constrain the properties of the material system.[18] Starting from the subjective level of the state a given subject may be in, leaves a number of unknown variables, such as, how accurate is the description of their experience, how do we know they are telling the truth, etc. Of course there are tests for consistency, but to enter into the mind of another is a completely different issue, which we have not learned to access to any greater degree than mere empathy.

One of the key components of IIT is this notion of integration. Information on its own will not tell us much of the phenomenal experience in terms of its physical manifestation, but this integration is what is important to the conscious experience. The question arises: Do we need some form of integration, even if minimal, to identify the point where consciousness originates in those primitive humans? Consciousness requires memory for recognition of self-existence, not only as an innate capacity but through self-introspection—it could not have been a completely natural state that those earliest humans found themselves in, as would be the case with lower animals, but a state that required self-reflection. So an act of self-knowledge requires a deliberation of thought and recognition of such a thought. It is an act of the intellect in unison with the will. Nevertheless, there must be a point where this was not possible for early hominids, since evolution reached its "boiling point," as Teilhard would say. Thus, some form of integration to get to that point seems to be necessary. But what is meant by integration in IIT? Balduzzi and Tononi explain:

> While the ability to distinguish among a large number of states
> is a fundamental difference between you and the photodiode,
> by itself it is not enough to account for the presence of con-
> sciousness. To see why, consider an idealized megapixel digital

16. See Rochat, "Five levels of awareness as they unfold early in life," 717–31.

17. For an exploration of functionalism, see Garfield, "Philosophy: Foundations of Cognitive Science.", 331–77.

18. See Tononi, "Integrated Information Theory," no pages.

camera, whose sensor chip is essentially a collection of a million photodiodes. Even if each photodiode in the sensor chip were just binary, the camera could distinguish among $2^{1,000,000}$ states, an immense number, corresponding to 1,000,000 bits of information. Indeed, the camera would enter a different state for every frame from every movie that was ever produced. Yet few would argue that the camera is conscious. What is the key difference between you and the camera?

According to the theory, the difference has to do with integrated information. An external observer may consider the camera chip as a single system with a repertoire of $2^{1,000,000}$ states. In reality, however, the chip is not an integrated entity: since its 1,000,000 photodiodes have no way to interact, the state of each photodiode is causally independent of that of the others: in reality, the chip is a collection of 1,000,000 independent photodiodes, each with a repertoire of two states. This is easy to prove: if the sensor chip were cut down into its individual photodiodes, the performance of the camera would not change at all. By contrast, your vast repertoire of conscious states truly belongs to an integrated system, since it cannot be subdivided into repertoires of states available to independent components. Thus, a conscious image is always experienced as an integrated whole: no matter how hard you try, you cannot experience the left half of the visual field of view independently of the right half, or colors independent of shapes. Underlying this unity of experience are causal interactions within your brain, which make the state of each element causally dependent on that of other elements. Indeed, unlike the camera, your brain's performance breaks down if its elements are disconnected. And so does consciousness: for example, splitting the brain in two along the corpus callosum prevents causal interactions between the two hemispheres and splits experience in two—the right half of the visual field is experienced independently of the left.

This phenomenological analysis suggests that, to generate consciousness, a physical system must have a large repertoire of available states (information) *and* it must be unified, i.e. it should not be decomposable into a collection of causally independent subsystems (integration).[19]

Integration is a necessary component to measure consciousness, but is this alone sufficient? As we will see below, the claim of PSII is that it is not. Nonetheless, IIT is one of the more promising theories of consciousness that has been developed in recent years. It not only proposes a way of

19. Balduzzi and Tononi, "Integrated Information in Discrete Dynamical Systems: Motivation and Theoretical Framework," no pages.

measuring consciousness, but it also takes into account how consciousness is recognized through the inner workings of the brain, why it diminishes when one enters into dreamless states but reappears in dream states. IIT lines up nicely with Dembski's notion of an informationally porous universe. It provides a potentially fruitful approach to understanding God's action through information and a viable scientific theory of consciousness.

The significance of this theory is that it takes consciousness as a real phenomenal experience and works from this phenomenal understanding of consciousness, to attempt to measure it with respect to the substrate (i.e., the brain's neural networking system). There are some further important features. One of its major champions, Christof Koch, believes that consciousness is a fundamental property of matter, neither emergent nor reducible.[20] It comes as no surprise that Koch is an avid supporter of panpsychism, which is compatible with Christian theism (panentheism), as we have examined with Teilhard's exposition of complexity-consciousness. There is also a strong affinity in the thought of Guilo Tononi toward the implications of panpsychism and its relation to IIT. Koch indicates that IIT is compatible with a specific kind of panpsychism, not a crude or naïve form, which involves consciousness in the most rudimentary forms of matter, but only those found in complex systems.[21] This raises some issues with respect to particular systems that exhibit high levels of integrated information such as the matrix multiplication system,[22] which do not, of course, have high levels of consciousness. In reference to panpsychism and its crude forms, Tononi states:

> How close is this position to panpsychism, which holds that everything in the universe has some kind of consciousness? Certainly, the IIT implies that many entities, as long as they include some functional mechanisms that can make choices between alternatives, have some degree of consciousness. Unlike traditional panpsychism, however, the IIT does not attribute consciousness indiscriminately to all things. For example, if there are no interactions, there is no consciousness whatsoever. For the IIT, a camera sensor as such is completely unconscious . . . [23]

The question arises as to whether one must concede to panpsychism in order to embrace IIT. The answer to this question, I would say, is no.

20. Koch is against both emergentism and reductionism. See, Koch, *Consciousness: Confessions of a Romantic Reductionist*," 119.

21. Christof Koch, "Ubiquitous Minds," 27–28.

22. See Aaronson, "Why I Am Not An Integrated Information Theorist (or, The Unconscious Expander)," no pages.

23. Tononi, "Consciousness as Integrated Information: A Provisional Manifesto," 216–42.

Perhaps this is off the mark (or perhaps the theory would need modification to avoid this pitfall; see below for PSII), but it requires further reflection, since you can use IIT to measure levels of consciousness without affirming a particular metaphysical explanation for why consciousness *is*. If it is to be taken strictly as a scientific theory, its implications can be wide-reaching without being relegated to a single interpretation. One could affirm IIT and see divine action, as Dembski envisions it, in information which provides the ability for organisms and systems to complexify in a given direction. Or, as envisioned by various theistic evolutionist/evolutionary creationists, it could have been infused with a planned method. "The main issue is whether the fundamental nature of information and its transferability through different means, is compatible with functionalism." Moreover consciousness, much like information "is substrate-independent."[24]

The central importance of information to IIT is what makes it seem promising as a theory of consciousness. This fact may aid us to discern its origin. But it is not without its difficulties. IIT seems to explain well the interdependence of complex functions and parts of particular systems, but it does not seem to provide a systematic explanation as to how consciousness arises from this simple interdependence. Much of the discussion about neuroscience, complexity, and consciousness is at an impasse; how do complex systems lead to conscious experience, whether phenomenal or in the sense of self-consciousness?

Information steals the show in biology. It was the necessary ingredient for the origin of life. What does IIT have to say about the origin of consciousness? Even if one were to grant the continuity assumed by panpsychism, what are we to make of human consciousness and its capacity for self-reflection, acknowledgment of one's own finitude, ability to do science and higher analytic thinking, etc.? Can we really calculate the amount of integrated information necessary for self-consciousness and higher cognitive abilities?

Since the origin of life, information has been increasing exponentially. One need only think about the Cambrian explosion, where the majority of body plans came into existence, to the first humans several hundreds of thousands of years ago, an event which has led to booming advances in technology, evolving at levels that are impossible for humans to keep up with.[25]

---

24. Koch, *Consciousness*, 121.

25. Some, like Ray Kurzweil and Michio Kaku, refer to this exponential increase in technology and artificial intelligence as a technological singularity, which we can only keep pace with by involving immersing ourselves in it physically and genetically. This is associated with a controversial idea that Teilhard supported and envisioned, through his understanding of transhumanism. See Kurzweil, *The Singularity is Near*.

7.3.2.2 *Psychophysical Semantic Information Integration (PSII)*[26]

Current work utilizing a neutral, monistic view of consciousness PSII (Psychophysical Semantic Information Integration) claims to avoid the pitfalls of both physicalism and dualism in order to bring us closer to a science of consciousness. It is worth pointing out that this theory of consciousness is undergoing many revisions, so its use is intended to be exploratory and tentative. It does demonstrate promise, but much further development is needed to show the extent of its explanatory scope and power. Many of the authors involved with PSII research and neutral monism suggest that neutral monism possesses several distinct advantages over substance dualism and physicalism when it comes to understanding consciousness. These include: "1. Resolves the mind-body problem without denying consciousness. 2. Avoids the problem of interaction and affirms mental causality. 3. The emphasis on organization confirms the importance of complexity research in neurodynamics, cognitive science, and non-linear dynamics, etc., while avoiding panpsychism."[27]

This work is still in progress but seems to demonstrate some promise. Adherents of neutral monism, such as Choate, Basti, and Frohlich, through utilizing PSII also claim to avoid panspsychism as is essential to the development of Phi/IIT (i.e., the view that consciousness is equivalent to information—Phi).[28] I have previously indicated that this aspect of IIT is not clear. The interesting claim of PSII is that it deals with semantic (meaning of) information as opposed to syntactic (order of) information (IIT claims rely solely on Shannon mathematical information [ordered information]). Choate, Basti, and Frohlich, who propose PSII as an alternative to IIT, suggest that it has a number of advantages over Phi/IIT as an empirical scientific theory of information, including:

1. If the world is composed of information (i.e., of the Shannon variety), then IIT would [necessarily] lead to pansypchism, i.e., everything is conscious.

2. Organisms, especially those with brains, do not process information; they sample information, construct meaning (semantics), and discard information.

---

26. Choate, et al. "Moving Towards PSII: A Proposal for a Psychophysical Science of Consciousness," abstract 36 (2016): 64.

27. Ibid.

28. John Searle has criticized this notion that consciousness is equivalent to information as circular. See John Horgan, "Can Integrated Information Theory Explain Consciousness?"

3. A justification of semantic information content and measure based upon Quantum Field Theory (QFT) and Category Theory Logic (CTL) exists.[29]

The connection between QFT and CTL has yet to undergo rigorous development. This leaves the robust and potential heuristic fruitfulness of PSII open, but uncertain. Nonetheless, this theory, in lieu of much more development, is compatible with a classic understanding of the Christian God and creation. The application of neutral monism as a theory of consciousness has striking similarities with Thomistic metaphysics.[30] It also seems to be sufficiently malleable and compatible with different interpretations of QMs and the understanding Dembski gives us of God's action through information and his Trinitarian Mode of Creation. There is an undeniably transcendent component regarding information, whether used in IIT or PSII. Yet, as intriguing and promising as PSII may sound on the surface, we must await further empirical evidence. IIT has amassed empirically observable evidence of having measured informational content of brain states and commences from a phenomenal understanding of consciousness, in order to avoid the "hard problem" of consciousness. IIT has gathered widespread attention from philosophers, cognitive scientists, and neuroscientists, as well as computational biologists. It remains to be seen whether PSII can provide better heuristics as a scientific theory of consciousness, while being capable of measuring and discerning the level of complexity, evident in something like the origin of consciousness. If PSII can measure the informational content required for organisms to formulate or construct meaning, as for instance, in a minimal threshold for self-consciousness, then we would have a scientific theory of consciousness. As to how this is scientifically quantifiable remains to be explored through empirically verifiable means using controlled observable evidence.

7.3.2.3 *Orchestrated Objective Reduction (Orch-OR)*

Orchestrated Objection Reduction theory is the product of the combined efforts of anesthesiologist Stuart Hameroff[31] and theoretical physicist Roger

---

29. Choate et al., "Moving Towards PSII"; Hameroff and Penrose, "Reply to Criticism of the 'Orch OR qubit'—'Orchestrated Objective Reduction' is scientifically justified," 94–100; Wheeler, *A Journey into Gravity and Spacetime*; Freeman, "How and Why Brains Create Meaning From Sensory Information," 513–30; Basti, "The Quantum Field Theory (QFT) Dual Paradigm in Fundamental Physics and the Semantic Information Content and Measure in Cognitive Sciences," 594–601.

30. For a treatment of Aquinas' monistic position in contrast with Cartesian dualism, see Klima, "Thomistic 'Monism' versus Cartesian 'Dualism,'" 92–112.

31. Hameroff has been a consistent presenter and organizer at the Science of

Penrose. This theory proposes that consciousness originates from the internal processes within neurons, as opposed to emerging from the causal connections between neurons. Hameroff and Penrose refer to the noncomputability[32] of conscious thought processes. They suggest that there is an inseparability between experiential phenomena (qualia, and I would include self-consciousness as well) and the physical universe (this would include our bodies). Thus, consciousness and physical reality are closely bound together. This is where they argue for OR (objective reduction), which is in the "phenomenon of quantum state self-reduction"[33] indicating that the quantum process of OR is orchestrated by what are known as microtubules. Some important points regarding Orch-OR will now be provided to help readers understand the implications and basic important features of Orch-OR.[34]

Microtubules can fall apart—which can cause loss of memory/consciousness—Alzheimer's disease would be an example. Microtubules act very similarly to computers, whereby proteins carry bits of information. The boundary between quantum mechanics and classical Newtonian mechanics is where Hameroff and Penrose claim that consciousness lies. This gets to the bottom of the Planck scale where single dimension objects known as strings reside. Hameroff and Penrose also suggest that information and Platonic wisdom may exist, i.e., abstractions such as "truth," "divine wisdom," "absolute knowledge," and "an intangible essence" may also reside at the bottom of the scale. I would contend this is where God's action comes into play through QM, and God's interaction through the Trinitarian Mode of Creation (introduced in chapter 6, section 4). Quantum computations refer to the threshold for consciousness occurring inside microtubules inside neurons. Both Hameroff and Penrose suggest that consciousness in the

---

Consciousness (previously known as Toward a Science of Consciousness) since 1994. He hosts the conference every second year in Tucson, Arizona. It attracts major thinkers on consciousness from around the world and from a variety of disciplines.

32. See Penrose, *The Emperor's New Mind*, 480. What is meant by non-computability is a reference to the Lucas-Penrose argument. This refers to the notion that because humans can understand or know the truth of Kurt Gödel's unprovable statements that human thought is necessarily non-computable. This is predicated on Kurt Gödel's notion that any theory capable of proving simple arithmetic can be neither consistent nor complete. This sounds completely paradoxical but it is illuminated when one accounts for the following statement: "This theory can't assert the truth of this statement." Such a statement is true or incomplete (unprovable) or the converse, false and provable (inconsistent). A major criticism of Orch-OR theory is Penrose's abductive reasoning, which associated quantum processes to non-computability. See Laforte, et al., "Why Gödel's Theorem Cannot Refute Computationalism," 265–86.

33. Hameroff and Penrose, "Conscious Events as Orchestrated Space-Time Selections," 791. The article is an adaptation of one that originally appeared in the *Journal of Consciousness Studies* 3.

34. See Hameroff and Penrose, "Consciousness in the Universe: An Updated Review of the "Orch-OR" Theory."

brain cannot be explained scientifically, i.e., through neither materialism nor methodological naturalism or any other conventional scientific approach. Moreover, Hameroff has suggested that the claim made by scientific materialists about the absurdity of the transcendence of consciousness has no real basis since it is not within their epistemic rights to bar such a possibility, if solely based on our knowledge of the structure and functioning of the brain. Quantum effects may connect the brain activity to a more basic and fundamental level of the universe. And finally, consciousness may exist non-locally, independent of biological functioning. I would add that Orch-OR is an interesting theory of consciousness, which could work well with IIT, PSII, dualist notions (see the next section) with scientific implications and informational structures.

7.3.2.4 Dualist Notions with Scientific Implications (A Spiritual Neuroscience?)

Over the years there have been prominent proponents of mind-body dualism, including distinct thinkers such as John Eccles, Karl Popper, Wilder Penfield, H. Stapp, Mario Beauregard, Jeffrey M. Schwartz, Eben Alexander, and Michael Egnor.

Interestingly, neuropsychiatrist Jeffrey Schwartz, who is world-renowned for his work with Obsessive Compulsive Disorder (OCD), recognizes the ability for humans to affect their own brain physiology to alleviate brain-locks, without the use of medication. Schwartz observes the power of mental force to reconfigure components (neuroplasticity) of the brain, which cause OCD (brain-locks).[35] He explains his position regarding the mind-body debate:

> We will explore the emerging evidence that matter alone does not suffice to generate mind, but that, to the contrary, there exists a "mental force" that is not reducible to the material. Mental force, which is closely related to the ancient Buddhist concepts of mindfulness and karma, provides a basis for the effects of mind on matter that clinical neuroscience finds. What is new here is that a question with deep philosophical roots, as well as profound philosophical and moral implications, can finally be addressed (if not yet full solved) through science. If materialism can be challenged in the context of neuroscience, if stark physical reductionism can be replaced by an outlook in which the mind can exert causal control, then, for the first time since the scientific revolution, the scientific worldview will become

35. See footnote 30 in the introduction, which outlines Schwartz's position and some of his writings.

compatible with such ideals as will—and, therefore, with morality and ethics. The emerging view of the mind, and of the mind-matter enigma, has the potential to imbue human thought and action with responsibility again.[36]

The principles Schwartz demonstrates through his work on OCD and his presupposition of the irreducibility of mind to matter (although espousing a substance dualism) can function to provide explanations for the causal interactions between the brain and mind.

Further to this, Schwartz's collaborative work with H. Stapp and M. Beauregard takes on the Von Neumann-Wigner interpretation of QM, whereby through conscious effort one can influence their own brain physiology by creating a template for action via neural activity. Stapp and Schwartz strongly indicate that this process is not a materialistic one. QM has opened the door to nonmaterialistic causation, whereby activity of mind or consciousness is not reducible to the brain. The Von Neumann-Wigner interpretation involves the suggestion that a particular particle exists in one position or another where they are "superimposed" on one another. When the experimenter observes and selects one particle position over another, the others are automatically ruled out inducing a "quantum collapse." Stapp, Beauregard, and Schwartz have used this conceptual framework analogously, indicating that:

> Attending to (measuring) a thought holds it in place, collapsing the probabilities on one position. The targeted attention strategy, which is used to treat obsessive-compulsive disorders, provides a model for how free will might work in a quantum system. The model assumes the existence of a mind that chooses the subject of attention, just as the quantum collapse assumes the existence of an experimenter who chooses the point of measurement.[37]

Mario Beauregard and Vincent Paquette have performed some interesting experiments involving the mystical experiences of Carmelite nuns.[38] Their work is part of a growing field of "spiritual neuroscience" which intersects psychology, religion, spirituality, and neuroscience. The main task of this field is to study the neural foundations for religious/spiritual/mystical experiences (RSMEs). Their study involved the use of functional magnetic resonance imaging (fMRI) and quantitative electroencephalography (QEEG) on fifteen nuns ranging from age twenty-three to sixty-four. Beauregard and Paquette's aims

---

36. Schwartz and Begley, *The Mind & The Brain*, 52–53.

37. Ibid.

38. See Beauregard and Paquette, "Neural Correlates of a Mystical Experience in Carmelite Nuns," 186–90; Beauregard and O'Leary, *The Spiritual Brain*, chapter 9: The Carmelite Studies: A New Direction?

were modest in that they wanted to gather information regarding the brain states induced by mystical experiences, specifically: "[they] wanted to know two things: whether brain activity during mystical consciousness is localized in the temporal lobe, as some have argued, and whether mystical contemplation produces brain states not associated with ordinary consciousness."[39]

Popular misconceptions exist revolving around neural correlates and mystical/religious experiences, Beauregard explains:

> The fact that mystical experiences and states may have identifiable neural correlates (which are the only aspect that neuroscience can actually study) has typically been interpreted by journalists as suggesting that the experiences are somehow a delusion. In itself, that is a confused idea, equivalent to assuming that if hitting a home run has identifiable neural correlates, the home run is a delusion. And of course, the results of our work are assumed to be a strike either for or against God.[40]

The existence or non-existence of God is completely independent of a neuroscientific study; it may have implications when interpreted one certain way or another but the effects on the brain evidenced by such experiences are independent of such questions. What Beauregard and Paquette's studies did indeed show is that there is no "God spot" in the brain located within the temporal lobes, but rather these mystical experiences involve several parts of the brain including the "inferior parietal lobule, visual cortex, caudate nucleus, and left brain stem as well as many other areas."[41] This is congruent with the subjects' accounts of RSMEs being multifaceted. Beauregard indicates that "the results of [the] fMRI and QEEG studies suggest that RSMEs are instantiated by neural activity in different brain regions involved in a variety of functions, such as self-consciousness, emotion, body representation, visual and motor imagery and spiritual perception."[42] They were able to measure brain activity through observation of the mystical states the nuns were known to experience. Much like in IIT, which starts from a phenomenological subjective state, the experimenter relies on the subjective experience of the subject in order to interpret the results. The neuroscientist cannot tell you what you experience, since the neural correlates will not provide such information. One cannot distinguish a particular thought from another thought based on neural interactions. What the Carmelite experiment does seem be indicative of is that a reductive explanation of RSMEs to a particular part of the brain like a "God spot" is demonstrably false. The

---

39. Beauregard and O'Leary, *The Spiritual Brain*, 265.

40. Ibid., 269.

41. Ibid., 272.

42. Ibid., 274.

experiment has also given neuroscientists sufficient data to compare other RSMEs and see the consistency with the results: "a complex pattern is not consistent with a simple explanation."[43]

These experiments and treatments are strong indications of a transcendent component to the brain—whether of a completely different substance (substance dualism) or of a different aspect (dual aspect monism) will require further reflection and exploration. Nonetheless it is consistent with the view that there is a spiritual dimension to reality and it seems to present a strong anomaly to reductive materialist explanations.

7.4 Non-Interventionist Objective Divine Action (NIODA)[44]

We now focus our attention on an important research program that undergirds Russell's CMI, NIODA. NIODA is intimately tied to both science influencing theology and vice versa. Russell has worked extensively on this program.[45] Our discussion of Lakatos's methodology of research programs continues and is highly relevant with respect to NIODA. Nancey Murphy's dissertation in theology focused on utilizing a Lakatosian methodology.[46] This has led Russell to a profound appreciation of this methodology. Indeed, he has applied it not only to NIODA as a research program, but also to several other research programs he is involved with.[47] A characteristic of a Lakatosian methodology is recognition of the fact that scientific theories contain in themselves a core scheme with a series of interrelated hypotheses.[48] As we have already seen, a major component of Lakatos's methodology is a criterion for evaluation of theories to determine whether one is more progressive than others.[49] The key criterion is the capacity for a theory to explain certain "novel facts" that are corroborated in the future.[50] Murphy's work extends Lakatos's methodology beyond the natural sciences, to its applicability to theology: "A fact is novel if it is one not used in the construction of theory T that is taken to confirm ... [that is] one documented after

43. Ibid., 276.

44. For an in-depth discussion on scholars involved in the science and theology dialogue regarding divine action and NIODA, see Russell, et al., *Quantum Cosmology and the Laws of Nature: Scientific Perspectives on Divine Action.*

45. See Russell, *Cosmology*, 151–11.

46. Refer back to sections 2.5 and 2.7 for a discussion regarding Lakatosian methodology. See also, Murphy, *Theology in the Age of Scientific Reasoning.*

47. See Russell, *Cosmology*, 17–19.

48. Ibid., 16.

49. Ibid.

50. Ibid.

T is proposed."[51] Clayton too has thought it useful to implement a Lakatosian methodology with respect to theological research programs. Key to
Clayton's position regarding Lakatosian methodology is the core concept of
explanation, which is applicable to the natural and social sciences as well
as theological inquiry.[52] He suggests that from a theological appropriation
of Lakatosian methodology, the key element lies in Lakatos's prerequisite
of criteria that has already been delineated by a particular community,
whereby rival hypotheses can be considered.[53]

Clayton and Murphy have been involved in a debate where they have
criticized each other's respective positions regarding Lakaotisan methodologies in applicability to theology.[54] As we have seen, Clayton does not
view CMI creating a problemshift[55] as an overall research program.[56] It is
my contention that a revision of NIODA may resolve such a tension, particularly in its application to the origin of consciousness.

It is worth noting that NIODA resulted because of a false dichotomy
that was imposed on theology and divine action. Murphy and others have observed this was influenced by "three elements that constitute the Newtonian
mechanistic worldview: the Laplacian/deterministic view of natural causality
embedded in classical mechanics, epistemic reductionism, and ontological
materialism (particularly atomism)."[57] This false dichotomy involved two
opposing views. In the first, "conservative" Christian theologians held that
God would suspend or break the laws of physics which He created. The other
position was opted for by "liberal" theologians. In that view, God appears to
be acting in creation, but this is nothing more than mere appearance and is
explicable through mere natural processes. NIODA seeks to override this false
dichotomy. First, I will consider Russell's proposal of a quantum mechanics
(QM) based method to NIODA (QM-NIODA),[58] followed by a critique by

51. As quoted in Russell, *Cosmology*, 16. For the original, see Nancey Murphy,
Theology in the Age of Scientific Reasoning, 68.

52. See Clayton, *Explanation from Physics to Theology*.

53. Ibid.

54. Murphy, "Response to Review by Philip Clayton of 'Theology in the Age of
Scientific Reasoning' by Nancey Murphy," 11; Clayton, "Review of 'Theology In the Age
of Scientific Reasoning' by Nancey Murphy," 29–31.

55. See section 1.6 for Clayton's quote.

56. Murphy does not see the CMI as a problemshift, either.

57. Russell, *Cosmology*, 16; Murphy, *Anglo-American Postmodernity*, especially
chapter 5.

58. It is worth noting that there are at least 11 distinct interpretations of QM—
physicists and philosophers of physics have great disagreement on which best describes
reality. See Collins, "The Many Interpretations of Quantum Mechanics." In part this
is why I have refrained from speaking specifically of one understanding over another. Russell's preference is the Copenhagen interpretation. As has been explained
earlier, some physicists and philosophers feel uncomfortable with this because of the

Alvin Plantinga. From there in a subsequent section, I will examine a position envisioned Dembski. The purpose of this section is to demonstrate that the pitfalls of "divine intervention" can be avoided through QM and the understanding Dembski gives us of information, in how God interacts with the material world including consciousness. The significance of Dembski's view of information allows for a coherent method of action for God to interact with the world and consciousness.

Russell suggests that QM-NIODA serves as the best explanation amongst its competitors but, as he admits, not completely without problems.[59] This concept of QM as applied to NIODA (QM-NIODA) entails that God created the universe *ex nihilo* in such a way that God can act within the universe without intervening or disrupting the laws of nature.[60] Russell explains that the appeal of QM-NIODA lies, from a Lakatosian perspective, in that it provides a "surplus of predictions in the realm of theistic evolution: quantum mechanics is integrally involved in genetic mutations."[61] Essentially,

---

measurement problem resulting in an sudden change to the wave function which violates the Schrödinger equation. Nevertheless, this has been foundational for Russell's NIODA program. Russell gives a more precise definition of measurement:

> It is crucial to note that, contrary to its term, the "measurement" process which triggers the collapse of the wave function is <u>not</u> limited to laboratory experiments. To avoid what is often taken to be this narrow meaning of the term "measurement" I have frequently used the term "quantum event" in its stead because the collapse of the wave function can take place throughout the subatomic world, and not just when scientists measure quantum systems. For example, the capture of an electron by a dust particle in interstellar space, the radioactive decay of a uranium atom in the core of the earth, the absorption of a photon by water molecules in the air, the making or breaking of molecular bonds involved in genetic mutations, the fusion of hydrogen nuclei in the center of the sun and the resulting emission of light—all these and countless other processes fall within the domain of quantum mechanics and represent the underlying ontological indeterminism of the atomic realm. In all these processes, the best inference is that there is genuine ontological indeterminism in the quantum domain of nature. Whether there is similar ontological indeterminism at one or many other levels, from those at the varieties of everyday nature to the universe as a whole, is an open question which other contributors to this volume will discuss. Indeed the exploration of such a possibility is one of the central reasons for this volume. Nevertheless, my theological proposal is that ontological indeterminism exists at the quantum level and that it provides a basis for a theological account of direct, objective, and non-interventionist / non-miraculous divine action. Russell, "What we've learned from quantum mechanics about non-interventionist objective divine action in nature—and what are its remaining challenges?", 10–11 (conference draft, April 2017—forthcoming publication).

59. See Russell, *Cosmology*, 251–52. Russell responds to common criticisms regarding utilizing a quantum mechanics approach to NIODA.

60. Ibid, 19.

61. Ibid.

the actual means by which genetic mutations transpire occurs at the quantum level, where a hydrogen bond is broken. This is a necessary condition for the development of a mutation. These mutations then are gradually built up and preserved through natural selection and lead to all the diversity we see around us. One of the main problematics with this proposal is that it can make God in a direct way responsible for all the genetic mutations, which according to the standard neo-Darwinian model, are said to be random with respect to the fitness of the organism. Not only are they random but most of them are deleterious and harmful to the organism. Only the rare instances of beneficial or neutral ones can lead to the preservation of biological complexity. Russell does not explicitly state this problem of deleterious mutations but acknowledges that this does "exacerbate" the problem of natural theodicy, because of God's intimate involvement with nature. Another problem that arises is that Russell presupposes the veracity of the Neo-Darwinian model. As we have already explored, there are various competing evolutionary models from the theistic perspective that may or may not include a full blown version of Neo-Darwinism (ND). Much of the advancement in evolutionary biology suggests that ND is a narrow view of evolution, especially theistic evolution. ND is fully compatible with theistic evolution, that is, once the relevant terms are properly defined. This is something that cannot be fully explored here. However, there is no logical contradiction between ND and theistic belief. It is only the metaphysical add-ons such as the claims that the process of evolution is unintended, impersonal and undirected, etc.; all of which are not part of the scientific theory, that may render it, by definition, incompatible with Christian theism. Nonetheless, Russell considers this to be a progressive example of a Lakatosian program of research on NIODA.

How does this research program affect the origins and emergence of consciousness? As we have already explored, this would depend on the ontological status we grant consciousness. If one were to adopt a position of eliminative materialism, then one would want to account for why evolutionary development would permit an illusory belief as advantageous for human adaptation and survivability. Even from a theistic perspective this would indeed be a peculiar thing but nonetheless imaginable and possible since there are Christians of all stripes, for example, quasi-physicalists (those who deny the existence of supernatural beings such as angels and demons exist, and even perhaps the existence of a real God). This book will not take that approach, but rather it will take consciousness as a real phenomenal human experience, which necessitates an explanation for its origins. This will be considered in chapter 8, in light of three differing proposals for the origin of consciousness from a Christian perspective: Moreland (substance dualist), Lonergenian-Helminiak (Tripartite), and Clayton (emergent monism). Moreland's position, as we shall see in chapter 8, could require divine action that could be deemed "interventionist" at some level, but could also work nicely under the umbrella of an emergentist substance dualism. As we have already considered, when it comes to an immaterial aspect or component of the human person such as the soul, there would be some sort of intervention needed.[62] This is the position offered by Christian evolutionary biologist and theologian Denis Lamoureux. Moreland adheres to traducianism. Perhaps Dembski's informationally porous universe can offer a way that is more consistent?

7.4.1 What is Meant by Intervention?

The question of intervention directly concerns the notion of divine action.[63] It will be useful to examine what is really meant by intervention and how it affects our understanding of divine action including NIODA. Traditionally, since the seventeenth century, an intervention is understood to be an act of God known as an instance of special creation after the initial creation of the universe. Intervention, it seems, could mean any action that God takes upon the created order. It is sometimes described as a suspension of the laws of physics.[64] One could ask why God would suspend the laws He created at one point, in order to intervene at another. In line with this thought, Murphy disapprovingly states: "the route of more conservative theologians who insist on God's miraculous contravention of the laws of nature, a route that often results in inattention to the results of science or, worse, to their outright rejection."[65] This, it seems to me, indicates a *prima facie* challenge to God's foreknowledge and turns God into a fumbler/tinkerer of sorts. But does intervention really necessitate a suspension or breaking of the laws of physics? As we shall see with Plantinga's criticisms, those supporting NIODA like Murphy and Russell are not entirely clear as to the meaning of intervention. Nonetheless, Murphy's concern is understandable, but is it a fair accusa-

---

62. See sections 3.6.2 and 3.6.3.

63. Look at chapter 7.4, in our discussion of NIODA.

64. For an interesting series of philosophical and theological essays on God's action in the world see Tracy, *The God Who Acts*. Certain interpretations of the cosmological sciences and evolutionary biological sciences have been seen to remove God from having any "influence," "intervention," or any discernible type of action. This is true with Pierre Laplace's work *Treatise on Celestial Mechanics*, Lyell's work in geology, and Darwin's work in evolutionary biology. Moreover, when this is coupled with the philosophy of David Hume and Immanuel Kant against the soundness of classical arguments for God's existence based on the observation of nature, it plays strongly into the materialistic/naturalistic interpretation of reality. Thus, scientific claims have been seen to trump claims of intervention ever since the philosophical and scientific development of a supposedly autonomous universe. See Meyer, "The Return of the God Hypothesis," 1–38.

65. Murphy, "Introduction" in *Neuroscience and the Person*, ii.

tion? The concept of divine intervention may seem unpalatable to many, particularly theologians,[66] because of the accompanying stigma of being labeled scientifically ignorant. But perhaps an intervention of God, or to put it in more acceptable terms, God's "action," is where a resolution may lie. In order to be intellectually honest with oneself, one must be able to at least entertain the possibility. What about God operating through the informational structure of the universe? Life as we know it depends on information-rich systems (specified information). We also know that information transcends the material component, so in essence this is a way God could interact with life and even complex brains without suspending or breaking the laws of nature. This could also be seen as an intervention, even if operating at the quantum level, but not one where God contravenes the laws of nature that He initially created. If God were to alter the physical state of a particular medium (i.e., the brain) then God would be involved in an "intervention." Russell's use of QM-NIODA with the Copenhagen interpretation suggests that an "intervention" can be avoided "if the media [the substratum where the information is being conveyed by God] lies at the quantum level and if God can collapse the wave function to a particular potential state." Russell also indicates that other interpretations of QM such as Bohm's views, many worlds/many minds, DCC (GRW) and others, would not avoid an intervention.[67] While I have left the issue of which interpretation to use quite open and I will appeal to future research to delineate precisely which one fits best with the evidence regarding the origin of consciousness; I can see the appeal of the Copenhagen Interpretation. But, what about the von Neuman-Wigner interpretation? This interpretation suggests that consciousness is the cause of the collapse of the wave function. This could be fitting with how God could potentially interact with the world as the transcendent observer of His creation—sustaining and conserving His creation but also acting within it (whether interventionist or non-interventionist). This is a notion worthy of further exploration but would run into difficulties regarding God's relationship to time and the fact that God does not take measurements since He is omniscient. Perhaps this could be a way that God views the totality of His creation. Nonetheless, the von Neumann-Wigner interpretation also suggests that the process of a quantum measurement can only be completed through consciousness (a conscious observer)—a "nonphysical mind." Nevertheless, both the von-Neuman-Wigner and the Copenhagen interpretations are appealing to Christian theism since they give a special status to the mind of the observer (whether God, or created persons), thus striking

---

66. Prominent twentieth-century theologians such as Langdon Gilkey and Rudolf Bultmann and also contemporary theologians such as Russell, Murphy, Clayton, and Thomas Tracy resist the label and notion of "intervention."

67. Private communication with Russell.

a blow at scientific materialism and physical determinism.[68] Murphy, as a physicalist, sees the explanation of all phenomena as being physical, but for our purposes is consciousness really reducible to some causal explanation from within the brain? Is emergence sufficient for its explanation? One must always take into consideration the standard objection of the god-of-the-gaps in the face of invoking an intervention as a mode of God's action. One way of avoiding this problem is to make an inference to the best explanation. This is a standard mode of reasoning we have already examined in chapter 2, discussing the role of philosophy in the sciences, specifically in a brief section regarding abductive logic.

Nancey Murphy and Jeff Schloss acknowledge one major problematic for physicalism: namely, explaining God's action with the material world, since God is understood as immaterial. It was much easier to explain God's action through other immaterial components such as the soul, but the interaction between immaterial and material is problematic in any form.[69] Those who support NIODA such as Murphy and Schloss (including also Russell of course) propose a downward causation because of the hierarchy of complexity, in an attempt to explain how God may interact without violating the laws of physics.[70] What is most troubling about the Christian physicalist position, if indeed they affirm God's omniscience, is that due to the very nature of a

68. See Stapp, "Quantum Theory and the Role of Mind in Nature"; Von Neumann, *Mathematical Foundations of Quantum Mechanics*; Davies and Brown, *The Ghost in the Atom*, 73. See also section 7.3.2.4 for further appeal of the von Neumann interpretation.

69. See Ryle, *The Concept of Mind*, chapter 1. He launches an attack on Cartesian Dualism, pejoratively naming it the "Ghost in the Machine"—purporting it explains nothing and exacerbates the problem of mind, since it is impossible to explain the causal relationship between the immaterial and the material. He also argues that dualism transforms into a form of solipsism, in either case, i) mind being the only knowable entity, or ii) the only existing one, but this criticism is applicable to any type of thought and can be problematic in any theory of mind.

70. See Russell, et al., *Neuroscience and the Person*; Juarrero, *Dynamics in Action*; Murphy and Brown, *Did My Neurons Make Me Do It?* Russell, nonetheless, is still relying on the Copenhagen interpretation of QM through God's action in relation to the collapsing of the wave function. He suggests there are 4 possible outcomes in terms of God's action in relation to the collapse of a wave function:

> option i) God's action is related to the collapse but it may or may not be related to the specific outcome. Instead the outcome might be due to natural causes.
> option ii) God's action relates to the specific outcome but it may or may not be related to the collapse. Instead the collapse might be due to natural causes.
> option iii) God's action is related to both the collapse and the specific outcome. Logically there is a fourth, rather deistic option: iv) God's action is not related to either the collapse or the specific outcome.

Russell, "What we've learned from quantum mechanics about non-interventionist objective divine action in nature—and what are its remaining challenges?", 11 (April 2017 Conference Draft).

materialistic universe, God is inaccessible to the inner moral conscience, i.e., our inner moral thoughts would be defined, in a strictly materialistic sense, as material. These thoughts, if you can call them that, would be nothing more than epiphenomenal or illusory activity (in the eliminative reductive position). This seems to pose a significant and perhaps even insurmountable problem. How can God possibly judge our internal moral conscience without any external manifestation? This is true especially if neuroscience is never able to overcome the "hard problem" of consciousness, i.e., revealing the contents of one's thoughts. Even if we take at face value what one says about sensations of pain, or how one experiences color or truth or perception in general, typically there is not a 100 percent correspondence between the real and these descriptions. So, if God is immaterial by the physicalist definition and cannot access thoughts, which are ultimately complex causal interactions with matter, understood as brain structure and neurons firing, then there can be no causal interaction between God and the material. Still, the informational content of the inner workings of the brain cannot be deduced by physicalist means. For instance, how does one distinguish the exact same neurophysiological inner workings, when a subject is claiming to have two very distinct thoughts? A serious problem develops for the Christian physicalist with respect to God's omniscience. Clearly, they must either alter their understanding of this or the traditional concept of omniscience must be dropped. Unless there is a way of reading the information in the brain, if it is indeed stored as it is in a USB key, hard drive, or any media-storing device, the information stored must be seen to transcend the material medium it is stored on; the transcendence of such information might perhaps, in principle, alleviate the difficulty of God knowing the information.

So, in essence, the physicalist position presents a peculiar but unavoidable conundrum to God's action and knowledge of our internal moral conscience. This also says absolutely nothing about whether we have free will or if we are just effectively matter in motion. Clearly there is confusion here, since this would deny any transcendent component of the human person even assuming a general physical composition. It is my contention that William Dembski, through his explorations concerning the metaphysics of information, has provided a plausible resolution to this issue of God's action, as explored with the arguments from systematic theology in chapter 6.

7.4.2 Plantinga's Criticism of NIODA

In his book on the relationship between science, religion, and naturalism, *Where the Conflict Really Lies*, Plantinga takes to task many of the intellectuals who support NIODA and DAP. The first thing to point out is that Plantinga believes that those who attack intervention are not clear about what they mean, and that this is the major source of discord. In other words, they attack or object to things that remain elusive, resulting in communication problems. One of Plantinga's greatest concerns is the fact that those involved with NIODA and DAP have not clearly defined what intervention means aside from "violating the laws," "setting aside natural law," or "overriding" physical laws.[71] Plantinga asks himself why God is unable to intervene, so to speak, within His own creation. Scholars involved in DAP and with NIODA such as Russell, Clayton, Murphy, Peacocke, George Ellis, and others allow for the creation and conservation of the universe, but not special action or direct intervention within the world.[72] Instead they seek to establish a means for God's action beyond creation and conservation of the world through intervention. What is also problematic is that these thinkers disregard significant actions of God, for example, His offer and gift of grace surely would constitute some kind of special divine action, but this is not clearly discussed. In a purely physicalist universe, would something like that be possible? How do those involved in NIODA/DAP understand the incarnation, resurrection, and other alleged miracles that are proper to classical Christianity?[73] To be sure, Russell has proposed a FINLONC for the resurrection.[74]

The question remains whether God can act in the world without following the predictability and regularity of the laws He established Himself.[75]

71. Plantinga, *Where the Conflict Really Lies*, 111; see Russell, "Divine Action and Quantum Mechanics," 295.

72. Plantinga, *Where the Conflict Really Lies*, 97.

73. While it is true that Russell does not deny miracles and accounts for them theologically following Pannenberg's thought as "proleptic manifestations of the eschatological New Creation within the processes of the present, fallen creation." This would be in line with Russell's FINLON/FINLONC. Russell indicates that "NIODA opens up a new, third category of divine action. It is a category that lies between general providence (God's action underlies but makes no difference to the flow of natural processes) and objective special providence / miracles (God's action does make a difference to the flow of natural processes by violating or suspending them, or as Aquinas writes in his third definition of miracle, God does what nature could do but God does it instead of letting nature do it). NIODA is a third category of divine action: it is not miraculous ("non-intervention") DA but it results in an objective change in the flow of nature."

Much of this clarification is due to a private communication with Russell (October 2018). I appreciate Russell's clarifications here, but I still ask myself how we are to avoid vague language or what Wittgenstein called "language games." In other words, how do we avoid the charge of speaking in ambiguities or what atheists may describe as nonsensical. Nonetheless, one would like to know how we can account for a variety of miracles given such a picture of the world and God's interaction within it. Is NIODA sufficient in terms of God's action? This is something I touch upon in section 2.7 with respect to the resurrection of Jesus as a FINLONC.

74. This will be discussed further in section 7.5.

75. Plantinga argues that even in a causally closed universe it is very difficult to "break" a law, but that this whole idea suffers from confusion. Plantinga responds to

I think Plantinga hits the nail on the head when he wonders what the differences are between intervention as conceived by those involved in NIODA and DAP and special divine action, when he states: "every case of special divine action will automatically be a case of intervention—thus making the whole project of trying to find a conception of special divine action that doesn't involve intervention look a little unlikely."[76] Even if one includes God's action within QM events, it is still unclear as to what is being referred to as divine action.

Plantinga explores the involvement of quantum mechanics in NIODA. The question arises whether it is relevant that QM gives the appearance or suggests unpredictability in our understanding and various interpretations of things, but does this really preclude any intervention? Most of the thinkers that hold to NIODA/DAP adhere to the Copenhagen interpretation[77] for quantum mechanics (as opposed to, at least ten other possible interpretations), which only holds to an indeterministic understanding with respect to "mysterious measurements."[78] This interpretation seems to amount to a

---

three main criticisms or objections to God's intervention. First there is a connection with the problem of evil whereby God only intervenes in some circumstances, but not others to alleviate human pain and suffering. The claim here is that we cannot make a reasonable deduction of God's intervention unless we have a certain criterion for deciding how God will miraculously intervene. Plantinga points out that by no means can or should we humans know God's reasons for intervening in one situation and not another. He illustrates this in the book of Job, where lack of understanding God's reasons for allowing suffering is clear. I would have to agree with Plantinga that such an expectation is wholly unreasonable. The second objection involves God's intervention or even interference with the regularity of the universe which infringes on free will. The concern here lies with regularity and predictability. Here again Plantinga points out that this need not necessarily be the case, since God could intervene in a regular and predictable manner. Even with the introduction of some irregularity, there needs to be a sufficient amount of regularity for human free deliberation. The third and the most common objection concerns God breaking the laws he ordained or "overriding" them. God establishes consistent and regular laws then seemingly acts contrary to them, as in the case of raising Lazarus from the dead or parting the Red Sea; this type of special action is deemed to be inconsistent with his already established created order. Plantinga views such an objection as being a theological one. God's special action could only be deemed inconsistent if he did not possess any special reason for intervening. Plantinga here envisions God acting as a "romantic" artist very active in His creation, as opposed perhaps, to an artist with more restraint, who operates through a universe which requires no guidance. Plantinga sees God "leading, guiding, persuading and redeeming people, by blessing them with 'the Internal Witness of the Holy Spirit' as Calvin would suggest, or 'the Internal Instigation of the Holy Spirit' as Aquinas has called it, and conferring upon them the gift of faith. Either option seems theologically consistent." Plantinga, *Where the Conflict Really Lies*, 108.

76. Plantinga, *Where the Conflict Really Lies*, 112.

77. We have already discussed the Copenhagen interpretation in the introduction, see page 39 footnote 110.

78. Plantinga, *Where the Conflict Really Lies*, 114–15.

meddling within the natural laws of QM. "Could it be that God acts in the unpredictable inner workings of QM?" How is one certain that this type of divine action does not conflict with their definitions of "intervention"? Is it solely our ignorance and human limitations which prevent us from accurately interpreting the findings of QM? Plantinga proposes a sort of resolution to the problematic of either a hands-off Creator or a constant meddler, as envisioned by those who support NIODA and DAP. Plantinga suggests a method of God's action through DCC.[79] This allows for God to act in a way that goes beyond mere creation and conservation of physical reality, "always acting specially."[80] The appeal of DCC is that God can interact with the microscopic physical reality, which supervenes on the macroscopic, namely through acting within the "right" microscopic collapse effects. This also offers a resolution to refraining from altering the nature of already created beings such as atoms, molecules, particular processes, animals, and humans. The DCC avoids the objections raised by proponents of NIODA and DAP.[81] This allows for the possibility of God's involvement in the origin of consciousness as well as another vital component: information. Moreover, it allows physical systems to undergo change between collapses according to the Schrödinger equation, which designates the changes of physical systems over time through quantum effects like wave-particle dualities.[82]

Although theories of physics are vital to understanding physical reality, we cannot reduce God's action to them. It may be that a particular interpretation of QM can provide a greater insight into *how* God has acted throughout the history of the universe and continues to act to this very day, but it would be theologically unsatisfactory to reduce His action in such a fashion. We must always keep in mind that we can only deal with the best scientific theories that we currently possess, as long they are consistent with the evidence, we cannot go any further. Thus, this is in line with the project of this book, searching for how theology can influence the sciences without reconstructing or constraining scientific theories, but allowing for creativity to decide which theories may best interpret the evidence while corresponding with a Christian theological understanding.

7.4.3 An Informationally Porous Universe

Alongside God's action through QM, there is a neglected but fundamental component to reality in discerning God's action: information. Throughout

79. Ibid., 116.

80. Ibid.

81. Koch, "Ubiquitous Minds," 27–28.

82. See Schrödinger, "An Undulatory Theory of the Mechanics of Atoms and Molecules," 1049–70.

his application of CMI, Russell has not utilized the notion of information to understand how God can act. This, it seems to me, would relieve much unneeded tension with respect to misconceived understandings of intervention and action. As Dembski rightfully notes, in the preface of his most recent book, *Being as Communion: The Metaphysics of Information*:

> Accordingly, the metaphysical picture that I'm painting attempts to make good on the promise of John Wheeler, Paul Davies and others that information poised to replace matter "as the primary 'stuff' of the world" and that in information we have "finally arrived at the 'right' metaphor that will unify" the sciences.[83]

Interestingly, a recent article from the *New York Times* provides a peculiar take on the nature of consciousness while ignoring the significance of information.[84] It was written by a prominent philosopher of mind, who adheres to an understanding of panpsychism, Galen John Strawson.[85]

What is important here is that information allows God to interact without "intervening" as feared by the scholars who support NIODA/DAP. This addresses the problem outlined by Murphy and Schloss regarding how an immaterial mind such as God can interact with a material mind like humans (assuming physicalism). The first thing to point out is that even in a physicalist picture of the universe, there is no reason to deny the reality of information

83. Dembski, *Being as Communion: A Metaphysics of Information*, xiv.

84. This it seems to me requires proper definitions of matter, information, and consciousness, which as we have seen are not easily defined. I follow Dembski, taking Karl Popper's lead in attempting to avoid problems of meaning for "real" ones, as Dembski states: "To be sure, I will provide definitions where they help to clarify. But I want to avoid the materialist trap in which nonmaterial realities such as intelligence, purpose and freedom—and, of course, information!—must be cashed out in materialist terms. This is a self-defeating game, and one I decline to play." See Dembski, *Being as Communion*, xv. Strawson claims that consciousness is not what is mysterious but rather our understanding of matter. He disagrees with both the eliminativists such as Dennett and Blackmore while rejecting substance dualism. He believes that perhaps something closer to Bertrand Russell's neutral monism is a better appropriation for understanding consciousness. What I found rather remarkable about the article is that it failed to account for the importance of information which, as we progress in thought as observed by Dembski, is a fundamental property of reality which transcends matter and its mere arrangement. Perhaps, information is this neutral entity? Nonetheless, without noting this, it is where I believe thinkers like Strawson blunder. He echoes Bertrand Russell that consciousness is just a matter of the inner workings of the brain. From this supposition, it seems like a difficult problem to crack, i.e., how one can distinguish one thought from the next particularly if the configuration or inner workings of the brain are identical but may generate two radically different thoughts. This problem seems to severely undercut Strawson's argument. See Strawson, "Consciousness Isn't a Mystery. It's Matter."

85. See Strawson, "Consciousness Isn't a Mystery. It's Matter."

and the fact that it transcends matter. This does not necessitate a dualism, but it suggests that information is not reducible to the medium it is embedded on. We know this from our experience of exchanging information. It can be contained on the pages of a book, a text message, an email, verbalized from one mind to another, it can be etched onto bark or even encoded into a bacteria's DNA. This is the versatility of the same specified information and its transferability. Given this, even if one wants to assume a physicalist position regarding the soul, one need not negate this transcendent nature of information. This would go against empirical observation. This mere fact moves us beyond Murphy's criticism that God cannot interact with material entities, since information by its very nature permits this.

The other point is that, as we have acknowledged with Plantinga's criticism, the universe is open to divine action, not closed to it as assumed in a deterministic and/or fully naturalistic universe—if God exists and interacts with His creation, the universe is open to His action, however that may appear. This is particularly true of a nondeterministic universe as envisioned by QM, as already discussed. An important point to make regarding a nondeterministic universe is that it is not synonymous with being a-causal as is often assumed. The precise cause may not be known, but it cannot be said there is no cause to a certain effect or phenomenon.[86] Some physicalists assume a position predominantly held by naturalists (those who deny the existence of any supernatural beings), but even if one assumes a causally closed universe as they do, there are ways around it and that should be kept in mind.

What if the universe was deterministic? What if a picture of the multiverse provided the probabilistic resources to explain away the apparent indeterminacy/non-determinant nature of QM? A causally closed universe may preclude God as an immaterial mind from interacting with a physical universe, by intervening in a way that the causal nexus may prevent on its own, but this by no means prevents God from acting in the world. Dembski paints a picture of God interacting within the world without "intervening" in a "substitutional"[87] way:

> Nonetheless, a world barring substitutional intervention cannot preclude God from prearranging the initial structure of the world so that desired material effects are achieved even if they appear

86. See Dembski, "Randomness by Design," 75–106. Dembski argues in this paper that randomness cannot make sense apart from certain inherent patterns and information in nature.

87. This demonstrates how God's action may bring forth about certain outcomes in the world, which on their own would be impossible, without necessarily involving direct intervention.

extraordinary and bespeak a deity active in the particulars of the moment. All that is required is that God build in the necessary information from the start so that it gets expressed at appropriate times and places. This is, in fact, an old idea. It comes up with Augustine's *Literal Commentary on Genesis*, where God is said to implant nature with seeds that come to fruition at appointed times and places. It is implicit in Leibniz's ideas about concurrence and pre-established harmony, in which divine purposes' material effects precisely track one another. Charles Babbage, the inventor of the modern digital computer, elaborated these ideas, arguing that God implanted nature with computational programs that activate at the right time and place. Babbage put forward this view in his *Ninth Bridgewater Treatise,* which predated Darwin's *Origins of Species* by more than twenty years . . . Accordingly, even in a world that is causally closed and fully deterministic, God, by carefully arranging the world from the start, could achieve all intended effects, up to and including acts of particular providence that appear to require direct, real-time intervention (though, in fact, they have been "front-loaded"). Note that even a full-throated physical determinism need not obviate libertarian free will: God could have arranged the physical world to reflect the freely made choices of free agents that have physical bodies.[88]

Dembski's proposition presupposes some kind of "front loading" is possible, but it would have to overcome or undercut Meyer's criticism of such scenarios as presented against the respective evolutionary creation viewpoints of Lamoureux and van Till. The question of where this information would be stored, to be unloaded at particular instances throughout natural history, arises since Meyer argues that the laws of physics are incapable of storing such rich informational content. Nonetheless, such a position is certainly consistent with classical theism and its view of God's omniscience.[89] It may be a matter of gaining further knowledge about information and the means by which it can be stored to fully understand if such a method could work. This view is also consistent with Aquinas's view that God operates through secondary causes.[90] Nonetheless, there are several options at our disposal to help us understand how God can interact with

88. Dembski, *Being as Communion,* 117–18; Dembski, *The End of Christianity,* chapter 15, "Moving the Particles," 113–21.

89. The following show the compatibility and coherence of divine foreknowledge with future contingent propositions Craig's discussion of Newcomb's paradox and divine foreknowledge. See Craig, "Divine Foreknowledge and Newcomb's Paradox," 331–50; Dembski, *The End of Christianity; Being as Communion,* 118–19n12.

90. For an up-to-date view of Aquinas' view of God's action through primary and secondary causation, see Dodds, *Unlocking Divine Action: Contemporary Divine Action.*

His creation through information, whether it is a causally open or closed system or through a deterministic or nondeterministic picture of the world. Regardless of which position one opts for, the universe will be as Dembski observes, "informationally porous."[91] This it seems is fundamental to understanding the origin of consciousness. If the brain is strongly linked to the mind and conscious states, then information will undoubtedly play a significant role in understanding different levels of consciousness. Moreover, recognition of God's action is what will provide a plausible explanation as to why self-consciousness arose when it did, in evolutionary history. It is precisely the interaction of God with his Creation that can impart information throughout the universe. This is allowed through His simplicity, meaning the lack of any parts. This is a concept that has been developed earlier.[92] This will also demonstrate the consonance of theories which take information seriously as it relates to consciousness, such as IIT and other theories of consciousness that have already been examined.

Before proceeding, a question on the necessity for a portrait of information regarding the origin of consciousness arises: Is it necessary to be tied to ID theory? I would answer that it is not necessarily the only way to understand information[93] and its relationship to consciousness. I do find Dembski's explanation of information extremely useful, but it is also not dependent upon IDT. I believe it can stand squarely outside of his work on ID since it can provide a plausible explanation for God's interaction with the universe. Dembski has in fact left the ID movement since 2015. Many ID proponents and others have disliked Dembski's work with QM and information theory to explain divine action, since God takes a "hands-off" approach. This would be true of scientific creationists. His Trinitarian Mode of Creation is also not dependent on ID, but rather is most certainly compatible.

91. Dembski, *Being as Communion*, 120.

92. This was developed in chapter 5 in the section on God's Simplicity and is connected to chapter 6 in the section on The Trinitarian Mode of Creation.

93. There are several considerations of information with respect to theology, but none as useful as Dembski's informationally porous universe or Trinitarian Mode of Creation. The following is interesting in the way it applies chaos theory which could bring some fruitful understanding of life and consciousness: See Huchingson, *Pandemonium Tremendum*. Another provides a series of different philosophical, theological, and scientific perspectives on information: See Davies and Gregersen, *Information and the Nature of Reality*.

7.5 The First Instantiation of a New Law of Nature (FINLON)

An important concept directly related to God's action, QM, and information is that of the FINLON. Though we have discussed this already in chapters 2, 3, and particularly 5, a brief review here will set the stage for understanding a significant further development. FINLONs represent singular events in the history of the universe which consequently become part of the regularity of nature once instantiated. The origin of human self-consciousness represents one such instance in the history of the universe. This we examined in chapter 5 on the concept of convergence alongside complexity and consciousness. Although phenomenal consciousness is manifested throughout biological organisms to varying degrees, the uniqueness of the high level of human self-consciousness indeed represents a FINLON particular to humans.

Russell has spent some time developing the concept of FINLON. This concept is vital since we are following Russell's CMI in order to understand how the conception of the Christian God and creation can influence the sciences, when it comes to the origin of consciousness. Russell relates FINLON to the concept of contingency, closely related to Pannenberg's idea that the laws of nature can be viewed as contingent, in a number of ways.[94] Russell has labeled this the "first instantiation contingency."[95] As mentioned before, the origin of life can also be seen as a FINLON since a law of something like Darwinian evolution, or some other process of evolution, is instantiated once a biological organism is present. Where Russell has focused his attention with respect to FINLON is on the resurrection of Jesus. He has more appropriately labeled this event as a FINLONC.[96] In light of the CMI, Russell's FINLONC faces two interesting challenges which include the challenge from cosmology to eschatology and the other from eschatology to cosmology.[97] The challenge from cosmology to eschatology represents how science influences and constrains theology (the first five pathways [1 to 5] represented by SRP à TRP). Whereas the challenge from eschatology to cosmology represents how theology can come to guide or influence science the last three pathways (6 to 8) represented by TRP à SRP. Russell expresses the concept of FINLONC through the following reflection:

> If it is impossible for Jesus to have risen from the dead (a la Hume) it cannot be true that he did. But if it is true that Jesus

94. Russell, *Cosmology*, 16.

95. Ibid., 16.

96. Ibid., 24.

97. Russell, "The Bodily Resurrection of Jesus as a First Instantiation of a New Law of the New Creation," 82.

rose bodily from the dead (a la the New Testament), it must be possible, and this in turn means that God must have been [sic] created the universe such that it can be transformed by God into the New Creation without a second *ex nihilo*. Finally, this idea can lead to very interesting scientific research programs . . .[98]

One wonders whether QM and an informationally porous universe would make the resurrection of Christ possible. A FINLONC for a general resurrection would be possible through the evolution of the universe into future eschatological scenarios that can be transformed. An important point Russell makes concerning nomological[99] contingency is that "perhaps all of the laws of nature have a first instantiation."[100] In reference to first instantiation contingency, Russell has made some other distinctions revolving around the notion of a "first instance" contingency which can be read either in a "mild" or "aggressive" way.[101] Russell points out that mild contingency is closely associated with the concept of emergence, for example, one can think of water and its property of wetness when a number of water molecules bond together. Emergence can be seen simply as when new processes and properties of complex systems are not reducible to simpler ones.[102] Many philosophers supportive of DAP such as Clayton, Murphy, and others would see consciousness as what Russell describes as a mild or weak form of a "first instance" contingency. So, the origins and emergence of consciousness can be considered a weak sense a FINLON since it is a new property or process that emerges from pre-existing properties and processes. It seems to me that the notion that consciousness, particularly, self-consciousness, as experienced by human persons is a radically novel phenomenon in the universe is indisputable. It seems G. K. Chesterton was correct, when he said, as we noted in the introduction, that would be a revolution rather than merely an evolution. For Russell, an aggressive or a strong form of "first instance" contingency represents the resurrection of Christ, which is indeed a FINLON but lays the foundation for the general resurrection of humanity, which is a FINLONC.[103] Russell suggests that with the world of matter and life there is continuity where emergence plays a fundamental role: "Thus biological phenomena evolve out of the nexus of the physical world: the organism is built from its underlying structure of cells and organs, the mind

---

98. Russel, *Cosmology*, 24.

99. Relating to or denoting certain principles, such as laws of nature that are neither logically necessary nor theoretically explicable but are simply taken as true.

100. Russel, *Cosmology*, 37.

101. Ibid.

102. Ibid.

103. Ibid., 309–10; Russell, *Time in Eternity*, 51, 81, 181.

arises in the context of neurophysiology, and so on."[104] Nonetheless, the origin and emergence of consciousness is indeed a FINLON even if in a weak sense in Russell's program.

7.6 Is the Origin and Endurance of Consciousness Consistent with NIODA or a Betrayal of It?

The question arises as to potential inconsistencies with NIODA, particularly with respect to the main objective of the book: the origin of consciousness. How is NIODA to accommodate the origin of consciousness in a way that is coherent? Certainly, as emergence is framed, it is consistent with NIODA and DAP, even though, the question remains whether the different understandings of emergence are sufficient to explain the origin of consciousness. As we have seen, it depends on how we define intervention. If we avoid these traps outlined by those supportive of DAP then we are in the clear, not necessarily side-stepping intervention, unless defined in a very narrow sense. Intervention in an open sense still allows for God's action through QM and informational processes. It could be as Dembski has iterated that no intervention is necessary as envisioned in NTE and PE outlooks on evolution.

Our examination of QM and God's action through information leaves it compatible with NIODA and DAP. Whatever the case may be, it does not deter the main objective of this book, namely, understanding the origins of consciousness through the Christian conception of God and creation. The simplicity of God can still explain—as we will show later in this book—how consciousness originates; without God the universe wouldn't exist, the laws of nature would not be as they are, and the various FINLONs such as the coalescing of matter, the origin of life, and consciousness would all be impossible since God is the source of all being.[105]

It is worth noting that philosopher Michael Arbib indicates the underlying tension and even coherence of NIODA/DAP in relation to the human person, the soul and future resurrection.[106]

Arbib states:

> Christian theology is diverse: even Catholic theologians may
> have views differing widely from each other's and the Pope's.

---

104. Russell, *Cosmology*, 309.

105. See conclusion and research guidelines (pathway 6) in this chapter, section 7.3.1. Recognizing the source of all being Who is ultimate simplicity, if there is a transcendent component to the human person then the principle of synonymy would explain such a thing (an argument which has been left to future research), see conclusion.

106. Arbib, "Towards a Neuroscience of the Person," 100.

While many Christians believe in an immaterial soul, most of the Christians writing in this volume [*Neuroscience and the Person*] do not, and see themselves as being in the mainstream of current Christian theology in rejecting dualism and embracing a belief in the resurrection of the body. They are therefore able to accept with equanimity the efforts of neuroscience to see mind [and consciousness] as a product of the brain (but with many caveats about reduction), since the New Creation would see the body resurrected in a more perfect form) by God, with mind thus recreated "automatically" without need for a disembodied spirit. Of course, this avoidance of the problem of dualism raises another problem: How does God hold "the pattern of the body" when the body decomposes in this creation? Neuroscience offers no support for reintegration of the nervous system after its decomposition following death. For this and further reasons, many other monists do not believe in immortality—the material of the body might be eternal in different forms of matter and energy, but the form of that material that gives rise to mind is temporary and loses its function at death.

Arbib raises some significant challenges for NIODA/DAP. If we can continue in this line of thinking, we can ponder even more challenges. Where is the personality of the person at the resurrection? Can it be merely transposed at the recreation? Some who rejected dualism support the endurance of the soul, such as Teilhard de Chardin and various interpretations of Aquinas suggest this as well. How does this work with NIODA/DAP? Despite the claims of neuroscience, the nature of consciousness and the mind remain elusive. Arbib is pointing out that God would have to "intervene" in some sense to arrange the particles to fit the same consciousness and personality in the brain and physical structure of the body prior to death in a perfected way for the New Creation. It is not that God is incapable, the criticism is that it fatally betrays the program of NIODA/DAP. Nonetheless, we have discovered other avenues than the strict definitional structure of NIODA/DAP with alternatives drawn from QM and the potential linkage with information systems.

7.7 Conclusion

It seems unlikely that these theories on their own or in combination will get us to the origin of self-consciousness. They all rely on a level of subjectivity to measure informational content within the brain through different inner workings such as certain neural states of the brain. What they do indeed show is the complexity of certain subjective states. But what else?

Is it actually possible to calculate the amount of integrated information, whether syntactic or semantic, necessary for self-reflection? Would one still be too reliant on the phenomenological experience of the subject to even begin to perform such a thing, so that we have no hope of overriding the "hard problem" of consciousness through IIT or PSII? What if we were to encounter a system or organism with the same calculated integrated information, whether syntactic or semantic, but possessed with self-reflective capabilities and another which did not? Would this suggest that the informational content, *form*, or structure of the brain/complexity of the organism would not be a good candidate for discerning the origin of consciousness as such? What would this say about the nature of self-consciousness? Would it be an indicator of substance dualism?

Even more questions still beg to be answered: What was the cause of the profound change from mere consciousness to self-consciousness? This is something a science of consciousness or natural science in general cannot answer. This would require a robust philosophical and/or theological program (as is being produced in this book). Are natural processes sufficient to account for singular events such as the advent of the functional information necessary to build a self-replicating system or the integrated information necessary for self-consciousness? God informationally interacting with creation could be a resolution. In a universe/multiverse created by God and in which God acts, one would expect an open system where God can interact with creation without "breaking" the laws of physics or intervening in a crude way. Russell and other theologians believe that the universe's indeterminacy as revealed by QM allows for such a possibility. Such an indeterministic universe is informationally porous and allows for God's action without any change in matter or energy given God's simple nature (disembodiment) as explored above.

How do we factor dualistic notions into neuroscience? Does the work of Schwartz, Stapp, and Beauregard suggest a duality in substance between the brain and consciousness? Or is it just another indication of the irreducibility of consciousness to the brain? Can their work operate in collaboration with any of the other scientific theories of consciousness? What are we to make of the different interpretations by different scientists of scientific finding? Does that enhance and facilitate scientific inquiry or inhibit it? Schwartz's supposition that the mind is separate from the brain has provided much fruitfulness to his medical work in curing people of OCD without medication. Regardless of whether his supposition is true or not, there is a powerful heuristic element to assuming that consciousness is separate from the brain (can assuming its irreducibility without necessarily resorting to separation potentially provide the same heuristic)? Whatever the case may be, it is Schwartz's religious beliefs (whether Jewish, Buddhist, or something else) that influence his selection of mind-body theories, which in turn affect his medical work in a positive manner. This is a definite example of theology influencing the sciences. Furthermore, scientists such as Beauregard and Schwartz are finding reductive explanations inadequate for explaining spiritual experiences and providing treatment for certain mental conditions.[107]

What about interconnecting IIT or PSII or Orch-OR with RSMEs? What could we find with respect to measurable informational content? What connections can be drawn from information, the origin of consciousness, QM, and the relationship with brain causal activities and microtubules? Which of these theories of consciousness are most plausible within the CMI framework as God causing the origin of consciousness? It is difficult to say since all these theories of consciousness seem quite tentative, but it could very well be that a combination of them or perhaps their strongest elements could function as a Lakatosian research program. This could perhaps give us a progressive problem shift if one of the theories were to accumulate more novel facts than anomalies to help explain the origin of consciousness.

Can the concept of God, as a transcendent and immaterial being, provide solutions to such difficult questions? Solutions to these difficult questions in the form of research programs are what need to be sought out by philosophers, theologians, scientists, and those who are interested in progressing the science-theology interaction in a bidirectional manner.

The question remains whether we can integrate several of these theories to produce a more robust scientific theory of consciousness. Each of them possesses valuable fruit. A combination could be the answer, but this remains for further research, since they all require further development particularly in discerning the origin of consciousness. The future of the science of consciousness remains open but these different positions seem to provide interesting potentialities in relation to theology. Theological doctrines of God's simplicity and God's action can lead us to theories like those we have explored to provide a fruitful connection between embodied self-consciousness and God.

It is the possibility of God's action through an informationally porous universe via QM indeterminacy, Plantinga's proposition of DCC, that provides some plausibility to the various possible scientific theories of consciousness. It demonstrates that these theories (IIT, PSII, Orch-OR, dualist notions with scientific implications) offer greater plausibility when in conjunction with a large measure of the Christian conception of God and creation (through the arguments in chapter 5 and 6 which are embedded within the pathways from science to theology and theology to science). In the following chapter we will examine three distinct frameworks of Christian thinkers for understanding consciousness and its origins. There are several possibilities that are compatible with Christian theism.

---

107. See Beauregard and Schwartz, "Non-Materialist Mind."

Chapter 8

Different Christian Understandings
of Consciousness

8.1 Introduction

IN THIS CHAPTER, WE will examine three different understandings of consciousness as they are expounded by three different Christian philosophers
(one understanding involves two thinkers): J. P Moreland, Bernard Lonergan
and Daniel Helminiak, and Philip Clayton.[1] In my estimation these are the
most robust and developed understandings of consciousness from a Christian
perspective. They may differ on their notions of God's interaction with the
world and how God created, but they all affirm the truth of Christian theism.
As I have outlined in earlier chapters, the main claim of my book, i.e., that
God and creation as understood through classical Christian theism (which
may encompass variations, i.e., views on evolution) provides the the most
plausible explanation for the existence of embodied human consciousness
in terms of self-reflective capacities, is compatible which each of three views
I will present even though they differ from one another. We have already
examined arguments from natural theology, philosophical theology, and
systematic theology, which are closely tied to the science and theology interaction. Now we will look at philosophical understandings of consciousness
also closely tied to that interaction. Moreover, since we have acknowledged
that philosophy acts as a mediator between science and theology, these three
understandings can provide an underpinning in our continual quest and
search for theology to provide something fruitful to say to the sciences, as
examined through the various research guidelines.

---

1. Helminiak has worked on Bernard Lonergan's theory of consciousness extensively. Given this, I have connected both their understandings of consciousness in this section. I have dubbed this understanding of consciousness as the "Lonergan-Helminiak
Tripartite Transcendent Model."

8.2 James Porter Moreland and Substance Dualism[2]

Moreland has written a number of articles and books defending substance dualism.[3] Moreland believes that God functions as "the best explanation for the finite examples of consciousness in creatures such as humans and various animals."[4] For Moreland, "consciousness is what you are aware of when you engage in first-person introspection."[5] Related to consciousness is the concept of the soul:

> The soul is a substance with an essence or inner nature, for instance, human personhood. This inner nature contains, a primitive unity, a complicated, structural arrangement of capacities and dispositions for developing a body. Taken collectively this entire ordered structure can be called the substance's *principle of activity* and will be that which governs the precise, ordered sequence of changes that substances will go through in the process of growth and development.[6]

Moreland tends to use the term consciousness and soul interchangeably, even though consciousness, for Moreland, is defined as stated above. He speaks of five types of conscious states that include sensation, thought, belief, desire, and act of will.[7] Similarly he discusses five states of the soul that are identical to his five types of conscious states: sensation, thought, belief, desire, and act of will.[8] Moreover, Moreland also discusses five faculties of the soul: sensory, the will, emotional, mind, and spirit. Thus,

2. Initially I was going to examine Charles Taliaferro's version of substance dualism, Integrative Dualism in his excellent book, *Consciousness and the Mind of God*, but felt that since there are sufficient crossovers with Moreland's work and that Moreland uses Taliaferro's argumentation to defend substance dualism, it would be redundant. Moreover, this is the case with many other thinkers who defend substance dualism such as Richard Swinburne, Robert Adams, George Bealer, Francis Beckwith, Mark Bedau, Roderick Chisolm, Stewart Goetz, William Hasker, Brian Leftow, Paul Mosser, Alvin Plantinga, Geoffrey Madell, Howard Robinson, and Eleanore Stump. I felt that Moreland's defense lined up closest to the project of this book with his AC (Argument from Consciousness). See also, Goetz and Taliaferro, *A Brief History of the Soul*.

3. See Moreland, *Scaling the Secular City*, 77–104; Moreland, *Consciousness and the Existence of God*; Moreland, *The Recalcitrant Imago Dei*; Moreland, "The Argument from Consciousness," 282–343.

4. Moreland, *The Recalcitrant Imago Dei*, 16; Moreland, *The Soul: How We Know It's Real and Why It Matters*.

5. See Moreland, *The Soul*, 77.

6. Moreland and Rae, *Body & Soul*, 204.

7. See Moreland, *The Soul*, 77–78.

8. Moreland, *The Soul*, 178–79.

Moreland understands states of the soul as equivalent to conscious states, but the soul is what unifies consciousness, mind, and spirit.

His line of thought is not so far from the one taken up in this book. As we have argued, finite consciousness, as it is embodied in the form of self-consciousness in humans, is plausibly explained by recourse to the Christian God. However, this book does not necessarily hold that there is a need to endorse substance dualism, although it is certainly compatible with it. Moreland also defends the argumentation that a broad generic theistic God best explains consciousness, but that the God not necessarily be the Christian God (although he is a Christian). Another point worth mentioning is that Moreland sees the findings of neuroscience as mostly irrelevant to the reality of mind, consciousness, and the soul. With respect to the neurosciences and theology, Moreland would hold to the domain of *Independence* (according to Barbour's typology in the science-religion interaction), which would come under Stephen J. Gould's famous view: Non-Overlapping Magisterium (NOMA).[9] This is not to say that Moreland holds this view for all of the interactions between science and theology; for instance, he holds to an old earth creationist (OEC) view,[10] whereby God intervenes directly with creation to create singular events, so that discontinuity is a large part of creation, as opposed to more continuity with the three TE models. So for Moreland, while neuroscience/cognitive science may tell us important factors concerning brain physiology and certain behaviors, it does not give an account for why there is a soul or consciousness (nor is science in a position to refute the soul or to suggest that consciousness is merely an illusion à la Dennett/Blackmore), as Moreland states:

> I find myself among the dissenters of this view [that science has provided evidence against the soul to explain life and consciousness] of the impact of modern science on issues in philosophy of mind. My thesis is that once we get clear on the central first and second order issues in philosophy of mind, it becomes evident that stating and resolving those issues is basically a (theological and) philosophical matter for which discoveries in the hard sciences are largely irrelevant. Put differently, these philosophical issues are, with rare exceptions, autonomous from (and authoritative with respect to) the so-called deliverances of the hard science.[11]

9. Gould, *Rocks of Ages*.

10. Moreland and Reynolds, *Three Views on Creation and Evolution*; Moreland, *Christianity and the Nature of Science*, 213–46.

11. Moreland, *Consciousness and the Existence of God*, 158; Moreland, "The Physical Sciences, Neurosciences and Dualism," 835–49.

Nonetheless, we must explain why there is disconnect and with regard to this book, which involves the science-theology interaction, the sciences do indeed put constraints on theological notions. Yet, in some sense, Moreland is right because philosophy is already heavily involved in scientific issues; not that science is necessarily irrelevant, but that philosophy becomes authoritative and trumps science in any argumentation that involves a single philosophical premise. The case with the neurosciences and the sciences in general is that there are always philosophical assumptions embedded within particular scientific theories. Moreland's support for arguing that the neurosciences are irrelevant to examining the nature and existence of the soul and consciousness includes the following arguments: 1) Neuroscience solely demonstrates a correlation between the mind and the brain—not that they are identical; 2) Near death experiences (NDEs) demonstrate that the soul is what possesses consciousness rather than the brain, and that the varied mental states of the soul have a two way connection with certain parts of the brain; 3) Both physicalism and dualism are empirically the same.[12]

I agree with Moreland on the irreducibility of consciousness to the brain but suggest that perhaps there may be another explanation aside from a strict physicalist interpretation or a substance dualism. Perhaps something in line with IIT, PSII, or a combination with Orch-OR theories or some of the principles examined within a dualist framework (without necessarily fully embracing substance dualism), might clarify the matter. So, this is one crucial area where I would part ways with Moreland's view of the science-theology dialogue in this book, when it relates to consciousness and its origins. Although there is agreement that science on its own cannot resolve such a question, there is a level of interaction between neuroscience, theology, and philosophy. I argue in this book that theology can provide a fruitful contribution of sorts, in order to discern the origin of consciousness. Nonetheless, Moreland has developed a rather rigorous argument he has dubbed the argument from consciousness (AC), which encompasses an argument for God's existence from consciousness.[13] Moreland outlines

12. Moreland, *The Soul*, 33–36.

13. This argument finds its ancestral roots in John Locke's insight in the radical difference between mind and matter. The following quote demonstrates that Locke recognizes, as we have argued in this book, the impossibility of order, structure, and the origin of mind/consciousness without an eternal mind/consciousness. See Locke, *An Essay Concerning Human Understanding*, 4.10.10. "Divide matter into as minute parts as you will, (which we are apt to imagine a sort of spiritualizing, or making a thinking thing of it,) vary the figure and the motion of it, as much as you please; a globe, cube, cone, prism, cylinder, etc. . . . and you may as rationally expect to produce sense, thought, and knowledge, by putting together in a certain figure and motion, gross particles of matter, as by those that are the very minutest that do anywhere exist. They knock, impel, and resist one another . . . So that if we will suppose nothing first, or eternal; matter can never begin to be: if we suppose bare matter, without motion, eternal; motion can never begin to be: if we suppose only

three different forms of AC: inference to the best explanation (IBE), Bayesian type argument, or a deductive argument (Moreland's favored type).[14] AC involves the following premises (in its deductive form):

1. Mental events are genuine nonphysical mental entities that exist.

2. Specific mental event types are regularly correlated with specific physical event types.

3. There is an explanation for these correlations.

4. Personal explanation is different from natural scientific explanation.

5. The explanation for these correlations is either a personal or a natural scientific explanation.

6. The explanation is not a natural scientific one.

7. Therefore, the explanation is a personal one.

8. If the explanation is personal, then it is theistic.

9. Therefore, the explanation is theistic.[15]

If one wanted to go further to argue for the Christian God, one would need to include more premises such as those that were discussed in the realm of systematic theology, which entail arguments to moral conscience concerning Christ. Moreland's argument involves a critique of rival philosophies/views of consciousness, including John Searle and contingent correlation,[16] Timothy O'Connor and emergent necessitation,[17] Colin

---

matter and motion first, or eternal; thought can never begin to be . . . Not to add, that though our general or specific conception of matter makes us speak of it as one thing, yet really all matter is not one individual thing, neither is there any such thing existing as one material being or one single body that we know or can conceive. And therefore if matter were the eternal cogitative being, there would not be one eternal infinite cogitative being, but an infinite number of eternal finite cogitative beings, independent of one another, of limited force, and distinct thoughts, which could never produce that order, harmony, and beauty which are to be found in nature. Since therefore whatsoever is the first eternal being must necessarily be cogitative; and whatsoever is first of all things, must necessarily contain in it, and actually have, at least, all the perfections that can ever after exist; nor can it ever give to another any perfection that is has not, either actually in itself, or at least in a higher degree; it necessarily follows, that the first eternal being cannot be matter." Locke's famous insights have since been developed by various other thinkers into the argument from consciousness for God's existence: see Swinburne, *The Existence of God,* 190–218; Swinburne, *The Evolution of the Soul,* 183–96; Swinburne, "The Origin of Consciousness," 355–78; Menuge, *Agents Under Fire*; Adams, "Flavors, Colors, and God," 225–40.

14. Moreland, *Consciousness and the Existence of God,* 32–37.

15. Ibid., 37. Moreland provides an overview of all these deductive premises, see 37–51.

16. Ibid., 53–69.

17. Ibid., 70–94.

McGinn and mysterian "naturalism,"[18] David Skrbina and pansychism,[19] Philip Clayton and pluralistic emergentist monism,[20] and finally, science and strong physicalism.[21] Before proceeding to an examination of our next philosopher's view of consciousness, let us examine Moreland's brand of substance dualism briefly.

Moreland's defense of AC and substance dualism involves a pointed critique of naturalism and its association to the physical sciences. He is also skeptical of any form of emergence being able to produce anything remotely close to consciousness.[22] He recognizes that naturalists have to either deny the reality of consciousness as *really* mental phenomenon or be moved into uncomfortable situations where they must re-examine their physical-ist commitments like other naturalists, such as in the case of Jaegwon Kim and David Chalmers, who espouse property dualisms.[23] In response, to such positions, Moreland states that:

> Kim's advice [namely, that we must re-examine our physicalist/ emergentist theories of mind are presented with nonphysical phenomena that resists physical explanation] to fellow natural-ists is that they must simply admit the irreality of the mental and recognize that naturalism exacts a steep price and cannot be had on the cheap. If feigning anesthesia—denying that con-sciousness construed along commonsense lines is real—is the price to be paid to retain naturalism, then the price is too high. Fortunately, the theistic argument from consciousness reminds us that it is a price that does not need to be paid.[24]

Aside from his critique of naturalism to explain consciousness away, as part of his AC, Moreland provides positive arguments to defend substance dualism. Moreland seeks to defend substance dualism, which encompasses property/event dualism but differs from it with respect to the immateriality of substance i.e., the self/soul. He argues that under a naturalistic frame-work, consciousness is a conundrum but under theism it is not, and that finite minds find their most warranted explication in a divine mind such as God. In building his case for substance dualism, Moreland first expounds and defends property dualism, showing that mental states are not at all

18. Ibid., 95–113.

19. Ibid., 114–34.

20. Ibid., 135–55. We will examine Clayton's views separately.

21. Ibid., 156–74.

22. See Moreland, *The Recalcitrant Imago Dei*, 28–40.

23. See Kim, *Mind in a Physical World* ; Chalmers, *The Character of Consciousness*.

24. Moreland, *The Recalcitrant Imago Dei*, 40.

physical because they possess five characteristics not had by physical states: 1) qualitative feel; 2) intentionality; 3) introspection; 4) subjective ontology; and 5) they cannot be adequately described with physical language.[25] Subsequently, Moreland expounds three crucial arguments for his defense of property/event dualism: 1) the argument from introspection; 2) the knowledge argument; and 3) the argument from intentionality. These arguments seek to undermine the veracity of physicalism and demonstrate the immateriality of mental properties and events. Moreland also provides both philosophical and scientific objections to property dualism, while providing logical rebuttals to each of these objections. He also provides critiques of various physicalist alternatives to property/event dualism, thereby making a compelling case for the immateriality of consciousness.

In order to discuss what consciousness is, if it is a substance itself or an aspect of the soul/mind, one would have to examine what sorts of properties such a thing might possess. Consciousness itself seems to possess certain properties if you do not reduce it to the brain or consider it to be an illusion.[26] It is a rather difficult task to speak of the properties of consciousness, but some seem to come forth, including immateriality, irreducibility, transcendence, (alongside its many features: self-reflection, memory, and emotions). Throughout his work, Moreland lists the different characteristics of substances,[27] properties,[28] and events.

Aside from unpacking pertinent terms relevant to the philosophy of mind, Moreland introduces a couple of notions that are crucial to his essential thesis: that substance dualism makes the best sense of the knowledge we have concerning the mind-body problem, i.e., in terms of understanding the connection between the brain/body and the apparent immaterial component regarded as mind. Moreland utilizes Leibniz's Law of the Indiscernibility of Identicals (LLII); whereby entities y and z exist, if y and z are the same, then any truth that is applicable to y will also be applicable to z.[29] His goal is to demonstrate that the brain and the mind are not identical entities by showing that if something is true of the mind or its states, but not true of the brain or its states, then physicalism is false (and dualism is true assuming no other alternatives). However, LLII has not been without criticisms in the history of philosophy. Max Black, an analytic philosopher of the twentieth

25. Moreland, *The Soul*, 78–79.

26. Blackmore, *Consciousness*, 1,8, 9, 132–33; Blackmore "Delusions of Consciousness," 52–64.

27. Moreland and Rae, *Body & Soul*, 70–85; Moreland, *The Soul*, 22–23.

28. Moreland and Rae, *Body & Soul*, 51.

29. Moreland, *The Soul*, 32.

century, criticized and attempted to falsify LLII by creating a thought experiment, through a hypothetical universe containing solely two spheres (numerically non-identical), possessing precisely the same properties. The example seems to fail since the demarcation of numerically non-identical is present. This demarcation violates LLII (i.e., by signifying they are not the same, nor are two "same" things solely being distinguished by descriptors), even though they share all properties (qualitatively) in common. Moreover, it seems completely counter-intuitive or even absurd, that this may be true and a refutation of LLII. Other arguments that attempt to undermine LLII include some differing interpretations of quantum mechanics, but quantum mechanics has at least eleven distinct interpretations, so at least as of yet, nothing can be really established in that domain (even though quantum mechanics itself has a high degree of accuracy mathematically, the differing interpretative frameworks for QM disqualify it).

There are three distinct positions regarding substance dualism, including three further categories: Cartesian substance dualism, Thomistic substance dualism,[30] and emergent substance dualism.[31] Moreland does not engage in the "in-house" debates amongst these three positions but rather focuses on demonstrating that the soul is immaterial and "bears" consciousness. The soul and the brain interact but are different substances with different properties. Moreland provides a series of arguments in support of this position, including: 1) awareness of self; 2) unity and first-person perspective; 3) conscious experience as best explained by a soul; 4) the modal argument; 5) the existence of free will, moral responsibility, and punishment; and 6) the sameness of self over time.[32] Moreland points out that in the philosophical literature concerning philosophy of mind, there has been minimal engagement with these relatively new developments with respect to arguments defending substance dualism. Most of the literature presents a caricature of such argumentation or sticks to outmoded critiques of Cartesian substance dualism.[33] Moreland, finally, considers why there is a prevalence of physicalism, whether through ardent scientific materialism, property dualism,[34] or other associated views. The

30. See Oderberg, "Hylomorphic Dualism," 70–99; Edward Feser, *The Last Superstition,* 120–23.

31. See Hasker, *The Emergent Self.*

32. Moreland, *Consciousness and the Existence of God,* 179–86; Moreland, *The Soul,* 118–37.

33. Moreland, *Consciousness and the Existence of God,* 186–94.

34. Which can entail epiphenomenalism whereby mental events are caused by physical ones without the mental having causal power over physical. This is construed in order to avoid the problem of how the immaterial can affect the material. One way

reason, he argues, is what Thomas Nagel has dubbed the "cosmic authority problem"; Moreland explains why he thinks that the failure of naturalism still persists in the minds of a variety of thinkers despite the evidence, essentially equating it with a fear of God and the consequent implications of the existence of a theistic God.[35]

Thus, essentially, for Moreland, "the self or ego" is what bears consciousness, which is in turn an irreducible and immaterial aspect of the human person. The soul entails conscious states and faculties, which involve both mind and spirit. Moreland's understanding of the soul is separate from our physical bodies. The soul and consciousness endure, while the body decays; the body itself is not what constitutes a human person, but it is this immaterial aspect, which is a finite mirror of the infinite divine mind. Moreland holds to a traducian view of the transmission of the soul. Although Moreland also holds to OEC, it is possible that one could be a substance dualist like Moreland while holding to some form of TE most likely either PE or DE.

Perhaps an emergent dualism[36] may be a more accurate position to explain the origination of self-consciousness in human embodied beings throughout the course of evolutionary development. William Hasker, for instance, who expounds emergent dualism, argues that consciousness cannot be solely explained by material processes, particularly with respect to its origins, but that it is not wholly distinct from the physical brain.[37]

---

of avoiding epiphenomenalism, which has three pitfalls, is to invoke informational processes which are immaterial but function with a material medium, as we have seen with Dembski's notion of an informationally porous universe where God as an immaterial mind can interact with the immaterial aspect whether separate (dualism) or holistic (monistic). The pitfalls include: 1) it's counterintuitive—pain is not the cause of my tears?; 2) If mental states do not have any function, then how did they evolve and have a selective advantage?; 3) We cannot justify other minds based on introspection if epiphenomenalism is true since "mental states do not explain my behavior and there is a physical explanation for the behavior of others. It is explanatorily redundant to postulate such states for others. I know, by introspection, that I have them, but is it not just as likely that I alone am subject to this quirk of nature, rather than that everyone is?" See Robinson, "Epiphenomenalism" section on "Dualism" in *Stanford Encyclopedia of Philosophy*, no pages.

35. See, Moreland, *Consciousness and the Existence of God*, 175–94.

36. See Hasker, *The Emergent Self*.

37. See chapter 4 on Teilhard. I would argue that the position of emergent dualism is not too distinct from Teilhard's holistic model since a level of complexity is required to emerge throughout the course of a teleological evolution. I have not devoted a whole section on Hasker's interesting view, since the process by which it came about is distinct from Moreland's; although God is the ultimate cause, the nature of consciousness (a dualistic view) is shared.

8.3 Lonergan-Helminiak: A Tripartite Transcendent Model

Philosopher and theologian Bernard Lonergan has written at length on consciousness.[38] Daniel Helminiak has done much work on consciousness and Lonergan's thought. This section will focus on Lonergan's thought but will take insight from Helminiak's propositions. An important distinction in Lonergan's thought between two modes of consciousness is given by Louis Roy, providing a more precise understanding of Lonergan's conception of consciousness:

> I am distinguishing consciousness (= consciousness-in) and self-awareness (= consciousness of consciousness) in a way a bit more precise than Lonergan's. In fact, he uses the two terms equivalently, although his preferred one is "consciousness". But he would entirely agree, I think, with my usage of "self-awareness" as indicating a stage beyond mere consciousness, namely, the stage wherein consciousness of mere consciousness begins to emerge.[39]

Lonergan's self-awareness, akin to what we have referred to as self-consciousness, is what we seek to understand in this book through the classical Christian conception of God and creation, in terms of its origins in embodied human consciousness. What is of interest in Lonergan's understanding of consciousness is what may be called a double awareness:

> I have used the adjective, present, both of the object and of the subject. But I have used it ambiguously, for the presence of the object is quite different from the presence of the subject. The object is present as what is gazed upon, attended to, intended. But the presence of the subject resides in the gazing, the attending, the intending. For this reason the subject can be conscious, as attending, and yet give his whole attention to the object as attended to.[40]

This involves awareness on the level of object and subject. This is what Helminiak describes as "simultaneous, concomitant, and inextricable."[41] Lonergan brings our attention to the duality and simultaneity of both our

---

38. Lonergan, *Insight*, chapters 11 and 18; Lonergan, *Method in Theology*, chapters 1 and 2.

39. Roy, *Mystical Consciousness*, 20.

40. Lonergan, *Method in Theology*, 8, see also 6–13.

41. Helminiak, *The Human Core of Spirituality*, 45.

intrinsically connected ability to possess "reflective" and "non-reflective" consciousness in such a way.[42] For Lonergan, consciousness is both intentional, in terms of being aware of a certain object as the reflective consciousness—reading of a text, driving, etc., while there is also an awareness of the subject, something we can call a non-reflective consciousness, since it is not directed toward an object that is oriented toward the subject, i.e, an awareness of self, a self-consciousness that occurs simultaneously to the awareness of the object. Thus, we have simultaneity of reflecting and non-reflecting consciousness. For Lonergan, this is innate to the human person's consciousness, but Lonergan goes further. He attempts to carefully not make this non-reflecting consciousness or as we call it, self-consciousness, into an object. We do attempt to objectify ourselves, in the sense of creating our subjective selves into objects of scrutiny and discernment, as Lonergan states:

> I have been attempting to describe the subject's presence to himself. But the reader if he tries to find himself as subject, to reach back and, as it were, uncover his subjectivity, cannot succeed. Any such effort is introspecting, attending to the subject; and what is found is, not the subject as subject, but only the subject as object, it is the subject as subject that does the finding.[43]

Helminiak explains the difficulty on objectifying ourselves as objects:

> Reflectingly aware of ourselves, knowing ourselves as objects, we can never fully appropriate ourselves because we are always more than what we are at present objectifying. We are, namely, the agent subjects who are doing the objectifying. Nonetheless, in non-reflecting awareness we do fully possess ourselves as aware subjects. In non-reflecting awareness, we are fully present "to" ourselves.[44]

Lonergan gives priority to what he calls "conscious" consciousness (non-reflective according to Helminiak), what we termed self-consciousness as having logical priority over reflective consciousness.[45] How does such dual

42. See Lonergan, *Insight*, 633–35; Helminiak, *The Human Core of Spirituality*, 45–56. Reflecting and non-reflecting are Helminiak's terms for Lonergan's intentional and conscious.

43. Lonergan, "Cognitional Structure," 226–27, as quoted by Helminiak, *The Human Core of Spirituality*, 46.

44. See, Helminiak, *The Human Core of Spirituality*, 49, figure 3.1. Helminiak uses the illustration of the ouroboros—the snake eating its tail—to demonstrate the dual nature of consciousness—reflecting (intentional) and non-reflecting (conscious).

45. Helminiak, *The Human Core of Spirituality*, 61–72.

consciousness, particularly, the element of non-reflective consciousness or self-consciousness as such, relate to God? In God's simplicity, can there really be any distinction in God's self whether reflective or non-reflective consciousness? God as a simple being is an undifferentiated being (with un-differentiated qualities/attributes), so that God's essence would be of pure self-consciousness/non-reflective consciousness or conscious activity as Lo-nergan would suggest. Our mirroring of this is exemplified in a finite capac-ity, while possessing the logical priority of this non-reflective consciousness (self-consciousness).

Helminiak, who follows much of Lonergan's thought, particularly on consciousness,[46] proposes a tripartite model as an alternative to the bipartite model of mind-body as we have seen with substance dualism as expounded by Moreland. The tripartite model includes spirit, psyche, and organism. Spirit encompasses what transcends space and time, such as "(1) conscious awareness, (2) intelligent understanding, (3) reasoned judge-ment, and (4) self-determining decision." Whereas psyche entails, accord-ing to Helminiak:

> a dimension of human mind, shared in common with other higher species and constituted by emotions (feelings, affect), imagery (and other mental representations), and memory. To-gether these determine habitual response and behavior, person-ality. Built on the internal functioning of the external perceptual system, psyche apprises the organism of its dispositional status within itself and within its environment. The requirement of psyche is to be comfortable, to feel good.[47]

Finally, organism refers to the physical body. Helminiak explains that the tripartite model helps distinguish psyche and spirit within mind. Moreover, this model is "necessary and sufficient" to account for human reality. Hel-miniak also suggests that while each component is distinct, "their distinc-tion does not imply separation."[48] Thus, the model that Helminiak proposes, which involves much of Lonergan's thought on consciousness, is a holistic model of the human person which differs from the substance dualist model.

---

46. Ibid., 14. Helminiak states the following on the influence of Lonergan's work in his thought on consciousness: "Lonergan claims to have understood human conscious-ness. Whether he is right or wrong (and I believe he is right), he presents a position that is unique, one that deserves a hearing. That position is the substance of the answer proposed in this book, the answer to the double question before us: What is a human being and What is spirituality?" These two questions are intimately linked to our ques-tion of the origin of self-consciousness.

47. Helminiak, *Religion and the Human Sciences*, 11.

48. Helminiak, *The Human Core of Spirituality*, 28.

The position of the endurance of the soul is unclear in this model, though there is the admittance that the body-soul model is useful in providing such an explanation.[49] Nonetheless, Helminiak is careful in his delineations of soul and the realm of mind, psyche, and consciousness, as he states:

> Depending on the context, soul could be used to replace any of the key terms in this study: mind, spirit, and psyche. Thus, in the formula *body and soul*, soul functions as synonym for mind and refers globally to the locus of inner human experience. In religious circles, soul generally refers to some immaterial and enduring aspect of the human being, the part that survives biological death (or even predates biological birth). To this extent, the term most closely parallels spirit as understood here. Indeed, presuming a synonym for soul, current religious usage often opines that one's spirit lives on after death . . . Because of its ambiguity, the term *soul* is not useful for technical discussion, but is very useful in poetic, suggestive, and evocative contexts.[50]

What and/or how are we to speculate regarding Lonergan's views on the origin of consciousness? As we have seen with Moreland's substance dualist model and his affirmation of OEC, this would require some sort of "intervention" in terms of God's action, most likely in a form contrary to that which is desired by those who support DAP. Although consistent, this proposition is problematic for any of the TE models, except perhaps DE, but still it is unsavory. Moreland seems to suggest we go where the evidence leads, regardless of how unsavory some theological conclusions may be. What are we to make of Lonergan's view on divine action and evolution? It seems to me, based on his writings in *Insight*, that Lonergan would support a view similar to those of Lamoureux and van Till, namely PE. Lonergan offers much praise to Darwin's theory of evolution.[51] Lonergan offers a more general view of evolution[52] as opposed to one strictly limited to Neo-Darwinism or biological change. His view would be closer to a view espoused by Teilhard; a cosmic evolution of sorts. Lonergan discusses the emergence of organized complexity, which is important if higher levels of complexity are going to be correlated to higher levels of consciousness.[53] Although Lonergan does not dispute the empirical data related to a theory like Neo-Darwinism or any other theory, his views on divine action and design

49. Ibid., 9.

50. Ibid., 26–27.

51. Lonergan, *Insight*, 154–55.

52. Byrne, "Lonergan, Evolutionary Science, and Intelligent Design," 899.

53. Lonergan, *Insight*, 471.

do not form a god-of-the-gaps or contradict any generally accepted scientific findings. Rather, Lonergan's position suggests something that grounds the whole enterprise of science and inquiry, namely an undergirding of intelligibility. It brings to mind the most sublime question of metaphysics and transposes it to epistemology—why does anything make sense at all? It is this very intelligibility that grounds all of the scientific method and any enterprise of knowledge, as Lonergan states: "Prior to the neatly formulated questions of systematizing intelligence, there is the deep-set wonder in which all questions have their source and ground."[54] For Lonergan, scientific theories, provide insight and inquiry, into an overall intelligibility of the cosmos. In his book, *New Proofs for the Existence of God*, Fr. Robert Spitzer further develops Lonergan's argument of intelligibility to argue for God's existence.[55] Lonergan's thought on acts of understanding, insight, inquiry, and intelligibility point to an ultimate source of perfect and "unrestricted"[56] knowledge. Lonergan's own argument is stated as such:

> If the real is completely intelligible, then complete intelligibility exists. If complete intelligibility exists, the idea of being exists. If the idea of being exists, then God exists. Therefore, the real is completely intelligible, God exists.[57]

Furthermore, Lonergan presents an argument for finite intelligibility (our ability in possession dual consciousness—reflecting and non-reflecting consciousness) as being grounded and mirroring an ultimate, unlimited, and unbounded consciousness—a pure unmitigated self-consciousness:

> [I]ntelligibility either is material or spiritual or abstract: it is material in the objects of physics, chemistry, biology and sensitive psychology; it is spiritual when it is identical with understanding and it abstract in concepts of unities, laws, ideal frequencies, genetic operators, dialectical tensions and conflicts. But abstract intelligibility necessarily is incomplete for it arises only in the self-expression of the spiritual intelligibility. Again, spiritual intelligibility is incomplete as long as it can inquire. Finally, material intelligibility necessarily is incomplete, for it is contingent in its existence and in its occurrences, in

54. Ibid., 208.

55. See Spitzer, *New Proofs for the Existence of God*, chapter 4: A Lonerganian Proof for God's Existence.

56. Spitzer, *New Proofs for the Existence of God*, 146–76. A term used by Lonergan to describe God's nature: "the unrestricted act of understanding coincides with Aristotle's conception of the unmoved mover." See *Insight*, 699.

57. Lonergan, *Insight*, 696.

its genera and species, in its classical and statistical laws, in its genetic operators and the actual course of its emergent probability; moreover, it includes a merely empirical residue of individuality, noncountable infinities, particular places and times, and for systematic knowledge of nonsystematic divergence. It follows that the only possibility of complete intelligibility lies in a spiritual intelligibility that cannot inquire because it understands everything about everything.[58]

Thus, Lonergan's argument of intelligibility is bidirectional. The fact that the universe demonstrates intelligibility requires conscious intelligent minds who can have the ability to possess self-consciousness and process information but point ultimately to an unrestricted transcendent intelligence grounding this mode of intelligibility. This provides a guarantor for why there is a synonymy between our consciousness and that of God's, both of which, though, can possess complex thoughts while remaining simple in nature.

When this is combined with Lonergan's views on cosmic evolution, it provides an uncanny similarity to the position propounded in this book, namely, that finite consciousness finds its ultimate source and grounding in an eternal consciousness through an intended evolutionary process. For Lonergan, complex processes or as he dubs them, "schemes," owe their complexity to simpler processes throughout the cosmos, as an ever-developing evolutionary process. As God's overall evolutionary design plan, Lonergan sees probabilities, shifting through intrinsic randomness with an inherent telos for man's purposes. He suggests that "since finality is an upwardly indeterminately directed dynamism and since man is free, the real issue lies not in the many possibilities but in the few principles on which man may rely in working out his destiny."[59] The working out of our destiny relies on our ability to deliberate and possess self-consciousness (non-reflective consciousness) and reflective consciousness. As the process continues, Lonergan suggests, similarly to Teilhard's law of complexity-consciousness, that "an incomplete universe [is] heading towards fuller being."[60]

A key to Lonergan's evolutionary view of the universe is his notion of "emergent probability." Knowledge and the scientific method provide the details as to how this has occurred (i.e., big bang cosmology/evolutionary biology) and will occur (i.e., eschatological scenarios of the universe/predictive capacity of science), but the overall project is not dependent on the specific

58. Ibid., 697.
59. Ibid., 659.
60. Ibid., 471.

details.[61] Lonergan explains the distinction between "emergent probability" and Darwinism (it could have been any other established theory—perhaps in the future, we will discuss the Extended Evolutionary Synthesis):

> Emergent probability affirms a conditioned series of schemes of recurrence that are realized in accord with successive schedules of probabilities. Darwinism, on the other hand, affirms a conditions series of species of things to be realized in accord with successive schedules of probability. The two views are parallel in their formal structures. They are related, inasmuch as species of living things emerge and function within ranges of alternative sects of schemes of recurrence.[62]

Essentially the difference lies in that "emergent probability" sketches out the intrinsic processes to which evolutionary biology adheres. The "schemes of recurrence" refer to the overall design undergirding physical, chemical, and biological processes. Philosopher Patrick Byrne further explains this notion of "emergent probability":

> "emergent," because cycles emerge, begin to function and survive as long as their requisite conditions are in place; "probability" because the non-systematic, random assembly of conditions nevertheless occurs according to ideal frequencies; "emergent probability" because once cycles at one level begin to function, they increase the probabilies of emergence of the next level of more complex cycles."[63]

The question of how exactly the tripartite view of the human person evolves from simpler organisms still remains a mystery. In terms of exactly how science can come to explain the immaterial aspects of the human person, whether these properties (or substances in the case of Moreland's view) can emerge, and how precisely this might happen, remains elusive. Nonetheless, Lonergan provides us with a coherent framework to understand how the intelligible structure of the universe reflects an ultimate consciousness so that finite consciousness can understand such a structure.[64]

61. Ibid., 145–49, 154–59; Lonergan makes a distinction between Darwinism and "emergent probability."

62. Lonergan, *Insight*, 156.

63 Byrne, "Lonergan, Evolutionary Science, and Intelligent Design," 911; Lonergan, *Insight*, 208.

64. It is worth mentioning an intriguing argument developed by Jay Richards and astrophysicist Guillermo Gonzalez, which is highly relevant to Lonergan's argument for God and intelligibility. This argument provides the scientific basis for Lonergan's onto-epistemic argument. In their book *The Privileged Planet*, Gonzalez and Richards

8.4 Philip Clayton's Emergent Monism

The first thing to keep in mind about Clayton is that he is a panentheist, but unlike Teilhard does not support panspsychism.[65] What is interesting about Clayton's panentheism is that he defends *creation ex nihilo*, as we too have argued throughout this book, as vital to the origin of consciousness.[66] In relation to mind and consciousness, Clayton provides an interesting analogy involving his panentheism:

> The highest level known to us in the emergence of mind or mental properties from the most complicated biological structure known to us, the human body and brain. So the relationship suggests itself: the body is to mind as the body/mind combination—that is, human persons—are to the divine.[67]

A problematic should be apparent with Clayton's panentheism and his view on consciousness. Due to his panentheistic views, Clayton correlates God's complexity with the complexity of the world.[68] The argument of this book is the reverse; namely, that the simple aspect of the human person, i.e., consciousness, although having certain correlates with complexity, is what is analogical to God, namely, God's simplicity. There is a confusion it seems with complex mental states and complex brain physiological

---

lay down a scientific argument with deep metaphysical implications. They provide a host of different lines of evidence to suggest that the earth occupies a special place in the cosmos. Their argument goes against the popular notion held by many scientists and popularized by Carl Sagan. He argued that the Earth had no special or privileged place in the cosmos and that it was merely an insignificant cosmic accident, which he dubbed a "pale blue dot." See Sagan, *Pale Blue Dot*. The book and the saying were inspired by a famous photograph taken of Earth on February 14, 1990, by the Voyager 1 space probe, which depicts Earth as a tiny speck in the vastness of space and bands of sunlight. This is strongly related to the misnamed Copernican Principle, which Gonzalez and Richards refute as well. Gonzalez and Richards argue that there is a deep correlation between habitability and scientific observability. So, the fact that we exist on a particularly special type of planet (Earth), is also related to the fact we are in such a place, with a purpose, to observe the universe and discover, measure, and understand much of the cosmos. They provide examples of the correlation between habitability and measurability. Richards and Gonzalez illustrate, in a scientific manner, the very intelligibility which Lonergan describes as being intrinsic to reality grounded upon the ultimate source of all intelligibility.

65. Clayton, *Mind & Emergence*, 4, 123–24, 130, 201.

66. Clayton, "Open Panentheism and Creatio ex nihilo," 166–83.

67. Clayton, "A Response to My Critics," 293. See editor's introduction to Clayton, *Adventures in the Spirit*, 15 and 273–274n70.

68. Clayton, *Adventures in the Spirit*, 15.

changes—between mental and physical properties.[69] Where Clayton sees panentheism as the resolution to God's interaction with mental states, this book adheres to informational structures as God's avenue for interacting without disrupting or "intervening" in a crude fashion within the created order. Criticisms have been laid that on one hand, Clayton's program does not need the divine to explain the origin of consciousness,[70] and on the other hand, that the program itself is incoherent and insufficient to bear the burden of the ambitious claims made in providing a plausible explanation of the origin of consciousness.[71]

Fundamental to Clayton's program is the concept of supervenience. Clayton indicates that anti-reductive materialists such as Kim argue well to maintain the real status of mental states against eliminative materialists (e.g. Dennett, Churchland), but they do not allow for the emergence of something "ontologically" novel since they hold that "the qualities of mental life are preserved, but the level of the mental is not really ontologically distinct."[72] Kim's understanding of supervenience entails a *weak supervenience*.[73] Clayton's program involves *strong supervenience*, which entails three steps.[74] First, strong supervenience entails that although the mental arises out of the physical it is not reducible (cannot be described in physical terms), but is dependent on the physical for its functioning, which is agreed by philosophers like Kim. This allows speaking of emergent properties. Second, Clayton argues, that new kinds of causal activity emerge, even though mental states depend on their "physical substratum" (the brain).[75] Clayton resists the notion that a new sort of substance emerges and maintains that humans are holistic beings as opposed to dual mind and body composites. His third step claims that "mental properties are not epiphenomenal but can in turn cause physical events."[76] This is significant

69. This is how this is framed by the editor in his introduction. See Clayton, *Adventures in the Spirit*, 15.

70. See editor's introduction in Clayton, *Adventures in the Spirit*, 18.

71. See Moreland, *Consciousness and the Existence of God*, 135–55. Moreland has leveled a very thorough critique, dealing with his concept of emergence, the theistic claims, his understanding of substance dualism and its overall program.

72. Clayton, *God and Contemporary Science*, 251.

73. Clayton indicates that Kim and he use weak and strong in an opposite sense: Clayton, *God and Contemporary Science*, 268n37; in reference to, Jaegwon Kim, "The myth of non-reductive materialism," 36—in this article Clayton claims that Kim reduced "the mental to the physical. . . a position this "strong" (in Kim's sense) threatens to reduce mental phenomena to mere epiphenomena."

74. Clayton, *God and Contemporary Science*, 252–57.

75. Ibid., 253.

76. Clayton, *God and Contemporary Science*, 255.

in terms of brain plasticity and arguing for the power of mental force (presented earlier in our section on Schwartz/Beauregard's dualist notions with scientific implications [A Spiritual Neuroscience?])[77]. It is also significant with regard to the idea that "the action of God upon human minds is certainly of great significance for theologians."[78] Clayton has made his case by arguing for the best explanation for human thought and behavior, not by appealing to theology. Nonetheless, this appeal is significant to the task of this book. As Clayton has noted, "no serious attempts have been made to suggest how theology can influence neuroscience, particularly in the science-theology dialogue and Russell's CMI."[79]

Interestingly, Clayton's defense of emergentist monism denies that reality is purely physicalist, mentalist, dualist (aspect theory), and/or substance dualist.[80] The question is, does Clayton's *strong supervenience* alongside his emergentist monism serve as a plausible explanation for the origin of consciousness? Is it sufficient to say that brain complexity reaches a certain point and then gives rise to consciousness as we have defined it? To say that consciousness can certainly interact and operate from a foundational basis of such complexity is one thing, but to suggest it originates from such complexity is another. Clayton's concern seems to be what is explicable within science. It could be that part of the problem in discussions about consciousness is that the standard methodologies of science itself are not adequate. Nonetheless, Clayton stresses the importance of analogy between God's infinite mind and human finite ones.[81]

Clayton's position demonstrates dissatisfaction with both substance dualism[82] and reductive materialism/physicalism.[83] He seeks to come up with a position that lies between these two boundaries in explaining the

---

77. Both Schwartz and Beauregard are mind/body dualists, while Clayton is not, but Clayton's program in conjunction with Schwartz/Beauregard allows for an argument against reductive materialism and materialism in general, since mental states affect brain states and the work of Schwartz and Beauregard provide the empirical scientific evidence for it.

78. Clayton, *God and Contemporary Science*, 256.

79. This has been explored in chapter 5.4 on divine simplicity and will be briefly mentioned in our conclusion with respect to the principle of synonymy (which was outlined in chapter 7.3.1 guideline 1b [path 6], where theology influences science: TRP à SRP).

80. See Clayton, "Toward a Constructive Christian Theology of Emergence," 317–18.

81. Clayton, *God and Contemporary Science*, 258. We will explore this further on the concept of divine simplicity and synonymy.

82. Clayton, *Mind & Emergence*, v, 1, 49 50, 53.

83. Ibid., 65, 158, 201.

nature and origin of consciousness. On the one hand, Clayton takes the datum from the neurosciences, which he believes suggest that substance dualism is unlikely, but he then equally resists reductive physicalism which has removed subjective conscious agents interacting within the world.[84] This position sharply differs with Moreland, who holds to the irrelevancy of the neurosciences on the nature/origin of consciousness but coheres to the non-reductive appeal. The Lonergan-Helminiak tripartite model seems to work well from a holistic framework, but with deep transcendent elements that also reject reductive approaches. Clayton's view attempts to answer the question of the origin of consciousness. Clayton holds to the view that mind emerges from the natural world as an additional component of the cosmic evolutionary process.[85] Another of the views which affects understanding of origin of consciousness that Clayton (as an emergentist) rejects is "the causal closure of physics."[86] Clayton explains the details behind his understanding of consciousness:

> On the view I am defending, consciousness is one more emergent property of this natural universe. Call this view *emergentist monism*. The position would be falsified if it turned out that, in the course of universal evolution, only one strongly emergent property appeared. In that case one would have to accept some sort of temporalized dualism [this suggestion would be akin to emergent dualism as defended by William Hasker]: the universe was fundamentally physical up to some point and then mental states arose, and after the universe (or at least some portion of it) was both physical and mental. By contrast emergentist monism is supported if—as seems in fact to be the case—natural history produces entities that evidence a range of hierarchically ordered emergent qualities.[87]

Clayton's position is appealing on the grounds that he does not shy away from the difficulty in understanding the origin of consciousness from an evolutionary perspective (assuming the mental is not separate from the

84. Ibid., vi.

85. Ibid., vi.

86. Ibid., 56.

87. Ibid., 128. It is worth mentioning that the origin of information necessary for any self-replicating system is an ongoing issue with origin of life studies, which emergentists also have to take seriously. It is closely linked to the origin of consciousness if we are to take IIT and PSII theories of consciousness seriously. The very nature of information and its influence on living systems is somehow bound to the question of the origins of consciousness. Information is not so much a mental state, but it seems to be dependent on or presupposes a mind for its existence.

evolutionary process). At least he acknowledges the problem, while not attempting to give way to reductive physicalism: "It is not possible to engage in reflection on the relationship of mind and brain without considering evolutionary history that produced brains in the first place."[88] This is correct if one assumes a direct correlation between complexity and consciousness as Teilhard had assumed, but was unable to fully explain from within his historic framework.[89] Yet, this is what Clayton seems to suggest is possible.[90] Clayton continues this line of thought later, when he suggests that:

> Understanding the dependence relation from the perspective of natural history represents a firm break with dualist theories of mind, which have generally denied that mind is essentially dependent on the history of biological systems. Focusing on the evolutionary origins of mind is therefore part of what distinguishes the emergence approach as a separate ontological option in the debate. At the same time, the dependent type– type relationship between the mental and the physical also allows one to give a more robust account of the nonreducibility of the mental than the competing accounts provide. Wherein, then, does this nonreducibility lie, and how can it best be characterized? Much turns on this question.[91]

Clayton affirms a neutral monistic position, when he asserts that mental properties emerge under his emergentist monism, which indicates that via

> a substrate that is neither 'physical' nor 'mental'. Emergent mental properties are dependent on the lower levels of the hierarchy, yet genuinely emergent from it. Hence thought is dependent on neurophysiology but not reducible to it. Critics of this view often argue that emergence theory comes closest to property dualism. Actually, it would be better to say that it is a form of property pluralism: many different and intriguing properties emerge in the course of natural history, and conscious experience is only one of them.[92]

88. Ibid., 107.

89. This resulted in his elusive proposal of "ultra-physics," which I have strongly suggested is worth examining further as part of a research program in the science-theology interaction with respect to the origin of consciousness.

90. Clayton, *Mind & Emergence*, 6.

91. Ibid., 127.

92. Ibid., 158. See section 7.3.2.2 for the position expounded earlier with PSII and a Thomistic understanding of neutral monism.

The question remains whether there is sufficient evidence to suggest that phenomena like consciousness and information systems might arise via emergence. Is emergence sufficient or a way of obfuscating the problem further? These and other questions are beyond the scope of our research, but can stimulate further thought, whether by way of confirmation, or refutation into further research. As Moreland observes concerning the serious problems in Clayton's understanding of emergentism:

> it boils down to an egregious *post hoc ergo propter hoc* fallacy. Indeed, for at least three reasons, there is no scientific evidence whatsoever for genuinely emergent properties. For one thing, the in-principle unpredictability of emergent properties from exhaustive knowledge of their alleged emergent bases entails that there is no empirical evidence for emergence. And the fact that there are no criteria for identifying a "sufficient degree of complexity" [a problem we witnessed in examining Teilhard's program] apart from slapping the label on whatever was present when the emergent property appeared in an *ad hoc*, after-the-fact manner, implies that there is no straightforward scientific evidence for emergence. This may be why Clayton equivocates on the nature of subvenient base, sometimes claiming that emergence is "out of matter" and most often asserting that it arises out of neutral monistic stuff. He also claims that emergent properties arise from the complex interactions among the parts of subvenient structures. None of these statements can be given one iota of empirical support . . . [Moreover,] Jaegwon Kim has convincingly shown, the appearance of emergent mental properties is consistent with numerous positions on the mind/body problem, e.g. substance dualism, type physicalism, epiphenomenalism, double-aspect theories (e.g. personalism). Thus, the scientific evidence is underdetermined with respect to these options, including emergentism.[93]

This is a heavily critical analysis given by Moreland on the status of Clayton's position.[94] I am not aware of Clayton's rebuttal, but naturalist philosopher Graham Oppy, in a critical review of Moreland's *Consciousness and the Existence of God*, has argued that there are plausible naturalistic

---

93. Moreland, *Consciousness and the Existence of God*, 148–49.

94. It is worth noting that Moreland only makes reference to Clayton's work *Mind & Emergence*, thus does not entail fully Clayton's position, nor his more recent work, as found in *Adventures in the Spirit*. See Moreland, *Consciousness and the Existence of God*, 212n1.

theories of consciousness.[95] Although Clayton, in a more recent text, still allows for a seamless type of evolution leading to the emergence of life and mind, his position is not that far removed from this book when he states: "In the end, it may be more accurate to analyze life not in terms of a single moment of emergence, but rather as a sort of family resemblance that ties together a large number of individual emergent steps."[96] As interesting as such a thing sounds, it still must confront the problem of functional information at the root of life. Clayton also weighs in on self-consciousness or self-awareness/"self-monitoring," (as he uses it):

> Some also distinguish reflective self-awareness from the generic self-awareness as a separate area of family resemblance. As the name implies, reflective self-awareness requires the ability to monitor one's own self-monitoring. If the feedback loop of self-awareness is a second-order phenomenon, then reflective self-awareness becomes a third-order phenomenon: being aware of *how* you are aware. Using more strongly mental predicates, we could describe it as knowing that one is thinking, or knowing one's own thoughts, or knowing that one is experiencing certain *qualia*.[97]

Again, this is not far removed from how we have viewed self-consciousness throughout this book and its link to both qualia and higher thought capacities (à la Damasio), such as deep reflective thought and moral awareness. For Clayton, he seeks to avoid any eliminativist reductionist positions such as those defended by Dennett or the Churchlands, while still being open to scientific advancements as carried forth with the neural correlates of consciousness.[98] Furthermore, Clayton's position lines up well with this book (and strangely does not sound too far off from Moreland's substance dualism, insofar that he acknowledges that science is impotent or even irrelevant when facing larger questions), as he states:

> At the same time, it gives us grounds to predict that these studies will not provide a complete explanation of actions in the world in which persons are agents.
>
>   There is a cost, of course. One can't speak of emergence of a new substance: a soul, metaphysical self, or *Geist*, at least not on the basis of science alone. But perhaps that is a cost one should

95. See Oppy, "Critical Notice of J. P. Moreland's Consciousness and the Existence of God," 193–212.

96. Clayton, *Adventures in the Spirit*, 86.

97. Ibid., 86.

98. Ibid., 87.

be willing to pay. This cost is, at any rate, far lower than the costs that one must pay if one adopts either a reductionist or dualist stance regarding mind and consciousness.[99]

Thus, Clayton would stand in opposition to Oppy and other naturalists/materialists when it comes to the truth of Christian theism. Clayton offers many arguments defending classical theism, while trying to defend a broad form of non-reductive physicalism, which seems to render his whole system of explaining consciousness inconsistent. Clayton seeks to affirm God's action in the world particularly with respect to consciousness. Although he supports panentheism, some of the lines of argumentation that he uses support classical theism. In a section of *Mind & Emergence*, entitled "What Naturalistic Explanations Leave Unexplained," Clayton provides a series of arguments against strong naturalism and reductive physicalism, including an explanation for why something exists rather than nothing, a transcendent cause of the big bang, the existence of objective moral values and duties, religious experience, the correspondence between our minds and truth/reality, and ultimate meaning in life. For Clayton, theism provides a better explanation for these than a strong naturalism/reductive physicalism.[100] So it seems that Clayton is seeking to find a conciliatory ground between naturalism and theistic dualism (which need not necessarily entail substance dualism), although as is argued in this book, theistic dualism (classical theism)[101] is to be preferred over panentheism and other notions.

Despite an inability to substantiate some of the claims regarding emergentism and the origin of consciousness, which may or may not be a cost higher than he has imagined (see above), Clayton does provide support for a couple of interesting arguments that line up quite closely with the aims of this book. Let us briefly examine them.

First, Clayton sees God as plausibly influencing "human moral intuitions and religious aspirations" as opposed to arguing "God fixed the broken plumbing system in one's house (unless one *also* calls a plumber to

99. Ibid.

100. See Clayton, *Mind & Emergence*, 172–79, with the exception of the transcendent cause argument to big bang cosmology found on page 205. See also Moreland, *Consciousness and the Existence of God*, 138. Moreland organizes all these reasons, which are scattered through Clayton's *Mind & Emergence*, together. However, Moreland does not further explain why or how he equates classic theism with theistic dualism. This is perfectly sensible, if by theistic dualism we mean to suggest God is spirit and the world is body, with God being both transcendent and immanent. This is in contrast to Clayton's panentheism, which suggests that God is the world's spirit and the world is his body.

101. It is to be preferred because it employs the classical conception of the Christian God.

come and do the repairs!) . . . If human action is indeed non-nomological, divine causal influence on the thought, will, and emotions of individual persons could occur without breaking natural law."[102] Clayton supports a double agency view, whereby human and other agents may function as "secondary" causes and God as a "primary" cause. God does not intervene, nor does He coerce human action, but rather He persuades.[103] This is similar to the systematic theology arguments we looked at earlier (Section 7.3.1 guideline 6b) regarding moral self-consciousness and the image-likeness to God, where humans through Scripture and personal relationship with God can be "persuaded" (using Clayton's term).

The second line of argument involves the difficulty we struggled with throughout this book, explaining God's action through evolutionary processes[104] to bring out His ends, specifically the origin of consciousness. Clayton recognizes the centrality of information theory in the biological sciences.[105] When examining theories involving information as a rudimentary component in applications such as IIT and PSII, it is of special interest when Clayton states:

> The informational approach clearly opens up significant parallels with information processing in the sphere of mental activity. No biological laws are broken if complicated biological systems such as the brain give rise to emergent mental properties and if these properties in turn constrain brain functioning. Since most cognitive activity concerns information retention, retrieval, and processing, it is natural to understand mental causation as involving the interplay of informational and biological causes. But the interplay of informational and biological causes does not occur only in thought.[106]

Clayton is right: informational and biological causes occur in many mental processes and extend to the very essence of life. Chalmers also astutely recognized this over twenty years ago.[107] That is why, as we have iterated on several occasions, for the purpose of producing the first self-replicating system, the origin of information is a fundamental question with respect to not only understanding life but also consciousness and its origins. Demonstration of a compatibility between evolution and mental activity for

102. Clayton, *Adventures in the Spirit*, 197.

103. Ibid.

104. Ibid., 198–203.

105. Ibid., 199.

106. Ibid.

107. Chalmers, *The Conscious Mind*, 276–309.

Clayton is an important factor in showing the reconciliation of evolution with theism. This is something that we have been struggling to do with the adaptation of various theories of consciousness such as IIT/PSII, Dembski's informationally porous universe, and the Trinitarian Mode of Creation. Possessing a theory of divine action based on information would operate nicely when it comes to the origin of consciousness and self-consciousness. The combination of these has at least opened the door to divine action, with respect to the phenomena at hand and has avoided what Clayton and those supporting DAP fear, namely that "a direct divine intervention to change the chemistry of a cell would be a troubling miracle."[108] Clayton's view on the origin of consciousness and his views on God have some problems with consistency. Clayton defends something close to the classical Christian conception of God but adheres to panentheism. His views on consciousness are nonreductive and emergentist; we wonder if they are sufficient to explain the origin of consciousness. Nonetheless, the important point is that Clayton allows for information to be crucial to divine action and opens the door for its role in the origin of consciousness. Despite the problems, this main point is certainly of critical importance. Information through divine action is crucial to all three. All three views on consciousness work with what we are attempting to demonstrate in this book; namely, that 1) theology can influence science ; and 2) that the classical Christian conception of God and creation is not only compatible but provides a plausible explanation for the origin of consciousness.

8.5 Conclusion

Having examined three prominent frameworks on consciousness that entail a wide range of views, we can see that the origin of consciousness could have originated through the means suggested by any of the three. This demonstrates that the Christian conception of God and creation need not be committed nor restricted by one narrow framework for understanding consciousness. This in turn emphasizes the importance of remaining sufficiently open to alternative views, within a given paradigm (Christian theism). Moreover, as we saw with Lakatosian problemshifts, it would be naïve to think that just because substance dualism, the tripartite model, or emergent monism may not provide sufficient explanatory scope, that sufficient warrant has been provided to discard any one of these Christian theistic perspectives in helping understand the origin of consciousness. Neither would an anomaly or other incongruent bits of evidence suggest

108. Ibid., 200.

that any of them should be discarded. As we saw in the guidelines in chapter 7 of this book, these understandings of consciousness are worth exploring further and can potentially incite further scientific research when coupled with PE or DE and/or various theories of consciousness that exist now or may come to be in the future.

Conclusion

THROUGHOUT THE DIFFERENT POSITIONS that we have examined, and in many others, there is no indication as to precisely *how* or by what process consciousness originates or emerges. This is true even though we have examined several different models of TE, where PE and DE were of interest. The other important point to note is that in this book, a modest claim has been made, namely that the Christian conception of God and creation functions as a plausible explanation for the origin of self-consciousness. We observed that through convergence this has manifested itself in varying degrees with an assortment of mammals but most strongly within humankind's self-consciousness. Let us recall the naturalist's claim that consciousness somehow emerges from matter, without a precise explanation as to how this is possible. This is in essence to suggest that something comes from nothing. We also examined the problems with panpsychism from a naturalist perspective (see combination problem in the introduction and chapter 7), though it appears to be more plausible from a theistic view. One cannot simply declare something by fiat, namely that it emerges from pre-existent matter or that it is conjoined to matter without some sort of explanation. We need to know why and how. This book provides the first inklings to that answer, though it still falls short of a definitive explanation (whether applying panpsychism or not). Moreover, we have no good reason to think that either phenomenal consciousness strongly linked to self-consciousness, or the lesser degrees of self-consciousness found throughout the animal kingdom, would have originated from purely naturalistic processes. Indeed, most academics in consciousness studies have given up on strictly materialistic explanations. Now, many people, such as David Chalmers, are exploring panpsychism. I see this as one of the final subterfuges of naturalism in the hopes of explaining consciousness.

It is widely acknowledged that consciousness studies sit at the uncomfortable boundary between philosophy and science. This book goes further to demonstrate that the study of consciousness sits at another uncomfortable boundary in addition to that of philosophy and science: that of theology. This is precisely why, when applied to Russell's CMI in studying the origin and nature of consciousness, all three disciplines have something profound to contribute. It is not to say that they are commensurate, but they do indeed interact and intersect in important ways. They are not epistemologically equivalent but cognitively similar. Recall that this book has a closer affinity to critical realism (chapter 2.6) than Russell's understanding of the CMI. Indeed, there has been quite a transformation of the CMI, one which Russell may not be comfortable with, but ideas and methods are not meant to be static, but rather to evolve and expand when other thinkers interpret and utilize them. There was a greater focus on critical realism with the application of natural theology (à la Barbour, Peacocke, Polkinghorne) than there was with Russell. Russell's approach prefers a theology of nature.

The Christian conception of God and creation provides a plausible explanation as to why things such as self-consciousness, moral aptitudes, volition, etc., exist, yet explaining the precise process is the difficult and quintessential question of the science-theology dialogue, particularly with respect to the origin of consciousness. It is what will create the ultimate problemshift that Clayton foresees in turning Russell's CMI into an actual research program, as opposed to merely a regulative ideal. I believe that integrating QM with a science and philosophy of information can lead to a discernment of its evolutionary origins.[1] Clayton admits that informational structures provide a useful outlook in understanding God's interaction with in-world mental activity. Utilizing theories such as IIT, Orch-OR, PSII, dualist notions, and others can aid in this quest. This is why I have presented research guidelines that can stimulate further thought. Perhaps my proposals miss the mark, but it is a step forward to get thinkers at an interdisciplinary level, focused more directly on the significance of the origin of consciousness. Nonetheless, we cannot know precisely how God interacts with the world in a "scientific" manner. We have philosophical and theological perspectives that may offer better explanations than naturalistic modes of thinking, but to say conclusively how God influenced or acted in evolutionary processes to produce a tripartite model, substance dualist, or emergent monist understanding of consciousness and the human person, may be an unattainable goal, given our physico-temporal embodied existence.

1. Trying to overcome such an impasse is not uncommon to deep scientific issues, i.e., the search for the theory of everything in overcoming the barriers between two seemingly incompatible scientific theories such as Quantum Theory and Einstein's General Theory of Relativity would be an example. Another example would be discovering the true mechanisms of evolutionary change responsible for all the living organisms and all the distinct features of every organism.

So, then how is the doctrine of divine simplicity related to the origin of self-consciousness? The objection can be raised at this point: How do these notions of consciousness, which appear to be quite complex, reflect divine simplicity? On one level, the response could be that the ability to have complex thoughts or its explanation of its functions may be complex but that does not make its nature complex. Both divine and finite consciousnesses are simple in terms of the non-possession of parts, despite the processes of deliberation, thought, reflection, non-reflection, etc. With respect to His relation to us, God as an ultimately simple being engages in interaction between complex beings given the duality of the compositional embodied natures of our simple immaterial aspect (our soul, mind, consciousness, spirit) with the complex multifaceted bodily aspect. Our existence is distinct from our essence, every created being is of both. As Dolezal notes: "No created essence is identical with its act of existence and is therefore relative and dependent in some sense. But God's essence is identical with his existence and therefore God is absolutely necessary and self-sufficient."[2] St. Thomas provides a succinct explanation:

> [T]he existence of a thing differs from its essence, this existence must be caused either by some exterior agent or by its essential principles. Now it is impossible for a thing's existence to be caused by its essential constituent principles, for nothing can be the sufficient cause of its own existence, if its existence is caused. Therefore that thing, whose existence differs from its essence, must have its existence caused by another. But this cannot be true of God; because we call God the first efficient cause. Therefore it is impossible that in God His existence should differ from His essence.[3]

Moreover, as Dolezal, explaining his work on divine simplicity suggests, the relationship between God's simplicity and its translation to complex humans in understanding God's essence (nature) through a multiplicity of distinctions in God's attributes, such as omnibenevolence, omnipotence, omniscience, omnipresence, etc. can be explained by understanding that:

> God manifests or reveals Himself to us complex, composite creatures in a complex and composite mode. So, that the true mode of the simple subsistent eternal God, the true mode of His being is not conveyed to us in our mode of knowing but rather he accommodates to our way of knowing and He puts the

---

2. Dolezal, *God without Parts,* 7.
3. Aquinas, "Summa Theologiae," I.3.4. As quoted in Dolezal, *God without Parts,* 7.

image of Himself in us under a mode of being that is fitting to us composite creatures.[4]

So, we go back to the respective notions of Pambrun and Clayton. In their analogy, we see that God can communicate in a way that is communicable to complex beings such as ourselves. We still have a finite stamp on our possession of self-consciousness through His image-likeness, though being eternal and transcendent. One speculative and possible exploration in the attempt to link this relation of God's simplicity to human self-consciousness can be examined through Aristotle's Principle of Synonymy. However, this is something that I would defer to future research. The development of an argument based on the principle of synonymy and God's simplicity as an agent, and humans as agents consisting of matter and form (as Aquinas would state it, *ST* Ia. 3.2.) would require rigorous intricacy beyond the scope of this text.[5]

Another loose end that can be left for future research is the biblical justification of *creation ex nihilo* as argued through the KCA. Even though there has been work done in this domain[6] there needs to be future re-

4. See YouTube Interview with James Dolezal, "God without Parts: The Doctrine of Divine Simplicity" between the 53–55 minute mark.

5. See Aristotle, *Metaphysics* XII, 1070a4: "Each substance comes to be from the synonymous." An interesting paper documents the debate between Franz Brentano and Eduard Zeller on the origin of mind in Aristotle. Essentially, what is argued is that mind does not come ultimately from finite human minds but is ultimately caused by a Divine Mind, in other words, God. See Novak, "The Zeller-Brentano Debate on the Origin of Mind." Additionally, given the finitude of the past, God, who encompasses a transcendent simple mind, is the best explanation for this. Ultimately, ECAs such as ourselves are synonymous with an eternal conscious being. We are created as finite versions of God. Our consciousness is synonymous with God's simple self-consciousness. The argument we have examined, and dubbed the CENTAC, is to the effect that consciousness originates ultimately from divine simplicity but through The KCA, the fine-tuning of the laws of physics and biology, and that the origin of information which is necessary to originate consciousness in embodied beings is ultimately through a principle of synonymy with finite minds, which reflect God's eternal simplicity. In a sense, we can argue that God serves as a highly plausible explanation for the origin of consciousness but cannot be reduced to a mere "explanation." To be clear, God infinitely transcends our impositions, understandings and explanations, but if God exists and has revealed Himself not only through Scripture, but also through nature, this is the sort of thing we would expect—God as being the ultimate cause of consciousness, even though God operates through secondary means, through the evolutionary process. God's intentions are manifested through secondary causes attested by His foreknowledge of the world. Thus, in a world which exemplifies evidence of mind, throughout its evolutionary development to the advent of self-conscious embodied beings, we come to expect existence undergirded by God's simplicity from all of the creation it ultimately originates from.

6. For a case supporting *creation ex nihilo* as supported biblically, see Copan, "Is

search to support the doctrine of *creation ex nihilo* in a serious exegetical way dealing with both OT and NT texts. An exegetical work of this sort should also take into serious account the cosmology of the times. It would also be important to look at how these biblical texts, that claimed to support *creation ex nihilo*, have been influential in the construction of the classical Christian conception of God.

Much of this book has been exploratory and speculative in nature since the origin of consciousness is indeed a difficult problem to unravel. Moreover, scientific theories of consciousness are a very recent development (less than ten years).[7] Consciousness has a variety of meanings, including what one is aware of in terms of first-person introspection. We have used the broad understanding of self-consciousness (self-awareness), the "I" realization, which entails moral consciousness through the will to discern between what is good or bad.

Throughout this book we have labored to respond to two main questions as they were outlined in the introduction. First whether theology, in particular the Christian conception of God and creation, can make a fruitful contribution to the sciences with regard to the question of the origin of consciousness. And second, whether the Christian conception of God and creation serves as a plausible explanation for the origin of consciousness.

As we have witnessed, the two questions are intimately intertwined as they both involve complex interactions between theology, science, and philosophy. We saw that philosophy plays an intimate role in the science-theology dialogue. It not only helps to protect the fruitfulness of the program from materialistic critiques, but also shows the soundness of the interconnectivity between seemingly disparate, broad disciplines such as science and theology.

In order to respond to the first, we proposed what, in my estimation, is the best research program involving the science and theology dialogue, namely Russell's CMI. Russell's CMI provides a bidirectional influence from science to theology and vice versa in a very plausible way. It is the latter of the two questions which is novel to the science and theology interaction. We looked at several creation and evolution models. The most applicable for reasons already examined were PE or DE, each still fraught with their own lacunae. For PE, the problem is the generation of information from the laws

---

Creatio ex nihilo a Post-Biblical Invention? A Response to Gerhard May's Proposal," 77–93; For a thorough case being made for the Old Testament, New Testament, and extra biblical witnesses, see Copan and Craig, *Creation out of Nothing*, chapters 1–4.

7. The first yearly conference on consciousness, established in 1994, then named Toward a Science of Consciousness, has now in 2016 officially been renamed The Science of Consciousness.

of physics and for DE the unsavory theological implications of "intervention" remain problematic. However, it seems to me that either of these TE models could work with respect to God's action. DE need not necessarily involve "intervention" as objected to by those who support DAP, but could involve God's action through informational processes, which as we have seen, may be intimately connected to consciousness.

After having examined Teilhard's synthesis of cosmic evolutionary notions and how they relate to God and Christian doctrine, we were able to tease out several useful ideas, in particular his emphasis on a holistic interpretation of the human person and his idea of "ultra-physics." This idea of 'ultra-physics' in a sense, seems to play into a neutral monistic idea that lay between matter and spirit. I believe this is grounded in our understanding of information. Information we saw, plays a vital role in the formation of life. Many who are working on the origin of consciousness recognize the place it has with respect to its connection to consciousness. We also saw fruitfulness in Teilhard's law of complexity-consciousness, as we developed our CENTAC.

From Teilhard's scientific theology and after examining arguments from natural theology, philosophical theology, and systematic theology, we moved on to applying Russell's CMI to the origin of consciousness in chapter 7, in an attempt to answer the first question. We saw how the findings of neuroscience place constraints on theology, with respect to brain damage/deterioration affecting memory and cognitive abilities. Still, theology helps to provide philosophical assumptions which undergird the sciences.[8] We provided research guidelines which point to the concept of divine simplicity functioning as the prime reality, from which all physical reality is ultimately derived—all complexity comes from simple beginnings.[9] We also saw that theological theories can provide motivation for new scientific theories. This is evident in one theological theory of divine action, where we take into account QM and Dembski's notion of God interacting with the world through informational processes. Scientific theories of consciousness like IIT and PSII take the concept of information seriously, when exploring the origin and nature of consciousness. We also saw how theology can create selection rules for choosing rival theories. For instance, the doctrine of God's simplicity can help us decide which understanding of consciousness fits better. If we indeed possess a transcendent nature similar to God, namely that our consciousness and soul are not reducible to the material then an understanding of consciousness which conforms to the doctrine of divine simplicity would be a better fit.

8. See path 6 in chapter 7.3.

9. This is exemplified through the KCA and our models of TE especially PE and DE. All entail simple beginnings preceding the advent of complex beings and processes.

We examined various guidelines that can stimulate further inter-disciplinary research. At the heart of the origin of consciousness are not only notions of evolution and creation but of God's action. How does God interact with the world? One of the main contentions of this book is that God interacts with the world in an objective manner. We base this on what we do know about science, not on what we do not know.[10] We know that information-rich systems have invariably come from intelligent sources. We know that information transcends matter and is not dependent upon it, since it can not only change material mediums but is also seemingly indestructible when the material medium is destroyed. The key question is how information itself transfers to matter, and where it originates from (before it gives the transformed matter its form).[11] We know that agents (minds) can interact with information through consciousness. Through examining all of the philosophical theology, systematic theological, and natural theological arguments, we built a cumulative case for the Christian conception of God and creation to explain the origin of consciousness (self-consciousness and moral consciousness).

In arguing for a plausible explanation for the origin of self-consciousness and moral consciousness, we considered a series of arguments from natural theology including the KCA, the fine-tuning of the laws of physics and biology and the origin of information (life) and convergent evolution. We saw that the most plausible explanation for these phenomena was grounded in a transcendent God who is the cause and reason for the existence of the universe, its evolution, and laws including life itself. From there we provided an argument for God's simplicity. These arguments cumulatively provide a single powerful argument for the existence of a transcendent God as the cause of the specific type of experience known as embodied self-consciousness. When the KCA is coupled with the doctrine of *creation ex nihilo* we gathered both philosophical and scientific support.

We also witnessed the doctrine of the image-likeness of God which corroborates our philosophical and scientific intuition that humans are unique. Our faculties of reason, self-knowledge, creativity, moral awareness, etc., mirror those of God. We also saw that the origin of moral consciousness exemplifies this image-likeness. Our moral consciousness has the propensity to long to love God, others, and ourselves. We then saw how the Trinitarian Mode of Creation fits nicely from a biblical context, into Dembski's ideas about what lay behind creation and God's interaction with the world through informational processes. The transcendent aspect

10. See Russell's quote regarding NIODA in section 2.7.

11. See Dembski, *The End of Christianity*, chapter 11.

of humans allows for God to interact through information, which also transcends mere physicality.

We then examined consciousness as it applies to origins, from three Christian understandings including Moreland's substance dualism, Lonergan-Helminiak's tripartite model, and Clayton's emergent monism. We observed that each were non-reductive and fit well with notions of God interacting through informational processes. Any of the three models could function well with TE models such as PE or DE. Moreland's understanding is more closely tied to DE (OEC is Moreland's preference) and the other two with PE, but it can conceivably function with either one, when considering minor alterations (i.e., emergent dualism for a PE system). Clayton's view allows for any of the three to function with QM and informational processes (chapter 8.4), as we demonstrated.

Recall Pambrun's argumentation in favor of analogy between theology and science in chapter 2.6. In a similar fashion, Philip Clayton in his book *God and Contemporary Science* has argued that panentheism is the best explanation for the analogy between divine and human agency:

> We found strong theological reasons to maintain an analogy between the human and the divine agent, and hence between human and divine agency. In previous chapters we developed the analogy in some detail: just as human consciousness (mental properties and their causal effects) can lead to changes in the physical world, so also a divine agent could bring about changes in the physical world—if this agent were related to the world in a way analogous to the relationship of our 'minds' to our bodies. With this analogy we found ourselves led again to the theological position developed in earlier chapters of this study: panentheism. A panentheistic account of God/world relation provides, I argued, the best framework for a theory of divine agency.[12]

As we explored earlier with respect to dualist notions with scientific implications, Schwartz approaches consciousness from a different supposition than Clayton, instead of espousing a monist position he defends a dualism. Schwartz, using empirical work with his treatment of Obsessive Compulsive Disorder (OCD), is convinced of a dualist picture of the mind and the brain. The point is to suggest that various approaches can exist. Here is one which does not necessitate a panentheistic view of God, since he can explain how the two can interact with one another through his pioneering work on OCD. Even if one does not accept his substance dualist interpretation, his work nonetheless, is clearly indicative of a transcendent component of the brain,

---

12. Clayton, *God and Contemporary Science*, 258–59.

i.e., the mind need not be completely or necessarily be separated. Further inquiry in not only theology and philosophy but also science, will potentially help illuminate the interaction with respect to agency and its influence on the physical. Nonetheless, it seems to me that this leaves the door open to Dembski's proposition that God acts through information within the material universe, which does not require a dualist position.

For reasons we have already examined, panentheism is no more viable than classical theism. The analogy between a divine agency and an embodied human agency need not collapse, depending on the mind-brain position adopted. It could apply with a variety of positions. The concept of divine simplicity and the principle of synonymy for the origin of consciousness do not necessitate the exclusion of dualist or monist theories of consciousness, and they may function with all.

Throughout the different positions we have examined and many others as well, there is no indication as to precisely *how* or by what process consciousness originated or emerged. I claim that the Christian conception of God plausibly explains why there are such things as self-consciousness, moral aptitudes, volition, etc., but to explain precisely by what process these have come to be, is the difficult task. This is the quintessential question of the science-theology dialogue, at least with respect to the origin of consciousness.

What about Clayton's concern with the CMI's ability to create a progressive problemshift from a Lakatosian perspective? Discerning the origins of consciousness, is what will create the problemshift[13] that Clayton emphasizes in helping turn Russell's CMI into an actual research program, as opposed to that of a mere regulative ideal. I believe that integrating QM with a science and philosophy of information can lead to discernment of its evolutionary origins. Clayton admits that informational structures are a useful outlook in understanding God's interaction with in-world mental activity. Utilizing theories such as IIT, Orch-OR, PSII, and others can aid in this quest. This is why I have presented research guidelines that can stimulate further thought.

Perhaps my proposals miss the mark, but they point to a step forward for thinkers at an interdisciplinary level, delving more deeply into the question of the origin of consciousness. Nonetheless, we cannot know precisely how God interacts with the world in a "scientific" manner. We have philosophical and theological concepts which may offer better explanations than naturalistic modes of thinking, but to conclusively determine exactly, how God influenced or acted in evolutionary processes to produce a tripartite

13. See section 1.6.

model, substance dualist or emergent monist understanding of consciousness and the human person may be beyond our ability to understand given our physico-temporal embodied existence. By what precise process God created consciousness will be a difficult task to ascertain, but it seems that understanding different models of evolutionary development and the science behind them, including the relationship of information to consciousness will be of tremendous aid. We learn about God's creation by studying the natural world itself, not through our gaps of knowledge. Nonetheless, it is clear that God's agency is involved in the history of the universe through an objective manner and not necessarily through "crude" intervention.

There are several other lingering problems/questions. For the PE model, how do the laws of physics produce novel information? For the DE model, how does God interact with the world without disrupting the complexity of a brain, even if through information? Can there be a science of the Trinitarian Mode of Creation? What is the precise relationship of complexity to consciousness? This still seems rather ambiguous. What is the connection between the origin of life and the origin of consciousness? Information seems like a strong connector between the two, but how? How do agents interact with information, and how does that relate to nature in a science of information and consciousness?

Inevitably, the following questions still haunt us: how can inanimate matter begin the process of self-replication without information to provide the instructions to do so? Does chance, physical law, or the combination of the two provide a sufficient explanation? Does agent causation provide a viable inference to the best explanation for the origin of life? Similarly, how do physical brain processes give rise to conscious subjective experience (qualia), i.e., the hard problem of consciousness? And finally, how does self-consciousness even emerge from qualia? Neuroscientist Antonio Damasio has argued that self-consciousness depends on phenomenal consciousness (qualia) for its evolutionary development but that to be fully conscious, organisms require both. In turn, as CENTAC suggests, qualia depend on the emergence of life and many steps in between. Each evolutionary step is dependent on its antecedent, at least in the case of embodied material existence. In my estimation, the unifying principle is information, i.e., information-rich and functional systems (as Meyer argues for). David Chalmers has iterated something similar in *The Conscious Mind*, where he stated: "I do not have any knockdown arguments to prove that information is the key to the link between physical processes and conscious experience, but there are some indirect ways of giving support to this idea."[14] Why should we agree

14. David Chalmers, *The Conscious Mind*, 287.

with Chalmers? Over twenty-two years after the publication of Chalmers's seminal text, we are still searching for this glue to reality. Are there some more direct ways available to us now? Which understanding of information? What is the connection between finite agents like humans and their interaction with the world, and that of God who we have claimed interacts with the world through informational processes? Understanding this seems like a tremendous task, but also an important quest which can incite further research programs. What is the informational content of self-conscious states? If a robot or artificial being were to experience self-consciousness, might we be able to measure something like that through quantifying the complexity of the substrate? What was it like for a prototypic hominoid who first experienced self-awareness?[15] What change if any would be seen in the complexity of the brain that might relay such information? What about moral consciousness? I believe research into these questions will help unravel some of the deep mysteries of the universe.

The origin of human self-consciousness through the process of cosmic evolution onward, from the origin of life to the wide diversity of organisms, represents an authentic example of a FINLON. Hopefully, future research will validate this claim and also recognize the importance of exploring the proposed guidelines of the CMI. I also believe the CMI can be expanded to utilize additional paths.[16] It is my anticipation that this book

15. The term hominoid refers to gorillas, chimps, orangutans and humans, and their immediate ancestors. In this instance, I am referring to both humans and their immediate ancestors that would have experienced a higher level of self-awareness; higher than modern apes currently experience. It is worth mentioning that some confusion surround related terms such as hominid and hominin (strictly human lineage); all are not interchangeable. Hominid refers to a group which consists of all the great apes including humans, orangutans, chimpanzees, and gorillas whether modern or extinct. And finally, hominin refers to a group of extinct human species such as genera Homo, Australopithecus, Kenyanthropus, Paranthropus and Ardipithecus. It is worth noting that these terms have undergone changes; 'hominid' had the same meaning that 'hominin' now has. Some textbooks have not yet been updated but scientific journals have begun using these new definitions. See *Hominoid Taxonomies*, no pages, http://cogweb.ucla.edu/ep/Hominoids.html.

16. I had some thoughts after an email exchange with a genetic scientist who sees a profound difference between viewing the universe as ultimately emanating from God, as opposed to the perspective of reductive materialist processes. The latter can lead one down heuristically unfruitful pathways to hastily sloppy conclusions, which can in turn blind us to potential cures for diseases and autoimmune deficiencies for instance. He made the point that the evidence is the same to the theist and the reductive materialist, but the *attitude* is the profound difference. I saw this as a lack of humility on behalf of the reductive materialist who thinks he's/she's explained all, once the bottom level of physics is reached, but of course in the history of genetics, as we have seen in the past twenty years, layer upon layer of complexity has been revealed with the discovery of epigenetics. Even Francis Collins, a theist latching onto Neo-Darwinism, realized

will inspire more research into the origin of consciousness through the use of the Christian conception of God and creation. A multi-disciplinary approach is vital for such an endeavor. Nonetheless, we must recognize first, that Christian theology indeed has something to say to the sciences, when it comes to the origin of consciousness. Secondly, we can conclude that the origin of consciousness based on all the arguments presented, plausibly affirms the Christian conception of God and creation.

---

that his supposition of junk DNA was wholly misguided. Thus, for a future path from theology to science, the attitude of humility that a good Christian theology can provide, would better investigative scientific research, encouraging an openness to discovery.

Diagram of The Method of Creative Mutual Interaction (CMI)

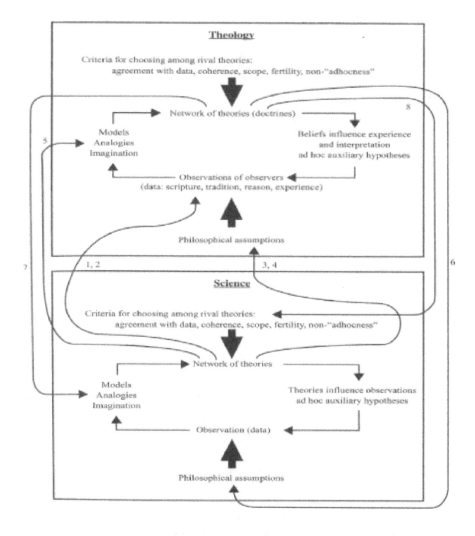

*As it appears on page 23 of Russell's *Cosmology*.

Appendix 2

The Trinitarian Mode of Creation represented by a schematic diagram of a general communication system

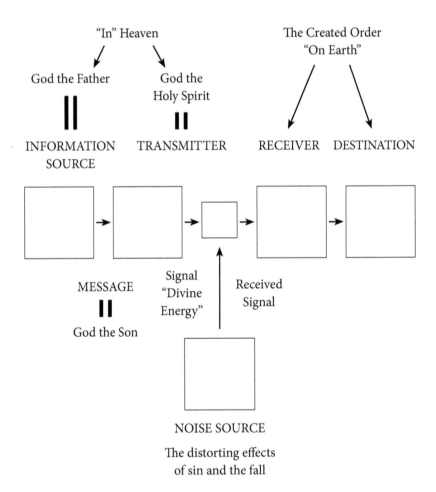

Claude Shannon's communication model; a schematic diagram of a general communication system.[1]

1. Shannon's communication diagram with the incorporation of Dembski's Trinitarian Mode of Creation. See William A. Dembski, *The End of Christianity*, 85–88; Shannon Weaver, *The Mathematical Theory of Communication* (Urbana, IL: University of Illinois Press, 1949), 34.

Bibliography

Aaronson, Scott. "Why I Am Not An Integrated Information Theorist (or, The Unconscious Expander)." http://www.scottaaronson.com/blog/?p=1799.

Aczel, Amir D. *The Jesuit and the Skull: Teilhard de Chardin, Evolution, and the Search for Peking Man.* New York: Riverhead, 2007.

Adams, Robert. "Flavors, Colors, and God." In *Contemporary Perspectives on Religious Epistemology*, edited by R. Douglas Geivett and Brendan Sweetman, 225–40. New York: Oxford University Press, 1992.

Albert, David. "On the Origin of Everything." *The New York Times*, Sunday Book Review (March 25, 2012).

———. *Quantum Mechanics and Experience.* Cambridge: Harvard University Press, 1994.

Allen, Paul. *Ernan McMullin and Critical Realism in the Science-Theology Dialogue.* Burlington, VT: Ashgate, 2006.

Allen, Paul. "A Philosophical Framework within the Science-Theology Dialogue: A Critical Reflection on the Work of Ernan McMullin." PhD diss., St Paul University, Ottawa, ON, 2000.

Allen, Paul. *Theological Method: A Guide for the Perplexed.* New York: T. & T. Clark, 2012.

Anselm of Canterbury. "Monologion." In *Anselm of Canterbury: The Major Works Including Monologion, Proslogion, and Why God Became Man*, edited by Brian Davies and G. R. Evans. Oxford: Oxford University Press, 1998.

Aquinas, Thomas. *De Aeternitate Mundi.* Translated by Robert T. Miller, 2009. http://dhspriory.org/thomas/english/DeEternitateMundi.htm.

———. "Questiones disputate De potentia." In *Questiones diputate.* Vol. 2. Edited by P. Bazzie, et al., 8th rev. ed. Rome: Marietti, 1949.

———. "Summa contra Gentiles." In *Sancti Thomae de Aquino Opera Omnia Iussu Leonis XIII*, Vols. 13–15 of 50 vols. edited by the Leonine Commission. Rome: 1882.

———. "Summa theologiae." In *Sancti Thomae de Aquino Opera Omnia Iussu Leonis XIII.* Vols. 4–12 of 50 vols., edited by the Leonine Commission. Rome: 1882.

Arbib, Michael. "Towards a Neuroscience of the Person." In *Neuroscience and the Person: Scientific Perspectives on Divine Action*, edited by Robert John Russell, et al., 77–100. Notre Dame, IN: University Notre Dame Press, 1999.

Aristotle. *The Complete Works of Aristotle.* 2 vols. Revised Oxford translation. Edited by J. Barnes. Princeton: Princeton University Press, 1984.

―――. *De Anima*. Translated by Michael Shiffman. Newsburyport, MA: Focus, 2012.

Asendorpf, J. B., et al. "Self-awareness and other-awareness II: Mirror self-recognition, social contingency awareness, and synchronic imitation." *Developmental Psychology* 32 (1996) 313–21.

Augustine. *The Trinity*. Edited by John Rotelle. Translated by Edmund Hill. New York: New City, 1991.

―――. *De trinitate*. Edited by John E. Rotelle. Translated by Edmund Hill, O.P. New York: New York City Press, 2010.

Ayer, Alfred Jules. "The Existence of the Soul." In *Great Thinkers on Great Questions*, edited by Roy Abraham Varghese, 48–49. Oxford: One World, 1998.

―――. *Language, Truth & Logic*. New York: Dover, 1952.

Aylward, E. H., et al. "Frontal Lobe Volume in Patients with Huntington's Disease." *Neurology* 50 (January 1998) 252–58.

Baker, Lynne Ruder. *Saving Belief: A Critique of Physicalism*. Princeton: Princeton University Press, 1987.

Balduzzi, David, and Giulio Tononi. "Integrated Information in Discrete Dynamical Systems: Motivation and Theoretical Framework." *PLOS Computational Biology* (June 13, 2008) http://dx.doi.org/10.1371/journal.pcbi.1000091.

Barbour, Ian G. *Myths, Models and Paradigms: The Nature of Scientific and Religious Language*. London: SCM, 1974.

―――. *Religion and Science: Historical and Contemporary Issues*. New York: HarperCollins, 1997.

―――. *Religion in an Age of Science: The Gifford Lectures 1989–1991 Volume 1*. New York: Harper & Row, 1990.

―――. *When Science Meets Religion: Enemies, Strangers, or Partners?* New York: HarperCollins, 2000.

Barrow John D., and Frank J. Tipler. *The Anthropic Cosmological Principle*. Oxford: Oxford University Press, 1986.

Bartlett, Johnathan, and Erica Holloway, eds. *Naturalism and Its Alternatives in Scientific Methodologies: Proceedings of the 2016 Conference on Alternatives to Methodological Naturalism*. Broken Arrow, OK: Blyth Institute, 2017.

Barzaghi, Amerigo, and Josep Corcó. "Ernan McMullin's Thought on Science and Theology: An Appreciation," *Open Theology* 1(2015) 512–23.

Basti, Gianfranco. "The Quantum Field Theory (QFT) Dual Paradigm in Fundamental Physics and the Semantic Information Content and Measure in Cognitive Sciences." (Paper presented at 40th Annual Convention of the Society for the Study of Artificial Intelligence and the Simulation of Behaviour, London) (April 1–4, 2014) 594–601.

Beardsley, Tim. "The Machinery of Thought," *Scientific American* (August 1997) 78–83.

Beauregard, Mario. *Brain Wars: The Scientific Battle Over the Existence of the Mind and the Proof That Will Change the Way We Live Our Lives*. New York: HarperCollins, 2012.

Beauregard, Mario, and Denyse O'Leary. *The Spiritual Brain: A Neuroscientist's Case for the Existence of the Soul*. New York: HarperOne, 2007.

Beauregard, Mario, and Vincent Paquette. "Neural Correlates of a Mystical Experience in Carmelite Nuns," *Neuroscience Letters* 405 (2006) 186–90.

Beauregard, Mario, and Jeffrey M. Schwartz. "Non-materialist mind" *The New Scientist*, letter to the editor, November 26, 2008. https://www.newscientist.com/letter / mg20026840–400-non-materialist-mind/.

Bedeau, Mark A., and Paul Humphreys, eds. "Introduction," in *Emergence: Contemporary Readings in Philosophy and Science*. Cambridge, MA: MIT Press, 2008.

Behe, Michael J. *Darwin's Blackbox: The Biochemical Challenge to Evolution*. New York: Free Press, 1996.

————. *The Edge of Evolution: The Search for the Limits of Darwinism*. New York: Free Press, 2007.

Beilby, James ed. *Naturalism Defeated? Essays on Plantinga's Evolutionary Argument against Naturalism*. Ithaca: Cornell University Press, 2002.

Benedict XVI. *Introduction to Christianity 2nd edition*, San Francisco: Ignatius, 1990.

Bergson, Henri. *Creative Evolution*. Translated by Arthur Mitchell. New York: Dover, 1911.

Berman, Marshall. "Intelligent Design: The New Creationism Threatens All of Science and Society." *American Physical Society News* 14 (October 2005). http://www.aps.org/publications/apsnews/200510/backpage.cfm.

Blackmore, Susan. *Consciousness: A Very Short Introduction*. Oxford: Oxford University Press, 2005.

————. "Delusions of Consciousness." *Journal of Consciousness Studies* 23 (2016) 52–64. https://www.susanblackmore.uk/wp-content/uploads/2017/05/2016jcs.pdf.

Block, Ned. "What Was I Thinking?" Review of *Self Comes to Mind: Constructing the Conscious Brain* by Antonio Demasio, *New York Times*, Sunday Book Review, November 26, 2010. http://www.nytimes.com/2010/11/28/books/review/Block-t.html?pagewanted=all&_r=0.

Blumenberg, Hans. *The Genesis of the Copernican World*. Second Printing. Translated by Robert M. Wallace. Cambridge, MA: MIT Press, 2000.

Bock, Walter J. "Reviewed Work: The Evolutionary Synthesis. Perspectives on the Unification of Biology," *The Auk: Ornithological Advances* 98 (1981) 644–46.

Boesiger, E. "Evolutionary Biology in France at the Time of the Evolutionary Synthesis." In *The Evolutionary Synthesis: Perspectives on the Unification of Biology*, edited by Ernst Mayr and William B. Provine. Cambridge: Harvard University Press, 1980.

Boghossian, Paul. "The Status of Content." *Philosophical Review* 99 (1999) 157–84.

————. "The Status of Content Revisited." *Pacific Philosophical Quarterly* 71 (1991) 264–78.

Borde, Arvind, et al. "Inflationary Spacetimes are not Past-Complete," *Physical Review Letters* 15 (2003) 151301-1–151301-4.

Bouteneff, Peter C. *Beginnings: Ancient Christian Readings of the Biblical Creation Narrative*. Grand Rapids: Baker Academic, 2008.

Brayton, Ed. "Exaptation vs Front Loading: Why Evolution Wins." http://scienceblogs.com/dispatches/2007/06/08/exaptation-vs-front-loading-wh/.

Brent, James. "Natural Theology." *Internet Encyclopedia of Philosophy: A Peer Reviewed Academic Resource*. http://www.iep.utm.edu/theo-nat/.

Brentano, Franz. "The Psychology of Aristotle." In *Essays on Aristotle's De Anima*, edited by R. George. Berkeley: University of California Press, 1977.

Brueggemann, Walter. "Genesis 1:1–2:4." In *Interpretation of Genesis*. Louisville, KY: Westminster John Knox, 1982.

Bruteau, Beatrice. *Evolution Toward Divinity: Teilhard de Chardin and the Hindu Traditions*. Wheaton, IL: The Theosophical Publishing House, 1974.

Byrne, Patrick H. "Lonergan, Evolutionary Science, and Intelligent Design." *Revista Portuguesa de Filosofia: Special Edition—Bernard Lonergan and Philosophy* 63 (2007) 893–913.

Caston, Victor. "Aristotle on Consciousness." *Mind* 111 (2002) 751–815.

Chalmers, David J. *The Character of Consciousness*. Oxford: Oxford University Press, 2010.

———. "The Combination Problem for Panpsychism." In *Panpsychism*, edited by G. Bruntrup and L. Jaskolla. Oxford: Oxford University Press, 2016.

———. *The Conscious Mind: In Search of a Fundamental Theory*. Oxford: Oxford University Press, 1996.

———. "The Puzzle of Conscious Experience," *Scientific American* 237(6) (December 1995) 62–68.

———. "Strong and Weak Emergence," In *The Re-Emergence of Emergence: The Emergentist Hypothesis from Science to Religion*, edited by Philip Clayton and Paul Davies, 244–56. Oxford: Oxford University Press, 2006.

———. "What is a neural correlate of consciousness?" In *Neural Correlates of Consciousness: Empirical and Conceptual Questions*, edited by Thomas Metzinger, 17–39. Cambridge, MA: MIT Press, 2000.

Chesterton, Gilbert Keith. *The Collected Works of G.K. Chesterton II: The Everlasting Man*. San Francisco: St. Ignatius, 1986.

Choate, R. A., et al. "Moving Towards PSII: A Proposal for a Psychophysical Science of Consciousness." Poster Presentation at the Science of Consciousness 2016 in Tucson, AZ.

———. "Moving Towards PSII: A Proposal for a Psychophysical Science of Consciousness." *The Science of Consciousness Program book*, abstract 36, (2016) 64. University of Arizona Center for Consciousness Studies. http://www.consciousness.arizona.edu/documents/TSC2016_BOOK_of_Abstracts_final.pdf.

Christensen, Jean Ann. "Aristotle and Philoponus on Light." PhD diss., Harvard University, 1979.

Churchland, Patricia S. *Neurophilosophy: Toward a Unified Science of the Mind/Brain*. Cambridge: MIT Press, 1986.

Churchland, Paul M. "Eliminative Materialism and the Propositional Attitudes." *Journal of Philosophy* 78 (1981) 67–90.

———. *Matter and Consciousness*. Cambridge: MIT Press, 2001.

Clayton, Philip. *Adventures in the Spirit: God, World, Divine Action*. Minneapolis, MN: Fortress, 2008.

———. "'Creative Mutual Interaction' as Manifesto, Research Program and Regulative Ideal." In *God's Action in Nature's World*, edited by Nathan Hallanger and Ted Peters, 51–64. New York: Ashgate, 2006.

———. *Explanation from Physics to Theology: An Essay in Rationality and Religion* New Haven: Yale University Press, 1989.

———. *God and Contemporary Science*. Grand Rapids: Eerdmans, 1997.

———. *Mind & Emergence*. Oxford: Oxford University Press, 2004.

———. "Neuroscience, the Person and God: An Emergentist Account." In *Neuroscience and the Person*, edited by Robert J. Russell, et al., 181–214. Vatican City: Vatican Observatory Publications; Center for Theology and the Natural Sciences, 1999.

———. "Open Panentheism and Creatio ex nihilo," *Process Studies* 1 (Spring/Summer 2008): 166–83.

———. "A Response to My Critics," *Dialog* 38 (1999) 289–93.

———. "Review of 'Theology in the Age of Scientific Reasoning' by Nancey Murphy," *CTNS Bulletin*, 11 (Winter 1991) 29–31.

———. "Toward a Constructive Christian Theology of Emergence," In *Evolution and Emergence: Systems, Organisms and Persons*, edited by Nancey Murphy and William R. Stoeger, SJ, 315–44. Oxford: Oxford University Press, 2007.

Cohen, Jack, and Steve Fuller, "Debate Over Teaching of Intelligent Design Between Steve Fuller and Jack Cohen at the University of Warwick." 2005. http://www.podcastdirectory.com/podshows/339033.

Collins, C. John. *Genesis 1–4: A Linguistic, Literary, and Theological Commentary.* Phillipsburg, NJ: P & R, 2006.

Collins, Francis. *The Language of God: A Scientist Presents Evidence for Belief.* New York: Free Press, 2006.

Collins, Graham P. "The Many Interpretations of Quantum Mechanics." *Scientific American* (November 19, 2017). https://www.scientificamerican.com/article/the-many-interpretations-of-quantum-mechanics/.

Collins, Robin. "God, Design, and Fine-Tuning." In *God Matters: Readings in the Philosophy of Religion,* edited by Raymond Martin and Christopher Bernard, 54–65. New York: Longman, 2002.

———. "The Fine-Tuning Evidence if Convincing." In *Debating Christian Theism,* edited by J. P. Moreland, et al., 35–46. Oxford: Oxford University Press, 2013.

———. "The Fine-Tuning of the Cosmos: A Fresh Look at Its Implications." In *A Companion to Science and Christianity*, edited by James Stump and Alan Padgett, 207–20. Malden, MA: Wiley-Blackwell, 2012.

———. "The Many-Worlds Hypothesis As an Explanation of Cosmic Fine-Tuning: An Alternative to Design?" *Faith and Philosophy* (Special Issue on God and Physical Cosmology), 22 (2006) 654–66.

———. "A Scientific Argument for the Existence of God: The Fine-Tuning Design Argument," In *Reason for the Hope Within,* edited by Michael J. Murray, 47–75. Grand Rapids: Eerdmans, 1999.

———. "The Teleological Argument: An Exploration of the Fine-Tuning of the Universe." In *The Blackwell Companion to Natural Theology,* edited by William Lane Craig and J. P. Moreland, 202–81. Malden, MA: Wiley-Blackwell, 2009.

Cooper, John W. *Panentheism, the Other God of the Philosophers: From Plato to the Present.* Grand Rapids: Baker Academic, 2006.

Copan, Paul. "Is Creatio Ex Nihilo A Post-Biblical Invention? An Examination of Gerhard May's Proposal." *Trinity Journal* 17 (1996) 77–93.

Copan, Paul, and William Lane Craig. *Creation Out of Nothing: A Biblical, Philosophical and Scientific Exploration.* Grand Rapids: Baker, 2004.

Corcoran, Kevin J. *Rethinking Human Nature: A Christian Materialist Alternative to the Soul.* Grand Rapids: Baker Academic, 2006.

Craig, William Lane. *The Cosmological Argument: From Plato to Leibniz.* Eugene, OR: Wipf and Stock, 1980.

———. "Divine Foreknowledge and Newcomb's Paradox." *Philosophia* 17 (1987) 331–50.

———. "God is Not Dead Yet." *Christianity Today* (July 2008) 22–27.

———. *The Kalam Cosmological Argument*. Eugene, OR: Wipf and Stock, 2000.

———. "Pantheists In Spite of Themselves." In *for Faith and Clarity*, edited by J. K. Beilby, 135–56. Grand Rapids: Baker Academic, 2006.

———. *Reasonable Faith: Christian Truth and Apologetics,* 3rd ed. Wheaton, IL: Crossway, 2008.

———. "Theism Defended." In *The Nature of Nature: Examining the Role of Naturalism in Science*, edited by Bruce L. Gordon and William A. Dembski, 901–20. Wilmington, DE: ISI, 2011.

———. *Time and Eternity: Exploring God's Relationship to Time*. Wheaton, IL: Crossway, 2001.

Craig, William Lane, and J. P. Moreland, eds. *The Blackwell Companion to Natural Theology*. Oxford: Wiley-Blackwell, 2009.

———, eds. *Naturalism: A Critical Analysis*. New York: Routledge, 2000.

Culp, John, "Panentheism." *Stanford Encyclopedia of Philosophy* (Summer 2015 Edition). http://plato.stanford.edu/archives/sum2015/entries/panentheism/.

Dalley, Stephanie. *Myths from Mesopotamia: Creation, the Flood, Gilgamesh, and Others*. Oxford: Oxford University Press, 2000.

Damasio, Antonio. *The Feeling of What Happens: Body and Emotion in the Making of Consciousness*. New York: Harcourt Brace, 1999.

———. *Self Comes to Mind: Constructing the Conscious Brain*. New York: Vintage, 2010.

Darwin, Charles. *The Descent of Man and Selection in Relation to Sex*, 2nd ed. London: John Murray, 1882.

———. *The Origin of Species*, 6th ed. London: John Murray, Albemarle Street, 1973.

Davidson, Herbert A. "John Philoponus as a Source of Medieval Islamic and Jewish Proofs of Creation," *Journal of the American Oriental Society* 89 (1969) 357–91.

———. *Proofs for Eternity, Creation and the Existence of God in Medieval Islamic and Jewish Philosophy*. Oxford: Oxford University Press, 1987.

Davies, Paul C. W. *The Fifth Miracle: The Search for the Origin and Meaning of Life*. New York: Simon & Schuster, 1999.

———. *The Mind of God: The Scientific Basis for a Rational World*. New York: Simon & Schuster, 1992.

Davies, Paul C. W., and J.R. Brown, eds. *Ghost in the Atom: A Discussion of the Mysteries of Quantum Physics*. Cambridge: Cambridge University Press, 1986.

Davies, Paul C. W., and Niels Henrik Gregersen, eds. *Information and the Nature of Reality: From Physics to Metaphysics*. Cambridge: Cambridge University Press, 2010.

Davis, Ellen F. *Scripture, Culture, and Agriculture: An Agrarian reading of the Bible*. New York: Cambridge University Press, 2009.

Davis, John Jefferson. *Frontiers of Science and Faith: Examining Questions from the Big Bang to the End of the Universe*. Downers Grove, IL: InterVarsity, 2002.

Dawkins, Richard. *The Blind Watchmaker: Why the Evidence of Evolution Reveals a Universe Without Design*. New York: Norton, 1986.

———. *The God Delusion*. New York: Houghton Mifflin, 2006.

———. "Is Science Killing the Soul?" An interview with Steven Pinker, *Edge* 53, www.edge.org/documents/archive/edge53.html.

———. "Put Your Money on Evolution." *New York Times*, April 9, 1989, sec. 7. 34.

de Lubac, Henri. *The Religion of Teilhard de Chardin*. Translated by Rene Hague. New York: Desclee Co. Inc., 1967.

———. *Teilhard De Chardin: The Man and His Meaning*. Translated by Rene Hague. New York: Hawthorn, 1965.

———. *Teilhard Explained*. Translated by Anthony Buono. New York: Paulist, 1968.

de Vries, Paul. "Naturalism in the Natural Sciences: A Christian Perspective." *Christian Scholar's Review*, 15 (1986) 388–96.

Delfour, F., and K. Marten. "Mirror Image Processing in Three Marine Mammal Species: Killer Whales (Orcinus orca), False Killer Whales (Pseudorca crassidens) and California Sea Lions (Zalophus californianus)." *Behavioural Processes* 53 (2001) 181–90.

Delio, Ilia. *The Emergent Christ: Exploring the Meaning of Catholic in an Evolutionary Universe*. Maryknoll, NY: Orbis, 2013.

———. "Evolution and the Rise of the Secular God." In *From Teilhard to Omega: Co-creating an Unfinished Universe*, edited by Ilia Delio, Maryknoll, 37–52. NY: Orbis, 2014.

———. "Evolution Toward Personhood." In *Personal Transformation and a New Creation: The Spiritual Revolution of Beatrice Bruteau*, edited by Ilia Delio, 109–34. Maryknoll, NY: Orbis, 2016.

———. *From Teilhard to Omega: Co-creating an Unfinished Universe*. Maryknoll, NY: Orbis, 2014.

Dembski, William A. *Being as Communion: A Metaphysics of Information*. Burlington, VT: Ashgate, 2014.

———. *The Design Inference: Eliminating Chance through Small Probabilities*. Cambridge: Cambridge University Press, 1998.

———. *The Design Revolution: Answering the Toughest Questions about Intelligent Design*. Downers Grove, IL: InterVarsity, 2004.

———. *The End of Christianity: Finding a Good God in an Evil World*. Nashville: B & H, 2009.

———. *No Free Lunch: Why Specified Complexity Cannot be Purchased without Intelligence*. Oxford: Rowman & Littlefield, 2002.

———. "Randomness by Design." *Nous* 25 (1991) 75–106.

Dembski, William A., and Michael Ruse, eds. *Debating Design: From Darwin to DNA*. New York: Cambridge University Press, 2004.

Dennett, Daniel C. *Breaking the Spell: Religion as Natural Phenomenon*. New York: Viking, 2009.

———. "Consciousness." In *The Oxford Companion to Mind*, edited by Richard L. Gregory and O. L. Zangwill. Oxford: Oxford University Press, 1987.

———. *Consciousness Explained*. New York: Basic Bay, 1991.

———. *Darwin's Dangerous Idea: Evolution and the Meanings of Life*. New York: Simon & Schuster, 1995.

———. *From Bacteria to Bach and Back: The Evolution of Minds*. New York: Norton, 2017.

———. *The Intentional Stance*. Cambridge, MA: MIT Press, 1987.

Denton, Michael J. "An Anti-Darwinian Intellectual Journey: Biological Order as an Inherent Property of Matter." In *Uncommon Dissent: Intellectuals Who Find Darwinism Unconvincing*, edited by William A. Dembski, 153–94. Wilmington, DE: ISI, 2004.

———. *Evolution: A Theory in Crisis*. Chevy Chase, MD: Adler and Adler, 1985.

————. *Fire-Maker: How Humans Were Designed to Harness Fire and Transform Our Planet*. Seattle: Discovery Institute, 2016.

————. *Focus on Origins*. Access Research Network video interview with Dr. Michael Denton (Senior Research Fellow, Biochemistry Department, University of Otago, New Zealand). Copyright 1993 by Access Research Network, Colorado Springs, CO 80937.

————. *Nature's Destiny: How the Laws of Biology Reveal Purpose in the Universe*. New York: Free Press, 1998.

Dewan, Laurence. "Saint Thomas, Alvin Plantinga, and the Divine Simplicity." *Modern Schoolman* 66 (1989) 141–51.

Dobzhansky, Theodosius. "Nothing in Biology Makes Sense Except in the Light of Evolution," *American Biology Teacher* vol. 35 (1973) 125.

Dodds, Michael. *Unlocking Divine Action: Contemporary Divine Action*. Washington, DC: Catholic University of America Press, 2012.

Dolezal, James E. *God without Parts: Divine Simplicity and the Metaphysics of God's Absoluteness*. Eugene, OR: Pickwick, 2011.

————. "God without Parts: The Doctrine of Divine Simplicity." YouTube Interview with James Dolezal, author of *God without Parts: Divine Simplicity and the Metaphysics of God's Absoluteness*. https://www.youtube.com/watch?v=-davnzphHdc.

Domning, Daryl P. "Teilhard and Natural Selection: A Missed Opportunity?" In *Rediscovering Teilhard's Fire*, edited by Kathleen Duffy, SSJ. Philadelphia: St. Joseph's University Press, 2010.

Domning, Daryl P., and Monika K. Hellwig. *Original Selfishness: Original Sin and Evil in the Light of Evolution*. Burlington, VT: Ashgate, 2006.

Douven, Igor. "Abduction." Stanford Encyclopedia. https://plato.stanford.edu/entries/abduction/.

Drees, Willem. *Religion, Science and Naturalism*. Cambridge: Cambridge University Press, 1996.

Dupuis, Jacques, SJ, and Josef Neuner, SJ. *The Christian Faith: in the Doctrinal Documents of the Catholic Church* 6th rev. ed. New York: Alba House, 1996.

Edwards, Denis. "Teilhard's Vision as Agenda for Rahner's Christology." In *From Teilhard to Omega: Co-creating an Unfinished Universe*, edited by Ilia Delio, Maryknoll, NY: Orbis, 2014.

Ellis, George F. R. "Intimations of Transcendence: Relations of the Mind and God." In *Neuroscience and the Person*, edited Robert J. Russell, et al., 449–74. Vatican City; Berkeley: Vatican Observatory Publications; Center for Theology and the Natural Sciences, 1999.

Erickson, Millard J. *Christian Theology*. Grand Rapids: Baker, 1994.

————. *Introducing Christian Doctrine*, 2nd ed. Grand Rapids: Baker, 2001.

Farabee, M. J. "Paleobiology: The Precambrian: Life's Genesis and Spread." https://www2.estrellamountain.edu/faculty/farabee/biobk/BioBookPaleo2.html#origin.

Faricy, Robert L. *Teilhard de Chardin's Theology of the Christian in the World*. New York: Sheed and Ward, 1967.

Feser, Edward. *The Last Superstition: A Refutation of the New Atheism*. South Bend, IN: St. Augustine's Press, 2008.

Flannery, Michael A. *Alfred Russel Wallace's Theory of Intelligent Evolution: How Wallace's World of Life Challenged Darwinism*. Riesel, TX: Erasmus, 2008.

————. *Nature's Prophet: Alfred Russel Wallace's Evolution from Natural Selection to Natural Theology*, Tuscaloosa, Alabama: University of Alabama Press, 2018.

Flew, Antony, R. M. Hare, and Basil Mitchell, "Theology and Falsification." In *New Essays in Philosophical Theology*, edited by Antony Flew and Alasdair McIntyre. New York: Macmillan, 1955.

Flew, Antony, and Roy Abraham Varghese, *There is a God: How the World's Most Notorious Atheist Changed His Mind*. New York: HarperOne, 2007.

Flynn, Mike. "Adam and Eve and Ted and Alice." http://tofspot.blogspot.ca/2011/09/adam-and-eve-and-ted-and-alice.htm.

Forrest, Peter. "The Epistemology of Religion." *Stanford Encyclopedia of Philosophy.* https://plato.stanford.edu/entries/religion-epistemology/#NatThe.

Fowler, Thomas B., and Daniel Kuebler. *The Evolution Controversy: A Survey of Competing Theories*. Ada, MI: Baker Academic, 2007.

Freddoso, Alfred J. "God's General Concurrence with Secondary Causes: Pitfalls and Prospects." *American Catholic Philosophical Quarterly* 67 (1994) 131–56.

Freeman, W. J. "How and Why Brains Create Meaning From Sensory Information." *International Journal of Bifurcation & Chaos* 14 (2004) 513–30.

Friederich, Simon "Fine-Tuning." *Stanford Encyclopedia of Philosophy.* https://plato.stanford.edu/entries/fine-tuning/#ExamPhys.

Frey, Cristofer. "Creation: Systematic Theology and Ethics." In *The Encyclopedia of Christianity* Vol. 1, edited by Erwin Fahlbusch, et al. Grand Rapids: Eerdmans, 1999.

Fuller, Steve. *Dissent over Descent: Intelligent Design's Challenge to Darwinism*. Thriplow, Cambridge: Icon, 2008.

————. *Science vs Religion? Intelligent Design and the Problem of Evolution*. Cambridge, UK: Polity Press, 2007.

Futuyma, D. J. *Evolutionary Biology*. Sunderland, MA: Sinauer Associates, 1998.

Galleni, Lodovico, and Marie-Claire Groessens-Van Dyck, "A Model of Interaction Between Science and Theology Based on the Scientific Paper of Pierre Teilhard de Chardin." In *Religion and the Challenges of Science*, edited by William Sweet and Richard Feist, Hampshire: Ashgate, 2007.

Gallup, G. G. "Chimpanzees: Self-Recognition." *Science* 167 (1970) 86–87.

Garcia, Robert K., and Nathan L. King, eds. *Is Goodness without God Good Enough? A Debate on Faith, Secularism, and Ethics*. Lanham, MD: Rowman & Littlefield, 2008.

Garfield, J. L. "Philosophy: Foundations of Cognitive Science." In *Cognitive Science: An Introduction*, 2nd ed., edited by N. A. Stillings, et al., 331–77. Cambridge: MIT Press, 1995.

Gauch, Hugh. *Scientific Method in Brief*. Cambridge: Cambridge University Press, 2012.

————. *Scientific Method in Practice*. Cambridge: Cambridge University Press, 2003.

Geisler, Norman L. *Systematic Theology*. Minneapolis, MN: Bethany House, 2011.

Gene, Mike. *The Design Matrix: A Consilience of Clues*. Berkeley: Arbor Vitae, 2007.

Ghirardi, G.C. et al., "A Model for a Unified Quantum Description of Macroscopic and Microscopic Systems." In *Quantum Probability and Applications*, edited by L. Accardi et al., Berlin: Springer Verlag, 1985.

Gish, Duane T. *Evolution the Fossils Say No!* El Cajon, CA: 1995.

Goetz, Steward, and Charles Taliaferro. *A Brief History of the Soul*. Oxford: Wiley-Blackwell, 2011.

Goff, Philip. "Why Panpsychism Doesn't Help Us Explain Consciousness." *Dialectica* 63 (2009) 289–311.

Gonzalez, Guillermo, and Jay Richards. *The Privileged Planet: How Our Place in the Cosmos is Designed for Discovery.* Washington, DC: Regnery, 2004.

Gould, Stephen J. *Rocks of Ages: Science and Religion in the Fullness of Life.* New York: Ballantine, 1999.

———. *Wonderful Life: The Burgess Shale and the Nature of History.* New York: Norton, 1989.

Gould, Stephen J. and Niles Eldredge, "Punctuated equilibria: the tempo and mode of evolution reconsidered," *Paleobiology* 3 (1977) 115–51.

Grant, Edward. "Science and Theology in the Middle Ages." In *God & Nature: Historical Essays on the Encounter Between Christianity and Science,* edited by David C. Lindberg and Ronald L. Numbers. Los Angeles: University of California Press, 1986.

Grenz, Stanley J., and Roger E. Olson, *Twentieth-Century Theology: God and the World in a Transitional Age.* Downers Grove, IL: InterVarsity, 1992.

Gray, Asa. "Natural Selection is not Inconsistent with Natural Theology." In *Asa Gray: Darwiniana,* edited by A. Hunter Dupree. Cambridge: Harvard University Press, 1963.

Grossman, Murray, et al. "Language Comprehension and Regional Cerebral Defects in Frontotemporal Degeneration and Alzheimer's Disease" *Neurology* 50 (1998) 157–63.

Grumett, David. *Teilhard de Chardin: Theology, Humanity and Cosmos.* Leuven: Peeters, 2005.

Guérard des Lauriers, O. P., Pere. "La Démarche du Père Teilhard de Chardin: reflexions d'ordre épistémologique. " *Divinitas* 3 (1959) 227–28.

Haarsma, Loren. "Is Intelligent Design 'Scientific'?" *Perspectives on Science and Christian Faith: Journal of the ASA* 59 (2007) 55–62.

Haarsma Deborah B., and Loren D. Haarsma, *Origins: Christian Perspectives on Creation, Evolution, and Intelligent Design.* Grand Rapids: Faith Alive Christian, 2001.

Hackett, Stuart C. *The Resurrection of Theism: Prolegomena to Christian Apology.* Eugene, OR: Wipf and Stock, 1957.

Hallanger, Nathan, and Ted Peters. *God's Action in Nature's World.* New York: Routledge, 2006.

Hameroff, Stuart, and Roger Penrose. "Conscious Events as Orchestrated Space-Time Selections." In *The Nature of Nature: Examining the Role of Naturalism in Science,* edited by William A. Dembski and Bruce L. Gordon, 790–814. Wilmington, DE: ISI, 2011.

———. "Consciousness in the Universe: A Review of the 'Orch OR' Theory." *Physics of Life Reviews* 11 (2014) 39–78.

———. "Reply to Criticism of the 'Orch OR qubit': 'Orchestrated Objective Reduction' is Scientifically Justified." *Physics of Life Reviews* 11 (2014) 94–100.

Hasker, William. *The Emergent Self.* Ithaca, NY: Cornell University Press, 1999.

Haught, John F. "Darwin's Nagging Doubt: What Thomas Nagel Could Learn from Theology." *Commonweal* 140.16 (2013) 11. Academic OneFile. Web. 2 Feb. 2016.

———. *Responses to 101 Questions about God and Evolution.* New York: Paulist, 2001.

———. *Science and Religion: From Conflict to Conversation.* Mahwah, NJ: Paulist, 1995.

———. "In Search of a God for Evolution: Paul Tillich and Pierre Teilhard de Chardin." *Zygon* 37 (2002) 539–54.

Hawking, Stephen, and Leonard Mlodinow. *The Grand Design*. New York: Random House, 2010.

Hiebert, Paul. "Epistemological Foundations of Science and Theology." *TSF Bulletin* 8 (1985) 5–10.

Helminiak, Daniel A. *Brain, Consciousness and God: A Lonerganian Integration*. New York: SUNY Press, 2015.

———. *The Human Core of Spirituality: Mind as Psyche and Spirit*. New York: SUNY Press, 1996.

Herbert, Nick. *Quantum Reality Beyond the New Physics: An Excursion into Metaphysics*. New York: Anchor Books, 1985.

Hess, Peter M., and Paul L. Allen. *Catholicism and Science*. Westport, CT: Greenwood, 2008.

Hilbert, David. "On the Infinite." In *Philosophy of Mathematics*, edited by Paul Benacarraf and Hilary Putnam, 183–201. Cambridge: Cambridge University Press, 1984.

Hodos, William, and Ann B. Hutler, "Evolution of Sensory Pathways in Vertebrates." *Brain, Behavior, and Evolution* 50 (1997)189–97.

Holten, Wilko van. "Theism and Inference to the Best Explanation." *Ars Disputandi* 2 (2002) 262–81.

Hooykaas, R. *Religion and the Rise of Modern Science*. Grand Rapids: Eerdmans, 1972.

Horgan, John. "Can Integrated Information Theory Explain Consciousness? A radical new solution to the mind–body problem poses problems of its own." *Scientific American*, (December 1, 2015). https://blogs.scientificamerican.com/cross-check/can-integrated-information-theory-explain-consciousness/.

Hubble, Edwin. "A Relation between Distance and Radial Velocity among Extra-galactic Nebulae." *Proceedings of the National Academy of Sciences* 15 (1929) 168–73.

Huchingson, James E. *Pandemonium Tremendum: Chaos and Mystery in the Life of God*. Eugene, OR: Wipf and Stock, 2001.

Hughe, Christopher. *A Complex Theory of a Simple God*. Ithaca: Cornell University Press, 1989.

Hume, David. *A Treatise of Human Nature*. Edited by L. A. Selby-Bigge. Oxford: Clarendon, 1888.

Hunter, Cornelius G. *Darwin's God: Evolution and the Problem of Evil*. Ada, MI: Brazos, 2001.

———. *Darwin's Proof: The Triumph of Religion over Science*. Ada, MI: Brazos, 2003.

Jablonka, Eva, and Marion J. Lamb, eds. *Evolution Beyond Neo-Darwinism, Evolution in Four Dimensions: Genetic, Epigenetic, Behavioral, and Symbolic Variation in the History of Life*. Cambridge: MIT Press, 2005.

Jabr, Ferris. "Self-Awareness with a Simple Brain." *Scientific American* (November 1, 2012). https://www.scientificamerican.com/article/self-awareness-with-a-simple-brain/.

Jaki, Stanley L. *The Origin of Science and the Science of its Origin*. South Bend, IN: Regnery/Gateway, 1978.

James, William. *The Principles of Psychology*. Vol. 1. New York: Cosimo, 1890/2007.

Jaynes, Julian. *The Origin of Consciousness in the Breakdown of the Bicameral Mind*. Boston: Houghton Mifflin, 1976.

Juarrero, A. *Dynamics in Action: Intentional Behavior as a Complex System*. Cambridge: MIT Press, 1999.

Immink, Frederik Gerrit. *Divine Simplicity*. Kampen, NL: Kok, 1987.

Irwin, Klee. "A New Approach to the Hard Problem of Consciousness: A Quasicrystalline Language of 'Primitive Units of Consciousness' in Quantized Spacetime (Part I)." *Journal of Consciousness Exploration & Research* 5 (2014) 483–97.

Johnson, Donald E. *The Programming of Life*. Sylacauga, AL: Big Mac, 2010.

Johnson, Philip E., and Denis O. Lamoureux, *Darwinism Defeated? The Johnson-Lamoureux Debate on Biological Origins*, edited by Robert Clements. Vancouver, BC: Regent College Publishing, 1999.

Johnson, Sterling C., et al. "Neural correlates of self-reflection." *Brain* 125 (2002) 1808–1814.

Kauffman, Stuart. *At Home in The Universe: The Search for the Laws of Self-Organization and Complexity*. New York: Oxford University Press, 1995.

Keenan, Julian Paul, et al. "An Overview of Self-Awareness and the Brain." In *The Oxford Handbook of Social Neuroscience*, edited by Jean Decety and John T. Cacioppo, 314–325. Oxford: Oxford University Press, 2015.

Kemp, Kenneth W. "Science, Theology, and Monogenesis." *American Catholic Philosophical Quarterly* 2 (2011) 217–36. http://www3.nd.edu/~afreddos/papers/kemp-monogenism.pdf.

Kim, Jaegwon. "Concepts of Supervenience." *Philosophy and Phenomenological Research* 45 (1984) 315–26.

———. *Mind in a Physical World*. Cambridge: MIT Press, 1998.

———. "The Myth of Nonreductive Materialism." *Proceedings and Addresses of the American Philosophical Association* 63 (1989) 31–47.

———. "Supervenience as a Philosophical Concept." *Metaphilosophy* 21 (1990) 1–27.

Kind, Amy. "Qualia." In *Internet Encyclopedia of Philosophy: A Peer Reviewed Academic Resource*. http://www.iep.utm.edu/qualia/.

King, Ursula. *Spirit of Fire: The Life and Vision of Teilhard de Chardin*. Maryknoll, NY: Orbis, 1996.

Klaaren, E. M. *Religious Origins of Modern Science*. Grand Rapids: Eerdmans, 1977.

Klima, Gyula. "Thomistic 'Monism' versus Cartesian 'Dualism.'" *Logical Analysis and History of Philosophy* 10 (2007) 92–112.

Koch, Christof. *Consciousness: Confessions of a Romantic Reductionist*. Cambridge: MIT Press, 2012

———. *The Quest for Consciousness: A Neurobiological Approach*. Englewood, CO: Roberts, 2004.

———. "Ubiquitous Minds." *Scientific American Mind*. (January/February 2014) 27–28.

Kragh, Helge, and Robert W. Smith. "Who Discovered the Expanding Universe?" *History of Science* 41 (2003) 145–48.

Krauss, Lawrence. *A Universe from Nothing: Why There Is Something Rather than Nothing*. New York: Free Press, 2012.

Kurzweil, Ray. *The Singularity is Near*. New York: Viking, 2005.

Laforte, Geoffrey, et al. "Why Gödel's Theorem Cannot Refute Computationalism." *Artificial Intelligence* 104 (1998) 265–86.

Lakatos, Imre. "Falsification and the Methodology of Scientific Research Programmes." In *Criticism and Growth of Knowledge,* edited by Imre Lakatos and Alan Musgrave, 91–196. Cambridge: Cambridge University Press, 1970.

———. *The Methodology of Scientific Research Programmes.* Vol. 1, edited by John Worrall and Gregory Currie. Cambridge: Cambridge University Press, 1978.

Lamoureux, Denis. *Evolutionary Creation: A Christian Approach to Evolution.* Eugene, OR: Wipf and Stock, 2008.

———. "Evolutionary Creation: A Christian Approach to Evolution." http://biologos. org/uploads/projects/Lamoureux_Scholarly_Essay.pdf.

———. *I Love Jesus & I Accept Evolution.* Eugene, OR: Wipf and Stock, 2009.

Lane, David H. *The Phenomenon of Teilhard: Prophet for a New Age.* Macon, GA: Mercer University Press, 1996.

Leftow, Brian. "God, Concepts Of," In *Routledge Encyclopedia of Philosophy*, Vol. 4, edited by Edward Craig, 3160–69. New York: Taylor & Francis, 1998.

Lederman, N. G. "Syntax of Nature of Science Within Inquiry and Science Instruction." In *Inquire Within: Implementing Inquiry- and Argument-Based Science Standards Grade 3 to 8*, 3rd ed., edited by L. B. Flick and N. G. Lederman, 301–37. Dordrecht, DE: Springer, 2006.

Lenhoff, Howard M., et al. "William's Syndrome and the Brain." *Scientific American* (December 1997) 68–73.

Lennox, John C. *God and Stephen Hawking: Whose Design Is It Anyway?* Oxford: Lion Hudson, 2011.

Leslie, John. *Universes.* London: Routledge, 1989.

Lindberg, David C., and Ronald L. Numbers. *God & Nature: Historical Essays on the Encounter between Christianity and Science.* Los Angeles: UCLA, 1986.

Lipton, Peter. *Inference to the Best Explanation.* New York: Routledge, 1991.

Locke, John. *An Essay Concerning Human Understanding* (first published 1689). Abridged and edited by Kenneth P. Winkler, Indianapolis: Hackett, 1996.

Lonergan, Bernard. "Cognitional Structure." In *Collection: Papers by Bernard Lonergan*, edited by Frederick E. Crowe, 223–39. Montreal: Palm, 1967.

———. *Insight: A Study of Human Understanding.* Collected Works of Bernard Lonergan, vol. 3, edited by Frederick E. Crowe and Robert M. Doran. Toronto: University of Toronto Press, 1992.

———. *Method in Theology.* Toronto: University of Toronto Press, 1992.

Lou, H.C., et al. "Towards a cognitive neuroscience of self-awareness." *Neuroscience & Biobehavioral Reviews* 83 (2017) 765–773.

Luskin, Casey. "The Facts about Intelligent Design: A Response to the National Academy of Sciences' Science, Evolution, and Creationism." http://www.discovery. org/a/4405.

Lonergan, Bernard. "Want a Good Grade in Alison Campbell's College Biology Course? Don't Endorse Intelligent Design." At *Evolution News & Science Today*, http:// www.evolutionnews.org/2011/03/want_a_good_grade_in_allison_c044581.html.

Lormand, Eric. "Consciousness." In *Concise Routledge Encyclopedia of Philosophy*. New York: Routledge, 2000.

Lyell, Charles. *Principles of Geology: Being an Attempt to Explain the Former Changes of the Earth's Surface, by Reference to Causes Now in Operation.* 3 vols. London: Murray, 1830–33.

Lyons, William. "Introduction." In *Modern Philosophy of Mind*, edited by William Lyons, London: Everyman, 1995.

Mackie, J. L. *The Miracle of Theism.* Oxford: Clarendon, 1982.

Macintosh, Douglas Clyde. *Theology as an Empirical Science.* New York: Macmillan, 1919.

Margulis, Lynn, and Dorion Sagan. *Acquiring Genomes: A Theory of the Origin of Species*. New York: Basic, 2002.

Maritain, Jacques. *The Degrees of Knowledge*. The Collected Works of Jacques Maritain, Vol. 7, edited by Ralph M. McInerny, translated by Gerald B. Phelan, Notre Dame, IN: University of Notre Dame Press, 1995.

——. *The Peasant of the Garonne: An Old Layman Questions Himself About the Present Time*. Toronto: Macmillan, 1966.

——. "Toward a Thomist Idea of Evolution." In *Untrammelled Approaches*, translated by Bernard Doering. Notre Dame: University of Notre Dame Press, 1997.

Marten, K., and S. Psarakos. "Evidence of Self-Awareness in the Bottlenose Dolphin (Tursiops truncatus)." In *Self-awareness in Animals and Humans: Developmental Perspectives*, edited by S. T. Parker, et al., 361–79. Cambridge: Cambridge University Press.

Mazur, Suzan. *The Altenberg 16: An Expose of the Evolution Industry*. Berkeley: North Atlantic, 2010.

McCarty, Doran. *Teilhard de Chardin*. Waco, TX: Word Inc., 1976.

McGrath, A. E. *A Scientific Theology*. 3 vols. London: T. & T. Clark, 2001–2003.

McKenzie, Ross H., and Benjamin Meyers, "Dialectical Critical Realism in Science and Theology: Quantum Physics and Karl Barth." *Science and Christian Belief* 1 (2008) 49–66.

McLaughlin, Brian P. "Emergence and Supervenience." In *Emergence: Contemporary Readings in Philosophy and Science*, Cambridge, MA: MIT Press, 2008.

——. "Philosophy of Mind: Consciousness." In *The Cambridge Dictionary of Philosophy*. Cambridge: Cambridge University Press, 1995.

McMenamin, M. A. S. *The Garden of Ediacara: Discovering the First Complex Life*. New York: Columbia Press, 1988.

——. "Teilhard's Legacy in Science." In *The Legacy of Pierre Teilhard de Chardin*, edited by James Salmon, SJ, and John Farina, 33–54. Mahwah, NJ: Paulist, 2011.

McMullin, Ernan. "Realism in Theology and Science: A Response to Peacocke." *Religion and Intellectual Life* 2 (1985) 39–47.

Menuge, Angus. *Agents under Fire: Materialism and the Rationality of Science*. New York: Rowman & Littlefield, 2004.

Meyer, Stephen C. "The Demarcation of Science and Religion." In *The History of Science and Religion in the Western Tradition: An Encyclopedia*, edited by Gary B. Ferngren, 18–26. New York: Garland, 2000.

——. "The Difference it Doesn't Make." In *God and Evolution: Protestants, Catholics and Jews Explore Darwin's Challenge to the Faith*, edited by Jay W. Richards, 147–64. Seattle, WA: Discovery Institute, 2010.

——. "DNA and the Origin of Life: Information, Specification and Explanation." In *Darwinism, Design and Public Education*, edited by John Angus Campbell and Stephen C. Meyer, 223–85. Lansing, MI: Michigan State University Press, 2003.

——. "DNA: The Signature in the Cell." In *The Nature of Nature*, Bruce L. Gordon and William A. Dembski, 293–345. ISI: Wilmington, DE, 2011.

——. "Evidence of Design in Physics and Biology: From the Origin of the Universe to the Origin of Life." In *Science and Evidence for Design in the Universe*, Proceedings of the Wethersfield Institute, vol. 9, 53–111. St. Ignatius: San Francisco, 2002.

——. "An Interdisciplinary History of Scientific Ideas about the Origin of Life." M. Phil. thesis, Cambridge University, 1986.

——. "Of Clues and Causes: A Methodological Interpretation of Origin of Life Studies." PhD diss., Cambridge University, 1990.

———. "The Origin of Biological Information and the Higher Taxonomic Categories." In *Darwin's Nemesis: Phillip Johnson and the Intelligent Design Movement*, edited by William A. Dembski, 174–213. Downers Grove, IL: InterVarsity, 2006.

———. "The Return of the God Hypothesis." *Journal of Interdisciplinary Studies*, Vol. XI (September 1999) 1–38.

———. *Signature in the Cell: DNA and Evidence for Intelligent Design*. New York: HarperOne, 2009.

———. "Teleological Evolution: The Difference It Doesn't Make." In *Darwinism Defeated? The Johnson-Lamoureux Debate on Biological Origins*, by Phillip E. Johnson and Denis O. Lamoureux, edited by Robert Clements, 89–100. Vancouver, BC: Regent, 1999.

Meyer, Stephen C., and Michael N. Keas, "The Meanings of Evolution." In *Darwinism, Design and Public Education*, edited by John Angus Campbell and Stephen C. Meyer, 135–56. Lansing, MI: Michigan State University Press, 2003.

Meyering, Theo C. "Mind Matters: Physicalism and the Autonomy of the Human Person." In *Neuroscience and the Person Scientific Perspectives on Divine Action*, edited by Robert J. Russell et al., 165–77. Vatican City: Vatican Observatory Publications; Center for Theology and the Natural Sciences, 1999.

Miller, Kenneth. *Finding Darwin's God: A Scientist's Search for Common Ground between God and Evolution*. New York: Cliff Street, 1999.

———. "Life's Grand Design." *Technology Review* (February/March 1994) 29–30.

———. *Only a Theory: Evolution and the Battle for America's Soul*. New York: Viking, 2008.

———. "Review of Darwin's Black Box." *Creation Evolution Journal*, 39 (1996) 36–40.

Mitchell, Basil. *The Justification of Religious Belief*. London: Oxford University Press, 1973.

Mitchell, Melanie. *Complexity: A Guided Tour*. New York: Oxford University Press, 2008.

Moltmann, Jürgen. *God in Creation: A New Theology of Creation and the Spirit of God*. Translated by Margaret Kohl. Minneapolis: Fortress, 1993.

Montgomery, John Warwick. *The Suicide of Christian Theology*. Minneapolis, MN: Bethany, 1970.

Monton, Bradley. *Seeking God in Science: An Atheist Defends Intelligent Design*. Peterborough, ON: Broadview, 2009.

Moore, James R. "Geologists and Interpreters of Genesis in the Nineteenth Century." In *God & Nature: Historical Essays on the Encounter between Christianity and Science*, edited by David C. Lindberg and Ronald L. Numbers, 322–50. Los Angeles: University of California Press, 1986.

Moreland, J. P. "The Argument from Consciousness." In *A Companion to Natural Theology*, edited by J. P. Moreland and William Lane Craig, 282–343. Oxford and Malden, MA: Blackwell, 2009.

———. *Christianity and the Nature of Science: A Philosophical Investigation*. Grand Rapids: Baker, 1989.

———. *Consciousness and the Existence of God*. New York: Routledge, 2008.

———. "God and the Argument from Consciousness." In *Debating Christian Theism*, edited by J. P. Moreland, Chad Meister, and Khaldoun Sweis, 119–30. New York: Oxford University Press, 2013.

———. "Intelligent Design and Evolutionary Psychology as Research Programs: A Comparison to Their Most Plausible Specifications." In *William A. Dembski and*

Michael Ruse in Dialogue, edited by Robert B. Stewart. Minneapolis, MN: Fortress, 2007.

———. "The Physical Sciences, Neurosciences and Dualism." *The Nature of Nature: Examining the Role of Naturalism in Science,* edited by William A. Dembski and Bruce L. Gordon, 835–49. Wilmington, DE: ISI, 2011.

———. *The Recalcitrant Imago Dei: Human Persons and the Failure of Naturalism.* Norwich, UK: SCM, 2009.

———. "A Response to a Platonistic and a Set-Theoretic Objection to the Kalam Cosmological Argument." *Religious Studies* 39 (2003) 373–90.

———. *Scaling the Secular City: A Defense of Christianity.* Grand Rapids, MI: Baker, 1987.

———. *The Soul: How We Know It's Real and Why It Matters.* Chicago: Moody, 2014.

Moreland, J. P., and William Lane Craig, *Philosophical Foundations for a Christian Worldview.* Downers Grove, IL: IVP Academic, 2003.

Moreland, J. P., Chad Meister, and Khaldoun A. Sweis, eds. *Debating Christian Theism.* London: Oxford University Press, 2013.

Moreland, J. P., and Scott B. Rae. *Body & Soul: Human Nature & the Crisis in Ethics.* Downers Grove, IL: IVP Academic, 2000.

Moreland, J. P., and John Mark Reynolds. *Three Views on Creation and Evolution.* Grand Rapids: Zondervan, 1999.

Moritz, Joshua M. "Human Uniqueness, the Other Hominids, and 'Anthropocentrism of the Gaps' In the Religion and Science Dialogue." *Zygon* 47 (2012) 65–96.

Morris, Henry M. *Scientific Creationism.* Green Forest, AZ: Master, 1974.

Morris, Simon Conway. *Life's Solution: Inevitable Humans in a Lonely Universe.* Cambridge: Cambridge University Press, 2003.

Muehlhauser, Luke. "The Kalam Cosmological Argument: Bibliography." http://commonsenseatheism.com/?p=1637.

Murphy, Nancey. *Anglo-American Postmodernity: Philosophical Perspectives on Science, Religion and Ethics.* Boulder, CO: Westview, 1997.

———. "Response to Review by Philip Clayton of 'Theology in the Age of Scientific Reasoning' by Nancey Murphy." *CTNS Bulletin,* Berkeley 11.1 (Winter 1991).

———. "Robert John Russell Versus the New Atheists." *Zygon* 45 (2010) 193–212.

———. "Supervenience and the Downward Efficacy of the Mental: A Nonreductive Physicalist Account of Human Action." In *Neuroscience and the Person,* edited by Robert J. Russell, et al., 147–64. Vatican City: Vatican Observatory Publications; Center for Theology and the Natural Sciences, 1999.

———. *Theology in the Age of Scientific Reasoning.* Ithaca, NY: Cornell University Press, 1990.

Murphy, Nancey, and Warren S. Brown, *Did My Neurons Make Me Do It?: Philosophical and Neurobiological Perspectives on Moral Responsibility and Free Will.* Oxford: Oxford University Press, 2007.

Murphy, Nancey, and George F. Ellis. "On the Moral Nature of the Universe: Theology, Cosmology, and Ethics." In *Theology and the Sciences Series.* Minneapolis: Fortress, 1996.

Nagel, Thomas. "What Is It Like to Be a Bat?" *The Philosophical Review* 83 (1974) 435–50.

———. *Mind & Cosmos: Why the Materialist Neo-Darwinian Conception of Nature is Almost Certainly False.* Oxford: Oxford University Press, 2012.

North S. J., Robert. *Teilhard and the Creation of the Soul.* Milwaukee: The Bruce, 1967.

Novak, Joseph A. "The Zeller-Brentano Debate on the Origin of Mind." *The Journal of Neoplatonic Studies* 3 (1995) 123–52.

Nowacki, Mark R. *The Kalam Cosmological Argument for God.* Westminster, MD: Prometheus, 2007.

Oderberg, David S. "Hylomorphic Dualism." *Social Philosophy and Policy* 2 (2005) 70–99.

Oppy, Graham. "Critical Notice of J. P. Moreland's 'Consciousness and the Existence of God.'" *European Journal for Philosophy of Religion* 1 (2011) 193–212.

Orgel, Leslie E. *The Origins of Life: Molecules and Natural Selection.* Somerset, NJ: John Wiley, 1973.

Orwell, George. *Nineteen Eighty-Four.* Fairfield, IA: First World Library Literary Society, 2004.

Padgett, Alan G. *Science and the Study of God: A Mutuality Model for Theology and Science.* Grand Rapids: Eerdmans, 2003.

Pambrun, James "Science, Theology and Acts of Understanding." *Science et Esprit* 58 (2006) 59–79.

Pannenberg, Wolfhart. *Basic Questions in Theology: Collected Essays.* Vol. II. Minneapolis: Fortress, 2008.

———. *Jesus: God and Man.* Translated by L. L. Wilkins and D. A. Priebe, London: SCM, 1968.

———. *Theology and the Philosophy of Science.* Translated by Francis McDonagh. Philadelphia: Westminster, 1973.

Peacocke, Arthur R. *All That Is: A Naturalistic Faith for the Twenty-First Century.* Edited by Philip Clayton. Minneapolis, MN: Fortress, 2007.

———. *Intimations of Reality: Critical Realism in Science and Religion.* Notre Dame: University of Notre Dame Press, 1984.

———. *Theology for a Scientific Age.* Minneapolis: Fortress, 1993.

———. "Welcoming the 'Disguised Friend': Darwinism and Divinity." In *Intelligent Design Creationism and its Critics*, edited by R. T. Pennock, 471–86. Cambridge: MIT Press, 2001.

Penn, Derek C., et al., "Darwin's mistake: explaining the discontinuity between human and nonhuman minds." *Behavior and Brain Science* 31 (208) 109–130. https://doi.org/10.1017/S0140525X08003543

Pennock, Robert T., ed. *Intelligent Design Creationism and Its Critics: Philosophical, Theological and Scientific Perspectives.* Cambridge: MIT Press, 2001.

Penrose, Roger. *The Emperor's New Mind: Concerning Computers, Minds, and the Laws of Physics.* New York: Oxford University Press, 1989.

Perakh, Mark. *Unintelligent Design.* Amherst, NY: Prometheus, 2004.

Peters, Ted. "Robert John Russell's Contribution to the Theology & Science Dialogue." In *God's Action in Nature's World: Essays in Honour of Robert John Russell*, edited by Nathan Hallanger and Ted Peters. New York: Routledge, 2006.

———. "Natural Theology versus Theology of Nature." *Theology and Science* 3 (2005) 1–2.

———. "Theology and Natural Science." In *The Modern Theologians*, second ed., edited by David Ford. Oxford: Blackwell, 1997.

Petto Andrew J., and Laurie R. Godfrey, eds. *Scientists Confront Creationism.* New York: Norton, 2007.

Phan, Peter C. "Creation." In *The Modern Catholic Encyclopedia*, edited by Michael Glazier and Monika K. Hellwig. Collegeville, MN: Liturgical, 1994.

Philoponus. *Against Proclus's "On the Eternity of the World 1-5."* Translated by Michael Share, Preface by Richard Sorabji. Ithaca, NY: Cornell University Press, 2005.

Pigliucci, Massimo, and Gerd B. Müller. *Evolution: The Extended Synthesis.* Cambridge, MA: MIT Press, 2010.

Pinker, Steven. *How the Mind Works.* New York: Norton, 1997.

Plantinga, Alvin. *Does God Have a Nature? The Aquinas Lecture, 1980.* Milwaukee: Marquette University Press, 1980.

———. *God and Other Minds: A Study of the Rational Justification of Belief in God.* Ithaca, NY: Cornell University Press, 1967.

———. *God, Freedom and Evil.* Cambridge: Harper & Row, 1974.

———. "When Faith and Reason Clash: Evolution and the Bible." *Christian Scholars Review* 21 (1991) 8–32.

———. *Warranted Christian Belief.* Oxford: Oxford University Press, 2005.

———. "What Is Intervention?" *Theology and Science* 6 (2008) 369–401.

———. *Where the Conflict Really Lies: Science, Religion & Naturalism.* Oxford: Oxford University Press, 2011.

Plato, *Phaedo.* Translated by David Gallop. Oxford: Oxford University Press, 1975.

Plotnik, J. M., F. B. M. de Waal, and D. Reiss, "Self-Recognition in an Asian Elephant." *Proceedings of the National Academy of Sciences* 103 (2006) 17053–57.

Poe, Harry Lee, and Jimmy H. Davis, *God and the Cosmos: Divine Activity in Space, Time and History.* Downers Grove, IL: IVP Academic, 2012.

Polkinghorne, John. *Belief in God in an Age of Science.* New Haven: Yale University Press, 1998.

———. *The Faith of a Physicist: Reflection of a Bottom Up Thinker.* Princeton, NJ: Fortress, 1996.

———. *Scientists as Theologians.* London: SPCK, 1996.

Pojman, Louis, and Michael Rea. *Philosophy of Religion: An Anthology.* Boston: Wadsworth Cengage Learning, 2011.

Popper, Karl R. *Realism and the Aim of Science: from the Postscript to the Logic of Scientific Discovery.* Edited by W. W. Bartley, III. New York: Routledge, 1983.

———. "Darwinism as a Metaphysical Research Program." In *The Philosophy of Karl Popper,* vol.1, edited by P.A. Schilpp, 133–43. La Salle, IL: Open Court, 1974.

Prior, H., A. Schwarz, and O. Güntürkün. "Mirror-Induced Behavior in the Magpie (Pica pica): Evidence of Self-Recognition." *PLoS Biology* 6 (2008) e202.

Rahner, Karl. "Christology with an Evolutionary View of the World," *Theological Investigations V.* London: Darton, Longman & Todd, 1966.

———. "Das Selbstverstandnis der Theologie vor dem Anspruch der Naturwissenschaft." Sonderheft, *Religionsunterricht an hoheren Schulen.* Dusseldorf: Patmos, 1963.

———. *Hominisation: The Evolutionary Origin of Man as a Theological Problem.* Translated by W. T. O'Hara. New York: Herder and Herder, 1966.

Ramirez, J. Roland E. "The Priority of Reason over Faith in Augustine." *Journal of Augustinian Studies* 13 (1982) 123–31.

Rau, Gerald. *Mapping the Origins Debate: Six Models of the Beginning of Everything.* Downers Grove, IL: InterVarsity, 2012.

Reiss, D., and L. Marino. "Mirror Self-Recognition in the Bottlenose Dolphin: A Case of Cognitive Convergence." *Proceedings of the National Academy of Sciences* 98 (2000) 5937–42.

Reppert, Victor. "Eliminative Materialism, Cognitive Suicide, and Begging the Question." *Metaphilosophy* 23 (1992) 378–92.

Richards, Jay. *The Untamed God: A Philosophical Exploration of Divine Perfection, Simplicity and Immutability.* Downers Grove, IL: InterVarsity, 2003.

———, ed. *God and Evolution: Protestants, Catholics and Jews Explore Darwin's Challenge to Faith.* Seattle, WA: Discovery Institute, 2010.

Rideau, Émile. *Teilhard de Chardin: A Guide to His Thought.* Translated by Rene Hague. Collins: London, 1967.

Rixon, Gordon. "Bernard Lonergan and Mysticism." *Theological Studies* 62 (2002) 479–97.

Roberts, John H. "Religious Reactions to Darwin." In *The Cambridge Companion to Science and Religion,* edited by Peter Harrison, 80–102. Cambridge: Cambridge University Press, 2010.

Robinson, William. "Epiphenomenalism." *Stanford Encyclopedia of Philosophy.* http://plato.stanford.edu/entries/epiphenomenalism/

Rochat, Philippe. "Five Levels of Awareness as They Unfold Early in Life." *Consciousness and Cognition* 12 (2003) 717–31.

———. "Layers of awareness in development." *Developmental Review* 38 (2015) 122–145.

———. *Others in Mind—Social Origins of Self-Consciousness.* New York: Cambridge University Press, 2009.

Rolston , Holmes. *Science and Origins: Probing the Deeper Questions.* Edited by Carl S. Helrich. Kitchener, ON: Pandora, 2008.

Ross, Hugh. *More Than a Theory: Revealing a Testable Model for Creation.* Grand Rapids, MI: Baker, 2009.

———. *Navigating Genesis: A Scientist's Journey through Genesis 1–11.* Covina, CA: Reasons to Believe, 2014.

Rowe, William L. "Does Panentheism Reduce to Pantheism? A Response to Craig." *International Journal for Philosophy of Religion* 61 (2007) 65–7.

Roy, Louis. *Mystical Consciousness: Western Perspectives and Dialogue with Japanese Thinkers.* Albany, NY: State University New York Press, 2003.

Ruse, Michael. *Can a Darwinian be a Christian? The Relationship between Science and Religion.* Cambridge: Cambridge University Press, 2000.

———. "Faith & Reason." *Playboy Magazine,* April, 2006, 52.

Russell, Robert John. "Arthur Peacocke on Method in Theology and Science and His Model of the Divine/World Interaction: An Appreciative Assessment." In *All That Is: A Naturalistic Faith for the Twenty First Century,* edited by Arthur Peacocke and Philip Clayton, 140–51. Minneapolis: Fortress, 2007.

———. "The Bodily Resurrection of Jesus as a First Instantiation of a New Law of the New Creation: Wright's Visionary New Paradigm in Dialogue with Physics and Cosmology." In *From Resurrection to Return: Perspectives from Theology and Science on Christian Eschatology,* edited by James Haire, Christine Ledger, and Stephen Pickard. Adelaide: ATF PACT Series, 2007.

———. "Cosmology, Evolution, and Resurrection Hope: Theology and Science in Creative Mutual Interaction." Proceedings of the Fifth Annual Goshen Conference on Religion and Science, edited by Carl S. Helrich. Kitchener, ON: Pandora, 2006.

———. *Cosmology: from Alpha to Omega: Theology and Science in Creative Mutual Interaction.* Minneapolis: Fortress, 2008.

———. "A Critical Response to Cardinal Schönborn's Concern over Evolution." *Theology and Science* 4 (2006) 193–98.

———. "Divine Action and Quantum Mechanics." In *Quantum Mechanics: Scientific Perspectives on Divine Action,* edited by Robert John Russell, et al., 351–404.

Vatican City: Vatican Observatory Publications, and Berkeley: Center for Theology and Natural Sciences, 2001.

———. "Eschatology and Physical Cosmology." In *The Far Future: Eschatology from a Cosmic Perspective*, edited by George F. R. Ellis, 266–315. Philadelphia: Templeton, 2002.

———. "Eschatology and Scientific Cosmology: From Conflict to Interaction." In *What God Knows: Time, Eternity and Divine Knowledge*, edited by J. Stanley Mattson and Harry Lee Poe, 95–120.Waco, TX: Baylor University Press: 2006.

———. An interview on a TV program entitled, "Faith and Reason." Broadcasted on September 11, 1998. Transcript at: http://www.pbs.org/faithandreason/transcript/bobr-frame.html

———. "Intelligent Design is Not Science and Does Not Qualify to be Taught in Public School Science Classes." *Theology and Science* 3 (2005) 131–32.

———. *Time in Eternity: Pannenberg, Physics and Eschatology in Creative Mutual Interaction*. Notre Dame, IN: University of Notre Dame Press, 2012.

———. "What we've learned from quantum mechanics about non-interventionist objective divine action in nature—and what are its remaining challenges?" Conference draft, April 2017—forthcoming publication.

Russell, Robert John, et al., eds. *Neuroscience and the Person: Scientific Perspectives on Divine Action*. Notre Dame, IN and Vatican City: Vatican Observatory Foundation and Center for Theology and Natural Sciences, 1999.

———, *Physics, Philosophy and Theology: A Common Quest for Understanding*. Notre Dame, IN: University of Notre Dame Press, 1989.

———, et al., eds. *Quantum Cosmology and the Laws of Nature: Scientific Perspectives on Divine Action*, second ed. Notre Dame, IN: University of Notre Dame Press, 1996.

Ryle, Gilbert. *The Concept of Mind*. Chicago: Chicago University Press, 2002.

Sagan, Carl. *Pale Blue Dot: A Vision of the Human Future in Space*. New York: Random House, 1994.

Sangiacomo, Andrea. "Divine Action and God's Immutability: A Historical Case Study on How to Resist Occasionalism." *European Journal for Philosophy of Religion* 7/4 (2015) 115–35.

Salmon SJ, James, and John Farina, eds. *The Legacy of Pierre Teilhard de Chardin*. New York: Paulist, 2011.

Sarfati, Jonathan. *Refuting Evolution: A Handbook for Students, Parents and Teachers Countering the Latest Arguments for Evolution*. Green Forest, AZ: Master, 1999.

Savary, M. *Teilhard de Chardin—The Divine Milieu Explained: A Spirituality for the 21st Century*. Mahwah, NJ: Paulist, 2007.

Shettleworth, Sara J. "Modularity, comparative cognition and human uniqueness." *Philosophical Transaction of the Royal Society B: Biological Sciences* 1603 (2012) 2794–2802. http://rstb.royalsocietypublishing.org/content/royptb/367/1603/2794.full.pdf.

Siewert, Charles. "Consciousness and Intentionality." *Stanford Encyclopedia of Philosophy*. https://plato.stanford.edu/entries/consciousness-intentionality/.

Suárez, S. D., and G. G Gallup. "Self-Recognition in Chimpanzees and Orangutans, But Not Gorillas." *Journal of Human Evolution* 10 (1981) 175–88.

Schaefer, Henry Fritz. *Science and Christianity: Conflict or Coherence?* Athens: University of Georgia Printing, 2003.

Schlesinger, George. *Religion and Scientific Method*. Dordecht, NL: D. Reidel, 1977.

Schoen, Edward L. *Religious Explanations: A Model from the Sciences.* Durham, NC: Duke University Press, 1985.

Schwartz, Jeffrey M. *Brain Lock: Free Yourself from Obsessive Compulsive Behavior—A Four-Step Self-Treatment Method to Change your Brain Chemistry.* New York: HarperCollins, 1996.

Schwartz, Jeffrey M., and Sharon Begley. *The Mind & The Brain: Neuroplasticity and the Power of Mental Force.* New York: HarperCollins, 2002.

Schwartz, Jeffrey M., et al., "Mindful Awareness and Self-Directed Neuroplasticity: Integrating Psychospiritual and Biological Approaches to Mental Health with a Focus on Obsessive Compulsive Disorder." In *The Psychospiritual Clinician's Handbook: Alternative Methods for Understanding and Treating Mental Disorders,* edited by S. G. Mijares, et al., chapter 13. Binghamton, NY: Haworth Reference, 2005.

Schwartz, Jeffrey M., and Rebecca Gladding. *You Are Not Your Brain: The 4-Step Solution for Changing Bad Habits, Ending Unhealthy Thinking, and Taking Control of Your Life.* New York: Avery, 2011.

Schwartz, Jeffrey M., H. P. Stapp, and M. Beauregard. "Quantum Theory in Neuroscience and Psychology: A Neurophysical Model of Mind/Brain Interaction." *Philosophical Transactions of the Royal Society of London, Series B,* 360 (2005)1309–27.

———. "The Volitional Influence of the Mind on the Brain, with Special Reference to Emotional Self-Regulation." In *Consciousness, Emotional Self-Regulation, and the Brain,* edited by Mario Beauregard, chapter 7. Philadelphia, PA: John Benjamins, 2004.

Schins, Juleon M. *Empirical Evidence for the Non-Material Nature of Consciousness.* Wales, UK: Edwin Mellen, 2004.

Schmaltz, Tad. "Occasionalism and Mechanism: Fontenelle's Objections to Malebranche." *British Journal for the History of Philosophy* 16 (2) (2008) 293–313.

Schrödinger, Erwin. "An Undulatory Theory of the Mechanics of Atoms and Molecules." *Physical Review* 28 (1926) 1049–70.

Searle, John R. A Reply to Daniel C. Dennett. "'The Mystery of Consciousness': An Exchange." *The New York Review of Books,* December 21, 1995. http://www.nybooks.com/articles/1995/12/21/the-mystery-of-consciousness-an-exchange/.

———. "Consciousness and the Philosophers." In *The New York Review of Books* 44 (1997) 43–44.

———. "Reductionism and the Irreducibility of Consciousness." In *Emergence: Contemporary Readings in Philosophy and Science,* edited by Mark A. Bedeau and Paul Humphreys, 69–80. Cambridge, MA: MIT Press, 2008.

Sebastián, Miguel Ángel. "What Panpsychists Should Reject: On the Incompatibility of Panpsychism and Organizational Invariantism." *Philosophical Studies* 172 (2015) 1833–46.

Shapiro, J. A. "How Life Changes Itself: The Read-Write (RW) Genome." *Physics of Life Reviews* 10 (2013) 287–323.

Sherry, Patrick. *Spirit, Saints and Immortality.* Albany: State University of New York Press, 1984.

Shermer, Michael. *In Darwin's Shadow: the Life and Science of Alfred Russel Wallace: A Biographical Study on the Psychology of History.* Oxford: Oxford University Press, 2002.

Shu, Frank H., "Friedmann-Lemaitre Models." Encyclopaedia Britannica. http://www.britannica.com/EBchecked/topic/139301/cosmology/27595/Friedmann-Lemaitre-models.

Simpson, G. G. *The Meaning of Evolution*. New Haven, CT: Yale University Press, 1967.

———. Review of Teilhard de Chardin, *The Phenomenon of Man*. *Scientific American* 202 (1960) 201–207.

Siniscalchi, Glenn B. "A Response to Professor Krauss on Nothing." *Heythrop Journal: A Bimonthly Review of Philosophy and Theology* 54 (2013) 678–90.

Smedes, Taede A. "Does Theology Have a Method? An Interview with Paul Allen." https://tasmedes.nl/does-theology-have-a-method-an-interview-with-paul-allen/

Smith, Wolfgang. *Teilhardism and the New Religion: A Thorough Analysis of the Teachings of Pierre Teilhard de Chardin*. Rockford, IL: Tan, 1988.

———. *Theistic Evolution: The Teilhardian Heresy*. Tacoma, WA: Angelico/Sophia Perennis, 2012.

Sorabji, Richard. "Infinity and Creation." In *Philoponus and the Rejection of Aristotelian Science*, 2nd ed., edited by Richard Sorabji, 195–237. London: Institute of Classical Studies, 2010.

———. "John Philoponus." In *Philoponus and the Rejection of Aristotelian Science*, 2nd ed., edited by Richard Sorabji, 1–81. London: Institute of Classical Studies, 2010.

Spitzer, Robert. *New Proofs for the Existence of God: Contributions of Contemporary Physics and Philosophers*. Cambridge: Eerdmans, 2010.

Stapp, H. "Quantum Theory and the Role of Mind in Nature." *Foundations of Physics* 10 (2001) 1465–1499.

Steel, Mike, and David Penny. "Origins of Life: Common Ancestry Put to the Test." *Nature* 465 (2010) 168–69. doi:10.1038/465168a. PMID 20463725.

Stewart, Robert B., ed. *Intelligent Design: William A. Dembski & Michael Ruse in Dialogue*. Minneapolis: Fortress, 2007.

Stich, Stephen. *Deconstructing the Mind*. New York: Oxford University Press, 1997.

Stoeger, William R. "Relating the Natural Sciences to Theology: Levels of Creative Mutual Interaction." In *God's Action in Nature's World*, edited by Nathan Hallanger and Ted Peters, 21–38. New York: Routledge, 2006.

Strawson, Galen John. "Consciousness Isn't a Mystery. It's Matter." *The New York Times*, May 16, 2016. http://www.nytimes.com/2016/05/16/opinion/consciousness-isnt-a-mystery-its-matter.html?partner=rss&emc=rss&_r=0.

Stump, Eleonore. *Aquinas*. New York: Routledge, 2003.

———. "God's Simplicity." In *The Oxford Handbook of Aquinas*, edited by Brian Davies and Eleonore Stump, 135–46. Oxford: Oxford University Press, 2012.

Stump, Eleonore, and Norman Kretzmann. "Absolute Simplicity." *Faith and Philosophy* 2 (1985) 353–91.

Suddendorf, T., and E. Collier-Baker. "The Evolution of Primate Visual Self-Recognition: Evidence of Absence in Lesser Apes." *Proc. R. Soc. B.* 276 (2009) 1671–77.

Sweetman, Brendan. *Evolution, Chance and God: Understanding the Relationship Between Evolution and Religion*. New York: Bloomsbury Academic, 2015.

Swinburne, Richard. *The Evolution of the Soul*. Oxford: Clarendon, 1986.

———. *The Existence of God*. 2nd ed. Oxford: Clarendon, 2004.

———. *Mind, Brain & Free Will*. Oxford: Oxford University Press, 2013.

———. "Nature and Immortality of the Soul." In *Concise Routledge Encyclopedia of Philosophy*. New York: Routledge, 2000.

———. "The Origin of Consciousness." In *Cosmic Beginnings and Human Ends*, edited by Clifford N. Matthews and Roy Abraham Varghese. Chicago and La Salle, IL: Open Court, (1995) 355–78.

———. "Soul." In *The Oxford Companion to Philosophy*, edited by Ted Honderich. Oxford: Oxford University Press, 1995.

Talbott, S. L. "Biology Worth of Life: Getting Over the Code Delusion." July 3, 2012. http://natureinsittute/txt/st/genome_4htm.

Taliaferro, Charles. *Consciousness and the Mind of God*. Cambridge: Cambridge University Press, 1994.

———. "Philosophy of Religion." *Stanford Encyclopedia of Philosophy*. https://plato. stanford.edu/entries/philosophy—religion/.

Teevan, Donna. *Lonergan, Hermeneutics and Theological Method*. Milwaukee: Marquette University Press, 2005.

Teichman, Jenny. *The Mind and the Soul: An Introduction to Philosophy of Mind*. Edited by R. F. Holland. London: Routledge and Kegan Paul, 1974.

Teilhard de Chardin, Pierre. *Christianity and Evolution*. New York: Harper & Row, 1965.

———. *The Divine Milieu*. New York: Harper & Row, 1960.

———. *The Heart of Matter*. Translated by Rene Hague, London: Collins, 1976.

———. *How I Believe*. New York: Harper & Row, 1969.

———. *Human Energy*. New York: Harcourt Brace Jovanovich, 1969.

———. "Letter of May 4, 1931: 'He Doesn't See That the Cosmos Holds Together Not by Matter But by Spirit.'"

———. *Man's Place in Nature*. New York: Harper & Row, 1966.

———. *The Phenomenon of Man*. Translated by Bernard Wall, New York: Harper & Row, 1975.

———. *Science and Christ*. Translated by Rene Hague. London: Collins, 1965.

———. Journal [26 août 1915–4 janvier 1919]. Paris: Fayard, 1975.

Than, Ker. "All Species Evolved from Single Cell, Study Finds." *National Geographic Society*, (14 May 2010). https://news.nationalgeographic.com/ news/2010/05/100513-science-evolution-darwin-single-ancestor/.

Thaxton, Charles B., Walter L. Bradley, and Roger L. Olsen, *The Mystery of Life's Origins*. Dallas, TX: Lewis and Stanley, 1984.

Theobald, Douglas. "A Formal Test of the Theory of Universal Common Ancestry." *Nature* 465 (13 May 2010) 219–22. doi:10.1038/nature09014. PMID 20463738.

Tipler, Frank J. *The Physics of Immortality*. New York: Anchor, 1994.

Tononi, Giulio. "Consciousness as Integrated Information: A Provisional Manifesto." *Biology Bulletin* 215 (2008) 216–42.

———. "Integrated Information Theory." *Scholarpedia*, 10 (2015) 4164. http://www. scholarpedia.org/article/Integrated_information_theory.

———. *Phi: A Voyage from the Brain to the Soul*. New York: Random House, 2012.

Tononi, Giulio, and Christof Koch. "Consciousness: here, there and everywhere?" Phil. Trans. R. Soc. B. 370:20140167.

Tormos, J. M., et al. "Lateralized Effects of Self-Induced Sadness and Happiness on Corticospinal Excitability." *Neurology* 49 (August 1997) 487–91.

Torrance, Thomas. "God and the Contingent World." *Zygon* 14 (1979) 329–48.

Tortorello, Frank. "What is Real about Reductive Neuroscience?" *Journal of Critical Realism* (May 5, 2017) 235–54. http://www.tandfonline.com/doi/full/10.1080/14 767430.2017.1312214.

Tracy, Thomas F., ed. *The God Who Acts: Philosophical and Theological Explorations*. University Park, PA: The Pennsylvania University State Press, 1994.

Tye, Michael. "Qualia." *Stanford Encyclopedia of Philosophy*. https://plato.stanford.edu/ entries/qualia/.

van Huyssteen, J. W. "'Creative Mutual Interaction' as an Epistemic Tool for Interdisciplinary Dialogue." In *God's Action in Nature's World*, edited by Nathan Hallanger and Ted Peters, 66–76. New York: Routledge, 2006.

———. *Essays in Postfoundationalist Theology.* Grand Rapids: Eerdmans, 1997.

van Inwagen, Peter. *The Nature of Rational Beings: Dualism and Physicalism*, 4th ed. Boulder, CO: Westview, 2015.

van Till, Howard J. "The Fully Gifted Creation." In *Three Views on Creation and Evolution*, edited by J. P. Moreland and John Mark Reynolds, 159–248. Grand Rapids: Zondervan, 1999.

———. "Functional Integrity (Fully Gifted Creation, Robust Formational Economy Principle)." http://www.asa3.org/ASA/education/origins/methods-hvt.htm.

Venter, J. Craig, et al. "The Sequence of the Human Genome," *Science* 291 (February 16, 2001) 1304–51.

Ventureyra, Scott. "Augustine as an Apologist: Is Confessions Apologetic in Nature?" *The American Journal of Biblical Theology* 32 (2015) 1–34. http://www.biblicaltheology.com/Research/VentureyraS03.pdf

Ventureyra, Scott. "The Cosmological Argument & the Place of Contestation in Philosophical Discourse: From Plato & Aristotle to Contemporary Debates." *Maritain Studies/Études maritainiennes* 32 (2016) 51–71.

Ventureyra, Scott. "Dawkins' Unholy Trinity: Incoherency, Hypocrisy and Bigotry." *Crisis Magazine*, Sophia Institute. November 26, 2014. https://www.crisismagazine.com/2014/dawkins-unholy-trinity-incoherency-hypocrisy-bigotry.

Ventureyra, Scott. "God's Simplicity, Evolution and the Origin of Consciousness." *Maritain Studies/Études maritainiennes* 32 (2016) 137–55.

Ventureyra, Scott. The Origin of Consciousness: A Research Program for the Science-Theology Interaction," *The Science of Consciousness Program book*, abstract 99, (2016) 94. University of Arizona Center for Consciousness Studies. http://www.consciousness.arizona.edu/documents/TSC2016_BOOK_of_Abstracts_final.pdf.

Ventureyra, Scott. "Science & Christian Spirituality: The Relationship between Christian Spirituality and Biological Evolution." *The American Journal of Biblical Theology* 43 (2015) 1–20. http://www.biblicaltheology.com/Research/VentureyraS06.pdf.

Ventureyra, Scott. "Scratching the Surface." Review of Alvin Plantinga, *Where the Conflict Really Lies: Science, Religion & Naturalism*, Convivium: Faith in Our Common Life 16 (October/November 2014) 38–40. https://www.convivium.ca/articles/scratching-the-surface.

Ventureyra, Scott. *Theology's Fruitful Contribution to the Natural Sciences: Robert Russell's 'Creative Mutual Interaction' in Operation with Eschatology, Resurrection and Cosmology.* MA Thesis, Faculty of Theology, Saint Paul University, Ottawa, 2009.

Ventureyra, Scott. "Warranted Scepticism? Putting the Center for Inquiry's Rationale to the Test." *The American Journal of Biblical Theology* 36 (2015) 1–26. http://www.biblicaltheology.com/Research/VentureyraS04.pdf.

Vilenkin, Alexander. "The Beginning of the Universe." *Inference: International Review of Science* 4 (2015). http://inference-review.com/article/the-beginning-of-the-universe.

Von Neumann, John and Robert T. Beyer. *Mathematical Foundations of Quantum Mechanics.* Princeton: Princeton University Press, 1985.

Wagner, Steven J., and Richard Warner, eds. *Naturalism: A Critical Appraisal.* Notre Dame: University of Notre Dame Press, 1993.

Wainright, William. "Concepts of God." *Stanford Encyclopedia of Philosophy*. http://plato.stanford.edu/entries/concepts-god/.

———. "Two (or Maybe One and a Half) Cheers for Perfect Being Theology" *Philo* 12 (2009) 228–51.

Wallace, Alfred Russel. "Sir Charles Lyell on Geological Climates and the Origin of Species." *Quarterly Review* 126 (April 1869).

Ward, Keith. "God as the Ultimate Informational Principle." In *Information and the Nature of Reality: From Physics to Metaphysics*, edited by Paul Davies and Niels Henrik Gregersen, 282–300. Cambridge: Cambridge University Press, 2010.

Wassermann, Christoph, Richard Kirby, and Bernard Rordorff. *The Science and Theology of Information*. Proceedings of the Third European Conference of Science and Theology, Geneva, March 29 to April 1, 1990. Geneva: Labor et Fides, 1992.

Watson, James D., and Francis H. Crick, "A Structure for Deoxyribose Nucleic Acid." *Nature* 171 (1953) 737–38.

Weaver, Shannon. *The Mathematical Theory of Communication*. Urbana, IL: University of Illinois Press, 1949.

Weigel, Peter. *Aquinas on Simplicity: An Investigation into the Foundations of his Philosophical Theology*. Bern: Peter Lang, 2008.

Wells, Jonathan. *Icons of Evolution: Science or Myth—Why Much of What we Teach About Evolution is Wrong*. Washington, DC: Regenery, 2000.

Wells, Jonathan. *The Myth of Junk DNA*. Seattle, WA: Discovery Institute, 2011.

West, John G. "Intelligent Design Could Offer Fresh Ideas on Evolution." *Seattle Post-Intelligencer*. December 6, 2002. http://www.discovery.org/a/1313.

Westergaard, Greg C., and C. W. Hyatt. "The Responses of Bonobos (Pan paniscus) to Their Mirror Images: Evidence of Self-Recognition." *Human Evolution*, 9 (1994) 273–79.

Wheeler, John Archibald. *A Journey into Gravity and Spacetime*. Scientific American Library, New York: Freeman, 1990.

Whitcomb, John C., and Henry M. Morris. *The Genesis Flood: The Biblical Record and its Scientific Implications*. Phillipsburg, NJ: P & R, 1961.

Whitehead, Alfred North. *Science and the Modern World*. New York: Macmillan, 1926.

Whitworth, Brian, "The Emergence of the Physical World from Information Processing." *Quantum Biosystems* 2 (2010) 221–49.

Wildberg, Christian. "John Philoponus." *Stanford Encyclopedia of Philosophy*, (fall 2008 Edition). http://plato.stanford.edu/archives/fall2008/entries/philoponus/.

Williams, Thomas. "Saint Anselm." *Stanford Encyclopedia of Philosophy*. https://plato.stanford.edu/entries/anselm/.

Wittgenstein, Ludwig. *Lectures and Conversation*. Berkeley: University of California, 2007.

Woodward, Thomas. *Doubts about Darwin: A History of Intelligent Design*. Grand Rapids: Baker, 2003.

Woodward, Thomas E., and James P. Gills. *Doubts about Darwin: A History of Intelligent Design*. Grand Rapids: Baker, 2003.

Wright, N. T. "Mind, Spirit, Soul and Body: All For One and Contexts." Presented at the Society of Christian Philosophers, Regional Meeting at Fordham University, March 18, 2011.

———. *The Resurrection of the Son of God*. Philadelphia: Fortress, 2003.

Yonezawa, Takahiro, and Masami Hasegawa. "Was the universal common ancestry proved?" *Nature* 468 (16 December 2010) E9. doi:10.1038/nature09482.

General Index

Scripture Index